Successful Science Communication

In the 25 years since the Bodmer Report kick-started the public understanding of science movement, there has been something of a revolution in science communication. However, despite the ever-growing demands of the public, policy-makers and the media, many scientists still find it difficult to successfully explain and publicise their activities or to understand and respond to people's hopes and concerns about their work.

Bringing together experienced and successful science communicators from across the academic, commercial and media worlds, this practical guide fills this gap to provide a one-stop resource covering science communication in its many different forms. The chapters provide vital background knowledge and inspiring ideas for how to deal with different situations and interest groups. Entertaining personal accounts of projects ranging from podcasts to science festivals to student-run societies give working examples of how scientists can engage with their audiences and demonstrate the key ingredients in successful science communication.

DAVID J. BENNETT is a Guest at the Department of Biotechnology of the Delft University of Technology in The Netherlands and a Visitor to the Senior Combination Room of St Edmund's College, Cambridge, UK. He has long-term experience, activities and interests in the relations between science, industry, government, education, law, the public and the media, and he works with the European Commission, government departments, companies, universities, public interest organisations and the media in these areas.

RICHARD C. JENNINGS is an Affiliated Research Scholar in the Department of History and Philosophy of Science in the University of Cambridge. His research interests are focused on the responsible conduct of research, and the ethical uses of science and technology. He is a member of BCS, the Chartered Institute for IT, has worked with the BCS Ethics Forum defining and refining the BCS Code of Conduct, and with four other members has developed a *Framework for Assessing Ethical Issues in New Technologies*.

Michael Faraday delivering a Christmas Lecture at the Royal
Institution in 1856

Successful Science Communication

Telling It Like It Is

Edited by

DAVID J. BENNETT
Delft University of Technology,
The Netherlands

RICHARD C.
JENNINGS
University of Cambridge, UK

CAMBRIDGE
UNIVERSITY PRESS

CAMBRIDGE UNIVERSITY PRESS
Cambridge, New York, Melbourne, Madrid, Cape Town,
Singapore, São Paulo, Delhi, Tokyo, Mexico City

Cambridge University Press
The Edinburgh Building, Cambridge CB2 8RU, UK

Published in the United States of America by
Cambridge University Press, New York

www.cambridge.org
Information on this title: www.cambridge.org/9781107003323

First published 2011

Printed in the United Kingdom at the University Press, Cambridge

A catalogue record for this publication is available from the British Library

Library of Congress Cataloguing-in-Publication Data
Successful science communication : telling it like it is / [edited by]
David J. Bennett, Richard C. Jennings.
    p.   cm.
    ISBN 978-1-107-00332-3 (Hardback) – ISBN 978-0-521-17678-1 (Paperback)
    1. Communication in science.   I. Bennett, David J.   II. Jennings, Richard C.
III. Title.
    Q223.S884 2011
    501′.4–dc22

ISBN 978-1-107-00332-3 Hardback
ISBN 978-0-521-17678-1 Paperback

'The time has come,' the Walrus said,
'To talk of many things:
Of shoes – and ships – and sealing-wax –
Of cabbages – and kings –
And why the sea is boiling hot –
And whether pigs have wings.'

from *Through the Looking-Glass and What Alice Found There*
Lewis Carroll (1872)

This book is dedicated to the memories of Stephen White and Stephen Schneider and to James Astley. Steve White died suddenly on 23 August 2010 at the age of 61 after writing his chapter on 'Dealings with the media' and before it was published. As Director of Communications at the British Psychological Society for many years he did a very great deal to further science communication with both his writings and his own kind dealings with his many friends, colleagues and course participants. Steve Schneider died also suddenly at the age of 65 on 19 July 2010 before writing his chapter on 'Tackling the climate communication challenge' which Andrew Revkin kindly took on at short notice. Steve Schneider was Professor of Environmental Biology and Global Change at Stanford University, and for long a renowned climate change researcher and eloquent communicator about the scientific evidence in the public arena. James was born on 29 October 2010 when the book's writing had just been completed, both having been carefully nurtured by his mother, Katrina Halliday, as Senior Commissioning Editor, and he has his life before him to build and enjoy.

Contents

      The colour plates are situated between pages 354 and 355

Foreword

The need for scientists to be able to communicate, and so engage with the public, is as important now, if not even more so, as it was when I chaired the Royal Society's 'Public Understanding of Science' committee in the mid-1980s. The final sentence of the Royal Society report was: *'But our most direct and urgent message must be to the scientists themselves: Learn to communicate with the public, be willing to do so and consider it your duty to do so.'*

Fortunately, the need for scientists to communicate is now widely recognised and no longer considered controversial by the scientific community. Indeed, it is now an accepted part of any scientist's activities and there is no longer any stigma for a scientist to be involved in the public communication of science.

This timely book is addressed to all those involved in any way in the enterprise of science, and makes a major contribution to promoting and supporting the need for science communication. It is full of good practical advice, as well as giving a wide-ranging background to the issues involved.

Some commentators on the 1985 report suggested, quite wrongly in my view, that all that was being proposed was for scientists to feed the public with the scientific facts and that they would then quietly support science. This came to be known as the 'deficit model' and led to an emphasis on public engagement.

But how can there be the dialogue that is, quite appropriately, implied by public engagement, without some understanding by the public, whoever they might, be of the scientific issues involved? It is necessarily the scientist who has the relevant information, especially of the latest advances whether pure or applied, and so the onus to explain the scientific issues must fall on the scientist. Without the scientist having the ability to explain science in a way that the non-expert can understand and a willingness to get involved in the dialogue, there can be no public engagement.

In the last 25 years there have been several major developments that impact on the issues of science communication and public engagement. The first is the huge increase in post-16 education and, especially in university participation, which is now almost 45% in the UK. This has inevitably led to a much higher proportion of the population having some science education beyond the age of 16. A second major change is the extraordinary explosive increase in information available on the web and the more recent opportunities this is now providing for social networking. A third change is in the proportion of the population that is over 65 and supposedly retired. In future these changes must be taken into account in any overall consideration of approaches to science communication and public engagement.

This book effectively covers most of these and other relevant topics and is written by authors with suitably diverse and appropriate backgrounds. The topics range from history, going back to the Greeks, through social science and philosophical questions, to measurements of public attitudes to science and methods for evaluating the impact of different approaches to science communication. Most importantly, it includes practical recommendations from the viewpoints of journalists, both from the UK and the USA, and from the experience of those working in environmental consulting, and for patient support organisations, funding agencies, consumer organisations, the pharmaceutical industries, the British Science Association and many others.

It is a book that should be recommended reading for all those who are involved in any way with science. There is no better current comprehensive and succinct source that gives such an excellent background to the issues around science communication and explains how to engage with the public, with much valuable practical advice.

Sir Walter Bodmer FRS

Authors' biographies

John Adams

John Adams is Emeritus Professor of Geography at University College London. He was a member of the original Board of Directors of Friends of the Earth in the early 1970s and has been involved in debates about environmental risks ever since. He is intrigued by the persistence of attitudes to risk: for the past 30 years, the same arguments, slogans and insults have been shouted past each other by the participants (or their descendants) in disputes about issues for which conclusive evidence is lacking. His current work on both risk and transport issues seeks to understand these attitudes and the reasons for their persistence, in the hope of transforming shouting matches into more constructive dialogues. He has a website: www.john-adams.co.uk.

David Bennett

David Bennett is now a Guest at the Department of Biotechnology of the Delft University of Technology in The Netherlands and a Visitor to the Senior Combination Room of St Edmund's College, Cambridge, UK. He has a PhD in biochemical genetics and an MA in science policy studies with long-term experience, activities and interests in the relations between science, industry, government, education, law, the public and the media. He works with the European Commission, government departments, companies, universities, public interest organisations and the media in these areas, having worked in universities and companies in the UK, USA, Australia and, most recently, the Netherlands. He was a founder member and secretary of the European Federation of Biotechnology Task Group on Public Perceptions of Biotechnology established in 1991 and one of the first organisations in this field. For the last 20 years or so he has been running many international network-based, multidisciplinary projects, courses, conferences, workshops, etc. funded by the European Commission and other bodies in biotechnology and, of late, nanobiotechnology.

Hayley Birch

Hayley Birch is a freelance science communicator and director of the not-for-profit science communication company Sounds of Science, which specialises in creative communication about science. She uses new media tools including podcasts, blogs and social networks to engage with audiences for Sounds of Science projects and has been involved in research in collaboration with the University of the West of England studying the use of new media in science communication. Hayley is the creator of Geek Pop, a music project focusing on commissioning and publishing science-inspired music online. She has written for publications including *New Scientist, Nature* and *Chemistry World*; edited several popular science books; been involved in European Commission-funded science, society and policy initiatives; and worked with music festivals and science festivals to produce shows as well as written and audio content. She has a keen interest in embedding science in culture and blogs about science at the intersection with the arts at wordsofscience.blogspot.com. Hayley graduated in biological sciences from the University of Warwick and received her master's in science communication from the University of the West of England.

Sir Walter Bodmer

Walter Bodmer studied mathematics at Cambridge University where, having become fascinated with genetics through courses taught by Sir Ronald Fisher as part of the final-year mathematics programme, he did his PhD with Fisher in population genetics. He then went as a Post-Doctoral Fellow in 1961 to work with Nobel Prize winner Joshua Lederberg at Stanford University and to learn molecular biology. While there, eventually as a member of the Faculty for eight years, he contributed to the discovery of the major human tissue-typing system. In 1970 Walter Bodmer returned to the UK to take up the chair of genetics at Oxford and in 1979 he left Oxford to become Director of Research at the Imperial Cancer Research Fund Laboratories in London and was appointed the first Director-General of the Fund in 1991. On retirement from the ICRF in 1996, he returned to Oxford University as Principal of Hertford College until 2005, and as head of the ICRF (now CRUK) Cancer and Immunogenetics laboratory at the Weatherall Institute of Molecular Medicine where he continues his research into cancer and human population genetics. Walter Bodmer was one of the first to suggest the idea of the Human Genome Project. He was elected FRS in 1974, knighted in 1986 for his contributions to science, is a Foreign Associate of the US National Academy of Sciences and is the recipient of more than 30 honorary degrees and memberships and fellowships of scientific and medical societies.

Tracey Brown

Tracey Brown is director of the UK-based charitable trust Sense About Science which equips the public to make sense of science and evidence. She joined Sense About Science in its founding year 2002. Tracey has a background in social research, and previously spent four years working on a European Commission programme to establish social research and teaching in the former Soviet Union and a year setting up a commercially based risk analysis centre. She is a trustee of Centre of the Cell and a trustee of MATTER for All. In 2009 she became a commissioner for the UK Drugs Policy Commission. She sits on the Outreach Committee of the Royal College of Pathologists and in 2009 was made a Friend of the College. She is a regular writer and commentator on science and society, peer review and publication of research data.

Nicola Buckley

Nicola Buckley is acting Head of Community Affairs at the University of Cambridge. She helps to convene the UK science festivals network and is a member of the European Science Communication Events Association. As well as managing the annual Cambridge Science Festival, she founded the Cambridge Festival of Ideas in 2008, which engages the public with arts, humanities and social sciences research. Prior to her current role at the University of Cambridge, Nicola worked as a fundraising manager for several health and social care charities. She has a BA in history and an MPhil in social anthropology from the University of Cambridge and an MSc in science in society from the Open University.

Michel Claessens

Michel Claessens was born in 1958 in Brussels. He has a PhD in physical chemistry, and has worked successively at the Free University of Brussels

(Department of Organic Physical Chemistry) and at the Erasme Hospital in Brussels (Department of Radiology), and then in the biotechnology and in the chemical industry. He has also been a freelance scientific journalist since 1980. Michel joined the European Commission in 1994. He was Deputy Head of the Communication Unit in the Research Directorate-General until March 2011. His main responsibilities concerned the organisation of major conferences and the Eurobarometer surveys on science and technology. He was also the editor-in-chief of the magazine research*eu of the European Commission. He is now Head of Communication at the ITER Organization (France, Cadarache) and teaches science communication at the Free University of Brussels. As a scientific journalist and writer, Michel Claessens has published 250 articles and eight books on science communication and several aspects of modern science and technology. He is also a member of the scientific committee of the international Publication Communication of Science and Technology network (PCST).

Sue Davies

Sue Davies is Chief Policy Adviser at Which?, working mainly on food issues. She is also a member of the Management Board of the European Food Safety Authority (EFSA). She has represented consumer interests on a range of government and industry committees and working groups at national and international level, including the Council of Food Policy Advisers, Science for All Expert Group, the Advisory Committee on the Microbiological Safety of Food (ACMSF) and Responsible Nano Code, and is the EU Chair of the Transatlantic Consumer Dialogue (TACD) Food Policy Committee. She was awarded an MBE in 2003 for services to food safety.

Peter Evans

Peter Evans is one of the UK's foremost science broadcasters, having spent over three decades presenting radio (and some television) programmes on all areas of research. After graduating from Oxford, he worked first in publishing as a commissioning editor, then became a freelance writer specialising in science, medicine and technology. He was the weekly 'voice' of radio science in the UK as presenter of the long-running magazine programme Science Now. He then started the prize-winning documentary strand Frontiers. Alongside this, he wrote and presented hundreds of programmes for the Open University from which he holds an honorary Master's degree for services to science communication. In addition, he has written or contributed to over 12 books and numerous articles; written and edited material for the

UK government; and run his own training and consultancy company, again specialising in scientific matters. Currently, he is carrying out academic research analysing the impact of radio science messages on lay audiences.

George Gaskell

George Gaskell BSc PhD, Professor of Social Psychology, is Pro-Director of the London School of Economics and Political Science. His research focuses on science, technology and society; in particular the issues of risk and trust; how values influence people's views about technological innovation, and the governance of science and technology. His research competencies include survey methodology and both quantitative analysis and qualitative inquiry. Since 1996 he has coordinated the series of Eurobarometer surveys on 'Biotechnology and the Life Sciences' for the Research Directorate-General. He was principal investigator of 'Life sciences in European society', a European comparative study of biotechnology in the public sphere funded by the European Commission and is now leading a project on 'Sensitive technologies and European public ethics'. He is a member of the Expert Group on Risk Communication of the European Food Standard Authority and chairs the International Advisory Group of the Centre for Genomics and Society in The Netherlands. He was vice-chair of the European Commission's Science and Society Advisory Committee and was also a member of the Science in Society Committee of the Royal Society.

Laura Grant

Laura first got involved in public engagement as a physics undergraduate at the University of Liverpool, developing shows and workshops to tour secondary schools in Merseyside. Since her early outreach work, Laura has developed an interest in what works and why when engaging audiences with science. Her PhD, entitled 'Comparative evaluation of science communication activities', addressed these questions and she has since spent most of her career on evaluation research. Laura approaches evaluation as a practitioner herself, which ensures the integrity and relevance of her recommendations. She has completed many evaluation projects for a diverse range of clients including the British Council, the Royal Society, the Engineering and Physical Sciences Research Council, AstraZeneca, the Institute of Physics and the Royal Academy of Engineering. One of Laura's research interests is in developing ways to meaningfully measure impact. She uses a range of tools to help clients develop strategies and impact frameworks to capture learning and measure success. Laura enjoys sharing her interest and enthusiasm in evaluation with others and is frequently called on to deliver training and write guides on the subject.

James Hannam

James Hannam graduated in physics at St Anne's College, Oxford before embarking on a career in the City of London. While working, he took his MA in historical research at Birkbeck College, London before taking time off to complete his PhD in the history and philosophy of science at Pembroke College, Cambridge. He now works for Ernst & Young LLP. His reviews and articles have appeared in academic journals as well as *History Today*, the *Mail on Sunday*, the *Guardian* and the *Spectator*. His first book *God's Philosophers: How the Medieval World Laid the Foundations of Modern Science* (Icon Books, 2009) was shortlisted for the Royal Society Book Prize 2010. James lives in rural Kent with his wife and two young children. He can be contacted at bede@bede.org.uk.

Richard Hayhurst

Richard Hayhurst has worked in science communications for over 30 years, starting in Finland as marketing communications manager for Labsystems, one of the first biotech companies which pioneered HIV testing. Having developed a taste for communicating the controversies being thrown up by a golden era in scientific discovery, Richard returned to the UK to set up a PR agency specialising in the life sciences. Over the next 20 years HCC De Facto was involved in many of the leading issues of the day including cloning, GM, stem cell research, the Human Genome Project and industrial biotechnology. The agency also famously launched 'Dolly the Sheep'. Clients included GlaxoSmithKline, Genzyme, Roslin, the UK BioIndustry Association, Johnson & Johnson and Cambridge Antibody Technology. In 2005 Richard founded Hayhurst Media which focused on early-stage biotechnology companies. The company was acquired by the leading US agency Schwartz Communications in 2009 and Richard now runs their life sciences and technologies practices. He has also participated in several European Commission-funded projects looking at communications issues in genetics and nanotechnology. He is a founding member of both the London Biotechnology Network and London Cleantech Network. He holds an MA in modern history from the University of St Andrews.

Wolfgang M. Heckl

Professor Dr. Wolfgang M. Heckl is the Director General of the Deutsches Museum and holder of the Oskar-von-Miller-Chair for science communication at the Technische Universität München. Previously he was professor of experimental physics and nanotechnology at the University of München (LMU) with a special interest in the field of organic self-assembly and the origin of life. His academic teachers include Nobel Prize winners Gerd Binnig and Theodor Hänsch. As a dynamic and charismatic science communicator he received the Communicator Prize in 2002 from the German Science Foundation and was awarded the first European Descartes Prize for Science Communication in 2004. He was the chairman of the pan-European Euroscience Open Forum in July 2006.

Paul Hix

Paul Hix is currently completing a transdisciplinary PhD in science communication and nanosciences in the Open Research Laboratory of the Deutsches Museum. The main element of his dissertation is the establishment of this novel laboratory concept in which he conducted nanoscale research in full public view for over two and a half years. From 1995 to 2003 he studied geophysics at the Ludwig Maximilian University of Munich and was awarded the Bavarian State Prize 2005 for his diploma thesis project: 'Scanning tunneling microscope for the International Space Station ISS'. In 1994 Paul Hix represented Great Britain in the luge competition of the XVII Winter Olympic Games in Lillehammer.

Sue Hordijenko

Sue began her career in public engagement with science in 1994 when she joined the Wellcome Trust to work on the public and schools programme for its permanent in-house exhibition on the biomedical sciences 'Science for life'. She joined the British Science Association in 1999 initially to manage the Association's special millennial festival 'Creating SPARKS', a month-long science and arts festival involving all of the cultural institutions of South Kensington, and then went on to manage the Association's 'Science in society' programme. This involved developing the annual national science communication conference and co-creating the online mass participation psychology experiment 'Laughlab'. In 2001 she moved to the Natural History Museum and worked with the Museum's scientific curators and researchers to instigate a programme of daily onsite and online public events involving museum researchers in the newly opened Darwin Centre. She returned to the British Science Association in 2004 in her current role as Director of Programmes where she has overall responsibility for the British Science Festival, National Science and Engineering Week, the Association's 'Science in society' programmes and its press and PR operation.

Richard Jennings

Richard Jennings is an Affiliated Research Scholar in the Department of History and Philosophy of Science in the University of Cambridge. His research interests are focused on the Responsible Conduct of Research, and the ethical uses of science and technology. He is a member of BCS, the Chartered Institute for IT, has worked with the BCS Ethics Forum defining and refining the BCS Code of Conduct, and with four other members has developed a *Framework for Assessing Ethical Issues in New Technologies*. He teaches philosophy of science to undergraduate natural science students and philosophy to undergraduate philosophy students. He lectures on ethics in science and runs graduate workshops on ethical conduct and ethical practice in science. He has a long-standing interest in the history of science and the history of philosophy of science, lecturing on the history of science for the Pembroke College International Programme. He is a member of Pembroke College and of Queens' College Cambridge.

Richard Jones

Richard Jones is Pro-Vice-Chancellor for Research and Innovation at the University of Sheffield. He has a first degree and PhD in physics from the University of Cambridge, and did postdoctoral work at Cornell University in the USA, before being appointed a lecturer in physics at the University of Cambridge. In 1998 he moved to the University of Sheffield. He is an experimental polymer physicist who specialises in elucidating the nanoscale structure and properties of polymers and biological macromolecules at interfaces. Richard Jones has written and lectured extensively for general audiences and has participated in a number of citizens' panels and other delib- erative forums about nanotechnology. He was the Senior Strategic Advisor for Nanotechnology for the Engineering and Physical Sciences Research Council from 2007 to 2009, and is a member of EPSRC's Societal Issues Panel. In 2006 he was elected a Fellow of the

Royal Society, and in 2009 he won the Tabor Medal of the Institute of Physics for contributions to nanoscience.

Alastair Kent

Alastair Kent is the Director of the Genetic Alliance UK, formerly Genetic Interest Group (GIG) – the UK alliance of charities and support groups for people affected by genetic disorders. Its mission is to promote the development of the scientific understanding of genetics and the part that genetic factors play in health and disease, and to see the speedy transfer of this new knowledge into improved services and support for the treatment of currently incurable conditions. Prior to joining GIG Alastair worked for a number of voluntary organisations on issues concerning policy, service development and disabled people.

Lise Kingo

Lise Kingo is Executive Vice President and Chief of Staffs, Novo Nordisk. She joined Novo Nordisk in 1988 and worked over the years to build up the company's Triple Bottom Line approach. Ms Kingo was appointed Senior Vice President in 1999 and Executive Vice President, Corporate Relations, in 2002. Ms Kingo serves as chair of the board of the Steno Diabetes Center A/S, Denmark. She is also associate professor at the Medical Faculty, Vrije Universiteit, Amsterdam, The Netherlands. Ms Kingo has a BA in religions and a BA in ancient Greek art from the University of Aarhus, Denmark from 1986, a BComm in marketing economics from the Copenhagen Business School, Denmark from 1991, and an MSc in responsibility and business practice from the University of Bath, UK, from 2000.

Rikke Schmidt Kjærgaard

Rikke Schmidt Kjærgaard is a research fellow at the Faculty of Science, Aarhus University, Denmark, and an affiliated research fellow at Harvard Medical School. She graduated in 2008 with her thesis 'Framing science and technology: Media, narratives and policy'. Since 2008, she has worked as a postdoctoral researcher at Harvard Medical School and as a research associate at the MRC Mitochondrial Biology Unit, Cambridge, UK. Her research is focused on visual communication. Her current research covers art and science, graphic design for science, and artistic license in scientific images. Besides a PhD in science communication she has an MSc in mathematics and art history.

Tanja Klop

After finishing her undergraduate study in biology, Tanja studied for her PhD at the Erasmus University of Rotterdam. She graduated in 2008 with her thesis 'Attitudes of secondary school students towards modern biotechnology'. Since 2008, Tanja Klop has worked as a postdoctoral researcher within the Biotechnology and Society Group at the Department of Biotechnology of the Delft University of Technology in The Netherlands. Her research is concerned with ethical and societal issues in emerging new technologies, with a main focus on innovative communication and education strategies.

Nicole Kronberger

Dr Nicole Kronberger is Assistant Professor at the Department of Social and Economic Psychology at Johannes Kepler University Linz (Austria) and Marie Curie Fellow at the London School of Economics and Political Science. Her research interests focus on social psychological phenomena – such as stereotypes, risk perceptions, moral reasoning and values – and how these relate to the processes of public understanding of technologies. She is currently working on the European Commission projects 'Sensitive technologies and European public ethics' and 'The landscape and isobars of European values in relation to science and new technology'.

Simon Lock

Simon J. Lock is a Teaching Fellow in the Department of Science and Technology Studies at University College London. His research focuses on historical, sociological and policy-related questions around the public dimensions of science with a particular focus on the public understanding of science, science communication, public engagement with science and technology, social and cultural representations of science and public attitudes to new technologies. Current projects include the history of the public understanding of science movement in the UK, and public attitudes and framings of carbon governance. He has also worked on projects concerned with public engagement with science and technology for the Royal Society, the Royal Society of Arts and the Government Office of Science.

Chris Mooney

Chris Mooney is the author of three books, including *The Republican War on Science* and *Unscientific America: How Scientific Illiteracy Threatens our Future* (with Sheril Kirshenbaum). He is also a host of the popular podcast *Point of Inquiry* (www.pointofinquiry.org), blogs for *Discovery* magazine (blogs.discovermagazine.com/intersection), and works as a science communication trainer.

Alfred Nordmann

Alfred Nordmann is a philosopher of science and of technoscience at Technische Universität Darmstadt, Germany, and University of South Carolina, USA. Since 2000, he has been studying the culture of research in nanoscience and converging technologies. This provides a grounding for the analysis of ethical and societal dimensions of technoscientific research. With Martin Carrier, Nordmann edited the volume *Science in the Context of Application* (Springer, 2010). With Andreas Lösch and Stefan Gammel he developed an institutional model for social learning from collective experiments with emerging technologies. He has contributed to numerous reports and projects commissioned by the European Commission.

Patricia Osseweijer

Patricia Osseweijer is Full Professor of Science Communication and Leader of the Biotechnology and Society Section of the Department of Biotechnology in the Faculty of Applied Sciences of Delft University of Technology. She also holds the Special Chair in Science Communication of the Dutch Royal Institute of Engineering (KIVI-NIRIA). She is Managing Director of the public–private partnership Kluyver Centre for Genomics of Industrial Fermentation, Principal Investigator of the Centre for Society and Genomics, and Flagship Manager of the socio-economic programme of the BE-Basic university–industry partnership for innovation in sustainable chemistry. Her research focuses on analysis of future societal (ELSA) issues underpinning design and evaluation of novel forms of public communication.

Andrew Revkin

Andrew Revkin is one of the most experienced and influential journalists covering climate change, biological diversity and other global environmental issues. Building on a quarter-century of prize-winning print work, he writes the Dot Earth blog for the Op Ed pages of *The New York Times*, creating a forum where several hundred thousand readers a month evaluate and discuss climate, biodiversity, population and related subjects. Revkin, who was a staff reporter at the paper from 1995 through 2009, is the senior fellow for environmental understanding at Pace University's Academy for Applied Environmental Studies. He has reported on the science and politics of global warming since the late 1980s, from the North Pole to the White House and the tumultuous treaty talks in Copenhagen. He is the author of three books on environmental subjects: *The Burning Season*, his prize-winning account of the life and murder of the rainforest defender Chico Mendes (Houghton Mifflin, 1990), *Global Warming: Understanding the Forecast* (American Museum of Natural History, 1992) and *The North Pole Was Here: Puzzles and Perils at the Top of the World* (Houghton Mifflin, 2006). Revkin has received journalism awards from many organisations, including the National Academy of Sciences, the American Association for the Advancement of Science, and Columbia University and has been awarded an honorary doctorate by Pace and a John Simon Guggenheim Fellowship. He lives in the Hudson Valley where, in spare moments, he is a performing songwriter and member of the roots band Uncle Wade. Background at: http://www.nytimes.com/revkin

Maarten van der Sanden

Maarten van der Sanden is an assistant professor in science communication at the Delft University of Technology. He worked as a science communication professional and head of science communication section at the marketing and communication corporate staff at the same university. His PhD thesis was on biomedical science communication on predictive DNA diagnostics. He started his science communication career as a science journalist after finishing his biology study both in experimental zoology and in biotechnology and society.

Piet Schenkelaars

In 1984 Piet Schenkelaars finished his studies in molecular sciences and philosophy of science at The Agricultural University Wageningen in the Netherlands. Thereafter he worked for many years for civil society organisations in The Netherlands. From 1990 to 1993 he worked as coordinator of the Clearinghouse on Biotechnology at Friends of the

Earth Europe in Brussels. Subsequently, he was employed by an environmental consultancy and a consultancy in societal communication, both located in The Netherlands. In 1998 he founded Schenkelaars Biotechnology Consultancy. Since then he has conducted many studies on regulatory and sustainability aspects of biotechnology. He has also coordinated EU research projects, organised conferences and moderated stakeholder dialogues.

James Shepherd

James Shepherd is currently reading for a PhD in theoretical chemistry at the Department of Chemistry, University of Cambridge, UK and is a graduate student at Gonville and Caius College. As an undergraduate studying natural sciences in 2006 he founded the Cambridge branch of an international organisation called The Triple Helix and in 2008, this work was recognised by the award of the Sir Harold Gilles Bursary. His passion for science communication stems from having been inspired towards science by the Royal Institution Christmas Lectures as a child. During his time at university so far, he has been lucky enough to be involved with several university initiatives, societies, newspapers and magazines. James is always on the look-out for new projects for the future, and is happy to receive correspondence to: js615@cam.ac.uk or jamesjshepherd@googlemail.com.

Chris Smith

Dr Chris Smith is a consultant medical virologist and a fellow of Queens' College at the University of Cambridge. He's also the founder and managing editor of *The Naked Scientists* radio show, podcast and website. Qualifying from the University of Cambridge combined MB/PhD programme in 2001, and having completed a thesis on the development of viruses as gene therapy vectors, Chris has forged his medical career in clinical virology. In parallel he has carved a niche as a science broadcaster and writer, publishing four popular science books internationally, including *The Naked Scientist* (Little Brown, 2010) and *Stripping Down Science* (Random House, 2010) and the hugely popular *Crisp Packet Fireworks* (New Holland, 2008), a book of kitchen science experiments co-authored with David Ansell. Outside of work, Chris enjoys gardening and travel and also has a young son and daughter who, together, ensure that his immune system remains on high alert by infecting him with everything circulating in Cambridge . . .

Sally Stares

Dr Sally Stares is a Research Fellow in the Methodology Institute at the London School of Economics and Political Science. Her research is based around the methodological theme of social measurement, with a focus on the measurement of social psychological concepts in cross-national social surveys, and an emphasis on the use of latent variable models to address common challenges encountered in this field of work, such as capturing complex constructs, taking account of 'don't know' responses, and exploring the comparability of measures between groups – particularly between countries. She works on public perceptions of various aspects of science and technology, as well as on public opinion and social attitudes and values more broadly, particularly as they relate to aspects of civil society. She works on a European Commission project 'Sensitive technologies and European public ethics', and on an ESRC-funded project 'Latent variable models for categorical data: tools of analysis for cross-national surveys'.

Susanne Stormer

Susanne Stormer joined Novo Nordisk in 2000 to ingrain the Triple Bottom Line (TBL) principle in the business. In 2001 she was appointed manager of corporate stakeholder relations, responsible for driving the company's sustainability reporting. In 2004 she also became responsible for internal brand strategy and brand culture programmes. In 2006 she was promoted to Director, Accountability and TBL Leadership, and in April 2008 she was promoted to her current position as Vice President, Global TBL Management. Susanne has an MA in English studies and a BA in East Asian area studies from the University of Aarhus, Denmark. She is a graduate of Stanford Graduate School of Business Executive Education Program (2006). From 1993 to 2007 she was an Associate Professor at Copenhagen Business School.

Stephen White

Stephen White, who died suddenly on 23 August 2010 aged 61 and to whose memory this book is dedicated, was Head of Communications for the British Psychological Society since 1985. He founded STEMPRA – Science, Technology, Engineering, Medicine Public Relations Association – in the early 1990s to provide an organisation and place where science communication professionals could network and learn from each other.

He organised and tutored numerous media and science communication skills courses for a wide variety of clients both in the UK and abroad, including the European Space Agency, Cancer Research UK, the Royal Society, the British Science Association, *Nature* and Unilever. His book *Hitting the Headlines* (White, Evans, Mihill, Tysoe, 1993) was the first to provide a practical guide to the media for scientists.

RICHARD A. L. JONES

Introduction

Public engagement in an evolving science policy landscape

WHY PUBLIC ENGAGEMENT WITH SCIENCE MATTERS

Many scientists think what they do is more important than anything else in the world. Science, in their view, is a system that provides an unrivalled way of thinking about the universe. They see the last five hundred years as a story of a world improved, indeed transformed, through science, and they look forward to a future defined by science's further advances. When we talk about the importance of communicating science, this enthusiasm of scientists for the intellectual, historical and practical importance of their subject is a good place to start. So, for many, it is with conveying the passion for science that science communication should begin. The Triple Helix, an undergraduate-run worldwide forum for science in society, and the Open Research Laboratory at the Munich Deutsches Museum described in other chapters of this book are perfect examples of such enthusiasm-stimulated activities.

This entirely positive view of science is, of course, not universally shared. The perception of a popular antipathy to some aspects of science means that defensiveness, as well as enthusiasm, can be seen as a motivation for communicating science to the public. This aspect of science communication comes to the fore when controversial issues hit the headlines; this gives rise to a reactive mode of science communication, in which it is seen as a tool for coping with science policy crises.

This is a substantially expanded and updated version of an article which first appeared in The Road Ahead: Public Dialogue on Science and Technology, Stilgoe, J. ed (2009) Sciencewise Expert Resource Centre, Department for Business Innovation and Skills, London. www.sciencewise-erc.org.uk/cms/assets/Uploads/Publications/ SWcollectionHIGH-RES.pdf

Successful Science Communication, ed. D. J. Bennett and R. C. Jennings. Published by Cambridge University Press. © Cambridge University Press 2011.

1

This reaction can even occur in anticipation of crises, as we have seen with nanotechnology and synthetic biology.

But there is much more to science communication than these two extremes. There are as many motivations for becoming involved in science communication as there are scientists so involved. Certainly, the desire to share one's enthusiasm for the subject is a good reason to want to communicate it, and it is this genuine passion for the subject that marks out some of the most successful media popularisers and evangelists of science. Some science communication is about the popularisation of well-established and uncontroversial science; sometimes, though, the popular media can be used to be provocative, or to advocate a particular point of view about a branch of science which isn't universally agreed on. Some of the most lasting and successful popular works of science fall into this category, being strengthened by the commitment of the author to a single, passionately held, position. If science is to take a central place in our culture, it must be positive when substantive intellectual arguments about science are carried out in the public domain. However, this presupposes that the difference between settled opinion and legitimate controversy, if this is a distinction that it makes sense to make, is made clear to the public and policy-makers, and that they can appreciate and live with the uncertainties resulting from the latter.

The 1985 report from the Royal Society chaired by Walter Bodmer, *The Public Understanding of Science*, brought a new urgency to the question of the communication of science to the public, and stressed a new set of very instrumental motivations for doing this (Bodmer *et al.* 1985). The report stressed that, in an increasingly technological society, it was a social imperative for the public to understand science better. With more widespread scientific literacy, workers would be able to do their jobs better, managers and government would make better decisions, and industry would become more competitive. In their personal lives, people would make better choices about their lifestyles, particularly if they understood risk better.

It may be that increased public understanding of science will lead to a more prosperous country with a healthier relationship to science and technology, but this is a long-term project. In the meantime, it has been crisis management that has caused some of the most urgent thinking about science communication. The acrimony surrounding the public debates about agricultural biotechnology and the Government's handling of the bovine spongiform encephalopathy outbreak led many to diagnose a 'crisis of trust' between the public and the world of science and technology (House of Lords 2000). This led to the idea that science communication should have a central role in maintaining public trust in the science that underpins possibly controversial policy.

A final motivation for science communication with the public stresses the two-way nature of the interaction, suggesting that the scientists involved should learn from the public as well as the public learning from the scientists. This turn to two-way engagement has followed a sustained and influential critique of some of the assumptions underlying the public understanding of science movement by social scientists, particularly from the Lancaster school associated with Brian Wynne (Wynne 2001).

According to the critique of Wynne and colleagues, the idea of 'public understanding of science' was founded on a 'deficit model,' which assumed that the key problem was a public ignorance of both basic scientific facts and the fundamental process of science. If these deficits in knowledge were corrected, it was assumed that the deficit in trust would disappear. To Wynne, this was both patronising, in that it disregarded the many forms of expertise possessed by non-scientists, and highly misleading, in that it neglected the possibility that public concerns about new technologies might revolve around perceptions of the weaknesses of the human institutions that proposed to implement them, and not on technical matters at all.

The proposed alternative was for the scientific community to reflexively engage the public in a genuine dialogue. And the time and place for such dialogue was upstream in the innovation process, while there was still scope to steer its direction in ways that had broad public support. These ideas were succinctly summarised in a widely read pamphlet from the think-tank Demos: *See-Through Science* (Wilsdon & Willis 2004).

The goal of this kind of public engagement with science, then, is to explore with the public what people want from technology in the future, with the aspiration that science and society can work together to shape that future. Seen in this way, public engagement is part of an explicit process of democratising science, in which research priorities and the trajectory of technologies are steered with reference to public values. Public engagement with science, in this view, should be seen neither as simply a way of promoting public support for the inevitable forward march of science and technology, nor as a mechanism by which a concerned public can put the brakes on progress. Rather, it imagines that the future is still open, and that society can have an influence on which of the many possible forking paths science and technology may take as the future unfolds.

In this introduction I will illustrate some of these issues as they have arisen in the context of nanotechnology, which, over the last ten years, has provided an excellent case study of the shift in emphasis from public understanding to public engagement.

THE CASE OF NANOTECHNOLOGY

Nanotechnology, from its very beginnings, has been a discipline in which the relationship between the science itself and the communication of science has been complicated, and often uneasy. The word 'nanotechnology' itself first entered wide circulation as a result of a popular science book, which described it as a potentially revolutionary new technology (Drexler 1986). On the negative side, the idea that the technology might pose serious threats to humanity was crystallised by a magazine article by the computer scientist and entrepreneur Bill Joy (Joy 2000).

Meanwhile, the academic enterprise of nanotechnology gained momentum, driven, in particular, by the announcement in the USA of a National Nanotechnology Initiative beginning in the year 2000. As the science progressed, an increasing divergence became apparent between the perceptions of nanotechnology in popular culture, which derived from science popularisations such as *Engines of Creation* (Drexler 1986) and which were imaginatively developed in science fiction, films and video games, and the directions that scientists in the field were pursuing.

My own involvement in science communication began in response to this divergence. I wrote a book about nanotechnology for the general reader (Jones 2004). My aim was partly to correct what I perceived as widely held misconceptions about the subject, and partly to present my own vision of a nanotechnology inspired by biology, in contrast to the mechanical paradigm which at the time dominated popular conceptions of the subject. Further science communication activities – such as public lectures and a blog – followed.

But what really brought nanotechnology into the public eye in the UK was the fear of another science policy crisis. In 2003, the Prince of Wales made the first of a series of high-profile media interventions that raised fears about nanotechnology (Lean 2004), drawing on a highly negative report from a campaigning NGO with a previous track record of opposing agricultural biotechnology (ETC Group 2003).

In response to the growing media profile of nanotechnology the government commissioned the Royal Society and the Royal Academy of

Engineering to carry out a wide-ranging study on nanotechnology and the health and safety, environmental, ethical and social issues that might stem from it. The working group included, in addition to distinguished scientists, a philosopher, a social scientist and a representative of an environmental NGO. The process of producing the report itself involved public engagement, with two in-depth workshops exploring the potential hopes and concerns that members of the public might have about nanotechnology.

The report – *Nanoscience and Nanotechnologies: Opportunities and Uncertainties* – was published in 2004, and amongst its recommendations was a whole-hearted endorsement of the upstream public engagement approach: 'a constructive and proactive debate about the future of nanotechnologies should be undertaken now – at a stage when it can inform key decisions about their development and before deeply entrenched or polarised positions appear.' (Royal Society 2004).

Following this recommendation, a number of public engagement activities around nanotechnology have taken place in the UK. Two notable examples were *Nanojury UK*, a citizens' jury which took place in Halifax in the summer of 2005, and *Nanodialogues*, a more substantial project which linked four separate engagement exercises carried out in 2006 and 2007.

Nanojury UK was sponsored jointly by the Cambridge University Nanoscience Centre and Greenpeace UK, with the *Guardian* as a media partner, and Newcastle University's Policy, Ethics and Life Sciences Research Centre running the sessions. It was carried out in Halifax over eight evening sessions, with six witnesses drawn from academic science, industry and campaigning groups, considering a wide variety of potential applications of nanotechnology (Nanojury 2005). As chair of the science advisory panel, I coordinated the science and industry based witnesses and took part in several sessions myself – thus this was my practical introduction into public engagement, as distinct to traditional science communication.

The *Nanodialogues* took a more focused approach (Stilgoe 2007). Each of its four exercises, described as 'experiments', considered a single aspect or application area of nanotechnology. These included a concrete example of a proposed use for nanotechnology – a scheme to use nanoparticles to remediate polluted groundwater – and the application of nanoscience in the context of a large corporation.

The Nanotechnology Engagement Group, which I was asked to chair, provided a wider forum to consider the lessons to be learnt from these and other public engagement exercises both in the UK and abroad (Gavelin, Wilson & Doubleday 2007). This revealed a rather consistent message from public engagement. Broadly speaking, there was considerable excitement from the public about possible beneficial outcomes from nanotechnology, particularly in potential applications such as renewable energy, and medical applications. The more general value of such technologies in promoting jobs and economic growth was also recognised.

There were concerns, too. The questions that have been raised about potential safety and toxicity issues associated with some nanoparticles caused disquiet, and there were more general anxieties (probably not wholly specific to nanotechnology) about who controls and regulates new technology.

Reviewing a number of public engagement activities related to nanotechnology also highlighted some practical and conceptual difficulties. There was sometimes a lack of clarity about the purpose and role of public engagement; this leaves space for the cynical view that such exercises are intended not to have a real influence on genuinely open decisions, but simply to add a gloss of legitimacy to decisions that have already been made. Related to this is the fact that bodies that might benefit from public engagement may lack the institutional capacity to make the most of it.

There are some more practical problems associated with the very idea of moving engagement 'upstream' – the further the science is away from potential applications, the more difficult it can be both to communicate what can be complex issues, whose impact and implications may be subject to considerable disagreement amongst experts.

CONNECTING PUBLIC ENGAGEMENT TO POLICY

The big question to be asked about any public engagement exercise is 'What difference has it made?' – has there been any impact on policy? For this to take place there needs to be careful choice of the subject for the public engagement, as well as commitment and capacity on behalf of the sponsoring body or agency to use the results in a constructive way. A recent example from the UK Engineering and Physical Science Research Council (EPSRC) offers an illuminating case study. Here, a public dialogue on the potential applications of nanotechnology to medicine and healthcare was explicitly coupled to a decision about where to target a research funding initiative, providing valuable insights that had a significant impact on the decision.

This initiative was part of a new approach to science funding at EPSRC, where I act as Senior Strategic Adviser for Nanotechnology. 'Grand Challenge' projects are large, goal-oriented interdisciplinary activities in areas of societal need. One of these was in the area of applications of nanotechnology to healthcare and medicine. This is a potentially huge area, so it was felt necessary to narrow the scope of the programme before asking the scientific community for research proposals. EPSRC drew on their Strategic Advisory Team – an advisory committee with about a dozen experts on nanotechnology, drawn from academia and industry, and including international representation. There was also a wider consultation with academics and potential research 'users', defined here as clinicians and representatives of the pharmaceutical and healthcare industries, and a 'town hall meeting' open to research and user communities.

This is a fairly standard approach to soliciting expert opinion for a decision about science funding priorities. Given the public engagement around nanotechnology up to this point, it seemed natural to ask whether EPSRC should seek public views as well. EPSRC's Societal Issues Panel – a committee providing high-level advice on the societal and ethical context for research – enthusiastically endorsed the proposal for a public engagement exercise on nanotechnology for medicine and healthcare as an explicit part of the consultation leading up to the decision on the scope of the Grand Challenge in nanotechnology for medicine and healthcare.

In the spring of 2008, the market research firm BMRB Ltd, led by Darren Bhattachary, ran a public dialogue on nanotechnology for healthcare. This took the form of a pair of reconvened workshops in each of four locations – London, Sheffield, Glasgow and Swansea. Each workshop involved 22 lay participants, with care taken to ensure a demographic balance. The workshops were informed by written materials, approved by an expert steering committee; there was expert participation in each workshop from both scientists and social scientists. Staff from EPSRC also attended, which was taken by many participants as a signal of how seriously the organisation was taking the exercise.

The dialogues produced a number of rich insights that proved very useful in defining the scope of the final call (Bhattachary, Stockley & Hunter 2008). In general, there was very strong support for medicine and healthcare as a priority area for the application of nanotechnology, and explicit rejection of an unduly precautionary approach. On the other hand, there were concerns about who benefits from the expenditure of public funds on science, and about issues of risk and the governance of technology. One overarching theme that emerged was a strong preference for new technologies that were felt to empower people to take control of their own health and lives.

One advantage of connecting a public dialogue with a concrete issue of funding priorities is that some very specific potential applications of nanotechnology could be discussed. As a result of the consultation with academics, clinicians and industry representatives, six topics had been identified for consideration. In each case, people at the workshops could identify both positive and negative aspects, but overall some clear preferences emerged. The use of nanotechnology to permit the early diagnosis of disease received strong support, as it was felt that this would provide information that would enable people to make changes to the way they live. The promise of nanotechnology to help treat serious diseases with fewer side effects by more effective targeting of drugs was also received with enthusiasm. On the other hand, the idea of devices that combine the ability to diagnose a condition with the means to treat it, via releasing therapeutic agents, caused some disquiet. This was seen as potentially disempowering. Lower down the list of priorities were applications of nanotechnology to control pathogens, for example through nano-structured surfaces with intrinsic antimicrobial or antiviral properties, nano-structured materials to help facilitate regenerative medicine and the use of nanotechnology to help develop new drugs.

It was always anticipated that the results of this public dialogue would be used in two ways. Their most obvious role was as an input to the final decision on the scope of the Grand Challenge call, together with the outcomes of the consultations with the expert communities. It was the nanotechnology Strategic Advisory Team that made the final recommendation about the call's scope. Their recommendation was that the call should be in the two areas most favoured in the public dialogue – nanotechnology for early diagnosis and nanotechnology for drug delivery. In addition to this immediate impact, the projects funded through the Grand Challenge will be expected to reflect these findings in how they are carried out.

WHERE NEXT?

In the case of nanotechnology, the motivation for much public engagement was the fear of a negative public reaction against what many thought was a promising, and powerful, emerging technology. We are now seeing the same pattern unfolding in the case of other emerging fields. Synthetic biology is one such area, where a series of very well-publicised results from the Craig Venter Institute have ensured a high media profile (Gibson *et al.* 2010). In anticipation of the announcement of the first synthetic organism, two UK research councils, EPSRC and the Biotechnology and Biological Sciences Research Council (BBSRC), had already begun a synthetic biology dialogue (Bhattachary *et al.* 2010).

Synthetic biology, as a topic, has an even more upstream character than nanotechnology. Not only is it very far from clear what applications will emerge from the technology, but the very definitions and underpinning philosophies of the field remain contested (Benner & Sismour 2005), and it remains possible that fundamental barriers may prevent the more optimistic projections for the technology from being realised (Kwok 2010). This has some echoes of the situation with nanotechnology. One negative feature of the nanotechnology debate was the way unlikely and implausible future projections for the technology gained undue credibility as a result of discussions of their potential societal implications. This phenomenon has been dissected by Alfred Nordmann who has criticised the kind of *'ethical discourse that constructs and validates an incredible future which it only then proceeds to endorse or critique'* (Nordmann 2007), and in his contribution to this volume calls for a 'responsible representation', which *'involves determinations of plausibility in light of ongoing trends rather than radical novelty'* and *'requires that communicators take responsibility for their representations by being prepared to defend their credibility'*.

If one danger of public engagement around technologies in their earliest stages is an excessive focus on a set of extreme, and rather unlikely, possible outcomes, another possible response is that people concentrate on wider concerns about emerging technologies in general. If one compares the outcome of the synthetic biology dialogue mentioned above with earlier dialogues about nanotechnology, there certainly seems to be a lot of common ground. The agricultural biotechnology debate which preceded these again appears to share many common characteristics. This suggests that it might be worthwhile systematically to draw out generic responses and lessons for all emerging technologies.

Perhaps the most highly charged areas of science communication arise in those fields where the results have major implications for public policy, and where those results are mediated by a wider variety of mass media with many different agendas of their own. The most important such area – arguably the most important area of science communication of all – is the debate about man-made climate change. Here the idea that simply communicating the results of consensus science to the public would lead to an informed policy debate has been tested to destruction. Instead, we have seen what are allegedly technical arguments being used as a proxy for disputes between quite profound political and ideological differences (Hulme 2009).

PUBLIC ENGAGEMENT IN AN EVOLVING SCIENCE POLICY LANDSCAPE

The current interest in public engagement takes place at a time when the science policy landscape is undergoing wider changes, in the UK and elsewhere. We are seeing considerable pressure from governments for publicly funded science to deliver clearer economic and societal benefits. There is a growing emphasis on goal-oriented, intrinsically interdisciplinary science, with an agenda set by a societal and economic context rather than by an academic discipline – 'mode II knowledge production' – in the phrase of Gibbons and colleagues (Gibbons et al. 1994). The 'linear model' of innovation – in which pure, academic science, unconstrained by any issues of societal or economic context, is held to lead inexorably through applied science and technological development to new products and services and thus increased prosperity – is widely recognised to be simplistic at best, neglecting the many feedbacks and hybridisations at every stage of this process.

These newer conceptions of 'technoscience' or 'mode II science' lead to problems of their own. If the agenda of science is to be set by the demands of societal needs, it is important to ask who defines those needs. While it is easy to identify the location of expertise for narrowly constrained areas of science defined by well-established disciplinary boundaries, it is much less easy to see who has the expertise to define the technically possible in strongly multidisciplinary projects. And as the societal and economic contexts of research become more important in making decisions about science priorities, we need to consider how to scrutinise the social theories of scientists. These are all issues that public engagement could be valuable in resolving.

The enthusiasm for involving the public more closely in decisions about science policy may not be universally shared, however. In some parts of the academic community, it may be perceived as an assault on academic autonomy. Indeed, in the current climate, with demands for science to have greater and more immediate economic impact, an insistence on more public involvement might be taken as part of a two-pronged assault on pure science values. As traditional gatekeepers between the experts and the public, media might not be sympathetic to such new forms of engagement. Then there are some who consider public engagement more generally as incompatible with the principles of representative democracy. Their view would be that the Science Minister is responsible for the science budget and he or she answers to Parliament, not to a small group of people in a citizens' jury. It is also clear that public engagement, done properly, is expensive and time-consuming. And 'properly' is the key word because otherwise such exercises succeed in attracting only the previously interested and committed, and not the majority of people who are very difficult to reach.

Many of the scientists (me included) who have been involved with public engagement, however, have reported that the experience is very positive. In addition to being reminded of the generally high standing of scientists and the scientific enterprise in our society, they are prompted to re-examine unspoken assumptions and clarify their aims and objectives. There are strong arguments that public deliberation and interaction can lead to more robust science policy, particularly in areas that are intrinsically interdisciplinary and explicitly coupled to meeting societal goals. What will be interesting to consider as more experience is gained is whether embedding public engagement more closely in the scientific process actually helps to produce better science.

CONCLUSION

The twenty-five years since the publication of the Bodmer Report have been very eventful from the point of view of those interested in science communication. That report was notably successful in establishing the need to put science communication at the heart of the scientific enterprise; in the intervening years we have seen a series of testing episodes in the relationship of science and society which have led us to refine our understanding of the aims and methods of science communication.

We can now recognise a very wide diversity of motivations, purposes and methods for science communication. The very proper desire of many scientists to convey to the public their passion for science remains important, and the need to cope with occasional science-related public policy crises is not likely to go away. But perhaps we can hope that science communication as a whole can move away from a defensiveness born of rather negative preconceptions of the relationship between the scientific enterprise and wider publics, towards a deeper project of more deeply rooting science in society. This does imply the continuing need for an understanding of science by those wider publics. But it also needs that deeper understanding, by scientists, of society in all its diversity, that comes from engagement and dialogue.

Key resources

J. Wilsdon & R. Willis, *See-Through Science: Why Public Engagement Needs to Move Upstream*, Demos, (2004) http://www.green-alliance.org.uk/uploadedFiles/Publications/ SeeThroughScienceFinalFullCopy.pdf (accessed 6/6/2011).
J. Stilgoe (ed.), *The Road Ahead: Public Dialogue on Science and Technology*. Sciencewise Expert Resource Centre (2009) http://www.sciencewise-erc.org.uk/cms/assets/ Uploads/Publications/SWcollectionHIGH-RES.pdf (accessed 6/6/2011).
S. Jasanoff, *Designs on Nature: Science and Democracy in Europe and the United States*. Princeton University Press (2005).
M. Hulme, *Why We Disagree about Climate Change*. Cambridge University Press (2009).

References

Benner, S. & Sismour, A. (2005) Synthetic biology. *Nature Reviews Genetics* 6 533–543.
Bhattachary, D., Calitz, J.P. & Hunt, A. (2010) *Synthetic Biology Dialogue*. http:// www.bbsrc.ac.uk/web/ILES/Reviews/1006-synthet-biology-dialogue.pdf (accessed 6/6/2011).
Bhattachary, D., Stockley, R. & Hunter, A. (2008) *Nanotechnology for Healthcare*. London: BMRB Ltd. http://www.epsrc.ac.uk/SiteCollectionDocuments/Publications/reports/ ReportPublicDialogueNanotechHealthcare.doc (accessed 6/6/2011).
Bodmer, W. *et al.* (1985) *The Public Understanding of Science*. London: The Royal Society.
Drexler, K.E. (1986) *Engines of Creation*. New York: Anchor.
ETC Group (2003) *The Big Down*. Winnipeg: ETC Group. http://www.etcgroup.org/ upload/publication/171/01/thebigdown.pdf (accessed 6/6/2011).
Gavelin, K., Wilson, R. & Doubleday, R. (2007) *Democratic Technologies? The Final Report of the Nanotechnology Engagement Group*. London: Involve. http:// involve.brilliantukhosting.com/assets/Uploads/Democratic-Technologies.pdf (accessed 6/6/2011).
Gibbons, M. *et al.* (1994) *The New Production of Knowledge: The Dynamics of Science and Research in Contemporary Societies*. London: Sage.
Gibson, D.G. *et al.* (2010) Chemically synthesized genome creation of a bacterial cell controlled by a chemically synthesized genome. *Science* 329 52–56.
House of Lords Select Committee on Science and Technology (2000) Third Report,Science and Society. London: Science and Technology Committee Publications. http://www.publications.parliament.uk/pa/ld199900/ldselect/ ldsctech/38/3801.htm
Hulme, M. (2009) *Why We Disagree about Climate Change*. Cambridge: Cambridge University Press.
Jones, R.A.L. (2004) *Soft Machines: Nanotechnology and Life*. Oxford: Oxford University Press.

Joy, W.N. (2000) Why the future doesn't need us. *Wired Magazine*, Issue 8.40.

Kwok, R. (2010) Five hard truths for synthetic biology. *Nature* **463** 288–290.

Lean, G. (2004) One will not be silenced: Charles rides into battle to fight a new campaign. *Independent on Sunday*, 11 July 2004. http://www.independent.co.uk/news/uk/this-britain/one-will-not-be-silenced-charles-rides-into-battle-to-fight-a-new-campaign-552772.html (accessed 15/7/2010).

Nanojury (2005) http://www.nanojury.org.uk/index.html (accessed 15/7/2010).

Nordmann, A. (2007) If and then: a critique of speculative nanoethics. *Nanoethics* **1** 31.

Royal Society (2004) *Nanoscience and Nanotechnologies: Opportunities and Uncertainties*. London: The Royal Society. http://www.nanotec.org.uk/finalReport.htm (accessed 15/7/2010).

Stilgoe, J. (2007) *Nanodialogues: Experiments in Public Engagement with Science*. London: Demos. http://www.demos.co.uk/files/Nanodialogues%20-%20%20web.pdf (accessed 6/6/2011).

Wilsdon, J. & Willis, R. (2004) *See-Through Science: Why Public Engagement Needs to Move Upstream*. London: Demos. http://www.demos.co.uk/files/Seethroughsciencefinal.pdf?1240939425 (accessed 6/6/11).

Wynne, B. (2001) Creating public alienation: expert cultures of risk and ethics on GMOs. *Science as Culture* **10** 445–481.

Part I   What it helps to know beforehand

SIMON J. LOCK

1

Deficits and dialogues: science communication and the public understanding of science in the UK

INTRODUCTION

In 1985 the Royal Society published a report on the public understanding of science (PUS), eponymously known as the Bodmer Report after Dr (now Sir) Walter Bodmer who chaired the working group which produced it and contributes the Foreword to this book (Royal Society 1985). This report problematised the public's knowledge of science and gave rise to a variety of science communication activities aimed at correcting a perceived lack of scientific knowledge by the public. Fifteen years later another key report by the House of Lords Select Committee on Science and Technology argued that society's relationship with science was in a critical phase (House of Lords Select Committee on Science and Technology 2000). Almost overnight, science communication activities practised by scientific and government agencies as 'public understanding of science', were replaced by encouragement for new methods of public engagement and dialogue under the new label of 'Science and Society'.

Many regarded this as a watershed moment in the public understanding of science movement. The idea that the public were deficient in scientific knowledge and should therefore be exposed to science communication by scientific experts was replaced by a dialogue model of communication which framed the public in a very different manner – a public who should be listened to, who had something meaningful to input into scientific policy-making and whose trust in scientists needed rebuilding – a view which continues to the present day.

Successful Science Communication, ed. D. J. Bennett and R. C. Jennings. Published by
Cambridge University Press. © Cambridge University Press 2011.

While activity and research into the public understanding of science is of course not limited to the UK, the initiatives in this area, particularly institutional programmes in the public understanding of science, have frequently become exemplars for other countries when developing their own. This is in part due to the involvement of well-known institutions in science communication having had a long history in Britain, for example by the Royal Institution's Christmas Lectures to general audiences continuing annually since 1825 and interrupted only during World War II, illustrated in the frontispiece to this book of Michael Faraday delivering a Christmas Lecture in 1856. Others followed such as the British Association for the Advancement of Science (now known as the British Science Association and previously as the BA) and the Royal Society, exemplified by Nicola Buckley and Sue Hordijenko in their Chapter 21 on science festivals. The more recent international concerns over the public understanding of science have also tended to follow from these involvements with a continued UK origin coupled with those of especially the American Association for the Advancement of Science stemming from the early 1960s.

THE BIRTH OF PUBLIC UNDERSTANDING OF SCIENCE

The 1970s was a low point for the scientific community in the UK for science communication. Many scientists felt the national press had taken a more critical stance on scientific issues, in part due to the increased awareness of environmental degradation caused by advances in science. At the same time the professionalisation of science journalists and broadcasters had resulted in them becoming more prominent in the public sphere (Gregory and Miller 1998).

Despite the scientific community having played a leading role in the popularisation of science over the previous 150 or so years, hostile headlines had made many cautious of sticking their head out of their ivory tower lest it be chopped off by these new critics of science. As Goodell suggested, this reluctance to engage in public communication was instilled in many scientists as a tacit part of their socialisation into the profession (Goodell 1977). The so-called 'unwritten rules of science communication' – that a scientist should not engage in public communication of their work before publication or, indeed, before their productivity as a researcher was over, and that they should stick only to their area of specialism – left popularisation of science mainly to a few strong-minded or senior scientists while the rest focused on their research.

The advent of the Thatcher Government in 1979 resulted in a squeeze on public finances, including scientific research. The 'brain drain' from the UK that resulted and falling numbers of students taking science at university added to the perception of a hostile environment for science in Britain. The Government looked to industry to take the lead on scientific decisions and to be the innovators and engine of the economy. The drop in financial support combined with perceived lack of public support precipitated concern within the science community that the popularisation efforts of scientists had had little effect. This perception however is to be set against the repeated findings of public opinion polls over the last 20 years that scientists are in fact held in considerable esteem and trust by the wider public, as Michel Claessens and David Bennett discuss in Chapters 8 and 15 respectively.

The late 1980s saw these concerns come to a head with the Royal Society setting up an *ad hoc* working group to *'investigate ways in which the public understanding of science (PUS) might be enhanced'* (Royal Society 1985, p. 7). Walter Bodmer, then Director of Research for the Imperial Cancer Research Fund and Fellow of the Royal Society, was appointed chair of the working group whose terms of reference were:

(i)   *to review the nature and extent of public understanding of science and technology in the UK and its adequacy for an advanced industrialized democracy;*

(ii) *to review the mechanisms for effecting the public understanding of science and technology and its role in society;*

(iii) *to consider the constraints upon the processes of communication and how they might best be overcome;*

(iv) *to make recommendations and report to Council.* (Royal Society 1985, p. 7)

The working group unanimously concluded that *'public understanding of science was inadequate'* and identified PUS as an important issue not only for the scientific community but also for the nation as a whole (p. 15). Scientific knowledge was needed by industrialists, policy-makers and individual members of the public if the UK was to be a competitive, prosperous, rational modern democracy. Most importantly, achieving this depended *'on the willingness and the ability of the scientific community to explain these aspects publicly'* (p. 10). Thus the main recommendations of the report were aimed at the scientific community, and its most direct and urgent message to scientists was for them to *'learn to communicate with the public, be willing to do so, indeed consider it your duty to do so'* (p. 6). In a clear break with the earlier period the Bodmer Report raised the profile of the public understanding of science from something that had been a relatively personal concern of a minority of scientists to something with which all should be concerned.

TAKING PUS FORWARD

The major outcome of the Bodmer Report was the formation of the Committee on the Public Understanding of Science (COPUS) in 1986 as a joint committee of the Royal Society, the Royal Institution and the British Association for the Advancement of Science. It was given the general aim of raising the profile and number of public understanding of science activities in the UK, particularly among scientists. Its initial activities included setting up a grants scheme to fund scientists in science communication activities, a Media Fellowship scheme, and the establishment of the Faraday Award for scientists or engineers who contributed significantly to the public understanding of science.

An Economic and Social Research Council (ESRC)-funded national survey of public attitudes and knowledge published in *Nature* in 1989 (Durant *et al.* 1989) suggested that the Bodmer Report's characterisation of the public as ignorant about science was correct. The main findings were that while levels of British interest in science, technology and medicine were relatively high, levels of knowledge were far lower.

CRITICISMS OF PUS

In parallel, though largely ignored by the scientific community's efforts, was the development of a research programme on Public Under-standing of Science established by the ESRC. This research, except for the surveys, approached PUS from a qualitative social science research perspective, and the results challenged many of the assumptions implicit in the approach which COPUS had been actively pursuing since 1985.[1] The physicist John Ziman, who had headed the ESRC research programme, criticised COPUS's actions as operating under a *'simple "deficit" model'* which was inadequate as an analytical framework for research into PUS, because it tried to *'interpret the situation solely in terms of public ignorance or scientific literacy'* (Ziman 1990). The ESRC research

[1] These qualitative projects examined issues of public understanding of science within specific practical social contexts rather than focusing on what the public did not know about science. Examples included a study of those who had inherited the familial hypercholesterolaemia, an investigation into two communities living close to hazardous industry, and an analysis of the role played by scientists in environmental organisations.

had shown a far more complex picture, emphasising the importance of the context within which the public was receiving scientific knowledge and questioning the assumption of ignorance on the part of the public. Science policy researcher Brian Wynne went further, arguing that it was the very institutional structures within which science was organised and projected that were part of the problem in public under-standing of science (Wynne 1990).

The 'contextual model' of PUS research which emerged ques-tioned many of the assumptions underlying the approach to PUS pro-moted by COPUS. It suggested that the lay public's understandings or misunderstandings of science was not the central point. Understanding how science was contextualised within people's lives, Wynne argued, was more *crucial to understanding the social authority (or lack of authority) of science*' than simply communicating abstract facts (Wynne 1990, p. 5). People did not use, assimilate or experience science as separate from other elements of knowledge, judgement or advice; supplementary knowledge, which could often be highly specialised, was always required to make any scientific understanding valid and useful in that context. The 'problem' of PUS, Wynne argued, lay with the scientific institutions themselves.

THE EXPANSION OF THE PUS AGENDA

The early 1990s was a period of expansion and consolidation of resources for both natural and social scientists involved in the public understanding of science. An academic journal entitled *Public Under-standing of Science* was launched in 1992 with John Durant as editor providing for the publication of both qualitative and quantitative research. He also established the first MSc course in science communi-cation at Imperial College London to provide professional training in the principles and practices of science communication[2] and was the founding chairman in 1991 of the European Federation of Biotechno-logy's Task Group on Public Perceptions of Biotechnology.[3]

---

[2] This was the first of many new academic courses in practical science communication set up around the UK and in many other countries.

[3] The Task Group was one of the first organisations active in this field and included among its members Brian Wynne (already mentioned) together with the authors or co-authors of several chapters of this book (George Gaskell, Chapter 4; Alastair Kent, Chapter 13; Piet Schenkelaars, Chapter 14; Lise Kingo, Chapter 20; and Patricia Osseweijer, Chapters 25 and 27) and its co-editor and author of Chapter 15, David Bennett, as secretary.

Criticism of the assumptions underlying the PUS agenda being pursued by COPUS grew from within the social sciences (Michael 1992, Collins and Pinch 1993, Wynne 1995, Irwin and Wynne 1996). The need for increasing PUS rested originally on the idea that lack of public understanding could be equated with lack of support for science (Thomas and Durant 1987). It was now suggested that underlying the democratic and economic claims for PUS made by COPUS was an implicit public relations exercise to solve the perceived problem of an ignorant and hostile public, and subsequently raise the fortunes of science in the UK (Lewenstein 1992).

However, COPUS's efforts continued with little or no engagement with these alternative characterisations of the problem of public understanding of science. The committee was given firm endorsement by the UK Government in its first White Paper on science for 20 years in 1993 (Office of Science and Technology 1993). A fund was set up administered by COPUS for small grants to cover part of the costs of activities to increase public understanding of science and technology, and the new Research Councils were charged with improving scientists' skills in communicating with the public. The following year the Government awarded funding for a national science, engineering and technology week overseen by the British Association for the Advancement of Science and in 1995 the *Wolfendale Report* argued that it should become mandatory for applicants for Research Council grants to show how they would communicate their research to the general public and why it was important (Office of Science and Technology 1995).

Ten years on, COPUS activities had gained widespread Government support and an evaluation revealed a large change in commitments to the public understanding of science since 1985, highlighting the large number of organisations and individuals now involved. Fifty-four per cent of Royal Society Research Fellows, for example, had taken part in PUS activities. The 1990s had also witnessed a boom in popular science books from scientists such as Stephen Hawking, Steven Jay Gould and Richard Dawkins becoming bestsellers. Yet despite these achievements perception and concern continued, particularly amongst senior scientists, that the public understanding of science was lamentable.

A HARD LESSON TO SWALLOW?

The politically damaging public crisis over BSE (bovine spongiform encephalopathy) in 1996 proved to be another watershed moment in the development of science communication in the UK. Government policies for disclosing, or in this case failing to disclose, information about risk to the public were blamed for the subsequent breakdown in consumer confidence. Rather than openly discussing the uncertainties of the science around BSE transmission, the Government had hidden behind presenting the science as certain and apolitical (Jasanoff 1997).

Further evidence that the relationship between public attitudes to science and technology and understanding was not as simple as previously assumed had also been published (Evans and Durant 1995). Analysis of survey data had shown there was relatively little evidence on whether or not the widespread assumption that greater knowledge of science leads to a greater support for science was correct (Durant, Bauer and Gaskell 1998). A British Social Attitudes Survey in 1996 further showed that levels of scientific literacy and attitudes to science had remained static since 1988 prompting questioning whether the PUS efforts had amounted to anything (British Social Attitudes Survey 1996).

Many have cited the BSE crisis as an indicator of declining public confidence in democratic structures and, more importantly, public trust in science and scientific advice. The political pressures highlighted by the episode certainly suggested that a new approach was needed: one that emphasised context, transparency and trust, many of the ideas that had been stressed as key to a healthy relationship between science and the public by those within the social sciences for years. Science communication post-BSE needed to be less about 'show and tell' and more two-way to ensure mutual trust and understanding. John Durant, now Professor of Public Understanding of Science at Imperial College London, called for a new programme in PUS, arguing that as long as it confined itself to what might be termed the missionary role – going out and looking for converts – the scientific community risked failing to address crucially important issues to do with the changing place of science and technology in our culture (Durant 1995). Many within the scientific community were starting to believe that if science and scientists were not to lose credibility as politics and politicians had done, then they needed somehow to renew their mandate with the public and work hard at building lost trust.

A NEW MOOD FOR 'DIALOGUE'

When genetically modified (GM) crops became a controversial issue in 1999, the UK Government, scientific institutions, the public, the media and industry were once more drawn into a public debate about scientific uncertainty, risks and how best to communicate science to the public. Despite a change of language within government in dealing with scientific uncertainty and risks post-BSE, differing ideas remained about managing relationships with science. Monsanto, for example, still assumed that by providing the scientific facts of genetic modification they could lead the public to accept it, not appreciating that much of the public dissent was over the ethical, social and political implications of the technology, on top of uncertainties about its safety to humans and the environment.

Following the controversy over GM foods, and the changing nature of the scientific advisory processes within government in response to the BSE affair, the House of Lords Select Committee on Science and Technology concluded in its report *Science and Society* in February 2000, that society's relationship with science was in a critical phase (House of Lords Select Committee on Science and Technology 2000, p. 11). It put forward many recommendations as to how this relationship could be improved, not least by advocating a shift away from *'simply giving information'* to *'engaging the wider public in dialogue about what science could and should be doing'* (p. 13). The Committee believed that the public, as evidenced in large-scale survey results and the high sales of popular science books, were interested in science, but they were also more sceptical and questioning of its uses.

The House of Lords report is a significant publication in many respects and marks yet another watershed moment in the history of the public understanding of science in the UK. What was striking was the level of input from social scientists in drawing up the report and the take-up of ideas such as trust and dialogue which both Government and the scientific community had for so many years ignored. The report made numerous arguments for the need to reconsider and renew the established public understanding of science agenda. Increasing the public understanding of science was no longer enough to solve the perceived problem in science/public relations, and scientists needed to engage the public to restore public confidence. Identifying what they called a *'new mood for dialogue'* within the public and the PUS community, they argued:

> Today's public expects not merely to know what is going on, but to be consulted;
> science is beginning to see the wisdom of this, and to move 'out of the laboratory and
> into the community' to engage in dialogue aimed at mutual understanding.
> Several of our witnesses agree that a shift along these lines is taking place.
> (House of Lords Select Committee on Science and Technology 2000, p. 37)

In comparison to the Bodmer Report, the issue of the public's relationship with science was to be managed less through educating and more by 'engaging' them in the policy-making process, yet both aimed for a positive change in public attitudes towards science and technology.

The next few years saw almost all government and scientific initiatives being relaunched with a new 'Science and Society' rhetoric. Several of the Research Councils reformulated their initiatives to fit in with, as the Natural Environment Research Council (NERC) described, the *'new approach to what was previously called "Public Understanding of Science", but which we now term "Science and Society"'* (NERC 2001). The Royal Society's response to the report was the establishment of a five-year 'Science in Society Initiative', set up as part of the Royal Society's commitment to respond to their growing concern and perception that *'the public's confidence in certain areas of science was failing'* (Royal Society 2001).

Perhaps the most obvious sign of all institutional changes to PUS at this time was the reconstitution of COPUS in 2001. Following extensive reviews, it was agreed by all the COPUS partners that it should be remodelled in this new climate as *'an inclusive partnership between the many sectors now involved in communicating science'* (COPUS 2001). COPUS was no longer to be used as an acronym but as a brand 'Copus' with a new expanded Council overseeing it. The new body made it clear that science communication was to be focused on *'supporting ways of increasing public engagement with the issues and processes of science'*. The COPUS grant schemes were reformulated under this new agenda to fund dialogue with the public. However, in May 2002, the chair of COPUS unexpectedly resigned and the COPUS founders disbanded it having reached the conclusion that the top–down approach was no longer appropriate to the wider agenda that the science communication community was now addressing (COPUS 2002).

With now no clear national strategy or co-ordinating body for science communication under the new 'Science and Society' agenda, the British Association conducted a study looking at how the Government should proceed with science communication policy and activity. The BA's consultation, however, also brought to light internal conflicts within the large science communication sector which had grown in the UK and which had increasingly been taken over by a new breed of professionals. The Royal Geographical Society criticised this so-called 'PUS industry' consisting of science communication degree graduates, Government officers and academics who understood *'meetings and mapping exercises, but nothing about communication proper, and a clutch of self-interested commercial pollsters, conference organisers and PR agencies eager to supply their services'* (Royal Geographical Society 2002). The criticism also raised the important distinctions between the multiple meanings of communication and dialogue, and between those institutions wishing to engage in either one-way or two-way conversations with the public and those trying to influence science policy, or restore confidence or trust.

PUBLIC ENGAGEMENT IN PRACTICE

A high-profile test of the UK Government's new commitment to public dialogue came in 2003 with the suggestion by the Agriculture and Environment Biotechnology Commission (AEBC 2001) that a different kind of consultation was needed for GM crops, arguing that the public should be given the opportunity to guide the way in which the issue was debated rather than respond to an agenda set by others. The Government, facing widespread media controversy over GM foods, accepted the AEBC's advice and the *GM Nation?* public consultation began in June 2003 reporting its findings later that year (Public Debate Steering Board 2003). Despite criticisms of the *GM Nation?* exercise, including in the UK Government's own report (Department of Trade and Industry 2003, Mayer 2003, Rowe *et al.* 2005), public engagement was moving up the Government agenda as a key component of policy-making. A Treasury report in 2004 announced that the budget for the Office of Science and Technology's Science and Society expenditure would be increased from £4.25 million per year in 2005–06 to over £9 million per year by 2006–07. As part of this, a new grants scheme was to be launched to *'build the capacity of citizens, the science community and policy-makers to engage in the dialogue necessary to establish and maintain public confidence in making better choices about critical areas in science and technology'* (HM Treasury 2004, p. 108).

UPSTREAM ENGAGEMENT

One of the criticisms levelled at the *GM Nation?* debate was that it had taken place too late to influence the direction of GM research and thus had failed as an example of 'true' public engagement (Mayer 2003). One answer to this problem was to hold public engagement at an earlier point 'upstream' in the innovation process, an idea promoted by the influential think-tank Demos in 2004 and which was quickly taken up throughout government and scientific agencies, appearing in both the

Treasury 10-year strategy document (HM Treasury 2004) and the Royal Society and Royal Academy of Engineering's report on nanotechnology (2004) (Wilsdon and Willis 2004). Their rationale for publishing the pamphlet had been to ensure that the lessons from previous attempts to manage the relationship between science and society were learned and the mistakes avoided. The challenge – and opportunity – for upstream engagement, as they saw it, was to try to force some of the social and political questions back onto the negotiating table, and at a point when the public was still able to influence scientific and techno-logical development.

An editorial in *Nature* lent further support, albeit qualified, to the idea (Nature 2004). For many researchers, it argued, the Demos pamph-let would make *'frightening reading'*, and for those scientists who believed the public to be easily swayed by *'misleading media'* on scientific issues, the proposal *'must seem close to giving the lunatics the key to the asylum'*. However, the editor felt that there were good reasons why scientists should *'ignore these fears and embrace upstream engagement'*.

CONCLUSION

Whilst it remains an ambiguous and therefore flexible term, there is no doubt that public engagement with science and technology has become the new 'orthodoxy' of science communication strategy within scien-tific and Government circles in recent years. The management of the science/society relationship has clearly shifted away from the encour-agement of scientists doing more one-way science communication towards a focus on problems about governance and political legitimacy of decision-making on scientific issues.

The institutional commitment to public engagement has con-tinued apace in the UK as elsewhere. The Sciencewise grants scheme has funded several 'upstream engagement' projects into nanotechno-logy which concluded that scientists, once involved in such exercises, found them rewarding and could see clear benefits to their research (Stilgoe 2007). In 2008 a four-year project to encourage all academic researchers, not just natural scientists, to engage the public with their research was set up by the Research Councils and the Wellcome Trust. Six Beacons for Public Engagement were established around the UK to help support, recognise, reward and build capacity for public engage-ment work within the higher education sector. That public engagement may well be included as an 'impact factor' for UK academics in the next Research Evaluation Framework raises more questions about how to encourage, train and reward already overstretched higher education staff in this field.

There has been a great deal of activity in public understanding of science over the past 25 years since the Bodmer Report was published. The report crystallised scientific interests in science communication and provided legitimacy for activities which had simply not been there at the time it was published. The assumption that we have all moved since then from a deficit model to a dialogue model is, however, questionable. Certainly the rhetoric has changed, as has the focus of scientific and Government concerns from education towards trust, confidence and political legitimacy. There remain, however, big questions around how public engagement with science will contribute to scientific research and policy and shape society's relationship with science. Much relevant work has been done in this area by social scientists yet it has often been ignored or discounted by policy-makers and scientists for being impenetrable (Lock 2009). Social scientists undoubtedly have a very great deal to contribute but may also need to learn how to 'communicate' or 'dialogue' with scientists, policy-makers and the wider public as they themselves recommend to others.

The discrediting of the deficit model has also led some to disapprove of those scientists who simply want to tell the public about what they do, yet there is, and always will be, a place for this sort of popularisation activity. Popularisation and dialogue are different kinds of activities and each is valid in its own right but for different reasons. Although there can be no dialogue without articulation of the scientific standpoint, the key is for scientists to remember that their views are only one way of framing any given issue. Without mutual understanding it becomes a 'dialogue of the deaf' so science communication and dialogue have to go hand-in-hand. With pressing contemporary scientific issues such as climate change, energy production and food security the calls for wider and more effective engagement between scientists, policy-makers and the public have never been more important to ensure that society advances in a sustainable and collectively acceptable manner. Whether future public engagement with science and technology exercises are genuinely meaningful and productive for everyone involved will depend on several key points. First, the organisers must be open and up-front about the motives underlying such exercises. Second, they will need to move beyond unsupported yet still sometimes entrenched ideas that dissemination of knowledge will necessarily lead to the public making the 'right' or 'rational' decision, nor must they think that ticking a box marked public engagement will legitimise predetermined policy decisions.

Key resources

Gregory, J. and S. Miller (1998), *Science in Public: Communication, Culture and Credibility* (New York: Plenum).

Holliman, R., Whitelegg, E., *et al.* (eds.) (2008), *Investigating Science Communication in the Information Age: Implications for Public Engagement and Popular Media* (Oxford: Oxford University Press).

Irwin, A. (2006), 'The Politics of Talk: Coming to Terms with the "New" Scientific Governance', *Social Studies of Science*, **36**: 299–320.

Irwin, A. and B. Wynne (1996), *Misunderstanding Science? The Public Reconstruction of Science and Technology* (Cambridge: Cambridge University Press).

Wilsdon, J. and R. Willis (2004), *See-Through Science: Why Public Engagement Needs to Move Upstream* (London: Demos).

Wynne, B. (2006), 'Public Engagement as a Means of Restoring Public Trust in Science – Hitting the Notes, but Missing the Music?' *Community Genetics*, **9**: 211–220.

References

AEBC (2001). *Crops on Trial: A Report by the AEBC*, London: Agriculture and Environment Biotechnology Commission.

British Social Attitudes Survey (1996). Economic and Social Data Service (University of Essex). www.esds.ac.uk/findingData/snDescription.asp?sn=3921 (accessed 6/6/2011).

Collins, H. and T. Pinch (1993). *The Golem: What Everyone Should Know about Science.* Cambridge: Cambridge University Press.

COPUS (2001). *A new direction for Copus.* www.copus.org.uk/copus_councilpaper. htm (accessed November 2001).

COPUS (2002). Press release: *Statement on Copus by the British Association, the Royal Institution and the Royal Society*, 9 December 2002. London: The Royal Society.

Department of Trade and Industry (2003). *GM Nation? The Findings of the Public Debate.* London: DTI.

Durant, J. (1995). *'A new agenda for the public understanding of science': An inaugural lecture given by John Durant, Professor of Public Understanding of Science*, 28 November 1995, Imperial College, London.

Durant, J., G. Evans and G. Thomas (1989). The public understanding of science, *Nature*, **340**: 11–14.

Durant, J., Bauer, M. and Gaskell, G. (1998). *Biotechnology in the Public Sphere: A European Source Book.* London: Science Museum Publications.

Evans, G. and J. Durant (1995). The relationship between knowledge and attitudes in the public understanding of science in Britain, *Public Understanding of Science*, **4**: 57–74.

Goodell, R. (1977). *The Visible Scientists.* Boston, MA: Little, Brown.

Gregory, J. and S. Miller (1998). *Science in Public: Communication, Culture and Credibility.* New York: Plenum Press.

HM Treasury (2004). *Science and Innovation Investment Framework 2004–2014.* London: HMSO.

House of Lords Select Committee on Science and Technology (2000). *Science and Society.* London: HMSO.

Irwin, A. and B. Wynne (1996), *Misunderstanding Science? The Public Reconstruction of Science and Technology.* Cambridge: Cambridge University Press.

Jasanoff, S. (1997), Civilization and madness: the great BSE scare of 1996, *Public Understanding of Science*, **6**: 221–232.

Lewenstein, B. V. (1992). The meaning of 'public understanding of science' in the United States after World War II, *Public Understanding of Science*, **1**: 45–68.

Lock, S. (2009). Lost in translations: discourses, boundaries and legitimacy in the public understanding of science in the UK. PhD thesis, University of London.

Mayer, S. (2003). *Avoiding the difficult issues: a GeneWatch report on the Government's response to the* GM Nation? *public debate.* www.genewatch.org/sub-531175 (accessed February 2007).

Michael, M. (1992). Lay discourses of science: science-in-general, science-in-particular, and self, *Science, Technology and Human Values*, **17**: 313–333.

Nature (2004). Editorial: 'Going public', *Nature*, **431**: 883.

NERC (2001). *Programme on Science and Society: A NERC policy paper.* www.nerc.ac.uk/insight/openness/scisocpolicy.asp (accessed October 2002).

Office of Science and Technology (1993). *Realising Our Potential: A Strategy for Science, Engineering and Technology.* London: HMSO.

Office of Science and Technology (1995). *Report of the Committee to Review the Contribution of Scientists and Engineers to the Public Understanding of Science, Engineering and Technology.* London: OST.

Public Debate Steering Board (2003). *GM Nation? The Findings from the Public Debate Report by the Public Debate Steering Board.* London: Department of Trade and Industry.

Rowe, G. *et al.* (2005). Difficulties in evaluating public engagement initiatives: reflections on an evaluation of the UK GM Nation? public debate about transgenic crops, *Public Understanding of Science*, **14**: 331–352.

Royal Academy of Engineering and The Royal Society (2004). *Nanoscience and Nanotechnologies: Opportunities and Uncertainties.* London: The Royal Society.

Royal Geographical Society (2002). *Response to the BA Report to the Office of Science and Technology, Science and Society.* www.rgs.org (accessed November 2002).

Royal Society (1985). *The Public Understanding of Science.* London: The Royal Society.

Royal Society (2001) *Science in Society* website. www.royalsoc.ac.uk/scienceinsociety (accessed September 2001).

Stilgoe, J. (2007). *Nanodialogues: Experiments in Public Engagement with Science.* London: Demos.

Thomas, G. and J. Durant (1987), Why should we promote the public understanding of science?, *Scientific Literacy Papers*, Summer 1987, 1–14.

Wilsdon, J. and R. Willis (2004), *See-Through Science: Why Public Engagement Needs to Move Upstream.* London: Demos.

Wynne, B. (1990). 'Knowledges in context', paper presented at the conference *Policies and Publics for Science and Technology*, Science Museum, London, 7–11 April 1990.

Wynne, B. (1995), Public understanding of science, in S. Jasanoff, G. E. Markle, J. C. Petersen and T. Pinch (eds.) *The Handbook of Science and Technology Studies*, pp. 361–388. Thousand Oaks, CA: Sage.

Ziman, J. (1990). 'Public understanding of science', paper presented at the conference *Policies and Publics for Science and Technology*, Science Museum, London, 7–11 April 1990.

2

Explaining the world: communicating science through the ages

The history of science communication is the story of how scientific practitioners have attempted both to educate the public and to project a positive image of themselves. They have especially sought to justify their activities in terms of what the public think to be useful or interesting.

SCIENCE AS STATUS: THE ANCIENT GREEKS

Nobody knows how the earliest Greek philosophers told the public about their ideas. Legend portrays them as disinterested sages thinking great thoughts without a care in the world. Thales of Miletus (c. 620 BC–c. 546 BC) supposedly fell down a hole because he had been looking up at the stars. But it seems likely that they valued the status that philosophy bestowed on them and actively tried to enhance it by disseminating their theories.

Later generations of Greek philosophers needed to earn a living. Plato (429 BC–347 BC) set up his own school called the Academy. He also wrote literary dialogues to spread his ideas, one of which, the *Timaeus*, is the earliest complete work of Greek natural philosophy that we possess. The polish that Plato applied to his dialogues, coupled with their non-technical nature, clearly shows that he intended them to reach as wide an audience as possible. His purposes were probably twofold. As a public intellectual he wanted to influence the policy of his rulers without running the risks of entering politics himself. And he needed money to live. His writings advertised his school and hopefully attracted students.

Successful Science Communication, ed. D. J. Bennett and R. C. Jennings. Published by Cambridge University Press. © Cambridge University Press 2011.

In contrast, the medical writings that we call the Hippocratic corpus, dating from the fifth century BC, do not seem intended to attract laypeople as readers. Since they are, in the main, anonymous (even if some were, indeed, composed by Hippocrates (c. 460 BC–c. 380 BC) himself), they would not have made effective advertising. A physician attracted patients thanks to his reputation for cures rather than as a writer. Later, as Greek medicine split into antagonistic schools, much of the output from medical writers became polemical. Physicians would defend their own medical ideology against their rivals. The public were probably nonplussed by these wars among doctors.

An alternative way of life for Greek philosophers who preferred not to teach students was to adorn the court of one of the many despots across the Greek world. The more extravagant the despot, the more plum the post in their palace. And no rulers were quite as despotic as the Ptolemies of Alexandria. Descended from one of the generals of Alexander the Great (356 BC–323 BC), the Ptolemies were a family of inbred Macedonians who somehow managed to install themselves on the throne of Egypt and keep themselves there until wiped out by the Romans three hundred years later.

As foreigners ruling a strange land, the Ptolemies wanted to encourage Greek immigration to their new capital of Alexandria. A logical way to achieve this was to attract Greeks to their city with a school and library generously endowed with professorships. The resulting Museum and Great Library have become the stuff of legend although, of the library in particular, we know remarkably little for certain. But they certainly fulfilled their purpose. The Museum became a beehive of scholarly activity and many of the ancient world's greatest mathematicians and natural philosophers worked in Alexandria. We need only mention the names of Euclid (c. 325 BC–265 BC) and Ptolemy (fl. 140 AD–170 AD) to make the point.

This reflected well on the ruling dynasty in Egypt, which was, of course, precisely the point. Natural philosophers and mathematicians no longer needed to explain their ideas to the public, as long as their work was prestigious enough to impress the pharaohs. The trouble was if the pharaoh of the day lost interest in his menagerie of scholars, there was no money to pay them. And if, like Ptolemy VIII Psychon (d. 116 BC), he was actively hostile, the whole institution might be shut down.

SCIENCE AS ART: THE ROMANS

By the end of the last century BC, the Greek world had come to be dominated by the Romans. Greek philosophy became a popular fad in

Rome and familiarity with its doctrines was a sign of being cultured. Many philosophers moved to Rome where they became teachers and servants to high-ranking Romans.

For the wider public, handbooks and encyclopaedias started to appear. The best-educated Romans could read Greek and they produced summaries of science for their monoglot countrymen. The best-known example is that massive compendium of knowledge, the *Natural History* by Pliny the Elder (d. 79 AD). Pliny himself was killed in the eruption of Vesuvius which destroyed Pompeii. His book remained the most complete description of the natural world in Latin until the Middle Ages.

Too large to be affordable by anyone except the rich, Pliny's encyclopaedia was later supplemented by smaller handbooks. These sought to hang their scientific content on some sort of literary peg, either as a commentary on Plato or Cicero (106 BC–43 BC), or else weaving the science through a story. During the early Middle Ages, Martianus Capella's *Marriage of Mercury and Philology*, written in the fifth century, was the most popular example of the latter technique. Capella gives us a comic account of a wedding where the bridesmaids each represent one of the seven liberal arts, including arithmetic, geometry, music and astronomy. As a bridesmaid arrives, she gives the guests a lecture on the rudiments of her subject. The final speech, by Astronomy, was often bound separately and used as a textbook in its own right.

SCIENCE AS HANDMAIDEN: THE MIDDLE AGES

After the fall of the Western Empire, the late Roman syllabus was inherited by monastic schools. Classical learning passed to the barbarian tribes that ruled the old imperial territories as part of a Christian package spread by missionaries. The seven liberal arts remained the backbone of education.

In the fourth century, St Augustine of Hippo (354–430) had insisted that Christians have some knowledge of science, if only so that they did not appear foolish to their pagan neighbours. Other church fathers underlined the importance of the seven liberal arts for a proper understanding of the Bible. Science was a handmaiden to theology – a subsidiary position certainly, but a privileged and protected one nonetheless. Thus, the old Roman encyclopaedias and textbooks continued to be preserved and studied through the early Middle Ages. But this was an elite activity that took place in monasteries and the imperial court of Charlemagne.

From the seventh century, much of the Roman Empire, including Egypt and Spain, fell under the rule of Islamic invaders. Briefly, all Muslims were joined into a single Caliphate, but even after it fragmented, Islam long supported a higher level of civilisation than Christian Western Europe. Arabic writers inherited and translated the best of Greek natural philosophy and mathematics before building on it to achieve advances of their own. Because science was not taught in *madrassa* (Islamic colleges), it always had to defend its position in Muslim society on the basis that it was useful knowledge. Among the ways it did this was through public displays of geometrical art, sundials to calculate the times for prayer and hospitals to cure the sick. But such demonstrations were for elite consumption because Arabic science almost always needed patronage to prosper.

Both Greek and Islamic science became available in the Latin West in the twelfth century. Christians began to reconquer Spain from its Berber masters and in the process captured the magnificent library of Toledo intact. At the same time, Greeks who still lived in Sicily and the Byzantine Empire were approached by northern European clerics desperate to obtain the masterpieces of Aristotle and Ptolemy. The newly discovered texts took their place as the advanced syllabus at the new universities, to be tackled once students had mastered the seven liberal arts.

For non-graduates and those not proficient in Latin, science remained a closed book. But gradually vernacular texts began to appear. Geoffrey Chaucer (*c.* 1343–1400) wrote an English treatise on how to use the astrolabe. This was an astronomical instrument that enabled the user to tell the time accurately from the position of the stars or else measure the relative position of the planets to calculate the date. A fantastical traveller's tale under the name of Sir John Mandeville (*fl.* fifteenth century) also contained some accurate information on cosmology as understood at the time. Sermons preached to common folk might also serve to elucidate some scientific topics that touched on the contents of the Bible. As a result, at least no one in the Middle Ages had any excuse for believing the Earth to be flat.

SCIENCE AS REFORM: THE EARLY-MODERN ERA

The trend towards science in the vernacular accelerated in the sixteenth century. Increasing numbers of books appeared and some enjoyed considerable success. *The Ground of the Art* by Robert Record (*c.* 1510–1558), an English-language arithmetic textbook, went through multiple editions. He followed it up with further guides to geometry and astronomy. On a less practical level, a deluxe English edition of Euclid's *Elements* was successfully marketed to wealthy clients who wanted to appear educated. Few of the surviving copies show much sign of ever having been read!

Most natural philosophers continued to work within universities. These institutions demanded that academics taught students to earn their salaries. This limited the time available for research. Galileo Galilei (1564–1642), a mathematician at the University of Padua, was desperate for the patronage that would enable him to conduct his cutting-edge investigations full time. He realised that the best way to get noticed by rich patrons was to give his work as wide an exposure as possible. The more famous he was, the more prestige he could supply to his employer.

Galileo was nothing if not an opportunist and in 1608 he saw a chance to make a big splash. He heard that the telescope had been invented in The Netherlands and set out to create his own version. Convincing the Venetian government of its military applications was not difficult, but Galileo had other uses for the instrument as well. He began to carry out observations on the heavens.

Galileo's pioneering discoveries of the mountains on the moon, the phases of Venus and the moons of Jupiter were a landmark of science. But just as important was the way he communicated his discoveries. Rather than send out letters to fellow astronomers, he chose to announce his work in a short book, *The Starry Messenger*.

As he had hoped, *The Starry Messenger* was a sensation and Galileo became an overnight celebrity. On the day of publication, the English ambassador in Venice wrote home to describe the excitement, noting that Galileo could expect either to find great fame or fall flat on his face. Shortly afterwards, Galileo was offered the job he wanted as scientific advisor to the Duke of Tuscany. Obviously, His Grace did not require much by way of scientific advice and his new advisor served merely as a well-remunerated ornament to his court. Installed in this sinecure, Galileo now had the leisure he needed for research.

Galileo deliberately made the public participants in scientific progress. When he wanted to bounce the Catholic Church into accepting the truth of the hypothesis that the Earth orbits the Sun, rather than the other way around, he wrote in vernacular Tuscan, the forerunner of modern Italian. This meant he could speak directly to the merchants and burghers of Florence, Pisa and other city states. For the first time, the general public was deliberately drawn into cutting-edge scientific debate. The resulting scandal saw Galileo convicted as vehemently suspected of heresy. But not even the Catholic Church could stop his ideas from spreading.

For Galileo, the public were there to be persuaded. In England, they were expected to take a more active role in the scientific process. The founders of the Royal Society saw science as analogous to law. When they did experiments, they wanted them to be witnessed as a way of validating what happened. Experiments did not just have to be repeatable, they had to be demonstrable. This meant that they conducted experiments in public meetings. Unfortunately, after some initial interest from King Charles II, the Royal Society found itself short of funds and public exposure.

Thomas Sprat (1635–1713) helped to drive forward the Royal Society project in its difficult early years by becoming its official propagandist. His book, the *History of the Royal Society*, was a public appeal for the kind of enquiry that he and his colleagues stood for. If people were not willing to get involved in science themselves, they could, at least, support the people who wanted to.

One of the founding fellows of the Royal Society, Robert Boyle (1627–91), decided to involve the public in science in a less demanding way. His books, such as *The Spring of the Air* and *The Sceptical Chemist*, described his experiments in great detail and urged his readers to repeat them. This meant that his results were not just validated by first-hand witnesses. He also challenged others to replicate his work and prove him wrong. But just in case they did not have the time, he told them what should happen too. And he warned his readers that if they could not reproduce his results first time round, they should try again until they got the 'right' answer.

Unfortunately, despite the pretensions of Francis Bacon (1561–1626), science still had very little practical effect on the common wield. This meant the need to justify natural philosophy as a worthwhile activity was a constant concern. One form of justification, wholeheartedly supported by Boyle, was natural theology. Traditional arguments for religion from nature had looked for the messages that God had implanted in the natural world for the edification of mankind. Thus, the beaver was said to bite off its testicles to evade the hunter much as man should cut out his sinfulness to escape damnation. Natural theology argued in the other direction. Instead of knowledge about God (primarily from scripture) being used to interpret nature, the wonders of nature were used as evidence for God. Boyle endowed public lectures that were intended to glorify both God and science by highlighting the links between the two.

SCIENCE AS ENTERTAINMENT: THE EIGHTEENTH CENTURY

Through the eighteenth century, people flocked to see scientific demonstrations dressed up as showmanship. Boyle's evacuated flask was used to near-suffocate and then revive small birds. Electricity could make people's hair stand on end, cause pyrotechnic displays and deliver shocks for the entertainment of the masses. From the 1750s, the invention of the Leiden jar enabled ever bigger jolts to be administered for the amusement of paying punters.

There was some educational value to all this, but that probably passed the majority of the spectators by. Its importance for the demonstrators was greater. Many were working researchers and even those who were employed by universities were expected to provide their own apparatus. Public displays were a good way of raising the necessary cash, as well as promoting the researcher's own activities. So while the public were no longer expected to be active participants in science, as the early Fellows of the Royal Society had hoped that they might be, they were now willing to finance it.

For some, the way that they could harness the powers of nature made the demonstrators into sinister figures. In his famous painting of the vacuum flask experiment, Joseph Wright of Derby (1734–97) defined the essence of the scientist as an individual apart and without human attachment. By seeking to thrill the public, and also scare them with his power, the public demonstrator established a character for himself that his successors would come to regret. This image was reinforced by the Romantic Movement and, most particularly, Mary Shelley's novel of 1818, *Frankenstein*. Shelley was inspired by demonstrations of galvanism where electricity was shown to cause dead muscle fibres, most notably frogs' legs, to twitch. Thus, among many ordinary people, cutting-edge science had acquired a reputation for pushing the boundaries of human knowledge further than they were meant to go. Men of science already stood accused of 'playing God'.

The thinkers who took science most seriously in the eighteenth century were the *philosophes* of the Enlightenment. They became fascinated by the implications of Isaac Newton's (1643–1727) discoveries and wanted to communicate them to a wider public. Newton had written his *Principia Mathematica* in Latin so that it would be accessible to an elite audience throughout Europe. But the *Optics*, less dependent on mathematics, was originally published in English and intended for readers without as much specialist knowledge.

In 1737, the Italian count Francesco Algarotti (1712–64) published a popularisation of Newton's optical work called *Newtonianism for Ladies*. The title, with its implication that women needed a helping hand to grasp scientific concepts, appears today doubly unfortunate given that one of the most notable experts on Newton's thought at the time was Madame du Châtelet (1706–49). She produced the only French translation to date of the *Principia* while her lover Voltaire (1694–1778) brought out his *Elements of Newtonian Philosophy* for general readers. This was a competent summary of Newtonian physics which introduced France to universal gravitation and helped to displace Cartesian mechanics with Newton's. It was even translated into English in the same year it was published in French.

Voltaire's book brought home the power of the new science to explain the world. It presented Newton's system as a comprehensive metaphysical explanation of reality. If one could obtain a total description of the current state of the universe, Newtonian physics could provide a complete description of its past, and of its future. This self-regulating universe, something that Newton had explicitly rejected, provided the philosophical justification for deism. Voltaire's fellow *philosophes* hatched a grand plan to communicate this world-view to the public, together with a state-of-the-art account of scientific knowledge. The result was the great encyclopaedia edited by Denis Diderot (1713–84) and Jean le Rond d'Alembert (1717–83), an ideological project cunningly disguised as objective knowledge.

The *philosophes* ensured that science was at home in the salons and tea houses of Europe, communicated through pamphlets and journals intended for educated but non-specialist readers. Even other scientists sometimes depended on these publications to keep up to date. Benjamin Franklin (1706–90) and his fellow electrical experimenters in Philadelphia first learnt about European results from an edition of the *Gentleman's Magazine*.

Science also had supporters who carried the flame of Francis Bacon's experimental philosophy. Without a scrap of evidence to support his claims, Bacon had believed knowledge about nature could drive forward human progress. Baconians were interested in the material benefits of science rather than the philosophical implications. The difficulty was that, even as late as the eighteenth century, these benefits had yet to materialise. It is true that industrialisation was gathering pace with the invention of steam engines, automated looms and new steel-making processes. But these advances were emphatically not applied science. They sprang from the traditions of craftsmanship and tinkering. Some industrialists, such as Josiah Wedgwood (1730–95), contributed scientific papers to the Royal Society, but these were the fruit of a hobby he took up after he developed his new manufacturing techniques in pottery. His success as a manufacturer flowed from the age-old process of trial and error, not from putting scientific theories into practice.

So if the new science was going to bask in the reflected glory of the industrial revolution and be associated in the public's mind with the resulting material benefits, a certain amount of historical gerrymandering was necessary. This was provided, probably unintentionally, by the Edinburgh professor John Robison (1739–1805). He claimed that Robert Hooke (1635–1703) had trained Thomas Newcomen (1664–1729), inventor of the earliest true steam engine. Robison also stated that the theory of latent heat advanced by his friend Joseph Black (1728–99) had aided the development of the separate condenser by James Watt (1736–1819). These claims were not refuted until the twentieth century, by which time science's fictional role in nurturing the industrial revolution was firmly entrenched in the public's mind.

SCIENCE AS PROGRESS: THE NINETEENTH CENTURY

By 1850, some of the grandiose claims that had been made for science by the Baconians finally began to appear realistic. Science and industry formed ever-closer links and the concept of 'applied science' became a reality. Lagging some way behind the invention of the steam engine, the new science of thermodynamics explained how heat could be transformed into motion. In Germany, the chemical industry sucked in the first graduates with PhDs to carry out research and development activities. Science ceased to be a branch of philosophy and morphed into a practical subject essential to the modern world.

Interest in science blossomed as people came to realise that it was a subject of importance to them. In 1799, the Royal Institution was founded on London's Albemarle Street as a forum for the public communication of science and a working laboratory. The lectures of Humphry Davy and Michael Faraday drew large and well-heeled crowds who financed the cutting-edge experimental work that took place downstairs. Albemarle Street became London's first one-way street in 1808, allegedly due to the crush of carriages trying to drop off their occupants for talks at the Royal Institution. In 1825, Faraday inaugurated the Christmas Lectures specifically for a younger audience and presented them himself on nineteen occasions, his lecture in 1856 being shown as the frontispiece of this book. A few years later, the British Association for the Advancement of Science (BAAS) held its first meeting, in York. This cultivated a deliberately provincial and democratic flavour, holding a meeting each summer in a different city, which had competed for the privilege of hosting it.

At the Cambridge meeting of the BAAS in 1834, the question was raised as to what men of science should call themselves. They no longer wished to be viewed as gentlemen–amateurs and those who had to earn their living through science could resent the dilettantes. So, the first thing that these new professionals needed was a name. The poet Samuel Taylor Coleridge (1772–1834) posed the question. The Cambridge meeting rejected 'philosopher' as too general a term, while 'savant' was thought to be too French. William Whewell (1794–1866) suggested 'scientist' which was rejected as well, but he started to use it in his own writings and it eventually caught on in any case.

In his *History of the Inductive Sciences*, Whewell also set out to provide science with a suitably heroic history intended to claim the great men of the past, such as Galileo and Newton, as prototypes for the new professionals. And as full-time scientists colonised the societies, journals and university positions, they drove out the amateurs. Many of the marginalised incumbents were members of the clergy who continued to practise science both for its own sake and to promote natural theology through publications like the *Bridgewater Treatises*. Occasional turf wars, such as when clergy were excluded altogether from the management of the new Cornell University in Ithaca, New York, were magnified in the eyes of the public into a conflict between science and religion. This impression was amplified by bestselling books that told a wholly mythical story of how science was held back by established superstition at every turn. It is this myth of conflict that continues to dominate public perceptions of science and religion to this very day.

None of this blunted the public appetite for news of the latest scientific advances. The Great Exhibition of 1851 became a 'must-see' attraction and cemented the marriage of science and technology in the public's mind. It portrayed scientists as agents of progress and modernity.

Unfortunately, the new status of science was also enjoyed by fields of research that today we consider less worthy of respect. Franz Anton Mesmer (1734–1815) used magnetism to produce cures on excitable ladies in Paris, but it was his secrecy rather than the crankiness of his theories which led to his downfall. Franz Joseph Gall (1758–1828) invented the new science of phrenology that analysed intelligence and personality through the shape of the skull, incidentally confirming prejudices about the superiority of Caucasians. In ante-bellum America, Samuel Morton (1799–1851) and others challenged the received wisdom (and the book of Genesis), by claiming that not all human beings were descended from the same primordial stock. This provided another excuse for racism since black people could be assigned to a different species. The public lapped all this up and the reputation of science as progressive and modern meant it could disguise a multitude of what we now recognise as sins. But at the same time, many of those whom we regard as mainstream scientists were also involved in what now looks like pseudoscience.

Among those who veered into parapsychology was Alfred Russel -Wallace (1823–1913), whose theorising about natural selection finally flushed out Charles Darwin (1809–82) and forced him to make public his own ideas. The publication of *On the Origins of Species* in 1859 came 15 years after *The Vestiges of the Natural History of Creation* written anonymously by the Scottish publisher and journalist, Robert Chambers (1802–71). *Vestiges* had already raised questions in the public's mind about traditional accounts of natural history and went some way towards softening up opinion for Darwin's great work. This meant that the concepts of evolution and deep time had already been considered, if largely rejected, by the reading public.

Darwin himself helped the spread of his ideas by writing a book that could be easily understood by general readers and even became a bestseller with repeated reprints. He was one of the few great scientists to communicate his ideas directly to the public in the same language that he used for his fellow experts. This probably made it easier for his ideas to spread so rapidly compared to what would have happened if promulgation had been left to polemical writers like Thomas Huxley (1825–95). Huxley's waspish prose and famous confrontation with the Bishop of Oxford make him an entertaining figure, but he did little for the standing of science in Victorian England.

SCIENCE AS PROFESSION: THE TWENTIETH CENTURY

Early in the twentieth century, a new kind of institution was founded in Munich (1903) and London (1909) – the museum of science.[1] In fact,

---

[1] See Chapter 24: 'Public understanding of research: the Open Research Laboratory at the Deutsches Museum', by Paul Hix and Wolfgang M. Heckl.

despite their names, both are really museums of technology and their function was initially nationalistic. Germany had come later to industrialisation than England, but had harnessed science to technology more effectively. These great museums told visitors that the technological prowess of their respective countries was something that they should be proud of. But by placing science in a museum in the first place, they increased its status, claiming parity of esteem with other branches of culture which already thrived in galleries and exhibitions. Science became a career option to which the educated classes could aspire. The British government wished to encourage this attitude and adopted the practice of ennobling those scientists, beginning with Lord Kelvin (1824–1907), who have reached the top of their profession. A Nobel Prize winner can now expect a knighthood by right while the President of the Royal Society is automatically elevated to the House of Lords.

Science could also be big news. In 1919, an expedition was despatched to West Africa and Brazil under the leadership of Arthur Eddington (1882–1944) to carry out observations on an eclipse of the Sun. They wanted to discover if the Sun's mass bent the light of distant stars as predicted in a recent paper by the German physicist Albert Einstein (1879–1955). The confirmation of Einstein's theory of general relativity made headlines in newspapers all over the world and turned the charismatic German into a celebrity. The public were fascinated by relativity even though, or perhaps because, they could not understand it. Previously, science communication had been about explaining the latest theories and discoveries to the public. In the twentieth century, elucidating concepts like the Copenhagen interpretation of quantum mechanics became more of a challenge. The strangeness of modern physics, soon coupled to its fantastic destructive power, increased the gulf between scientists and the public.

Luckily, as the century progressed, there were scientists ready to rise to the challenge. Fred Hoyle (1915–2001) harnessed the media to explain modern physics though the persona of an avuncular Scotsman. Through his radio talks on the BBC in 1949 and then on television, he reassured the public that science was in the hands of sensible down-to-earth people like him. Television initially supplied an uncritical platform for science to communicate to the world. In the 1970s, major series such as Jacob Bronowski's (1908–74) *The Ascent of Man* and Carl Sagan's (1934–1996) *Cosmos* reinforced the nineteenth-century narratives of the history of science as a story of progress. *Tomorrow's World* showcased new technology and the latest biomedical research in bite-sized segments. More in-depth science programmes, such as the deservedly long-running *Horizon*, allowed scientists to educate the public about developments in their fields. Science could promulgate its self-image as professional, progressive and benign without too many awkward questions being asked.

And yet surprisingly, none of this has really worked. The public has indeed continued to view 'scientific proof' as the gold standard of truth and to lap up its technological benefits. But that has not stopped science communication suffering catastrophic setbacks in recent years. Against the communication skills of the tabloid media and well-funded pressure groups, scientists have fallen short.

Andrew Wakefield (b. 1956) remains a hero to many for continuing to support his claims, now comprehensively falsified, of a link between the MMR vaccine and autism. He has successfully hijacked the narrative of the brave scientist fighting against establishment dogma, casting himself as Galileo. Genetically modified (GM) crops are now being grown again after being effectively banned for many years in Europe which can probably afford the luxury of doing so. But, as a result of European influences, Third World governments have become suspicious of GM crops when their people certainly do need the agricultural benefits that the technology can provide. In the arena of climate change, scientists have allowed themselves to become associated in the minds of the public with environmentalist political movements. This allowed global warming sceptics to claim that the science of climate change is ideologically tainted and, as a result, cannot be trusted. Finally, in conservative Christian circles, and increasingly among Muslims, creationism has dressed itself in clothes that scientists had tailored for themselves. Intelligent Design theorists use the language and accoutrements of mainstream science even as they attempt to undermine it.

The publishing genre of popular science has become the most effective way to explain complicated ideas to a wide audience. There have been books about science for the general reader since Pliny the Elder, but authors like Brian Greene (b. 1963) and Richard Dawkins (b. 1941) have been able to explain their fields of string theory and evolution in language that both enlightens and entertains. The disadvantage is that the public can be given the impression that ideas that may be of marginal significance to working scientists are central to the discipline. Furthermore, good popular science can remain in print rather longer than its contents remain current. *A Brief History of Time* by Stephen Hawking (b. 1942) kicked off the current trend for books by distinguished scientists on difficult topics. It continues to sell even though cosmology has moved on considerably in the 20 years since it first came out. Nonetheless, science publishing for the general reader is currently enjoying a golden age communicating the full breadth of modern science to the public.

Selected further reading

James McClellan and Harold Dorn, *Science and Technology in World History: An Introduction*, Second Edition (Baltimore, 2006).

David Lindberg, *The Beginnings of Western Science: The European Scientific Tradition in Philosophical, Religious, and Institutional Context, Prehistory to AD 1450*, Second Edition (Chicago, 2008).

James Hannam, *God's Philosophers: How the Medieval World Laid the Foundations of Modern Science* (London, 2009).

Steven Shapin, *The Scientific Revolution* (Chicago, 1998).

John Henry, *The Scientific Revolution and the Origins of Modern Science*, Third Edition (London, 2008).

Thomas Hankins, *Science and the Enlightenment* (Cambridge, 1985).

David Knight, *The Making of Modern Science: Science, Technology, Medicine and Modernity 1798–1914* (Cambridge, 2009).

3

Science: truth and ethics

INTRODUCTION

People are inquisitive. It is only natural to ask what the world[1] is made of, and how it works. These questions have occupied humankind for millennia – they were among the central questions asked in the earliest years of philosophical inquiry. What we now call science has its origins in the efforts made to answer these questions. And when we now ask these questions it is to science that we turn. People are interested in science for what it tells them about the world in which they live – what it is made of, and how it works. Science communication surely has a role in satisfying this natural curiosity, in fulfilling this need. We trust the scientist to tell us truly about the world and we value science for what it tells us. We welcome the light that it can cast on our understanding of the world.

But in generating knowledge of the world, especially knowledge of how it works, the scientist also acquires the ability to do things, to make things happen. We are often surprised by what can be done – technology, the uses of science, is another great interest we have in science. And this too is something that we want to know about – we want to know what can be done with science and what is going to be done with it. We appreciate the many benefits that science, engineering and technology (SET) have bestowed upon humanity, but we are also wary of the dangers that can result from ill-considered uses of science. For that reason we are not so entirely trusting of science in its uses. The fruits of science are often sweet, but sometimes they are bitter.

---

[1] I take 'world' in the old-fashioned sense of the universe and everything in it, that is, everything that you think is real.

Successful Science Communication, ed. D. J. Bennett and R. C. Jennings. Published by Cambridge University Press. © Cambridge University Press 2011.

The desire to know about what the world is made of and how it works stems from an interest in truth, a desire to satisfy curiosity. But in wanting to know what science can do and what is going to be done with it we have a practical interest, and generally we have a view concerning the right way and the wrong way to use science – in other words, we look at the uses of science in an ethical context. Both of these facets of science need to be communicated – what science has discovered and how it is to be used. And each aspect of science is valued differently – scientific discoveries, the light of science, are valued for their truth, the uses of science, its fruits, are valued ethically.

In this chapter I speak not as a scientist but as an observer of science. I am a philosopher and historian of science – I do not do science, but I study science – from the outside, as it were. So I speak more as a member of the audience in the science communication process, and I also speak as a member of an audience that is affected by what scientists do. Thus, though I do not do science, I am concerned with what is done with science. As an observer of science I want to know what science is up to, but I also want to have some say in what it is doing. I am willing to trust the scientist to tell me the truth, but I'm not always willing to trust the scientist to use his knowledge in the best way.

WHAT IS SCIENCE?

In the early nineteenth century phrenology was a thriving science. Its advocates saw it as an answer to social ills and the way to understand an emerging social order. It gave the promise of greater job satisfaction and a scientific method for finding the perfect mate. It sustained a programme of empirical research and made lasting contributions to science as we know it (Shapin 1979). Whatever happened to phrenology?

Most of us have a pretty good idea what is a science and what is not. And phrenology is not a science. Why not? One obvious reason is that it does not appear in any university science curriculum, nor does it appear in any contemporary list of the sciences. What counts as science is what is generally agreed to be a science. If there is any doubt, there are enough well-established scientists around for us to go and ask. And if we ask, we find that phrenology is not a science. But again, why not? The most immediate answer is that it doesn't work like science, people do not practice phrenology according to the scientific method. Everyone knows that science is practised according to a method – the scientific method – and if it doesn't use the scientific method it is not a science. Generally speaking the scientific method is taken to be a method for finding out the truth about the world. But when we ask what, specifically, that method is, we find it remains an enigma. Philosophers of course delight in such enigmatic puzzles, and over the centuries there have been a variety of answers to this question. There are a number of historically well-established accounts of the scientific method, and anyone who has an inkling of what the scientific method is will doubtless have one or other of these historical accounts in mind. When discussing science it is well to have a grasp of these various accounts – it provides the background from which your listener or reader may be coming.

THE SCIENTIFIC METHOD

In fact there are only a few accounts which are likely to be at work. The first, and most traditional, is the inductive method traditionally associated with Francis Bacon and which has a venerable and distinguished history. The inductive method doubtless captures an important aspect of science, and Francis Bacon was for centuries heralded as the founder of the scientific method. But the twentieth century saw a proliferation of alternative theories of the scientific method, and a number of these have managed to travel beyond the philosophical quarter.

Bacon's method dominated popular thinking about science well into the twentieth century. In the early twentieth century it was further supported by the Vienna Circle which aimed to prove scientific claims on the basis of the secure foundation of immediate experience. Karl Popper reacted strongly against both Bacon's and the Vienna Circle's claim that science could prove its theories inductively and offered another method, that of falsificationism. Popper was a charismatic speaker and writer, and he developed a large following for his falsificationist method. This in turn was rejected by those such as Carnap and Hempel who argued that even if science could not prove its theories it could at least do more than just falsify them. By the mid twentieth century philosophy of science was beginning to look like scholastic logic chopping until the historian of science Thomas Kuhn, and the iconoclast Paul Feyerabend, offered alternative ways of thinking about the method of science.

FRANCIS BACON: THE LIGHT OF SCIENCE

The idea that science uncovers the truth about the world, discovers nature's secrets, has a venerable history going back to the very origins of empirical science as we know it. In the early seventeenth century Francis Bacon (1561–1626) laid down the rules for the practice of empirical natural philosophy, as science was then known. These rules, the rules of inductive logic, had a lasting impact on the practice and understanding of science, an impact that is still felt today, not least because they do capture an important element of scientific thinking. Indeed, the image of science that Bacon created is one that still dominates much contemporary thinking about science today.

Bacon's image of science was that of a growing body of truth, a body of truth that was generated from empirical observations, and especially from experiments. Bacon emphasized the importance of experiments in contrast to the purely observational method recommended by Aristotle, because experiment gave the scientist access to the secrets of nature. Bacon spelt out his method in his *Novum Organum* and developed his vision of the scientific community in his *New Atlantis*.

The method consists of gathering facts from observations and experiments and compiling them in great catalogues. Then the inductive method is applied to these collections of facts. For a phenomenon we want to understand, a list is compiled of circumstances in which this phenomenon occurs (the 'table of presence'), and another list is compiled of circumstances like those in the first list but in which the phenomenon does not occur (the 'table of absence in proximity'). The first table indicates the possible laws of the phenomenon, and the second table eliminates possible errors that result from coincidence. For Bacon, this process generates the true laws of nature. It was a method for discovering laws of nature and it was also, at the same time, a method which proved the laws of nature. For Bacon, and for those who followed him, the truths of science were not mere conjectures, or hypotheses, they were proven truths. This is a view of scientific truth that dominated thinking for centuries and still has a hold on our thinking today.

When we turn to science to learn about the world, we generally take what we're told at face value – we trust science to tell us the truth. And of course that is how the science textbooks are written – they tell us what the world is made of and how it works. But since the seventeenth century, when science as we know it began, this view has suffered some serious blows, so that now we recognize that science is never really certain that it has finally established the truth. Scientists there may be, who are certain that they have the truth, but that is a common mistake – the Scholastics were as certain that the Earth was the centre of the universe as many contemporary scientists are certain of their own beliefs. I once put to a fairly eminent Cambridge scientist the view that science can never be certain about the truth of its theories. He retorted that surely nobody could doubt Newton's theory of gravity. I muttered something about Einstein's theory of general relativity and we changed the subject!

Philosophers of science, who make it their business to understand the nature of scientific knowledge, argue back and forth about the foundations of scientific belief. But none of them any longer try to claim that science can prove the claims it makes. At best it can give support to those claims, and there are even those who say the rational thing to do is to suspend belief.[2] Reasons for doubting the certainty of scientific claims have been around since the beginnings of scepticism in the fourth century BC. Modern arguments have their origin in the sceptical arguments of David Hume in the mid eighteenth century. Hume argued that whatever our laws of nature, and however convinced of them we are, we can always imagine things turning out differently from what they predict and therefore we can never be 100% certain they are right. But wholesale reaction against the idea that science establishes certain truth did not take hold until Karl Popper's reaction against the logical positivism of the Vienna Circle.

THE VIENNA CIRCLE AND THE QUEST FOR CERTAINTY

At the turn of the twentieth century, physics underwent a radical transformation in its vision of the world. Classical physics, dominated by Newtonian mechanics and the more recent theories of electromagnetism, was suddenly turned over by the advent of special, and then general, relativity and then by the bizarre quantum theory. This transformation shook the confidence of the scientific community to the roots, and gave rise to a Viennese movement to reconstruct the foundations of science. This movement began with the reflections of the physicist Ernst Mach (1838–1916) and developed into what we now call logical positivism. Here we find the interplay of science and philosophy – the impact that developments in science have on philosophy and vice versa. Mach introduced an ultra-empiricist view of science. Taking immediate sensations as the foundation of knowledge he envisioned constructing scientific knowledge from these immediate sensations alone. This philosophy, sensationalism as he called it, or phenomenalism as it is sometimes called, provided the starting point for the logical

---

[2] Karl Popper – quoted below.

positivist tradition. For Mach and the logical positivists science was the study of relations among these sensations, in particular, the patterns and regularities between them.

This view of science led the followers of Mach to adopt a view of the world that is often simply characterized as the positivist view – that the role of science is to find the patterns in our experience of the world and that laws of nature are simply reports or summaries of observed regularities. In addition to this view, the positivists held two additional views. The first was that experience is self-evidently true – there could be no doubt about what is experienced. Experiences are reported by observation statements. The second view was that scientific claims could be deduced (or constructed) from these observation statements. Putting these two together implies that, rightly done, science can attain certain truth. Self-evident observations are reported by observation statements and thus provide the firm foundation for science. Scientific claims are in turn deduced from these firm foundations. Since the foundations are secure, and logically imply the scientific claims, these claims must be true. This was the logical positivist programme.

KARL POPPER AND THE GLORIFICATION OF SCEPTICISM

Karl Popper (1902–94) offered a radical alternative to the inductivism of the Baconian/positivist tradition. Popper was philosophically active during the heyday of the positivist movement, but he was not himself a positivist. In fact he raised serious problems with this philosophy and in the process developed a wholly new method of science, the method of falsification. Popper was a powerful and charismatic advocate of his theory of falsificationism, and through the central decades of the twentieth century he developed a strong following in his critique of inductivism. Two observations lie at the heart of Popper's falsificationism. The first is that the laws of science cannot be proved, or deduced, from the observations on which they are based. The second is that laws are not derived from observations, they are not simply generalizations over observations. More generally, scientific claims are, according to Popper, only ever conjectures. Science for Popper is a matter of conjectures, and these conjectures are the product of scientific creativity. In a word, Popper disputed, indeed refuted, two of the most basic traditional ideas about science that we inherited from Bacon and which were built into the positivist view of science – the idea that scientific claims are derived from observations by some kind of scientific method, and that by this derivation their truth is guaranteed.

The reaction of the positivists to Popper's critique was mixed. Some of them, in particular Moritz Schlick (1882–1936) who was leader of the Vienna Circle, concluded that the 'laws of nature' were not so much truths about the world, but rules of inference – rules to enable us to infer from observation of current events in the world to predictions about subsequent events in the world. Others, such as Rudolf Carnap (1891–1970) took on board Popper's critique and reassessed the status of laws of nature, arguing that they really were statements about the world, but because of their generality could not be proved to be true. Carnap however argued that the observations on which these general-izations were based provided evidence for the generalizations – the observations confirmed, but did not prove, the truth of the generaliza-tions. In a word, the observations provided reason, if not conclusive reason, to believe the laws are true. At this point Popper and Carnap had a parting of the ways. Popper never accepted that there could be reason for belief in scientific theories – indeed he says 'Belief, of course, is never rational: it is rational to suspend belief' (Popper 1974, p. 69).

Carl Hempel (1905–97) followed Carnap in thinking that we could have reason to believe in these generalizations. He developed his ideas into the very influential and successful model of science called by various names including 'the deductive–nomological model' and 'the hypothetico-deductive model'. The model takes on board the two points that Popper opposed in the positivist programme, that laws of nature are neither proved nor derived from observations, but rejects Popper's claim that belief is never rational. Science, according to this model, is a process of creative hypothesis formation followed by testing the deduct-ive consequences of the hypothesis. Crudely speaking, false predictions show the hypothesis is false, true predictions confirm (but do not prove) the hypothesis.

This model has been so widely accepted that it has been incorpor-ated into school teaching of science. One of the first things primary school students learn about doing science is the importance of formulat-ing and testing of hypotheses. Insofar as people have any understanding of the scientific method, it is probably one of these three – Bacon's inductivism, Popper's falsificationism or Hempel's logical empiricism. In fact, of course, science is not done according to any of these idealized models. There is an art to doing science as much as a logic. And this art is something that needs to be communicated, as much as the products of the art. This is a point that is clearly and strongly made in Tracey Brown's

Chapter 5. This is also a point that philosophers of science have come to recognize as a result of their growing knowledge of the history of science.

THOMAS KUHN AND THE HISTORICAL TURN

In 1962 Thomas Kuhn (1922–96) published his now classic, but quite short and readable, book, *The Structure of Scientific Revolutions* (SSR). Kuhn was writing as an historian of science, and SSR was a theory of scientific change, based on his understanding of the history of science. The nature of science as presented by Kuhn was entirely different to the nature of science as seen in the logical empiricist tradition. In fact Kuhn saw science as a social activity more than a philosophical activity – he did not look at science as a logical process of conjectures and refutations, or the formulation and testing of hypotheses. Rather he looked at science as a practice, a culture, that was learned as part of a tradition. The tradition he called a paradigm, a term which is notoriously both vague and ambiguous. But the term captured something about science that the logical empiricist tradition missed, it introduced the social dimension into the discussion of the nature of science. It also introduced an idea that undermined the logical empiricist conception of science, the idea that in many ways logic could not capture the activity of doing science. Kuhn recognized that establishing scientific 'truth' is more than a simple matter of logical argument; he saw that there is a social dynamic involved. This is evident whenever scientific controversy develops, for example in the three-dimensional structure of the DNA molecule or the controversy over the GM crops, discussed by Piet Schenkelaars in Chapter 14. Initially Kuhn gave little credit to rationality in the settling of scientific disputes, emphasizing the social processes involved. This led to considerable criticism from the logical empiricist camp, and Imre Lakatos (1922–74) described Kuhn's theory as a theory of mob psychology (Lakatos 1970, p. 178).

TWO REACTIONS TO KUHN'S THEORY

In place of mob psychology, but recognizing that science is a practice, a culture, learned as part of a tradition, Imre Lakatos introduced the idea of a scientific research programme (SRP). The SRP embodies all of the cultural and traditional beliefs and practices of the science, all the aspects that are taken for granted and not so easily subject to empirical support or criticism. Scientific activity then takes place within the research programme, proposing theories, testing them, falsifying and revising them, and generally doing what is considered rational science. But this can only be done in the context of the shared assumptions that constitute the SRP. Lakatos then distinguished SRPs that are progressive and those that are degenerating. Progressive ones succeed in making novel predictions which sometimes turn out to be true; degenerating ones either fail to make novel predictions, or, if they do, the predictions turn out to be false. Lakatos incorporates Popper's falsification into a framework of SRPs which are very like Kuhn's paradigms.

Paul Feyerabend (1924–94), friend and ally of Kuhn, emphasizes the dangers of getting bogged down in a paradigm or SRP. Feyerabend counsels us to question our culture, to consider alternatives to the traditional beliefs that we inherit from our teachers. For Feyerabend anything goes – any belief is open to criticism, any assumption can be questioned. The only thing we must do is engage in the discussion – defend our own views, and try to improve them. Even traditional standards of rationality are cultural assumptions and open to question. One argument that Copernicus produced for his heliocentric theory was based on Hermetic worship of the Sun and another on belief in divine harmony. Kepler's theories were based on his belief in a mathematical God who created a mathematical universe. What we now regard as irrational was successful in the past and so, argues Feyerabend, we should not feel constrained by current criteria of rationality.

WHAT METHOD THEN?

I have discussed four main theories of the rationality of science, or scientific method, ranging from the optimistic inductivism of Bacon and the logical positivists, through Popper's negativistic falsificationism and the moderately optimistic logical empiricism that grew out of it, to Kuhn's historically based theory of science and the pessimism about rationality that it implies. I then briefly considered Lakatos' attempt to reconstruct the rationality of science and Feyerabend's delight in questioning anything, including the criteria of rationality.

By the end of this discussion of how truth is established in science we may begin to wonder if there is anything more to science than speculation and socially sanctioned fairy tales. But to do so would be to overlook what is perhaps the most impressive fact about scientific knowledge – that science DOES DO things, that it is an integral part of science, engineering and technology (SET). Engineering and technology (ET) without the science would be just so much trial and error. One could hold the view that theory is just so much fairy tale, a story made up to tie together the incrementally acquired successes of the trial and error process. But these stories *might* be true, and certainly many scientists are convinced they *are* true. Insofar as we have good reasons to believe anything we have good reasons to believe these stories, so we might as well believe them. But whether we do or not, the inescapable fact is that those who act on these stories can do some pretty remarkable things. ET does not depend on these stories being true. If they were true that would go a long way to explaining the success of ET, but they need not be true for ET to work. So let us leave the discussion of truth and look at what SET does. And this is where our values come into play – this is where we cease to have a disinterested appreciation of the knowledge that is generated by SET and begin to have an interest in the applications of this knowledge. And this is also where we leave behind the deficit model of science communication and embrace the interactive, or engagement, model.

As a brief aside to those who would communicate science, I would recommend learning a bit about the history of science, the philosophy of science and the sociology of science. All are very interesting subjects, especially for scientists, and each contributes to a broader context of understanding into which current beliefs can be placed.

ETHICS AND THE FRUITS OF SCIENCE

Beyond a general interest in what the world is made of and how it works, people have an interest in what scientists are doing, and what they can do, with their science. This interest is often focussed on the ethics or morality of scientific behaviour and the uses of science. Broadly speaking, there are three areas of ethical concern in science, two of which are more relevant to science communication than the other. The area that is probably of less concern to the wider public is that which concerns the professionalism of the scientist, the behaviour that is appropriate for scientists working within the scientific community. The second area of ethical interest to the wider public is scientific work that involves sentient, or feeling, beings – humans and other animals. And finally, the third area that attracts the most interest from the wider public is the applications of science – the uses to which science is put.

RESPONSIBLE CONDUCT OF RESEARCH

Ethical questions arise in more ways than simply how science is used or applied. In addition to the uses or applications of science, there is considerable interest in the study of the responsible conduct of research devoted to the honesty and integrity of the professional scientist. This includes such issues as the traditional concern with falsification, fabrication and plagiarism; and it also includes issues concerning the proper allocation of credit, ownership of ideas, and conflicts of interest. Broadly speaking I regard these as ethical issues that arise within the community of science rather than with the wider society in which the science community is embedded. This area is more relevant to the truth claims of science – fabrication of experimental results, or vested interests in the outcome of experiments, can seriously undermine the truth of scientific claims. In the last decades a number of cases have emerged where the responsible conduct of research was threatened by political and industrial interests (Thompson *et al.* 2001, Baylis 2004, Union of Concerned Scientists 2004, and Jackson 2005). And in these cases the truth claims of science have been genuinely threatened.

THE USE OF SENTIENT BEINGS IN DOING SCIENCE

An area of ethical concern where the wider community has an interest in how science is actually done is in the use science makes of living subjects with feelings in experiments. This divides into two main sub-areas, the use of humans in scientific experiments and the use of other animals. The former area is addressed by the well-studied subject of medical ethics, and the latter includes the highly volatile discussion of animal welfare and animal rights.

In medical ethics the two primary ethical concerns are that the subject of the experiment gives informed consent to their participation in the experiment, and that their confidentiality be respected with regard to any information about them that may be gathered or discovered. Informed consent is notoriously difficult to define, and in a litigious society such as the USA, it tends to be defined through legal process in the courts. Confidentiality can be problematic in genetic investigation not just because of the implications it has for family members, but for what it may reveal about family relations.

The use of non-human animals in science is a highly contentious practice with extreme views both for and against such use. The discussion and debate has raged for nearly two centuries with a gradual shift in public opinion, as well as in legislation, toward the protection of animals. In fact most of the practices of animal abuse that are attributed to science by the radical animal rights activists are illegal under current legislation. Scientists sometimes feel that they should keep quiet about their use of animals in science so as not to stir up problems. But it is my view that this only exacerbates the problem by suggesting there is something to hide. When use of animals is then discovered, the worst is expected and the use of animals is regarded as unusual and outrageous. Instead of keeping quiet about the uses of animals, scientists need to be quite open and clear about the care that is taken of the animals, and that the suffering of animals is scrupulously avoided. Of course this is also legislated for, but in my experience those scientists who work with animals feel a good deal of empathy with the animals, and this is a feature of their work that needs emphasis.

THE USE AND APPLICATIONS OF SCIENCE

The third area of ethical concern with science is in its use and applications – its technological side. Gone are the days when science was a disinterested search for the truth, a purely curiosity-driven exercise pursued by aristocrats with time and money to spare for it, or by ivory tower academics. Now the study of science is clearly directed to the practical ends of increasing benefit to society and national wealth. In the UK this was enshrined in the 1993 Government White Paper *Realizing our Potential* in which five out of six scientific research councils were given missions of '*enhancing the United Kingdom's industrial competitiveness and quality of life*' (pp. 29–31). The only research council whose mission was '*improved understanding of the concepts and principles underlying physical phenomena*', the Particle Physics and Astronomy Research Council (PPARC), has since been dissolved. Science is funded by government and industry for the practical consequences that flow from it. The scientist and many in the public may be primarily interested in what the world is made of and how it works, but those who fund science look to the fruit that they can harvest from their investment in science.

It is the application of science that draws the greatest ethical scrutiny and to which the greatest attention is paid – it is the wonderful new applications of science which elicit the biggest headlines. But new applications also elicit the greatest objections – GM crops are a classic case, but mobile phone masts, the noise of the windfarm turbines, and numerous other applications of science raise ethical issues. Those who communicate science must be prepared to engage with the ethical issues raised by the applications of science. I will take as an example of the kinds of ethical issues that arise the case of nanoscience and nanotechnology (which I will simply call nanotech). In the wake of the

GM crops controversy and the polarization of opinion that resulted from that controversy, a number of studies and reports were published on the ethical issues of nanotech. The first thing to note is that these issues are not particularly specific to nanotech. Instead these are issues that generally apply to any new technology – issues of health and safety, environmental degradation, distribution of wealth, and so on. In other words, the example of nanotech serves as a model for the ethical issues of any science.

The most basic question that is raised about any new technology is whether it is safe – will the fruits of this technology have any adverse effect on our health and welfare? In the case of nanotech the worry is that the very small particles that are produced are able to enter the human body in ways that have not previously been possible – the worry is that nanoparticles may be the new asbestos. Are there regulations in place that will control the use of nanomaterials in ways that will protect our health, both in the actual products we use, and in the safe manufacture, transport and use of nanomaterials in the production process? There are also environmental concerns. One possible environmental benefit of nanotech is in soil or water remediation. Such remediation may effectively remove toxic chemicals and heavy metals, but the impact that it has on plants, animals and microorganisms in the ecosystem is unknown. Are there any regulations governing the release of nanoparticles into the environment? Suppose a nanotech method of dispersing oil from the Deepwater Horizon oil leak disaster were proposed – who would decide whether or not to try it out? Will nanotech be used in the military – will it be used to produce more devastating weapons, or can it be used to reduce the incidence of suffering and 'collateral damage' that result from warfare? What about human rights to privacy – will our privacy be invaded by tiny cheap cameras and microphones? Will research developments in nanotech be monopolized by industry and used for the benefit of shareholders? Further worries concern intra- and international inequity – will the technology make the rich richer and the poor poorer, or will it be used for the benefit of the most needy?

These are questions that raise ethical issues about nanotech, but they are not confined to nanotech. These are ethical questions that apply to any new development in science and technology. If we wish science to be socially acceptable we need to create a science which gives socially acceptable answers to these questions. What those answers are is not up to science, it is up to the society which supports and accommodates the science. If we are to avoid a widespread anti-science movement we are well advised to listen to what society wants and govern science in an ethical manner. But society is not an homogeneous mass – different members of society have different desires. At this point what counts as ethical governance becomes a political issue. The politics of science governance is still in its early stages. In his introduction to this volume, Richard Jones describes some of the recent developments in the process of engaging the public in the governance of science. Philosophers too (e.g. Kitcher 2001 and Alfred Nordmann, Chapter 7 in this book) are beginning to try to figure out how this can best be done. It appears that, one way or another, science is beginning to be responsible to the public which depends on it, and on which it itself depends.

Key resources

John Desmond Bernal (1969) *Science in History*, 4 vols., Harmondsworth: Penguin. This is old, but ties the history of science into the social and economic history of the world and provides a broad perspective for understanding the role of science in contemporary society.

Samir Okasha (2002) *Philosophy of Science: A Very Short Introduction*, Oxford: Oxford University Press.

The Royal Society and The Royal Academy of Engineering (2004) *Nanoscience and Nanotechnologies: Opportunities and Uncertainties.* http://www.nanotec.org.uk/finalReport.htm (accessed 17 September 2010).

Nuffield Council on Bioethics (May 2005) *The Ethics of Research involving Animals.* A well-balanced and thorough discussion of the issues. Available as a whole (2.8 Mb) or as individual chapters from: http://www.nuffieldbioethics.org/animal-research (accessed 17 September 2010).

Thomas Kuhn (1970) *The Structure of Scientific Revolutions,* 2nd edition, Chicago, IL: University of Chicago Press.

Carl Hempel (1966) *Philosophy of Natural Science,* Englewood Cliffs, NJ: Prentice-Hall.

References

Françoise Baylis (2004) 'The Olivieri debacle: where were the heroes of bioethics?' *J Med Ethics* 30 44–49; and http://jme.bmj.com/content/30/1/44.full (accessed 17 September 2010 – may require Athens or Institutional login).

Melissa Jackson (2005) 'Sponsors "manipulate" scientists'. http://news.bbc.co.uk/1/hi/education/4379457.stm (accessed 17 September 2010).

Philip Kitcher (2001) *Science, Truth, and Democracy,* New York and Oxford: Oxford University Press.

Imre Lakatos (1970) 'Falsification and the methodology of scientific research programmes' in I. Lakatos and A. Musgrave (eds.) *Criticism and the Growth of Knowledge,* London: Cambridge University Press, pp. 91–196.

Karl Popper (1974) 'Intellectual autobiography' in P. A. Schilpp (ed.) *The Philosophy of Karl Popper, Book I,* La Salle, IL: Open Court Publishers, pp. 3–181.

Steve Shapin (1979) 'Homo phrenologicus: anthropological perspectives on an historical problem' in B. Barnes and S. Shapin (eds.) *Natural Order: Historical Studies in Scientific Culture*, Beverly Hills, CA: Sage, pp. 41–71.

Jon Thompson *et al.* (2001) *The Olivieri Report*, Toronto: James Lorimer.

Union of Concerned Scientists (2004) 'Scientific integrity in policy making'. http://www.ucsusa.org/scientific_integrity/abuses_of_science/reports-scientific-integrity.html (accessed 6/6/2011).

4

The public's view of science

WHY TAKE THE PUBLIC SERIOUSLY?

The focus in this chapter is on public perceptions of science, taking biotechnology and the life sciences as an exemplar. From almost its outset in 1974, with the application to patent recombinant DNA, biotechnology has been understood as having far-reaching implications for the lives of us all. In 1975, scientists agreed at the Asilomar Conference in California to a voluntary moratorium on their research, such was the scale of their concern about the potential and unknown health and safety issues associated with this new technology. But the economic benefits of biotechnology soon became its focal point, and the moratorium was soon lifted. In 1979 a European Community report entitled *The Biosociety* described biotechnology as central to economic competitiveness in subsequent years. But even at that time, the European public was uneasy and troubled by the idea of gene technology. As Mark Cantley, then a senior member of the European Commission, wrote, '*what the sector ignored above all was public perception . . . the public were learning to see gene technology, genetic engineering, biotechnology and so on as a single, vague and disquieting phenomenon*' (Cantley 1992). A Eurobarometer survey in 1979 found that 49 per cent of the European public saw genetic research as an unacceptable risk and a similar percentage thought the same about 'synthetic food', or what we now call GM food (Gaskell 2004).

However, the early warning signals from the public went unheeded. In the 1990s, the life sciences project, embracing medical, pharmaceutical, industrial and agri-food technologies based on

Successful Science Communication, ed. D. J. Bennett and R. C. Jennings. Published by Cambridge University Press. © Cambridge University Press 2011.

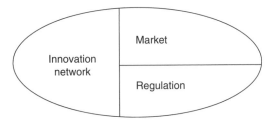

Figure 4.1 Market model of innovation.

recombinant DNA, took off led by European and North American multinational companies. They based their strategy on the market model of innovation, depicted in Figure 4.1 (Gaskell 2008). Here success in the process of innovation is contingent on gaining the support of the regulators and the market forces.

In the event the strategy foundered, the life sciences project collapsed and increasingly the 'red' (medical) and 'green' (agricultural) biotechnologies bifurcated. This was not due to a change in heart of the regulators or the farmers turning against GM crops. Rather it was, as Harold MacMillan, sometime UK prime minister, described the things that blow governments off course – 'events, dear boy, events'. In the context of GM, the events were a mixture of history and contemporary issues, some of which were only indirectly related to biotechnology.

As noted above, the European public had been troubled by the idea of gene technology since the 1970s. This unease grew in the 1990s with a number of high-profile food crises in Europe – bovine spongiform encephalopathy (BSE), foot and mouth disease in cattle, and dioxin traces in chickens. In particular the BSE crisis evidenced the emergence of the risk society (Beck 1992), as the disease was clearly a consequence of human action and one that did not respect national boundaries. The BSE crisis challenged the public's confidence in farming, in scientific expertise and in the regulators. Then in 1996 the first shipment of Monsanto's GM soya arrived in Europe to enter the food chain. Activists protesting about the environmental impacts of GM were joined later on by consumer groups protesting about the absence of labelling and the denial of consumer rights.

A few months later, in February 1997, the public announcement of the cloning of Dolly the sheep was accompanied by a maelstrom of media coverage with dystopian visions of human cloning. Over the following years research was widely reported claiming evidence for risks to the symbolic North American monarch butterfly and purporting to

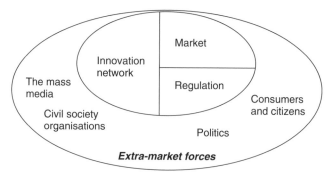

Figure 4.2 The societal model of innovation.

show health risks to rats fed on GM food. As sections of the European media and public became more polarised against GM agriculture, mounting public concern was accompanied by the disruption of GM field trials, supermarket boycotts of GM food, declarations of GM-free zones, and eventually a Europe-wide de facto moratorium on the commercialisation of GM crops across the European Union – against a ruling of the World Trade Organization. The saga of GM crops continues: in 2010 the European Commission proposed that Member States should have the legal right to decide whether to cultivate GM crops or not (European Commission 2010). Whether this will satisfy those for or those against GM crops is an open question.

What was the mistake of the life science companies? Essentially, they failed to appreciate that their innovation – GM crops and food – was entering a more complex environment than the market models of innovation suggests. Robert Shapiro, Monsanto's CEO, admitted as much in an interview in 1999: 'We did proceed on the basis of our confidence in the technology and we saw our products as great boons both to farmers and to the environment. I guess we naively thought that the rest of the world would look at the information and come to the same conclusion' (Globe and Mail 1999).

Figure 4.2 depicts technological innovation as a societal process, where success is contingent not merely on the reactions of those who are directly affected, but also on other sections of the wider public arena. Here we find a number of actors with a variety of agendas and interests: the public as potential consumers (choosing in the market) and as citizens (voting in elections); politicians; the mass media; and civil society organisations operating in between these other actors. The reactions of the public, then, need to be understood in this broader scheme.

MAPPING PUBLIC PERCEPTIONS

One key tool in understanding public perceptions is the social survey, which has had a continuous and influential presence in public understanding of science (PUS) research since its early days (von Grote and Dierkes 2000). For example, Withey's public opinion survey of 1957 is often cited as marking the start of modern PUS research in the USA (Miller 1983), and from 1979 onwards the US National Science Board's biennial Science Indicators surveys have had considerable impact on the field. In the UK, significant survey research began with a study by Durant and colleagues in the late 1980s (Durant, Evans and Thomas 1989), and continued with several surveys either partially or completely dedicated to PUS topics, including modules in the British Social Attitudes series, a survey sponsored by the Wellcome Trust, and a number by government departments and government-commissioned bodies. These are just some examples of many country-level surveys, from Canada through Europe to Japan and Brazil, to name but a few. From an early point in the use of national surveys, efforts have been made to replicate questions in different countries and within countries at different time points, in order to study comparative patterns and trends in opinions. The European Commission sponsored Eurobarometer surveys arguably have the leading edge in this approach (Durant *et al.* 2000), beginning to address topics of science and technology as early as 1977, and including modules on biotechnology and the life sciences in 1991, 1993, 1996, 1999, 2002, 2005 and 2010, covering an ever-expanding set of European countries – from 12 in 1991 to 32 in 2010.

The most recent Eurobarometer in 2010, to which we refer in later sections of this chapter, provides trends on technological optimism; perceptions of GM food; regenerative medicine including human embryonic stem cell research; and trust in the various actors developing, exploiting and regulating biotechnology. New questions address emerging issues such a biobanks, synthetic biology, nanotechnology and cisgenics.

It is well known that question wording should always be carefully borne in mind when interpreting survey results: striking biases in responses can be produced by leading or ambiguous or convoluted phrasing, as well as by priming effects of the questions asked before the one of interest (Schuman and Presser 1981). The crucial quality indicator for surveys that is too often overlooked is the sampling strategy used. In order for a survey sample to adequately represent the population from which it is drawn, it needs to be selected using a formal sampling procedure that draws on well-established and sophis-ticated literature on sampling theory. Survey samples that are not based on some form of random selection run the real and serious risk of providing a biased rather than a balanced picture of the communities they are supposed to represent, and this will happen if the people who participate in surveys differ systematically in their views from those people who do not.

If a probability sample is drawn, it need not be as large as many people think. In the context of the Eurobarometer surveys, for example, around 1000 respondents are selected per country. This may seem a surprisingly small number to represent populations of, in some cases, many millions. However, statistical theory allows us to calculate the possible error attached to any generalisation from a sample to the wider population, and it turns out that in survey samples of 1000 respondents where 50 per cent think X and 50 per cent think Y, we can be 95 per cent confident that the true contrast in the population is captured within the interval $+/-$ 3.1 per cent. If the sample were to be increased to 10 000 the sampling error would only decrease to $+/-$ 1.0 per cent. Thus, where very precise figures are not needed, for public opinion surveys are not referenda, there is no reason to opt for larger samples with all the additional costs that would entail.

Now some emphasise, and rightly so, that survey research is an imperfect instrument. Typically in surveys a set of standardised ques-tions are posed, and people asked to respond to them by choosing one of a few predetermined answers – these are called 'closed questions'; 'open questions', which allow respondents to answer freely, are used only rarely since they take more time to administer, and require a great deal of work post-hoc to code responses for the purposes of analysis. How-ever, one might justifiably say, isn't there more to public perceptions than some headline percentages of responses to a set of fixed questions? We agree wholeheartedly with this view. Surveys provide low-resolution portraits of the broad panorama, and are clearly limited when it comes to the very fine detail – the shades of light and colour revealed only through close inspection. For this, other types of social research are needed to provide the complementary perspective. However, we would stress that surveys are invaluable in providing this broad type of infor-mation: survey research is the only reliable way of mapping the con-tours of public perceptions, and of assessing how opinions are distributed across a population. When comparative and trend data are available, their informative potential is even greater.

In the PUS community a number of high-profile researchers object to the use of survey research (Bauer, Allum and Miller 2007). Their critiques of surveys illustrate some important points. Surveys represent the world in particular ways. Depending on the perspective adopted, the representations will differ. Some of the anti-survey school argue that survey research on public views of science sustain the infamous 'information deficit model' that Richard Jones points to in his Introduction and Simon Lock discusses in Chapter 1, cultivating a caricature of the public as ignorant, distrustful and risk-averse, and pointing the finger of blame, for example for the problems over GM food, exclusively at the public and away from systemic institutional and political failings in the governance of science. We are not sympathetic to this claim, as it confuses conceptions of the public and research methods. Fundamentally, survey results, like all social research, do not have a single, obvious and unequivocal meaning. Whether the glass is half full or half empty is a matter of judgement. Responsible survey researchers are all too aware of this, and will be careful to be transparent in their reports, conveying clearly the rationale for their interpretations, and the extent of their confidence in them, and making the data publicly available such that others can assess the empirical warrants for the conclusions drawn. Equally, survey researchers also have a natural aversion to those narratives that are constructed merely from a 'laundry list' of headline percentages question by question, opinion-poll style, popular as they are with their various consumers and users, as well as to the 'horse-race' version, which ranks responses to questions by country. What emerges very clearly from cross-national analyses of survey data is that there are patterns of concerns among the public that are situated in broader social and cultural norms and priorities. We now turn to a few of the key concerns for understanding public sentiment towards the life sciences.

RISKS: SCIENTIFIC AND PUBLIC LOGICS

One of the most important lessons learned through public opinion research in PUS is that scientific and societal thinking about risk and uncertainty are different in their logics and manifestations (Gaskell and Allum 2001). Take the example of GM crops; confronted by the same hazard, the scientific assessment differs markedly from the position taken by sections of the public.

The scientific logic begins from a simple definition of risk as the probability of an unacceptable loss. Expert risk assessment typically involves probabilistic models that estimate the likelihood of negative outcomes and the potential impacts of these outcomes, as John Adams points out in his Chapter 6. Such risk assessment is underpinned by the scientific method, assuming that there are facts about the world to be discovered and that knowledge progresses through empirical research, leading over time to a closer approximation to the truth (Jaeger *et al.* 2001). Research that follows these canons of the scientific method is seen as objective and unbiased by human motivations and agency. It therefore provides almost a universal currency, transcending place and time. A risk is a risk is a risk, whether one is in Britain, Belgium or Burundi. Of course, there may be different levels of risk acceptability, and different ways of managing risk, but these are different, external issues.

The public's logic of risk assessment is a different matter. Tetlock notes that much research in the aftermath of the so-called 'cognitive revolution' in social psychology (and including studies of the public perception of technologies) has construed people as *intuitive scientists* or *intuitive economists*, seeking, respectively, to understand the science or to maximise expected utility (Tetlock 2002). However, people are not only self-interested utilitarians. There are at least two other important metaphors for understanding how everyday people think: *intuitive politicians* and *intuitive ethicists*. Intuitive politicians are concerned with fairness, the balancing of social interests, distributional and procedural justice and the avoidance of social exploitation. They ask questions such as, 'Who is affected?', 'For whom are technologies potentially risky and beneficial?', 'Is the technology in safe hands?'. Intuitive ethicists are concerned with the core values and beliefs that are essential to the fabric of society, as Alfred Nordmann discusses in his Chapter 7. These values sometimes need to be defended from challenges which may arise from science and technology amongst other sources. They ask questions such as, *'Should science trump social values?', 'It may be safe but is this the sort of society we wish to live in?'*. All 'intuitive experts' are able to evaluate technologies as either good or bad. However, it is only the intuitive scientist/economist that can be expected to base judgements primarily on expected consequences, on utilitarian grounds. Intuitive politicians and ethicists may well base their approach on non-consequentialist arguments, such as procedural fairness or other core values.

While some people may be more inclined to think in terms of one logic rather than another, they will recognise the others and sometimes switch between them, on occasion confronting dilemmas. Thus, for example, people may struggle with dual sympathies for the idea of respect for nature (as an intuitive ethicist) and the imperative to con-quer or master it in the interest of progress (as an intuitive scientist/economist) (Rozin *et al.* 2004).

The intuitive logics lead to a concept of risk that goes beyond sound science. In the public sphere risks may take on political, ethical and emotional dimensions (Douglas and Wildavsky 1982). For the intui-tive public, the essence of perceptions of risk are not cold, calculating, cognitive decisions but rather fears, hopes, pleasure and anger. Culture, stereotypes, trust in experts and social values (amongst other things) all play a part in the identification of risks and in the amplification or attenuation of risk perceptions (Renn 1998).

In the 2010 Eurobarometer we asked respondents about three technologies: GM food, nanotechnology and cloning animals for food products. For all three technologies, we find that the issue of safety (risk) is the paramount concern for the European public (Gaskell *et al.* 2010). However, in deciding whether the development of a technology should be encouraged, other considerations are also relevant – will the technology bring benefits? Are the risks and benefits likely to be fairly distributed in society? Is there a choice whether to use it or not and what regulatory control is there? And finally, is the technology per-ceived to be intrinsically unnatural or worrying?

CONFRONTING UNCERTAINTY

There are many new technological developments where the potential risks are beyond the frontiers of current scientific knowledge. Current examples are the toxicological effects of nanotechnologies and of endo-crine disruptors such as bisphenol A. Confronted by such uncertainties, Sir Robert May, a former Chief Scientific Advisor to the UK government, captured the essence of the scientific thinking: *'There are so many unknown factors and so much scientific ignorance, that top calibre advisers are needed to guide us through the fog'* (Royal Society 1999). In other words, even when the scientists know that they don't know, they still know better than anyone else.

But how does the public respond to uncertainty? For suggestive evidence we turn to Daniel Ellsberg (Ellsberg 1961) who, simply put, offered people a choice between two proposed bets based on the toss of a coin. In the first proposition an unbiased coin is used, thus the probability of heads is 0.5, as is the probability of tails. In a single toss of the coin, if it comes up heads you win €100, and if it comes up tails you get nothing – let's call this bet A. The second proposition also offers the opportunity to win €100 or to get nothing based on a single toss of a coin. But here, crucially, the probability of heads is created by a random number generator, with the probability of heads falling anywhere between 1.0 and 0.0, and the combined probability of heads and tails summing to 1.0 – let's call this bet B.

Offered a choice between these two bets to win €100, which would you prefer? The so-called Ellsberg paradox is that the majority of people have a confident preference for bet A. It is a paradox because the result runs counter to rational choice. The expected values of both bet A and bet B are identical at €50, so the choice between the two should be split 50/50 among decision-makers. Ellsberg suggests that the reason why people tend to prefer bet A over bet B is that the latter is ambiguous. We prefer to reason that bet B appears to be more uncertain than bet A, and for most people that is unattractive.

The implication of the so-called Ellsberg paradox for technological innovation is that uncertainties make people uneasy. In a world of increasing uncertainty, moreover, discussing socially acceptable thresholds of uncertainty might be a worthwhile concern of science communicators. When scientists and specialists say that they consider a technology to be safe, albeit with potentially unknown consequences, to be addressed if and when they arise, we suspect that the public is not greatly reassured. However, this might be mitigated if the intuitive economist in us perceives that there are substantial benefits to offset the uncertainties.

WEIGHING UP GAINS AND LOSSES

Kahneman and Tversky's prospect theory (Kahneman and Tversky 1979) elaborates a general framework for understanding why people's decisions about risk depart from the predictions of rational choice theory. Acting as intuitive economists, people tend to give too much weight to low-probability events (and, incidentally, too little weight to high-probability events). Apparently, that something is conceivable appears to be sufficient to give it a reality beyond its objective probability. The implication for new technologies is that even a hint of potential problems may loom significantly in the public mind.

Kahneman and Tversky define a value function for this kind of decision making in terms of gains and losses from a reference point (see Figure 4.3). For gains, the function is concave, and while the same holds for losses, in this context the slope of the curve is much steeper. Consider, for example the first cup of coffee in the morning – it is just

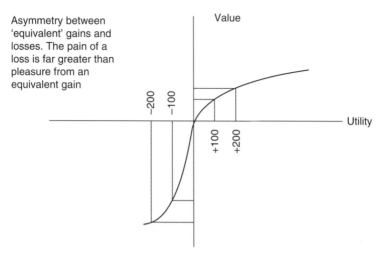

Asymmetry between 'equivalent' gains and losses. The pain of a loss is far greater than pleasure from an equivalent gain

Value

Utility

−200 −100 +100 +200

Figure 4.3 Prospect theory: weighing up gains and losses.

what is needed to get going. But by the sixth cup, the shakes set in and one suffers diminishing marginal utility. By contrast, if one is looking forward to the 'lift' from the first cup, the pain of the realisation that someone else has finished all the coffee beans is far in excess of the pleasure that the cup would have brought. In other words, the utility weighting leads to an imbalance between objectively equivalent gains and losses.

Thus the pain from a small loss from one's current position far outweighs the pleasure from an equivalent small gain. In terms of the way people think about biotechnology or nanotechnology, it follows from prospect theory that potential harms might loom larger for the public even if weighed against apparently equivalent gains in efficiency, reduction in price, and so on. The benefits of any innovation need to be great in order to justify taking any risks.

When GM crops were introduced, industry claimed they would bring a range of benefits to producers in both developed and developing countries, and to the environment in general. But, using data from the Eurobarometer 2005, we found that what drives the European public's opposition to GM food is the perceived absence of benefits rather than their misperception of the scientific risks (as was widely thought to be the case). In the minds of a large proportion of the European public, GM foods are a 'non-innovation' about which risk communication is more or less an irrelevance. Without the perception of an improvement on the status quo in terms of quality, price or other attributes there is simply no incentive to deliberate further on the issue. But by contrast, in the same survey we find that while human embryonic stem cell research is controversial, the prospects of new medical treatments to alleviate diseases appear to outweigh the public's ethical concerns.

HOW DOES THE PUBLIC ENGAGE WITH SCIENCE?

On reflection, promoting the benefits of science has always been a fundamental issue for science communicators, even if not articulated explicitly as such. Public understanding of science research typically urges for more science education in order to equip people for engagement and to increase support. The 'Science and Society' critique to this approach argues against concentrating on scientific knowledge as a prerequisite for engagement, focusing instead on increasing opportunities for participation – getting people involved in dialogue about science and technology, regardless of anything else (Bauer, Allum and Miller 2007).

But some argue that, normatively, these approaches are both important elements of scientific citizenship, which should be a matter of competence – having the ability to contribute meaningfully, and participation – actually doing so (e.g. Horst 2007). In other words the two apparently competing approaches (Michael and Brown 2005) may in fact be complementary. Eurobarometer 2005 survey data indicate to us that, empirically speaking, competence and participation are two sides of the same coin: they are elements that are analytically and empirically distinct, yet statistically associated with each other. Moreover within those two concepts, competence and participation, it can be useful to note two further subtleties (Mejlgaard and Stares 2010).

Firstly, it makes sense to distinguish between *objective* competence, reflected in knowledge of basic scientific facts, and *subjective* competence, that is the extent to which people are interested and feel well informed about science. These concepts are only moderately associated with each other. So it is not straightforwardly the case, for example, that all those who lack knowledge about science lack enthusiasm for it. And for participation, a useful distinction is to be made between *horizontal* forms, such as reading and talking with others about science – modes of engagement that reflect the general climate for participation, and *vertical* forms, such as attending public debates or consultation exercises – modes of engagement that are intended to have an actual impact on science policy. Looking at patterns of participatory behaviour, we can identify some people as non-participative on both counts, some as participative only in the horizontal, more passive forms, and some as participative in both horizontal and vertical forms.

Overall, among the European public, competence and participation appear to be positively associated: those who participate in both horizontal and vertical forms are most likely to be identified as highly competent. But the distribution of these characteristics varies from country to country. In some countries, levels of both tend to be high and in some both are low, but in others we see a mixture. The implication of this for science communicators is that the public is a heterogeneous audience, and moreover, not an audience that should be classified on a unidimensional scale of 'most engaged' to 'least engaged'. Some bring more scientific knowledge to the table than others; some feel more connected to science and some less so; some are passively exposed to science issues while some actively take part in consultations. These elements of citizenship are not very strongly related to each other – so there are pockets of enthusiasm, pockets of background knowledge, pockets of active dialogue, and pockets of uninterest.

PUBLIC ETHICS, SCIENCE AND TECHNOLOGY

We know that people integrate new information into their existing world-views and everyday concerns. But what hooks or frameworks guide the public's understanding of unfamiliar developments in the biosciences – the sciences of life? One such hook takes us back to the intuitive politicians and ethicists. People's beliefs about fairness in society and moral imperatives about what it is to be human and how society should be governed provide a shared framework for judging what is right or wrong in different domains of life – in the family, at work, in broader social and political issues, and in developments in science and technology.

To date, we know little about the role of intuitive politicians' and ethicists' concerns in perceptions of science and technology. As a suggestive, introductory example of some empirical analysis to address this question, we use a cluster analysis of the 2010 Eurobarometer to identify groups of countries where broadly similar views are shared on moral and ethical issues in relation to science and technology. The analysis (Gaskell et al. 2010) is based on country scores for the following indicators of moral and ethical sensitivities:

- The percentage of respondents who think that in a disagreement between science and ethics in the context of regenerative medicine, the ethical view should prevail (*ethics over science or science over ethics*).
- For GM food, nanotechnology and animal cloning, the average level of concern about distributional fairness – whether 'it will benefit some people but put others at risk' and whether 'it will help people in developing nations' (*distributional fairness*).
- The percentage of respondents who would want to know about the moral and ethical issues involved in synthetic biology if they were deciding how to vote in a referendum (*interest in ethics*).
- The percentage of respondents who think that the governance of science, in relation to synthetic biology, and separately, animal cloning, should be based on moral and ethical considerations rather than scientific evidence (*moral governance versus scientific governance*).

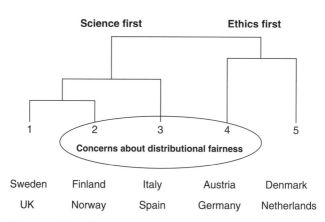

Figure 4.4 Clustering countries by ethical sensitivities.

Figure 4.4 summarises the results of a five-cluster depiction of these items, with two example countries for each cluster.

Looking from the top of the figure downwards, the first split is fundamental. It distinguishes between countries whose publics tend to prioritise science over ethics ('science first': clusters 1, 2 and 3) versus those countries who tend to prioritise ethics over science ('ethics first': clusters 4 and 5). Moving down the figure, the next split is between cluster 4 and 5. Here the key difference is that countries in cluster 4 have high concerns about the sharing of benefits and risks, with a wide-ranging moral and ethical imperative. Countries in cluster 5 are interested in ethical issues, but, in comparison to cluster 4, apparently less concerned about distributional fairness. The next split contrasts clusters 1 and 2 versus 3, with countries in cluster 3 opting for a stronger position on scientific governance relative to moral governance. Lastly, cluster 2 differs from cluster 1 in having higher concerns about distributional fairness (a characteristic shared by countries in clusters 3 and 4).

If these patterns of ethical concerns are the hooks on which unfamiliar technologies are hung, are they related to broad evaluations of them? We investigate how they vary with three indicators:

- Technological optimism – the average number of technologies that people say will improve our way of life in the coming years (optimism).
- Support for GM food, nanotechnology and animal cloning for food products – total percentage of supporters (bio-nano).
- Support for the various regenerative medicines; total percentage of supporters (regenerative medicine).

What we find is that, generally speaking, optimism about technologies and support for bio-nano and regenerative medicine are linked to a combination of two aspects of moral and ethical concerns. Where ethics is prioritised over science and there are concerns about distributional fairness (cluster 4; Germany and Austria) support for the technologies is relatively low. But giving priority to ethics over science does not lead to pessimism about technologies in general, or low support for biotechnologies. In cluster 5 (Denmark and The Netherlands) ethics are prioritised over science, but distributional fairness is less of a concern – and here, support for the technologies is high.

Amongst those countries where science is prioritised over ethics, general enthusiasm for technologies tends to be higher, although moderated by distributional fairness. Cluster 2 (Norway and Finland) and 3 (Italy and Spain) are both concerned about distributional fairness and here technological optimism is moderate. By contrast, cluster 1 (Sweden and the UK), with lower concerns about distributional fairness, has relatively high technological optimism.

This analysis shows how broader ethical and moral considerations are, in quite complex ways, associated with people's perceptions of biotechnology and the life sciences. Such ethical concerns do not necessarily turn people against science.

COMMUNICATING SCIENCE TO THE PUBLIC

A traditional view of science communication is the requirement of a good speaker with the ability to make the science accessible, interesting and even exciting, with appropriate reference to the expected benefits to society. In the light of our conceptualisation of the public in terms of intuitive logics, such an approach is designed to appeal to the public audience when they are thinking along the lines of the intuitive scientist and the intuitive economist.

On the whole, in many domains of pure science, addressing the intuitive scientist/economist may be sufficient. But in the life sciences and, more generally where science interfaces with technologies for everyday life, values come into question and the relevant public logics extend beyond the intuitive scientist/economist. As has been illustrated from the findings of Eurobarometer 2010, what may be described as 'sensitive technologies' raise issues of concern to the intuitive politician and the intuitive ethicist. As such, science communication that focuses solely on the science and its benefits is but a partial picture. Depending on the characteristics of the technology, people as intuitive politicians want to hear about fairness – who will benefit and who will carry the burden of risk? They also may want to know, as intuitive ethicists, about potential challenges to assumptions about the moral order and the environmental consequences.

While it is accepted that these issues are outside the scope of traditional science, and indeed they may be relatively recent public concerns concentrated in some but not all European national publics, scientists cannot bury their heads in the sand. With sensitive technologies – regenerative medicine, genetic modification and synthetic biology for example – the intuitive logics of politics and ethics are likely to take on greater prominence. If they are ignored in science communication then science will not carry the confidence of the public.

What emerges from our analyses of the Eurobarometer survey is a complex picture of the ways in which intuitive logics relate to views about sensitive technologies. Those who lean more often toward the intuitive scientist/economist logics are not always amongst the confirmed supporters of science and technology. And by the same token those who tend to lean toward the logic of the intuitive ethicist are not always in the opposition camp. But, what is also clear is that benefits arising from the technology are important, and that for a sizeable proportion of the European public, fairness of the distribution of both benefits and risks is a particular concern.

If it is accepted that science is a part of society and that some science and technology is more sensitive than other fields on account of its societal impacts, then science communication must accommodate to this reality. While it may be unrealistic to add sophistication in ethics and other related issues to the training of scientists, it is surely not unrealistic to envision science communication as a coalition of different competencies that collectively address the public in the guises of intuitive scientists, economists, politicians and ethicists.

Key resources

For the most recent general report of public perceptions of biotechnology in Europe:
Gaskell, G., Stares, S., Allansdottir, A., et al. (2010). *Europeans and Biotechnology in 2010: Winds of Change?* A report to the European Commission's Directorate-General for Research. http://ec.europa.eu/research/science-society/document_library/pdf_06/europeans-biotechnology-in-2010_en.pdf

For access to more Eurobarometer data and reports:
http://ec.europa.eu/public_opinion/index_en.htm

For some views from across the Atlantic:
US National Science Board's Science and Engineering Indicators. http://www.nsf.gov/statistics/seind08/c7/c7h.htm

For tips on how to spot problematic wording in survey questions, and general advice on leading-edge survey methodology:
de Leeuw, E., Hox, J.J. and Dillman, D.A. (eds.) (2008). *International Handbook of Survey Methodology*. London: Taylor and Francis.

References

Bauer, M. W., Allum, N. and Miller, S. (2007). What can we learn from 25 years of PUS survey research? Liberating and expanding the agenda. *Public Understanding of Science*, **16**, 79–95.

Beck, U. (1992). *Risk Society: Towards a New Modernity*. London: Sage.

Cantley, M. (1992). Public perception, public policy, the public interest and public information: the evolution of policy for biotechnology in the European Community, 1982–92. In J. Durant (ed.) *Biotechnology in Public*, pp. 169–201 London: Science Museum.

Douglas, M. and Wildavsky, A. (1982). *Risk and Culture: An Essay on the Selection of Technological and Environmental Danger*. Berkeley, CA: University of California Press.

Durant, J., Bauer, M. W., Gaskell, G. et al. (2000). Two cultures of public understanding of science and technology in Europe. In M. Dierkes and C. von Grote (eds.) *Between Understanding and Trust: The Public, Science and Technology*, pp. 131–156. Amsterdam: Harwood Academic Publishers.

Durant, J., Evans, G. and Thomas, G. (1989). The public understanding of science. *Nature*, **340**, 11–14.

Ellsberg, D. (1961). Risk, ambiguity, and the savage axioms. *Quarterly Journal of Economics*, **75**, 643–669.

European Commission (2010). *Commission Recommendation on Guidelines for the Development of National Co-Existence Measures to Avoid the Unintended Presence of GMOs in Conventional and Organic Crops*. Brussels, 13.7.2010, C(2010) 4822 final. http://ec.europa.eu/food/food/biotechnology/docs/new_recommendation_en.pdf

Gaskell, G. (2004). Science policy and society: the British debate over GM agriculture. *Current Opinion in Biotechnology*, **15**, 241–245.

Gaskell, G. (2008). Lessons from the bio-decade: a social scientific perspective. In K. David and P. B. Thompson (eds.) *What can Nanotechnology Learn from Biotechnology?*, pp. 237–259. London: Academic Press.

Gaskell, G. and Allum, N. (2001). Sound science, problematic publics? Contrasting representations of risk and uncertainty. *Notizie di Politeia*, **XVII**, 63, 13–25.

Gaskell, G., Stares, S., Allansdottir, A. *et al.* (2006). *Europeans and Biotechnology in 2005: Patterns and Trends*. A report to the European Commission's Directorate-General for Research. http://ec.europa.eu/public_opinion/archives/ebs/ebs_244b_en.pdf

Gaskell, G., Stares, S., Allansdottir, A. *et al.* (2010). *Europeans and Biotechnology in 2010: Winds of Change?* A report to the European Commission's Directorate-General for Research. http://ec.europa.eu/research/science-society/document_library/pdf_06/europeans-biotechnology-in-2010_en.pdf

Globe and Mail (1999). Robert Shapiro's reality check. 22nd December.

Horst, M. (2007). Public expectations of gene therapy: scientific futures and their performative effects on scientific citizenship. *Science, Technology and Human Values*, **32**, 150–171.

Jaeger, C. C., Renn, O., Rosa, E. A. and Webler, T. (2001). *Risk, Uncertainty, and Rational Action*. London: Earthscan.

Kahneman, D. and Tversky A. (1979). Prospect theory: analysis of decision under risk, *Econometrica* **47**, 263–291.

Mejlgaard, N. and Stares, S. (2010). Participation and competence as joint components in a cross-national analysis of scientific citizenship. *Public Understanding of Science*, **19**, 545–561.

Michael, M. and Brown, N. (2005). Scientific citizenships: self-representations of xenotransplantation's publics. *Science as Culture*, **14**, 39–57.

Miller, J. D. (1983). Scientific literacy: a conceptual and empirical review. *Daedalus*, Spring, 29–48.

Renn, O. (1998). Three decades of risk research: accomplishments and new challenges. *Journal of Risk Research*, **1**, 49–71.

Royal Society (1999) *Science, Technology and Social Responsibility*. London: Royal Society.

Rozin, P., Spranca, M., Krieger, Z. *et al.* (2004). Preference for natural: instrumental and ideational/moral motivations, and the contrast between foods and medicines. *Appetite*, **43**, 147–154.

Schuman, H. and Presser, S. (1981). *Questions and Answers in Attitude Surveys*. New York: Academic Press.

Tetlock, P. E. (2002). Social functionalist frameworks for judgment and choice: intuitive politicians, theologians, and prosecutors. *Psychological Review*, **109**, 451–471.

von Grote, C. and Dierkes, M. (2000). Public understanding of science and technology: state of the art and consequences for future research. In M. Dierkes and C. von Grote (eds.) *Between Understanding and Trust: The Public, Science and Technology*, pp. 341–362. Amsterdam: Harwood Academic Publishers.

5

The common language of research

Science is a way of thinking much more than it is a body of knowledge.

Carl Sagan (1986, p. 15)

INTRODUCTION

When there is a lot of activity, it is easy to assume that this is translating into benefits and advances. We certainly seem to be in a second golden age when it comes to the action around communicating science. Looking back to the publication of the Bodmer Report, and even back just a decade to the publication of the House of Lords Report on Science and Society (House of Lords 2000), there was a palpable absence of scientific voices in civil society; by comparison, we now find ourselves in much more of a 'can do' environment.

Researchers embark on their careers with some expectation of their work having a public interface, in many countries research grants now regularly stipulate it, colleagues more often support it and institutions run outreach programmes and festivals to promote it. Communication theory, training and governance advice have become crowded academic marketplaces, initially in the UK and parts of Europe but increasingly elsewhere. There has been a significant promotion of science as a leisure activity and cultural interest. There have been sustained efforts to make the public interest case for investment in scientific research and development. Yet, if we look at all the engagement activity and theory according to its purpose, we find that, in all societies, we have barely begun to explore popularising science as a tool for empowering civil society.

Successful Science Communication, ed. D. J. Bennett and R. C. Jennings. Published by Cambridge University Press. © Cambridge University Press 2011.

Sense About Science, the charitable trust I work for, has been striving to do this, working with over 5000 scientists and hundreds of civic groups in the UK where it is based, and with other organisations similarly interested in civil society elsewhere, including the USA, South Africa, Portugal and Slovenia. Our experiences have produced some insights into how to frame questions about scientific and medical matters so that the underlying assumptions become clearer and more useful to civil society.

People – and organisations who interact directly with the public – are asking for help about a wide range of science-related subjects, to sort through scare and hype stories, to determine which products and practices are effective or what might be a scam, and to come to conclusions about the reliability of scientific claims and assess controversies. Many of the questions that people seek help on are about establishing the reliability or 'meaning' of research claims: what do scientists actually know about this? Can I find out what tests have been done?

This is the public language of research and it needs more attention. It surely should be the starting point of science communication. In the 1950s, the great populariser Jacob Bronowski talked about the dangers of losing 'a sense of science as a social activity' and noted that chief among its symptoms was the decline of a common language (Bronowski 1978, p. 62). It is a language that emerges when we lay bare the reasoning behind different claims about science and evidence, not in the sterile and cynical way that rests at 'who funded what' or that satisfies itself with narrow-minded glee at pointing out limits and errors as though scientific inquiry is just a pretension, but in a way that empowers us to question our assumptions and received wisdom.

Viewed from the broader historical aspirations of science popularisers, it is surprising to find, amid the more recent proliferation of science communication initiatives, that the popularisation of scientific *reasoning* has been relatively neglected. Why is this? Perhaps in part it is that too little of the communication activity or theory stems from what people are actually asking or debating. More significantly, it may be a product of defensiveness. The recognition by Bodmer and others that the relationship between science and society needed attention also occurred in the context of a loss of confidence in science, a bruised mood which has led to losing sight of what scientific reasoning contributes to the public interest and instead focusing on more anxious, defensive, and often somewhat self-regarding, questions of trust.

STARTING WITH THE PUBLIC DEBATE

Scientists often ask *'What are we to do when commentators or products can make sweeping, unsupported assertions but our responses must be tentative and full of caveats?'* There seems to be a tendency in science and policy communications to be coy about taking up misconceptions even when the purpose of a report or commentary is to address them. By moving away from this rather defensive position and starting with the public discussion, it becomes possible to give a more socially meaningful response. We may not know everything about the immune system, for example, but we know that the fashionable food-intolerance tests which are heavily promoted on the Internet and by some alternative health therapists produce arbitrary results, are not supported by evidence and defy basic physiology.

Addressing misconceptions and discussing the nature of evidence for claims, in the experience of Sense About Science and in the view of the hundreds of early career researchers who have come together to form the associated Voice of Young Science network, is an integral part of being a civic scientist. This means addressing directly the claims that are in circulation, whether in advertising material, advice columns, campaign statements, public health schemes, policy proposals, common prejudice or celebrity health fads, for example.

When there is a significant difference between scientific reasoning and the way that a particular subject, such as food-intolerance testing, appears in wider society, it requires a bit of work with scientists in related fields and with different civic groups to identify the assumptions that are being made. We go in search of the insights that can equip people better to weigh things up for themselves, both specific to the subject area and more generally to scientific methods.

This was an approach that first developed with *Making Sense of Chemical Stories* in 2006, when Sense About Science and the Royal Society of Chemistry took a group of chemical scientists and asked them to work out the most common misconceptions behind inaccurate claims about chemicals (Sense About Science 2006). By evaluating a year of media stories, campaign material and product claims, it appeared that there were six misconceptions that accounted for the majority of misleading claims. We found, on testing these with the public, that they had counterintuitive power. For example, the inaccurate (and dangerous) idea that natural chemicals are good and synthetic chemicals are bad, which had been raised by the chemists as an aside in their commentary, was identified in public trials as the most useful thing to find out, leading people to recall a range of products and stories which they had found believable and which they were now inclined to re-evaluate.

It was a similar story with work on *Making Sense of GM* in 2009, when we collated media records, online discussions and the Sense About Science enquiries log to identify recurring questions (Sense About Science 2009a). We then asked the UK's leading plant science institutes to explain what they were doing with genetic modification and why – reasoning that had been almost impossible for any curious inquirer to find amid the polemical GM row. It is also how we put together *Making Sense of Screening*, when we asked members of the public to tell us which of the insights and arguments from clinicians helped them to evaluate the somewhat frenzied calls to widen screening programmes which had followed Jade Goody's death from cervical cancer (Sense About Science 2009b).[1]

In similar work on radiation, our group of physicists and epidemiologists worked out that the main difference between their reading of a WiFi scare story and that of a school governor confronted with a campaign against WiFi introduction in schools was that they saw radiation as a spectrum and not as all the same thing. This led to *Making Sense of Radiation*, which is used by local authorities and community groups to discuss WiFi, phone masts and other concerns (Sense About Science 2008). Similarly, working out that the most common misconception about homeopathy was that it contained an active ingredient ('a herb or something') has helped to develop effective interventions into that debate.

Collaborative projects to make sense of statistics, to clarify the meaning of scientific uncertainty, and to weigh up stories claiming 'links' to causes and cures are emerging from the same process of starting with the public discussion and pinning down misconceptions and insights with scientists and members of the public.

The public use of these kinds of insights has shown that there is an appetite for understanding how others (notably scientists and policymakers) have reasoned something through. It should be noted that it is very rare that scientists have themselves immediately identified the insights that best equip the public to make sense of claims they encounter. It is often only through a persistent review of public discussion that their different assumptions become clear. It requires a process of liaison through networks of civic groups to establish useful insights, and then some use of their counterintuitive character to generate a broader

---

[1] Jade Goody was an English television celebrity who died in March 2009 from cervical cancer.

discussion, in the national media and elsewhere, to see them taken up in public discussions of research and claims about science and medicine. Starting more directly with a review of the claims and views in circulation can also avoid much wasted effort in science communication. Unless contributions are a clear response to what people are actually talking about and deciding, they don't tend to notice or use them. People often ask questions relating to evidence about subjects on which long reports or Government consultation documents are widely available. It seems that if people (including journalists and other opinion-formers) cannot see direct links to the debates and claims they encounter, they just do not see these materials. Or perhaps put another way, what people are looking for is not to be taken back to school but some straightforward reasoning to help them sift claims and decide where their concerns lie.

HOW DO WE KNOW?

How do we know: a review of knowledge themes in public enquiries to Sense About Science 2006–2007

Help me get to grips with it

- *Is this something parents should be worried about?* (Midwife responding to news story on plasticisers in babies' bottles)
- *Can I get something from the scientists about this?* (UK town councillor on WiFi radiation; AIDS meals on wheels group about miracle diets and superfoods stories)
- *Is this another scare story?* (Women's magazine on skin absorption of make-up; allotment holders on stories about growing food near main roads)
- *Is this something we should warn people about?* (Jobs agency hosting ads for clinical trials after a clinical trial at Northwick Park Hospital in the UK left six people in intensive care)
- *Do scientists do any work on this kind of thing?* (Parent–teacher association on option to site wind turbine on school)
- *Is it the scientists or the companies who say it's safe?* (Parish council and local newspaper on mobile phone masts)

How much do we know?

- *What do the scientists actually know about this?* (Local residents association on chemical residues in brown-field site; gym instructor on steroid use)

- *Can I find out what tests have been done?* (TV celebrity on homeopathy, education writer on WiFi, mental health group on use of the herbal remedy St John's wort to treat depression)
- *How sure are they that they're right?* (Most common call on vaccine safety)

Balance of scientific opinion

- *Do these people represent the majority of scientific opinion?* (UK advertising company responding to TV programme on global warming; members of the public with the same question; youth clubs on the effects of illicit drugs following a BBC TV Newsnight programme)
- *How are the scientists split on this?* (Local horticultural society on GM 'superweeds' story, parenting magazine on 5-in-1 vaccine, a UK County Council on fluoride)

Legitimacy

- *Is it a proper study?* (Self-help breast cancer group on whether stories about underarm deodorants causing cancer are true; teachers on reports of 'brain gym' success in schools)
- *How can I tell whether it's proper research?* (Patients responding to stories about full-body scans preventing disease; carers responding to story that the UK National Institute for Health and Clinical Excellence (NICE) does not approve Alzheimer's drugs for prescription; community café on the effects on children of colourings in foods)
- *It says here it's from scientific research – how can I tell whether that's true?* (Most common question about Internet advertisements for health cures)
- *Are they only listening to one group of scientists?* (Conservation group on fishing quota decision)
- *Have they talked to the scientists?* (Parents on decision to allow WiFi in schools)
- *How should we explain to helpline callers what kind of studies these are?* (Neurological disease societies on flurry of unfounded claims in media)

The questions that people ask about scientific issues, or which are begged by public discussion, are often quite generic. They are concerned with what is known and how (see Box). Researchers also ask these kinds of questions when judging scientific claims, such as, has it been peer reviewed? What has other research in the field found? How likely are these findings to be superseded? Have they been replicated?

However, scientists rarely make this reasoning clear when talking about research. In fact our working groups have shown that they do not spontaneously see it. But we have found it to offer precisely the language to enable people to have an adult discussion, rather than a science lesson, whether about the likelihood of nuclear fusion, or the basis of nutritional therapy or the safety of MRI scans. When trying to discuss what they know, and how they know it, researchers seem to start drawing on a far more socially creative (and less defensive) language, one that is socially shared and dynamic and very much the opposite of a translation into lay terms of scientific statements.

The encouragement of scientists, policy-makers and opinion formers to explain the scientific reasoning and the evidence on which conclusions are based will only work if it is mirrored by encouraging the public, journalists and civic groups to ask searching questions that can help them follow scientific reasoning and question the status of research claims.

The main focus of this attempt to find and promote a public language to talk about the status of research claims has been the creation and dissemination of a short guide, *I Don't Know What to Believe*, which explains peer review and the value of knowing whether a research claim has been published in a scientific journal (Sense About Science 2005). In 2005, the scientific community's reaction to the suggestion of popularising peer review was largely dismissive and sceptical, so much so that the initial print run of this guide by Sense About Science was set at just 10000 copies. What if, said many scientists, we were seen to be saying that peer review means a paper is right? How can people contemplate consideration of research according to its validity, significance and originality?

Eight reprints on, over a quarter of a million people from 40 different countries have requested copies of the guide and intermediaries such as patient help-lines, libraries, teachers, and online resources now use it to explain why some research claims are more significant than others. They find that it is quite possible to do this without suggesting that if a paper is peer reviewed it is flawless, just as people know very well that a washing machine with a quality mark might still break down.

The appeal of such tools to the public seems to be that you don't, for example, have to become a gastroenterologist to ask searching questions about the status of claims regarding the measles–mumps–rubella (MMR) vaccine and autism – you can talk about peer review, replication, consensus, stability of the science, levels of confidence and certainty, all of which help to navigate a debate. In short, the experience of this kind of civic activity is that people are not looking to be treated as alternative experts, but for scientific reasoning and indications that high standards are being followed to be brought into wider discussion and held up to the light.

The potential for this nascent shared language around evidence and scientific inquiry to develop is supported by some survey research, which shows that people without a background in science readily perceive questions about evidence and scientific enquiry. In a survey of attitudes and awareness of medical research conducted in 2009 and published in 2010, the Wellcome Trust Monitor found that 70% of adults correctly identified that the scientific way to test the effectiveness of a drug was to give it to some patients but not others and compare their outcomes (Butt *et al.* 2009). An even higher number (79%) answered questions about probability correctly. Conclusions drawn from other surveys of understanding of the scientific process, such as the Eurobarometer (Eurobarometer 1973–2010) and the US National Science Foundation (National Science Board 2008) surveys, have been more pessimistic, putting the figure for 'scientific literacy' at around a fifth of the population. Putting aside differences in how this was assessed and the extent to which the surveys tested prior knowledge, it is worth noting that a fifth of the adult population already being able to discuss the nature of a scientifically designed test is far from a disaster or a limit to the development of a sceptical and engaged civil society.

There is now a distinct move towards organising some areas of science communication with reference to 'how do we know?' The new climate gallery of the London Science Museum has been designed to encourage visitors to consider climate change in the context of how we expect scientific knowledge to develop, through peer review, challenge and self-correction. Director Chris Rapley has contrasted this to the less helpful framing of climate discussions as a debate in which one side has the right answer (Rapley 2010). Journalists and broadcasters are also contributing to fuller discussions about the status of scientific claims.

Sense About Science has also led efforts with the UK Parliament and Government, since 2005, to forge recognition that the status of a claim about scientific research is as important as the claim itself.

From our interactions we have found that the idea of a balance of evidence is now better understood, peer review is reasonably well recognised but that replication, consensus and stability might usefully be developed as part of the language of public and policy discussion. There seems to have been a lack of language for talking about research and the quality of science or the status of conclusions. The BSE experience, and focus of the subsequent Phillips Inquiry on the nature of what was known and with what certainty (Phillips *et al.* 2000), clearly began to introduce more of these considerations into exchanges about science in public policy, but talking about research in these terms is not a common language yet, even for policy-makers.

THE 'SCENE' AND CONTEXT

Starting with the claims in public circulation and formulating the different assumptions behind them in these ways has exposed many areas where people find themselves ill-equipped by all the communication activity to work out what is going on. Chief among the things we take for granted is the 'science scene', its networks, institutions and experts. Knowing this kind of context is the way that many of us follow pathways to further information. As such, it is empowering and enabling. It is, however, a missing component in much science communication. Until the past couple of years, few of the authors of popular factsheets and public reports thought to provide an outline of who is who, and how to pursue a question.

This sounds like a minor point but to imagine how alien and unquantifiable the science scene can be, do a little thought experiment. Assuming you have no familiarity with law, imagine that you are asked to write an article about the legal implications of the community blog Mumsnet, a website that is hugely popular with young mothers, being sued for libel, by tomorrow afternoon. Where do you look? What questions do you ask? Think of that huge edifice of the legal world and just imagine trying to formulate what you are looking for, never mind find it. Even if you get as far as the existence of the Defamation Act, subsequent amendments, and what they do, how sure would you be about who to call and how much of the picture their view would be giving you? Now consider being a jobbing writer on a parenting magazine, living outside London and wanting to write about plasticisers in babies' bottles. Or a head teacher looking at a promotion of brain-training products to improve pupil performance or reviewing a request for permission to conduct clinical research in the school. Many phone calls

to Sense About Science from people in these circumstances begin with *'I'm not really sure who to ask, I'm not really sure how to ask this.'*
It is also useful to remember that understanding institutional and professional dynamics is the preserve of people who follow particular kinds of news, hear gossip, read other organisations' newsletters and who know who is influential or a reliable source of information. In the absence of this kind of context, it is perhaps not surprising that commentators set out many scientific and medical controversies in an over-simplified world, for example of big companies and consumers.

There are now, though small in number, some attempts to provide a snapshot of sources of help and some context, notably in the area of medicine. The UK National Health Service *Behind the Headlines*, which produces online rapid commentary on medical stories, frequently situates single claims from scientific papers in the broader questions being investigated by the research team concerned and highlights others working in the field. But with dialogue buzzing on everyone's lips, many people in the science communication world are shocked to learn that they are still incredibly insular in this regard.

SCIENCE AS A PUBLIC TOOL

What all of this goes towards is another purpose in the science and society relationship, one which is universal in character: science as a public tool of truth-seeking, reasoning and debunking. Popularising science for this purpose involves giving people the tools to question claims and to identify pseudo-science. It enables people to share the scientific reasoning and evidence that help to transcend the noise around a scientific or medical issue. It appeals to people – from the bar-stool pedant to the worried parent – who want to cut through the presentation of a subject to ask *'How do we know?'*

The challenge for science and society is to reformulate the many questions and assertions in public circulation in order to spell out and weigh up the assumptions behind them. But this common language of research and evidence requires a level of civic aspiration that struggles to show itself in all the activity to popularise and communicate about science.

There has been a proliferation of activity that might be described as 'Wow Science'. This kind of popularisation covers a wide spectrum of cultural activities, from books about star birth and interactive exhibitions, to television programmes on the mating rituals of poisonous frogs and home chemistry. Wow Science introduces people to the manipulation of natural forces, for education and enjoyment. We do not know what effect it has on the number of pupils enrolling for science courses or whether anyone who makes a 'volcano' with sodium bicarbonate is spurred on to reacquaint themselves with the periodic table and electrons. It may be wrong to think in terms of such goals. It seems good and important that science should be publicly entertaining and that many researchers divert energy and imagination into maintaining the public's cultural or educational interest in the natural world, though we recognise that some activities are also motivated by advancing particular arguments, or policy 'messages'. But whether there is a unique case for education in science is debatable. One could equally argue that the public should understand compound interest rates or the principle of equality before the law, as that they should be more familiar with soil structure or super-colliders.

Then there have been significant efforts to achieve popular support for science as a *sector*: the university expenditure code and the research budgetary allocation. This is where 'science' refers to the labs and infrastructure, the research programmes and the funding of researchers, which must compete for national favour and finance with the arts or international policy. Science, in this sense, is necessarily particular. Why, say, a chemistry department over an archaeological dig? While there may be public-spirited arguments around the relative merits of what should be pursued or funded, it is driven by the pragmatic considerations of departments, businesses, institutions and national economies.

Instead of maintaining that scientific inquiry is a better way for everyone to understand the natural world than subjective perception (such as political intuition or anecdotal experience), science has been increasingly relegated to these less presumptuous roles of being a cultural pursuit and an economic interest.

Perhaps this is the result of reverberations of the more defensive mood of the last decade, following a succession of debates about scientific issues 'going wrong' and public forums being characterised by hostile campaigns and media scare stories. Discussions following the 2000 House of Lords report prompted several initiatives for putting the relationship between science and the public on better terms. Sense About Science was among them. Born into the fire of debates raging about cloning, GM, 'man-made' chemicals, the MMR vaccine, organ donation, alternative medicine, mobile phone radiation and more, it was faced with the huge question: how can the public get a handle on the scientific evidence?

In the years since, with the relative luxury of thousands of scientists giving up their time, and with a body of experience in equipping the public with questions and evidence on a wide range of subjects, we have realised that those anxieties about the science and society relationship reined in the democratic impulses of earlier popularisers. On the one hand, the resulting more critical and hesitant attitude towards science appears to have led to welcome reflection and openness in many scientific and medical institutions. The Bodmer Report of 1985 both typified and catalysed this kind of reflection.

On the other hand, the defensiveness and anxiety that it has also produced in the scientific community have been of doubtful benefit. Into the crisis in confidence in scientific institutions and policy bodies has flowed a wide array of communication theories, and the rapidity with which they flow has brought with it confusion and a degree of over-complication about how to communicate with people. Experience in workshops with mid-career researchers also suggests that this complication has added to fears about public engagement. It amplifies the defensiveness. Communication theories develop in a fairly self-referencing way, often by definition against one another more than as the result of learning and insights generated by interaction in public discussion; they tend to have a passive relationship with the public via social research and exercises.

Watching the public is attractive because it involves less risk-taking, but it also yields less in terms of social imagination.

The result seems to be that we have a golden age of science in society, but at the moment it has a high ratio of tentative facilitators and consultants to bold popularisers. Communication theories can't compensate for engagement. Scientists forget to draw on their most straightforward resource – how they themselves engage in society, as arguers, debaters, consulted relatives, frustrated viewers, curious citizens or self-critical thinkers.

The many questions that people have about the scientific basis for assertions are testament to the public's desire to find a way into discussions from climate change to mercury in vaccines. As the author Thomas Berger is reported to have said, *'the art and science of asking questions is the source of all knowledge'.*[2] We can respond to this only by rediscovering science as a public tool for testing the plausibility of competing claims, and by encouraging a sceptical and inquiring public that readily asks 'How do we know?'

[2] See http://thinkexist.com/quotes/thomas_berger

Key resources

Bronowski, J. (1978) *The Common Sense of Science*. Cambridge, MA: Harvard University Press. (First published 1951.)

Brown, J. R. (2001) *Who Rules in Science? An Opinionated Account of the Wars*. Cambridge, MA: Harvard University Press.

Gregory, J. and Miller, S. (1998) *Science in Public: Communication, Culture and Credibility*. Cambridge, MA: Perseus Publishing.

Laird, F. N. (1989) The decline of deference: the political context of risk communication. *Risk Analysis*, **9**: 543–550.

Marquand, D. (2004) *The Decline of the Public: The Hollowing Out of Citizenship*. Cambridge, UK: Polity Press.

References

Bronowski, J. (1978) *The Common Sense of Science*. Cambridge, MA: Harvard University Press. (First published 1951.)

Butt, S., Clery, E., Abeywardena, V. and Phillips, M. (2009) *Wellcome Trust Monitor: Tracking Public Views on Medical Research*. London: Wellcome Trust.

Eurobarometer surveys (1973–2010) European Commission. http://ec.europa.eu/public_opinion/index_en.htm

House of Lords (2000) *Select Committee on Science and Technology Third Report: Science and Society*, HL Paper 38. London: HMSO.

National Science Board (2008) *Science and Engineering Indicators*. Arlington, VA. NSB 08–01; NSB 08–01A. Ch.7 Science and technology: public attitudes and understanding.

Phillips, Lord Justice, *et al.* (2000) *The BSE Inquiry Report*, Vol. 1. http://collections.europarchive.org/tna/20090505194948/http:/bseinquiry.gov.uk/report/index.htm

Rapley, C. (2010) A forum to make sense of climate science. *Guardian*, 27 May. http://www.guardian.co.uk/environment/cif-green/2010/may/27/science-museum-climate-gallery

Sagan, C. (1986) *Broca's Brain: Reflections on the Romance of Science*. New York: Ballantine.

Sense About Science (2005) *I Don't Know What to Believe*. London: Sense About Science in collaboration with Elsevier, Blackwell Publishing, Medical Research Council, Royal Pharmaceutical Society of Great Britain and the Institute of Biology.

Sense About Science (2006) *Making Sense of Chemical Stories: A Briefing for the Lifestyle Sector on Misconceptions about Chemicals*. London: Sense About Science.

Sense About Science (2008) *Making Sense of Radiation: A Guide to Radiation and Its Health Effects*. London: Sense About Science in collaboration with the Institute of Physics and Engineering in Medicine, the British Institute of Radiology and the Institution of Mechanical Engineers.

Sense About Science (2009a) *Making Sense of GM: What is the Genetic Modification of Plants and Why Are Scientists Doing It?* London: Sense About Science in collaboration with the Genetics Society, John Innes Centre, Lawes Agricultural Trust, BBSRC, Institute of Food Research and Institute of Biology.

Sense About Science (2009b) *Making Sense of Screening*. London: Sense About Science in collaboration with the Association for Clinical Biochemistry, the Institute of Biomedical Science and the Royal College of Pathologists.

6

Not 100% sure? The 'public' understanding of risk

All knowledge is provisional, subject to revision in the light of new information. Knowledge is probabilistic. Some beliefs might be assigned infinitesimal probabilities – creationism and intelligent design perhaps – but all probabilities must be treated as revisable in the light of new evidence. Where knowledge (belief) relates to potential future harms or benefits, as it usually does in situations where science communication is seen as problematic or contentious, the issue can be framed as one of risk communication.

WHAT IS RISK?

There are many ways in which one can categorize problems of risk and its management. Typing the single word 'risk' into Google produces hundreds of millions of hits. One need sample only a small fraction in order to discover unnecessary and often acrimonious arguments caused by people using the same word to refer to different things and shouting past each other. Figure 6.1 proffers a typology that has proved helpful in clearing away some unnecessary arguments.

Some risks are visible to the naked eye. We manage them using *judgment*. We do not undertake a formal probabilistic risk assessment before crossing the road; some combination of instinct, intuition and experience usually sees us safely to the other side.

Others are perceptible only to those armed with microscopes, telescopes, surveys, scanners and other measuring devices, and the data they produce. This is the realm of quantified risk assessment. In this realm uncertainty comes with numbers attached in the form of probabilities.

Successful Science Communication, ed. D. J. Bennett and R. C. Jennings. Published by Cambridge University Press. © Cambridge University Press 2011.

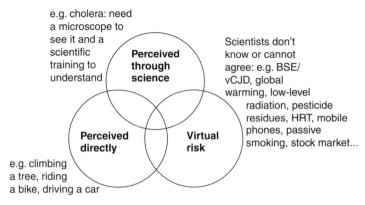

Figure 6.1 Different kinds of risk.

In this circle one also finds attempts to attach magnitudes to the conse-quences of a risk materializing – often expressed in monetary terms. So commonly we find the expression Risk = Probability × Magnitude.

Virtual risks may or may not be real – scientists disagree – but beliefs about them have real consequences. The uncertainty is liberat-ing; if science cannot settle the issue people feel free to argue from their beliefs, convictions, prejudices or superstitions. Here we are thrown back, as in the first circle, on judgments that cannot be objectively validated.

THE RISK THERMOSTAT

Figure 6.2 proffers the essence of the process of risk management. It describes the Risk Thermostat. 'Propensity' in this diagram represents the setting of the thermostat. Some are set high, others low. I have yet to meet anyone with a thermostat set to zero; life would be unutterably boring.

Propensity leads to risk-taking behaviour that leads, by definition, to accidents: to take a risk is to do something that carries with it a probability of an adverse outcome. Through surviving accidents and learning from them, or seeing them on television, or being warned by mother, we acquire our perception of safety and danger. The model postulates that when propensity and perception get out of balance we behave in a way that seeks to restore the balance. Why do we take risks? There are rewards, and the model proposes that the magnitude of the reward influences propensity.

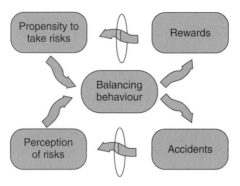

Figure 6.2 The Risk Thermostat with perceptual filters.

For most economists and psychologists today the idea of 'risk compensation', as this process is commonly known, is axiomatic; while in pursuit of opportunities, we scan our environment for evidence of safety and danger and modify our behaviour in response to what we observe. The insurance industry knows the phenomenon as 'moral hazard'; if you have house contents insurance you are less careful about locking up, or if you are the president of a bank that is too big to fail you will sell more sub-prime mortgages. Where the phenomenon is still the subject of debate, the argument now is usually not about its existence but about the magnitude of its effect – is the behavioural response to perceived changes in risk, partial, complete, or more than complete?

Most institutional risk management, outside the offices of venture capitalists, hedge funds managers and sub-prime mortgage brokers, is devoted to the prevention of bad things happening. It is focused on the bottom loop of Figure 6.2. It is risk averse.

This bottom loop bias colours the reporting of most scientific risk stories – '*if it bleeds it leads*' in journalistic parlance. But not always and everywhere. Reporting of the 'sub-prime credit crunch' frequently identified top-loop bias – incentive structures that offer enormous rewards for taking risk-free risks with other people's money – as an important inflator of the financial bubble that burst with such devastating effect.

PERCEPTUAL FILTERS

It is commonly alleged by people struggling to put across scientific messages that 'the public' craves certainty and cannot cope with the provisional nature of scientific knowledge. This seems unlikely. The public after all buys millions of pounds worth of lottery tickets every week[1] and a significant number regularly visit bookmakers. A more likely explanation of the difficulties encountered by those charged with communicating scientific information to the public is that there is no such beast as 'the public'. There are many publics and they perceive and respond to uncertainty differently.

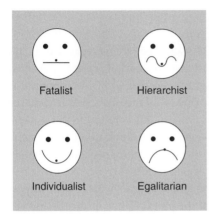

Figure 6.3 A typology of perceptual filters.

The Risk Thermostat of Figure 6.2 comes equipped with perceptual filters. Cultures and individuals vary widely in their perception of risks. Figure 6.3 proffers a cartoon version of a typology of commonly encountered responses to risk developed in a branch of anthropology called cultural theory. These are caricatures, but nevertheless recognizable types that one encounters in debates about threats to safety and the environment. With a little imagination you can begin to see them as personalities. In a report for Britain's Health and Safety Executive (HSE) (Adams and Thompson 2002) they are described as follows:

- Individualists are enterprising 'self-made' people, relatively free from control by others, and who strive to exert control over their environment and the people in it. Their success is often measured by their wealth and the number of followers they command. They are enthusiasts for equality of opportunity and, should they feel the need for moral justification of their activities, they appeal to Adam Smith's Invisible Hand which ensures that self-interested behaviour in

---

[1] It is sometimes argued that this behaviour in the face of such daunting odds demonstrates a failure to understand quantified uncertainty, but where else can one buy so much fantasy for £1?

a free market operates to the benefit of all. The self-made Victorian mill owner or present-day venture capitalist would make good representatives of this category. They oppose regulation and favour free markets. Nature, according to this perspective, is to be commanded for human benefit. They are prone to top-loop bias.

- Egalitarians have strong group loyalties but little respect for externally imposed rules, other than those imposed by nature. Human nature is – or should be – cooperative, caring and sharing. Trust and fairness are guiding precepts and equality of outcome is an important objective. Group decisions are arrived at by direct participation of all members, and leaders rule by the force of their arguments. The solution to the world's environmental problems is to be found in voluntary simplicity. Members of religious sects, communards and environmental pressure groups all belong to this category. Nature is to be obeyed and respected and interfered with as little as possible. They are advocates of the precautionary principle and prone to bottom-loop bias.
- Hierarchists inhabit a world with strong group boundaries and binding prescriptions. Social relationships in this world are hierarchical with everyone knowing his or her place. Members of caste-bound Hindu society, soldiers of all ranks and civil servants are exemplars of this category. The hierarchy certifies and employs the scientists whose intellectual authority is used to justify its actions. Nature is to be managed. They are devotees of cost–benefit analysis and nervous in the presence of uncertainties that preclude the possibility of attaching uncontested numbers to the variables they are supposed to be managing.
- Fatalists have minimal control over their own lives. They belong to no groups responsible for the decisions that rule their lives. They are non-unionised employees, outcasts, refugees, untouchables. They are resigned to their fate and see no point in attempting to change it. Nature is to be endured and, when it's your lucky day, enjoyed. Their risk management strategy is to buy lottery tickets and duck if they see something about to hit them.

In our report we explained to the HSE that in the terms of this typology they were statuary Hierarchists; they make the rules and enforce the rules. For the foreseeable future we predicted they could expect to be attacked from the Egalitarian quadrant for not doing enough to protect society, and from the Individualist quadrant for over-regulating and suffocating enterprise.

Figure 6.3 represents a first-order categorization; within each quadrant many further sub-categories can be found. Occupants of all four quadrants are all familiar with the concept of uncertainty but respond to it very differently. Consider this exchange, reported in Hansard, during the House of Lords inquiry into the safety of genetically modified organisms:

> Lord Reay (Chairman) *Your opposition to the release of GMOs, that is an absolute and definite opposition? It is not one that is dependent on further scientific research or improved procedures being developed or any satisfaction you might get with regard to the safety or otherwise in future?*
>
> (Lord Melchett) *It is a permanent and definite and complete opposition based on a view that there will always be major uncertainties. It is the nature of the technology, indeed it is the nature of science, that there will not be any absolute proof. No scientist would sit before your Lordships and claim that if they were a scientist at all.* (House of Lords Select Committee on GM Crops, Minutes of Evidence, 3 June 1998)

Here the difficulty for advocates of genetic modification is not Lord Melchett's failure to understand uncertainty; indeed he prays it in aid. It lies in his assessment of the potential costs and benefits of the technology. As noted above risk approached scientifically is often presented as an equation: Risk = Probability × Magnitude. With novel technologies there is limited evidence upon which to base estimates of probability, and even less upon which to base estimates of magnitude – positive or negative. So long as genetic modification remains in the virtual risk category of Figure 6.1, participants in debates about it will remain free to imagine the worst.

Or the best. Matt Ridley (2010) argues that its safety has been proven – '*More than a trillion GM meals have been eaten worldwide and nobody is known to have had a tummy upset as a result*' – and focuses on the potential rewards of the technology: higher yields, more efficient use of water, less fertilizer, herbicides and pesticides, and '*spectacularly good for wildlife*'.

Ridley is one of Britain's best-known science communicators. The varied response to his most recent book *The Rational Optimist* highlights the challenge of virtual risks. His book was the focus of a two-page interview in *New Scientist*[2] – Britain's leading popular science journal. The interview compares him to Voltaire's Doctor Pangloss. It does not challenge his contention that for billions of people life has improved over the past 50 years – *'we've seen extraordinary improvements in human health, income and lifespan'* – but concludes pessimistically that *'past performance is no guide to the future.'* Sadly in the face of scientific uncertainty we don't have many better guides.

WHAT KILLS YOU MATTERS

Figure 6.4 illustrates another way of classifying risks that can also help clear out of the way some unnecessary arguments.

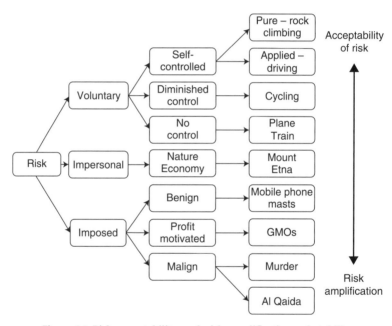

Figure 6.4 Risk acceptability and risk amplification: what kills you matters.

Acceptance of a given actuarial level of risk varies widely with the perceived level of control an individual can exercise over it and, in the case of imposed risks, with the perceived motives of the imposer.

With 'pure' voluntary risks, the risk itself, with its associated challenge and rush of adrenaline, is the reward. Most climbers on

---

[2] When optimism know no bounds, *New Scientist*, 12 June 2010.

Mount Everest and K2 know that it is dangerous and willingly take the risk (the fatality rate on K2 – fatalities/those reaching the summit – is reported to be 1 in 4).

With a voluntary, self-controlled, applied risk, such as driving, the reward is getting expeditiously from A to B. But the sense of control that drivers have over their fates appears to encourage a high level of tolerance of the risks involved.

Cycling from A to B (I write as a London cyclist) is done with a diminished sense of control over one's fate. This sense is supported by statistics that show that per kilometre travelled a cyclist is much more likely to die than someone in a car. This is a good example of the importance of distinguishing between relative and absolute risk. Although much greater, the absolute risk of cycling is still small – 1 fatality in 25 million kilometres cycled; not even Lance Armstrong can begin to cover that distance in a lifetime of cycling. And numerous studies have demonstrated that the extra relative risk is more than offset by the health benefits of regular cycling; regular cyclists live longer.

While people may voluntarily board planes, buses and trains, the popular reaction to crashes in which passengers are passive victims suggests that the public demand a higher standard of safety in circumstances in which people voluntarily hand over control of their safety to pilots, or bus or train drivers.

Risks imposed by nature – such as those endured by people living on the San Andreas Fault or the slopes of Mount Etna – or by impersonal economic forces – such as the vicissitudes of the global economy – are placed in the middle of the scale. Reactions vary widely. Such risks are usually seen as motiveless and are responded to fatalistically – unless or until the risk can be connected to base human motives. The damage caused by Hurricane Katrina to New Orleans is now attributed more to wilful bureaucratic neglect than to nature. And the search for the causes of the economic devastation attributed to the 'credit crunch' has become focused on the enormous bonuses paid to the bankers who profited from the subprime debacle.

Imposed risks are less tolerated. Consider mobile phones. The risk associated with the handsets is either non-existent or very small. The risk associated with the base stations, measured by radiation dose, unless one is up the mast with an ear to the transmitter, is orders of magnitude less. Yet all around the world billions of people are queuing up to take the voluntary handset risk, and almost all the opposition is focused on the base stations, which are seen by objectors as impositions. Because the radiation dose received from the handset increases with distance from the base station, to the extent that campaigns against the base stations are successful, they will increase the distance from the base station to the average handset, and thus the radiation dose. The base station risk, if it exists, might be labelled a benignly imposed risk; no one supposes that the phone company wishes to murder all those in the neighbourhood.

Even less tolerated are risks whose imposers are perceived to be motivated by profit or greed. In Europe, big biotech companies such as Monsanto are routinely denounced by environmentalist opponents for being more concerned with profit than the welfare of the environment or the consumers of its products.

Less tolerated still are malignly imposed risks – crimes ranging from mugging to rape and murder. In most countries in the world the number of deaths on the road far exceeds the numbers of murders, but far more people are sent to jail for murder than for causing death by dangerous driving. In the United States in 2002 16000 people were murdered – a statistic that evoked far more popular concern than the 42000 killed on the road – but far less concern than that inspired by the zero killed by terrorists.

Which brings us to terrorism and Al Qaida. How do we account for the massive scale, worldwide, of the outpourings of grief and anger attaching to its victims, whose numbers are dwarfed by victims of other causes of violent death? In London 52 people were killed by terrorist bombs on 7 July 2005, about six days' worth of death on the road. But thousands of people do not gather in Trafalgar Square every Sunday to mark, with a three-minute silence, their grief for the previous week's road accident victims. The malign intent of the terrorist is amplified by governments who see it as a threat to their ability to govern. To justify forms of surveillance and restrictions on liberty previously associated with tyrannies, 'democratic' governments now characterize terrorism as a threat to Our Way of Life.

WHO'S TO BLAME?

The drunk notoriously searches for his keys not in the dark where he dropped them, but under the lamp-post where he can see (Figure 6.5). This is an apt metaphor for much of what is written on the subject of risk management.

Lord Kelvin famously said, '*Anything that exists, exists in some quantity and can therefore be measured.*' This dictum sits challengingly alongside that of another famous scientist, Peter Medawar (1967) who observed,

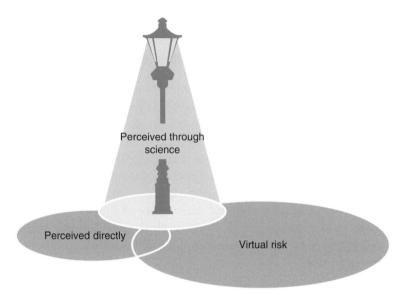

Figure 6.5 Risk: where are the keys?

If politics is the art of the possible, research is the art of the soluble. Both are immensely practical minded affairs. Good scientists study the most important problems they think they can solve. *It is, after all, their professional business to solve problems,* not merely to grapple with them. *[emphasis added]*

Risk is a word that refers to the future. It has no objective existence. The future exists only in the imagination. There are some risks for which science can provide useful guidance to the imagination. The risk that the Sun will not rise tomorrow can be assigned a very low probability by science. And actuarial science can estimate with a high degree of confidence that the number of people killed in road accidents in Britain next year will be 2500, plus or minus a hundred or so.

But these are predictions, not facts. Such predictions rest on assumptions; that tomorrow will be like yesterday; that next year will be like last year; that future events can be foretold by reading the runes of the past. Sadly, the history of prediction contains many failures – from those of stock market tipsters to those of volcanologists seeking to predict eruptions, earthquakes and tsunamis. In the area lit by the lamp of science one finds risk management problems that are potentially soluble by science. Such problems are capable of clear definition relating cause to effect and characterized by identifiable statistical regularities.

On the margins of this circle one finds problems framed as hypotheses, and methods of reasoning, such as Bayesian statistics, which guide the collection and analysis of further evidence. As the light grows dimmer the ratio of speculation to evidence increases. In the outer darkness lurk unknown unknowns. Here lie problems with which, to use Medawar's word, we are destined to 'grapple'.

The problem for science communicators is that we, scientist and non-scientist alike, do not respond blankly to uncertainty. We impose meaning upon it. The greater the uncertainty the greater becomes the influence of the perceptual filters in Figure 6.2. The different perspectives summarized in Figure 6.3 have deep cosmological roots and are not easily shifted. Perhaps the best that a science communicator can hope for is that introspection might assist recognition of one's own biases, and an awareness of the inevitability of different biases in others. Self-knowledge and an ability to stand metaphorically in the shoes of others are key ingredients of the empathy essential to effective communication.

Key resources

My website – www.john-adams.co.uk
My latest book – *Risk*, first published, 1995, UCL Press; third impression 1996, fourth impression 1998, fifth impression 2000; first published, 2001, Routledge: Taylor & Francis e-Library 2002 – ISBN-13: 978-1857280685
Simon Jenkins (http://www.guardian.co.uk/profile/simonjenkins) and Ben Goldacre (http://www.badscience.net/) are journalists who routinely do a good job of dealing with risk.

References

Adams, J. and Thompson, M. (2002). *Taking Account of Societal Concerns about Risk: Framing the Problem*, Health and Safety Executive, Research Report 035. Available online at http://www.hse.gov.uk/research/rrpdf/rr035.pdf
House of Lords Select Committee on GM Crops (1998). Minutes of Evidence, 3 June 1998. Available online at http://www.parliament.the-stationery-office.co.uk/pa/ld199899/ldselect/ldeucom/11/8060312.htm
Medawar, P. (1967), *Art of the Soluble*. London: Heinemann Young Books.
Ridley, M. (2010) Why ban genetic modification? *Wired*, 20 January. http://www.wired.co.uk/wired-magazine/archive/2010/02/start/matt-ridley-genetic-modification?page=all

ALFRED NORDMANN

7

The ethos of science vs. ethics of science communication: on deficit and surplus models of science–society interaction

First, there is the communication of science that involves a communal effort to get at the truth in a deliberative manner. It presupposes a mutual commitment to comprehensibility, truth, adequacy, and sincerity. Then there is science communication which seeks to ensure that our knowledge societies provide a supportive environment for the responsible development of science and technology. In order to be trustworthy, science communication has to meet certain ethical requirements. These two kinds of communication are radically different in character – and this is a dilemma and moral struggle for all scientists who engage in science communication, and for all science communicators who wish to communicate not just the results and promises of technoscientific research but also wish to retain the Enlightenment ethos of science as an exemplary deliberative enterprise. This is, in short and in summary, what calls for elaboration in the following pages.

INTRODUCTION: DISCOURSE ETHICS, SCIENCE, AND DEMOCRACY

One cannot formulate an ethics of science communication without considering the ethics of discourse more generally. What else is there, after all, in the communication of science or any other kind of communication: be clear and comprehensible, say what is correct or true, adhere to what is rightful or adequate to the situation, convey your sincerity and honesty! It would appear that an ethics of science communication urges

Successful Science Communication, ed. D. J. Bennett and R. C. Jennings. Published by
Cambridge University Press. © Cambridge University Press 2011.

adherence to norms such as these. Things are more complicated, however, and so is the current practice of what has come to be the business of science communication. The complication starts right here: the four imperatives stated above are not, in fact, norms of discourse that are more general than those of science – they originate within science itself and the tradition of the Enlightenment. It is for the sake of the intellectual progress of humankind in its pursuit of truth that the clarity, veracity, adequacy, and honesty of what we say to one another matters so much.[1] Arguably, however, this tradition of science as pursuit of truth and of general Enlightenment has lost sway in the contemporary world of innovation, of research and development, of science centers, stakeholder involvement, and public engagement – and thus, perhaps, the four norms are anything but self-evident and have little to do with the standards of appropriateness for science communication.

In order to better understand this predicament, let us take a closer look at clarity or comprehensibility, correctness or truth, adequacy or rightness, sincerity or honesty. In discussion with Karl-Otto Apel, Jürgen Habermas introduced these not as norms that are brought to communication but as implicit expectations that accompany all communication (Apel 1973; Habermas 1990, 1991). In the tradition of the Enlightenment, Habermas assumes that the goal of communication is ideally to reach a rational consensus. By entering into communication people are joining in a common process. This process fuses questions of knowledge (epistemology) with questions of practice (ethics and politics): in order to produce a consensus in which everyone can join on their own conviction, each participant in the conversation must assume that they are understanding the others, that the others are speaking the truth, that they are as open as the process requires, that they are sincere in their dedication to a rational consensus. This is not to say, of course, that these assumptions are always correct – in fact, we usually do not know for sure whether they are. But as soon as these assumptions are questioned or break down, the very nature of communication changes: when we are not sure whether we understand each other and whether the condition of comprehensibility is met, we start debating the meanings of words and concepts. When we are not sure whether the others are saying what they hold to be true, social cohesion and the very idea of a joint process of rational consensus formation breaks down. Similarly, when relevant information is withheld or when ulterior motives for engaging in

---

[1] These norms do not matter much in paternalist settings, for example, where heads of family or state or congregation say what is good for their charges to hear.

communication are suspected, the process needs to be repaired and the basis of trust restored. The sincere commitment to veracity is therefore a precondition that creates an ideal situation in which equals can join together to forge a consensus regarding scientific theories or arrangements for social justice.[2] This a necessary precondition because a consensus is legitimate only to the extent that all concerned can assent in their capacity as free rational agents. Discourse ethics is therefore dedicated to the overarching goal of establishing and maintaining the conditions where such rational consensus can be formed by free agents, and where everyone aims for comprehensibility, truth, openness, and sincerity.

It is easy to see that this discourse ethics is indebted to science and the tradition of the Enlightenment. From Immanuel Kant, John Stuart Mill, Max Weber, or Charles Sanders Peirce to John Dewey, Karl Popper, Robert Merton, or Jürgen Habermas one encounters idealized conceptions of the scientific community as a vanguard of deliberative and democratic society. The scientific community was thought to be exemplary because it is composed of free rational agents who are united in their pursuit of truth and who will not settle for anything that does not draw the consensus of all. This pursuit of truth by a community of equals then serves as a model also for a democratic society that seeks to establish a rational consensus on fair and equitable social arrangements.

This eighteenth-, nineteenth-, and twentieth-century conception of rational deliberation and its larger civic significance also informed the move towards public understanding of science and especially the deficit model of scientific communication discussed elsewhere in this book. The advocates of public understanding of science sought to include the public in rational consensus formation regarding matters of science and technology. According to the deficit model, if all citizens had available to them in a comprehensible manner the information available to scientists, they would come to the same rational conclusion as did the scientific community. Thus, if there is resistance to the findings of science, it must simply be due to a deficit of knowledge about the facts and the methods of science – and once this deficit is reduced, the fruits of science and technology will automatically gain legitimacy and

---

[2] To be sure, democratic societies are characterized by a rational consensus on the principle that, after sufficient debate, the opinion of a majority confers legitimacy on certain decisions. Indeed, the "ideal speech situation" is an idealized image of deliberative democracy – it serves as an implicit standard by which actual democracy can be evaluated and is not meant to be a literal description of human behavior.

at the same time, democracy will be strengthened because citizens no longer simply defer to the authority of science.

But, alas, today's "technoscientific" research communities are dedicated primarily to economic and social innovation rather than the development of theory in the pursuit of truth.[3] Accordingly, science communication accepts the strategic brief to create a supportive environment for the development of emerging technologies, and the deficit model has been superseded by a surplus model that smothers or overwhelms the target audience by drawing it into a fun-filled space of sensory and informational overload. These developments are radically incompatible with discourse ethics as presented so far. Of course, science communicators may well be tempted to have it both ways, that is, to first accept the strategic brief to promote public acceptance of technological development and then to add on to this that one might pursue this brief with a commitment to comprehensibility, truth, adequacy, and sincerity. There is no such easy way out, however. The following pages aim to show that science communicators are faced with a stark alternative. If for ethical and political reasons they wish to hold on to the ideals of the Enlightenment and assert the attendant norms of deliberative discourse, they need to rebel against the various tendencies that produced the demand for effective science communication – against the values of the innovation-oriented technosciences and in favor of the old-fashioned ideals of basic science, against the strategic goal of science communication to initiate a discourse about opportunities and risks that is generally favorable towards innovation, and against the huge arsenal of media technologies that provide an experience of immersion in the wonderful world of exciting scientific and technical possibilities at the expense of critical distance.[4] If, in contrast, science communication mostly aims to foster enthusiasm and engagement, the question of ethics becomes a different one entirely. It is now concerned with the issue of trustworthiness. In order to achieve its goals, this kind of science communication must earn trust by being responsible, that is, for example, not too

---

[3] This claim requires empirical evidence and conceptual work to be fully persuasive. In the present context, one can do no more than point to the pervasiveness and policy relevance of the notions of technoscience, mode-2 research, or post-academic science (Nowotny et al. 2001; Forman 2007; Carrier and Nordmann 2010; Nordmann 2010).

[4] An empirical investigation of different approaches to science communication would probably reveal ambivalence and traces of the just-mentioned rebelliousness among those who engage in science communication, especially among the scientists themselves, but also among those who come from the field of science and technology studies.

patronizing, not beholden to incredible promises or visionary expectations. In particular, the responsible representation of technoscientific
research needs to include the communication of ignorance and of what
is and might remain unknown. But one way or the other – whether one
wishes to promote the deliberative ideals of discourse ethics or gain
trust for the achievement of strategic communication goals in support
of the technosciences – it is not an option to obscure the predicament
by painting a picture of science as a noble and disinterested pursuit that
only happens to drive technological and economic innovation and thereby
to shape our natural as well as social world.

In order to elaborate the stark alternative between communication in the service of deliberative ideals and of strategic goals, each of
the next four sections looks at one of the four ideals and how it fares
amidst the current realities of technoscience.

1 SINCERITY AND STRATEGIC COMMUNICATION

As mentioned above, a general goal of communication is to achieve
rational consensus. In other words, to communicate is a form of action
in the realm of opinion and thought and any genuine, uncoerced consensus in this realm will be justified in terms of the reasons that are
given and the reasoning process as a whole. By distinguishing this form
of communicative action from instrumental action, Jürgen Habermas
gives voice to the tradition of the Enlightenment and its familiar way
of juxtaposing science and technology. Instrumental action is technological in that it seeks to bring about a certain end. Instrumental rationality is therefore concerned with means–end relations: what do we need
to do if we want to attain this or that specific goal? While communicative
action in the realm of knowledge, opinion, and law requires good reasons
and persuasive evidence, instrumental action requires above all the
selection of an appropriate means. And while communicative action is
not prejudiced at all but may involve the questioning of all hitherto
accepted truths, instrumental action is prejudiced by its unquestioned
ends, be they economic growth, a cure for cancer, the spread of democracy, more fuel-efficient automobiles, or the conquest of space. All such
ends are already supposed to be good, and from here on one needs to do
no more than select the appropriate means to promote these goods.

On this understanding, communication is deliberative like science, instrumental action strategic like technology. Their difference,
even antagonism, is important because the ends we assume to be
unquestionably good deserve to be taken up, questioned, and deliberated

in the sphere of communicative rationality. But yet, how awfully out-dated will this division of communicative vs. instrumental action appear to readers of this handbook – hasn't Habermas ever heard of advertising, of communication strategies and tools, of science communication as a business and a profession, and shouldn't he recognize that the juxtapos-ition of pure science and its technological application has long been superseded by strategic research, application-oriented basic science, the so-called technosciences like pharmacy, synthetic chemistry, materials research, ICT, nano- and biotechnologies?

Indeed, one might ask, how can one communicate anything at all without having some strategy for it? Isn't non-strategic communi-cation just about a contradiction in terms? But therein lies the rub – "to communicate something" is not at all the same as engaging in communicative action.

Communicative action presupposes that two or more parties ascribe to each other sincerity about the communicative process. In other words, they come together on the basis of the assumption that they have no other interests but the achievement of rational consensus. In the case of science, this is the assumption that everyone who pub-lishes an article in a scientific journal has no other interest but the advancement of knowledge or truth.[5] In contrast, when one sets out to "communicate something," there is here a message to be communi-cated in an instrumental way. With this instrumental purpose comes a clear understanding of what it means to communicate successfully.

---

[5] The sociologist of science Robert Merton articulated in the early 1940s the ethos of science as itself in the context of the Enlightenment tradition (Merton 1979). One of the four norms that shape the image of science as an ideal community of truth-seekers is that of "disinterestedness." Of course and as a matter of fact, even for the most noble scientists there are always other interests at play (money, fame, ideology, priority, prestige), and Merton himself explored the resulting ambivalence. Merton's point and that of Habermas or even Immanuel Kant is that participants in rational deliberation need to treat each other *as if* there were no other interests at play. They therefore adopt certain constraints in their ways of reasoning. Accordingly, scientists might be motivated by considerations of ideology and prestige, but they present their theories in such a way that these theories will stand or fall on the basis of empirical evidence and this in accordance with the universal criteria accepted by all scientists. Many observers have pointed out that, for better and worse, the Mertonian norms are not characteristic of contemporary R&D because "disinterestedness" is no longer considered an important value (Ziman 2000; Radder 2010). Researchers are not invited primarily to advance theories and deliberate their truth, but to develop capabilities of controlling complex situations that may, in the long run, address societal needs or advance national economies.

Success does not consist in a deliberative reflection, even critique of that message, but ideally in a measurable effect showing that the message has gotten across. Frequently in science communication, this desired outcome is also a consensus, but one that is manufactured by an instrumentally effective communication strategy rather than one that is discovered in the give and take of reasons during a deliberative process (Jasanoff 2003). By definition, those who set out to communicate something (the advancement of science, the promise of nanomedicine, the environmental impacts of GMOs) are not sincere in the sense of being interested only to foster deliberation and debate. Of course, science communicators can earn trust by being open and honest about the fact that there is something which they want and need to communicate. Through this, however, they enter a paradoxical situation: by acknowledging openly and honestly their vested interest in the outcome of the communication process, they become trustworthy individuals precisely by declaring themselves unfit for a genuine process of non-strategic rational deliberation.[6]

One telling example of this is a 2010 science policy document by the European Commission: *Communicating Nanotechnology: Why, to Whom, Saying What and How? – An Action-Packed Roadmap towards a Brand New Dialogue* (Bonazzi 2010).[7] This is a state-of-the-art report in that it reflects recent developments in social studies of science and in science communication, including a critique of the deficit model, for example. One of the problems with the deficit model was its assumption that science arrives at a rational consensus, that publics are often irrational, and that this gap between science and publics could be closed if publics knew more about scientific methods and facts. As it turns out, however, the questions that are of public and political interest may originate in science and technology but are not questions of scientific fact alone: for example, whether genetically modified organisms should be incorporated into agricultural systems involves far more than scientific determinations of safety or risk of physical harm. In order to engage these questions, therefore, one needs to address a deficit not only on the side of science-illiterate publics but also on the side of policy-makers, researchers, and developers who are similarly illiterate when it comes

---

[6] To be sure, this paradoxical situation arises for just about anyone who brings commitments and convictions to a process of communication in which contrary commitments and convictions might prevail.

[7] This document was chosen not because it is naïve or crude but, on the contrary, because it reflects the state of the art and exhibits the tension between competing ideals of science communications (see notes 4 and 6 above).

to understanding publics. Aside from "public understanding of science" one therefore needs "science (and science policy) understanding of publics," that is, an understanding of where these publics are coming from and what their concerns are. So far, so good – this critique and extension of the deficit model is fully in the realm of classical discourse ethics with its interests in maintaining the conditions for a deliberative process that may engender a rational consensus.

Communicating Nanotechnology takes this state of the art and adds a small, but decisive twist which catapults it into the strategic domain of advertising nanotechnology. From the call for scientists to enter deliberations with a better understanding of public concerns, the report shifts to the notion that a "scientific understanding of publics" will afford in a purely instrumental fashion the more effective targeting and delivery of its message. Consider the problem of condescension, for example:

> *Any conventional approach, so far based on the 'public understanding of science' has to be redressed now. It needs to be turned around into the trickier concept of a 'scientific understanding of publics'. These different audiences could not simply stand any tone they might remotely perceive as condescending. They would just turn you off and tune you out in no time. Clearly, a new mode of communication is required.* (Bonazzi 2010, pp. 9, 31–33, 105)

In a deliberative context people cannot stand condescension because it is a violation of sincerity and signals a refusal to enter the deliberative process as an equal partner. From the idealistic point of view of discourse ethics this problem can therefore be solved only by ceasing to be strategic and by entering the process in good faith as a partner. In contrast, the proposed scientific understanding of publics makes publics an object of study and analysis and prepares a communication strategy that successfully avoids the appearance of being condescending. This communication strategy may well include the injunction that communicators have to learn to listen to publics. This injunction, however, does not make for equal partners, if only because the clever communicators are making use of what they learned about unsuspecting publics as their objects of study and targets of intervention. Also, though the communicators are listening, they rarely pass on what people are telling them, all the while holding fast to their message, not sincerely prepared to question that message or to seek out the grounds for its legitimacy. What is that message? In the case of *Communicating Nanotechnology*, the overarching message is "nano revolution coming" which encompasses the more particular messages that *"nano*

is not magic; nano is a new phase of technology exploiting nanoscale effects; it
deals with new beneficial applications and markets, impacting on health, safety,
privacy, ethics and the socioeconomic divide; it must and can be controlled and
driven conscientiously" (Bonazzi 2010, p. 106). But is nano a revolution and a
new phase of technology, or is it business as usual in the quest for faster,
cheaper, stronger, more efficient, and more powerful products? Who is
suggesting that nano is magic, and why might they be doing this? And if
it really is a revolution, how do we know that it can be controlled – or,
for that matter, that it is really all about beneficial applications? What is
here taken for granted as the message to be communicated might be
precisely the questions in need of rational deliberation.

According to this conception of nano communication, one needs
to learn a great deal about the public but nothing about nanotechnology:
the report does not recommend a deliberative process of assessing the
meaning and significance of nanotechnology, but the communication
of nanotechnology as if it were a known entity.[8] And indeed, the report
is clear that it concerns the communication of an *"image"* by adapting
specific tools to specific target groups, using *"communication and dialogue*
recipes" that appeal to all the senses and the emotions and thereby promote
"public social consensus" (Bonazzi 2010, pp. 9, 81, 112). Adopting a scientific
marketing approach, this communications roadmap straddles a very
fine line between gaining public trust by doing all the right things and
losing it again for its strategic manner of getting things just right.

2 COMPREHENSIBILITY AND UNDERTAXING THE PUBLICS

The authors and many readers of *Communicating Nanotechnology* will
object that it is simply unfair to equate this effort with marketing or
advertising. After all, isn't it about taking citizens more seriously? In
particular, attempts to attain a scientific understanding of publics serve
to fully appreciate public attitudes and take them into account.[9]
Indeed, what is wrong with this and related approaches to science
communication is not that they are top–down or presumptuous,
manipulative, or cynical, but that they are too sophisticated for their

---

[8] For a more general reflection on the communication of nanotechnology,
see the report of the DEEPEN project (Macnaghten *et al.* 2009) and its critical
reflection in a special issue of the journal *Nanoethics*, 4:2 (2010).

[9] See Bonazzi (2010, p. 81). However, for all the talk about communication being a
two-way street there is astoundingly little in this and related documents about
the sequencing of information and opinion flow back from publics to
decision-makers.

own good. They are overproduced and undertax their intended audience and thereby exemplify what is here called the surplus model of science communication. The deficit model failed for its belief that scientific and public representations would converge if "just the facts" became available to all. The surplus model cannot be accused of such naïveté. Generously equipped with glossy pictures, lively scenarios, social science research, high production values, it overwhelms its audience. It does not so much seek to represent scientific and technological developments as objects for public deliberation but, instead, provides the immersive experience of new, perhaps future worlds.[10]

One of the most eloquent criticisms of the surplus model can be found in a short text by Helga Nowotny. It points to the fact that prior to all the technological promise of scientific research and prior to its large and small success stories there is hard piecemeal work, a considerable investment of labor and equipment with many frustrations, nonstarters, and setbacks. This aspect of struggle and failure has long been considered a defining feature of science as an unending quest to gradually approach but never quite reach the truth. According to Nowotny, however, this aspect of science is not captured by most contemporary science communication:

> Scientific knowledge constructs high-cost reality, usually based on a densely organized system of concepts, facts, rules, interpretation, methodological skills, equipment, and evidence. As such, the knowledge is not directly accessible to laypersons and remains esoteric. Low-cost realities may be expensive to produce, but are "cheap" to consume. They depend on the immediate experience of the flow of images and sounds. They become the shared means by which the public conceives, imagines, remembers, thinks, and relates or acts in politics. They allow the public to simulate the witnessing of real events without the trouble of being actually there. Low-cost reality is a spectacularly successful commercial product in our culture. (Nowotny 2005, p. 1117)

According to the faulty deficit model, the public understanding of science is cheap to produce – just provide the missing bits of knowledge – but expensive to consume as it requires citizens to work through the information and make up their minds. As Nowotny points, the surplus model inverses the picture: the glossy brochures, traveling exhibits, science centers, video games, 3D simulations, and documentary films of today's science communications are expensive to produce, but cheap

---

[10] The shift from a representational to an immersive mode is a more general feature of the transition from classical Enlightenment science to today's technosciences (Nordmann 2006).

to consume. They seek clarity and comprehensibility by being quick and easy to grasp, by making the complicated appear easy and unambiguous while providing a rich sensory experience. They operate on the assumption that publics primarily want assurances of certainty and information to latch onto rather than representations of difficulties, unsolved problems, and uncertainties. And this might be in line, on the face of it, with the demand for comprehensibility as a norm that underpins deliberative discourse.

However, the discourse ethical conception of comprehensibility has nothing to do with simplification, straightforwardness, non-ambiguity.[11] Instead, it expresses the requirement that we can and should make each other understood, a requirement that underpins every public negotiation of difficult and complex issues. In the surplus model of science communication, comprehensibility serves primarily to draw everyone into the task of "responsible development," be it by creating illusions of empowerment, be it by creating a "hands-on, minds-on, hearts-on" experience, or be it by creating easy access to complex issues.

> *Sexy communication is not going to be enough to inform good decision-making. [. . .] Successful communication can begin to be measured through short-term indicators, such as improvements in public opinion polls on trust in science or increases in enrollment figures for undergraduate physics or chemistry programs. In the longer term, we will need to measure evolution in the direction of scientific citizenship, which presupposes rights and duties on the part of citizens as much as on the part of political and scientific institutions.* (Nowotny 2005, p. 1118)

3 TRUTH AND RESPONSIBLE REPRESENTATION

No matter how stark the contrast between rational deliberation as envisioned by discourse ethics and commissioned science communication, it would appear that a commitment to "truth" is shared by both. But here, too, a stark difference must be noted between a deliberative

---

[11] This bears remembering in light of the fact that "comprehensibility" is the first principle in a code of conduct for research in nanoscience and nanotechnologies that was proposed by the European Commission (2008). The traditional ethos of science as identified by Robert Merton includes as one of its four norms the notion of "communism" or shared ownership within the community of science in the theories and hypotheses, methods and procedures of science. Comprehensibility as conceived by discourse ethics and, presumably, by the European Code of Conduct creates shared ownership in ideas.

process that seeks to get at the truth and a communication strategy that sticks to the truth in the sense of reporting only what someone has actually said. As the development of science and technology is motivated to a considerable extent by visionary rhetoric, simple-minded extrapolation, and the general promise of healing societal and environmental ills, a lot is being said about so-called scientific breakthroughs, and accurate reporting even of what respected scientists say does not make it so. Though it does not usually engage in a kind of collective inquiry that gets at significant truths, there arises here for strategic science communication a problem of trustworthiness that calls for a notion of responsible representation.[12]

The previous section emphasized that stakeholders who are introduced to the latest technoscientific developments as well as visitors of science centers are frequently overwhelmed by overproduced power-point presentations, simulated environments, hands-on anticipations of technical control, and the like. This can create a condition of credulity or else a feeling of unease and disorientation that wants to know how things are in truth. One symptom of credulity has been discussed under the heading of "speculative ethics" which is said to arise when ethicists argue from a position of credulity and leapfrog countless scientific and technical problems in order to discuss the ethical implications of a far-fetched envisioned application (Nordmann and Rip 2009). The example of a traveling science center serves to illustrate how the speculative stance can disorient the intended audience.[13] By entering the windowless space of the exhibit, its visitors are leaving the real world of their lived experience behind and may as well be stepping into a totally fictitious world. This impression is confirmed by the immersive architecture of the exhibit which presents short- and long-term technological prospects side by side with experimental demonstrations of capability next to simulated proofs of concept next to visionary programs. All the while the visitors are confronted with questions that sound open-ended but require an imaginative leap that

---

[12] Merton's ethos of science includes "organized skepticism." The philosopher Karl Popper singled it out as the single most effective method of getting at the truth. The notion of "responsible representation" that is proposed at the end of this section takes a small step in this direction but serves primarily as a corrective to wishful thinking and unrealistic expectations.

[13] The case in question is the 2009 *Science Express* that was developed primarily by the German Max-Planck-Gesellschaft. Twelve train carriages offered an expedition into the future; for a bilingual catalogue see Max-Planck-Gesellschaft (2009).

dissociates them from the present, questions such as *"Will we be living in a world without disease?"*[14] This experience produces disorientation regarding limits of understanding and technical control – what these limits are today, what it would take to overcome them, or whether they might prove insurmountable: is everything technically feasible that appears to be physically possible? It also induces disorientation regarding temporal horizons: will I really live to see this, and when? It finally induces disorientation regarding the role of the citizens who are invited to participate, reflect, leave comments, and who are at the same time confronted with images of the future, that is, of what is thought to be coming their way, more or less inescapably.

This kind of disorientation is not limited to unwitting publics who become overwhelmed by images of the future. The famous proposal of an elevator into space could serve as a case study to demonstrate that journalists, policy-makers, and scientists do not know whether to consider this an extremely far-fetched or rather more plausible technical prospect. When strategically effective communication nevertheless produces disorientation, it is for its own good to establish mechanisms to assure the responsible representation of science and technology. Before one can sensibly talk about the responsible development of emerging technologies, considerations of responsible representation ought to determine what is robustly communicable in the first place. This involves determinations of plausibility in light of ongoing trends rather than under the assumption of discontinuous novelty, it requires that communicators take responsibility for their representations by being prepared to defend their credibility, it might include watchdog activities and societal monitoring of the quality of science communication.

---

[14] Neither the catalogue nor the website with its virtual walk-through can substitute for the actual immersion in such a well-designed space. The website provides glimpses of the rhetorical strategy by which technological futures are presented as simultaneously inevitable and radically disconnected from the present: *"Genetic technology is viewed critically, particularly in industrialised nations, and its practical application is moving faster than its ethical-moral integration. In terms of global nutrition, significant interest will be focused in [the] future not only on 'how' but also on 'what'. Diet-related illnesses, like obesity and diabetes, are a burden on the health systems in industrialised countries and are spreading like an epidemic in threshold countries. This shows how closely our nutrition is linked to health. In the age of genetics, we are also becoming aware that our own genetic make-up dictates what is healthy for us. In [the] future, it will be possible to prevent or even heal illnesses through individually-tailored nutrition with customised foodstuffs"* (http://de.expedition-zukunft.org/, English description of carriage 8, accessed May 23, 2011).

4 ADEQUACY AND THE COMMUNICATION OF IGNORANCE

Responsible representation also involves notions of proportionality, appropriateness, and adequacy. In discourse ethics and the context of communicative action, these concern respect for the other and tactful cognizance of the situation. For strategic communication and the context of responsible development of emerging technologies adequacy is reduced to primarily the question of inclusiveness. The rightness of a communication and its adequacy to the communicative situation is judged by its ability to reach out and include most everyone. Accordingly, one of the main functions of science communication (publications, stakeholder events, consumer conferences, public engagement exercises) is to create a large public that provides the proper environment for the responsible development of emerging technologies. In the case of nanotechnology, at least, the large and largely supportive public that is created through the communicative strategies of "responsible development" is characterized by the inclusion from the start of societal and ethical considerations. As has been pointed out, the careful maintenance of trustworthiness is a different undertaking from creating a public sphere for rational deliberation on the Enlightenment model (Nordmann and Schwarz 2010). And what should go without saying in attempts primarily to get at the truth is far from self-evident in the attempt to build a supportive environment for technoscientific innovations – for example, the communication of limits of knowledge and of the piecemeal, incremental, circuitous character of research and development. The rightness or adequacy of communication in the search for knowledge and rational agreement depends not only on whom to include and exclude but also on what is included or excluded.[15] However, communication of technoscientific developments shares the predicament of much contemporary research in that there is no incentive and no language for communicating failure and for ignorance as a rightful and important part of the full story (Nordmann 2008). As opposed to traditionally conceived classical science, technoscientific research is dedicated not primarily to hypothesis-testing but to the control of complex situations. Accordingly, the role of negative evidence

---

[15] When Robert Merton identified "universalism" as one of the four norms that characterize the ethos of classical science, this is primarily the injunction to admit anyone to rational deliberation irrespective of their social standing. However, it refers more generally to the creation of conditions that allow everyone to participate. And this, in turn, implies that all relevant information is made available and none withheld.

has diminished greatly: it is of great scientific significance when a well-designed experiment fails to confirm a hypothesis, but it is a mere temporary setback when some attempt to control a process or a phenomenon has failed. In the latter case, only success stories are meaningful and are immediately interpreted as proofs of concept, with no definite conclusions drawn from failure or difficulty.[16]

Accordingly, contemporary science communication does not dwell on inscrutable mysteries of nature, on limits of knowledge, of technical control, or growth. Instead, it celebrates the seemingly unlimited capacity of science and technology to master complexity and to solve problems of global warming, environmental degradation, or resource depletion.[17] And yet, where the goal of science communication is to build a supportive environment and broadly inclusive public, responsible representation demands the communication of ignorance. The importance of a reflection on current as well as structural limits of understanding and control was pointed out already. Also, in order to assess the technical or therapeutic promise of a supposed breakthrough, one needs to know how much or how little has been achieved and what remains to be done before this breakthrough can acquire practical significance. Most importantly, perhaps, it is not helpful to speak exclusively of remaining knowledge gaps that remain to be closed. The condition of ignorance and uncertainty about toxicological, economic, or social implications of emerging technologies are defining features of our so-called knowledge societies: when knowledge gaps cannot be closed any time soon, it is not an option to wait for science until it has done its job and eradicated ignorance about risks and benefits. Instead, our knowledge societies need to develop tools for dealing with ignorance and uncertainty as part of an ongoing experiment with emerging technologies (Felt and Wynne 2007). Science communication fails to achieve its strategic aim of creating a robust environment for social and technical innovation if it does not counteract the one-sided triumphalism of contemporary technoscience and if it does not

---

[16] According to Merton's and Popper's "organized scepticism" (see note 15 above), failure to confirm a hypothesis may be the single most important element of scientific method.

[17] The major accident at the Fukushima nuclear power plant may have called into question whether this technology can be successfully controlled. It also brought to the fore, however, the implicit faith that there are plenty of technologies that can do the job and substitute for nuclear power. This unfettered technological optimism may well be an effect of the celebration of unlimited possibility by science communicators.

empower its publics to question presumed benefits, to relate hope and risk, and to assess the achievements of control within the larger horizon of ignorance – allowing them to determine where scientific and technological solutions can and cannot be relied upon to tackle our social, political, technological, or environmental problems.

Acknowledgment

I would like to thank Christopher Coenen and Arianna Ferrari for helpful comments.

Key resources

Nerlich, Brigitte, Richard Elliott, and Brendon Larson (eds.) (2009) *Communicating Biological Sciences: Ethical and Metaphorical Dimensions*. Aldershot, UK: Ashgate.

Special issue on the ethics of science journalism of *Ethics in Science and Environmental Politics (ESEP)* **9**: 1 (2009).

Latour, Bruno (2008) *What is the Style of Matters of Concern?* Amsterdam: Van Gorcum.

Nisbet, Matthew C. (2009) "Framing Science: A New Paradigm in Public Engagement," in LeeAnn Kahlor and Patricia Stout (eds.) *Communicating Science: New Agendas in Communication*, pp. 40–67. New York: Routledge.

Nowotny, Helga (2008) *Insatiable Curiosity: Innovation in a Fragile Future*. Cambridge, MA: MIT Press.

Shapin, Steven (2008) *The Scientific Life: A Moral History of a Late Modern Vocation*. Chicago, IL: University of Chicago Press.

Benhabib, Seyla and Fred Dallmayr (eds.) (1990) *The Communicative Ethics Controversy*. Cambridge, MA: MIT Press.

References

Apel, Karl-Otto (1973) "Das Apriori der Kommunikationsgemeinschaft und die Grundlagen der Ethik: Zum Problem einer rationalen Begründung der Ethik im Zeitalter der Wissenschaft," in Karl-Otto Apel, *Transformation der Philosophie*, vol. **2**, pp. 358–435. Frankfurt: Suhrkamp.

Bonazzi, Matteo (2010) *Communicating Nanotechnology: Why, to Whom, Saying What and How? – An Action-Packed Roadmap towards a Brand New Dialogue*. Luxembourg: Publications Office of the European Union, available at: ftp://ftp.cordis.europa.eu/pub/nanotechnology/docs/communicating-nanotechnology_en.pdf

Carrier, Martin and Alfred Nordmann (eds.) (2010) *Science in the Context of Application*. Dordrecht: Springer.

European Commission (2008) *Commission Recommendation of 07/02/2008 on a Code of Conduct for Responsible Nanosciences and Nanotechnologies Research*. Brussels: European Commission, available at: ftp://ftp.cordis.europa.eu/pub/fp7/docs/nanocode-recommendation.pdf

Felt, Ulrike and Brian Wynne (eds.) (2007) *Science and Governance: Taking European Knowledge Society Seriously*. Brussels: European Commission, Brussels, available at: http://ec.europa.eu/research/science-society/document_library/pdf_06/european-knowledge-society_en.pdf

Forman, Paul (2007) "The Primacy of Science in Modernity, of Technology in Postmodernity, and of Ideology in the History of Technology," *History and Technology* **23**: 1–152.

Habermas, Jürgen (1990) "Discourse Ethics: Notes on a Program of Philosophical Justification." In Jürgen Habermas, *Moral Consciousness and Communicative Action*. Cambridge, MA: MIT Press.

Habermas, Jürgen (1991) *Erläuterungen zur Diskursethik*. Frankfurt: Suhrkamp.

Jasanoff, Sheila (2003) "Technologies of Humility: Citizen Participation in Governing Science," *Minerva* **41**: 223–244.

Macnaghten, Philip *et al.* (eds.) (2009) *Reconfiguring Responsibility: Lessons for Public Policy and Lessons for Nanoethics*. Durham, UK: Durham University; compare also a critical reflection of this report in a special issue of *Nanoethics* 4:2, 2010, 131–189.

Max-Planck-Gesellschaft (ed.) (2009) *Expedition Zukunft/Science Express: Wie Wissenschaft und Technik unser Leben verändern*. Darmstadt: Wissenschaftliche Buchgesellschaft.

Merton, Robert K. (1979) *The Sociology of Science: Theoretical and Empirical Investigations*. Chicago, IL: University of Chicago Press.

Nordmann, Alfred (2006) "Collapse of Distance: Epistemic Strategies of Science and Technoscience," *Danish Yearbook of Philosophy* **41**: 7–34.

Nordmann, Alfred (2008) "Philosophy of Nanotechnoscience," in G. Schmid, H. Krug, R. Waser, V. Vogel, H. Fuchs, M. Grätzel, K. Kalyanasundaram, L. Chi (eds.) *Nanotechnology*, vol. **1**, G. Schmid (ed.) *Principles and Fundamentals*, pp. 217–244. Weinheim: Wiley.

Nordmann, Alfred (2010) "A Forensics of Wishing: Technology Assessment in the Age of Technoscience," *Poiesis and Praxis* **7**: 5–15.

Nordmann, Alfred and Arie Rip (2009) "Mind the Gap Revisited," *Nature Nanotechnology* **4**: 273–274.

Nordmann, Alfred and Astrid Schwarz (2010) "Lure of the 'Yes': The Seductive Power of Technoscience," in Mario Kaiser, Monika Kurath, Sabine Maasen, Christoph Rehmann-Sutter (eds.) *Governing Future Technologies: Nanotechnology and the Rise of an Assessment Regime*, pp. 255–277. Dordrecht: Springer.

Nowotny, Helga (2005) "High- and Low-Cost Realities for Science and Society," *Science* **308**: 1117–1118.

Nowotny, Helga, Peter Scott, and Michael Gibbons (2001) *Rethinking Science: Knowledge and the Public in an Age of Uncertainty*. Cambridge, UK: Polity.

Radder, Hans (ed.) (2010) *The Commodification of Academic Research*. Pittsburgh, PA: University of Pittsburgh Press.

Ziman, John (2000) *Real Science: What It Is, and What It Means*. Cambridge, UK: Cambridge University Press.

Part II Policy-makers, the media and public interest organisations

8

Research and public communication in EU policy and practice

INTRODUCTION

Along with the United States, Japan and China, Europe is today one of the major international players in science. Since 1984, the European Union (EU) has been implementing research policy through successive so-called Framework Programmes (FPs). The Seventh Framework Programme (FP7) covers the period from 2007 to 2013 and has a budget of €53 billion, representing a 63% increase compared to the Sixth Framework Programme (FP6, 2002–2006). Still, EU R&D expenditures remain, in relative terms, quite low. The latest available data (Eurostat 2008) shows that the EU's 27 Member States, even though together the world's largest economy, devote only an average 1.90% of their gross domestic product (GDP) to R&D compared to 2.76% and 3.44% for the USA and Japan, respectively.[1]

Publicly funded support for research in Europe increasingly encourages and even requires the beneficiaries to engage with the public and the media. For example, most of the UK Research Councils promote scientific outreach activities and provide the training needed by scientists to allow them to carry out those activities effectively. In particular, grant-holders have to develop a public communication strategy and in doing so they can get help from Research Council information and press staff.

As both science and science communication have become increasingly globalised, Europe's role in research has become increasingly visible outside Europe as well as within it. In addition, the EU has made important efforts to study and develop the science–society interface and to improve communication between scientists and the European

---

[1] 2007 data.

Successful Science Communication, ed. D. J. Bennett and R. C. Jennings. Published by
Cambridge University Press. © Cambridge University Press 2011.

public in order to assure that public awareness keeps pace with rapid scientific and technological development.

In the EU's Framework Programmes, dissemination of results is a contractual obligation for participation in research initiatives. What are commonly referred to as the 'participation rules' lay down not only the rules for participation in FPs but also the rules for dissemination of research results.[2] The rules specify in particular that the quality of the planned dissemination is assessed at the proposal evaluation stage, and Article 20 states that '[the grant agreement requires] the submission to the Commission of a plan for the use and dissemination of foreground [generated results, author's note]'.

Since FP6, beneficiaries of EU funding are also bound to develop public communication activities. With a view to enhancing the impact of research funded by the EU, and to foster dialogue and debate, the FP7 grant agreement requires project participants to communicate and engage with actors beyond the research community.[3] Plans for these outreach activities should also be outlined at proposal stage. These plans are taken into account during the evaluation process.

The specific aims of this provision are to promote knowledge-sharing, greater public awareness, transparency and education. Consortia of researchers are required to provide tangible proof that collaborative research not only exists, but also pays dividends in terms of academic excellence, industrial competitiveness, employment opportunities, environmental improvements and enhanced quality of life for all.

---

[2] Regulation (EC) No 1906/2006 of the European Parliament and of the Council of 18 December 2006 laying down the rules for the participation of undertakings, research centres and universities in actions under the Seventh Framework Programme and for the dissemination of research results.

[3] General Conditions, II.2, Organisation of the *consortium* and role of *coordinator*: 'Beneficiaries shall fulfil the following obligations as a consortium: [. . .] engage, whenever appropriate, with actors beyond the research community and with the public in order to foster dialogue and debate on the research agenda, on research results and on related scientific issues with policy makers and civil society; create synergies with education at all levels and conduct activities promoting the socioeconomic impact of the research. 'General Conditions, II.12, Information and communication: '1. The *beneficiaries* shall, throughout the duration of the *project*, take appropriate measures to engage with the public and the media about the *project* and to highlight the *Community* financial support. Unless the *Commission* requests otherwise, any publicity, including at a conference or seminar or any type of information or promotional material (brochure, leaflet, poster, presentation etc), must specify that the *project* has received *Community* research funding and display the European emblem. [. . .]'

Being almost halfway through FP7 now at the time of writing, the experience collected so far shows that engaging with the public and the media brings benefits to project management such as increasing public visibility and awareness of the science, achieving successful integration with stakeholders, promoting internal communication, networking and marketing the consortium and disseminating research results. Some participants also argue that having a good communication/dissemination plan increases the success rate of a proposal. At a higher (policy) level, the activities also contribute in bridging the gap between scientists and the public and making European research more attractive.

EUROPEAN BACKGROUND

The European Commission has published a new Eurobarometer public opinion survey (European Commission 2010) which has been carried out in 32 European countries[4] with 26 671 people interviewed in January–February 2010 to evaluate European citizens' general attitudes towards science and technology, and to see if this perception has changed significantly from 2005 when the previous survey was carried out. According to the new results, European citizens appear to have a clear and positive view about the image of science and technology. However, Europeans have a less clear insight into the work of the scientist, what a scientist actually does, or the structure of the scientific community. They feel slightly less informed about science and technology than they were in 2005 and feel less well informed than their level of interest deserves. There is no clear view on the effectiveness of European research. The perception of the current level of investment in scientific research at the EU level is also not clear. However, for a large majority of Europeans, collaborative research is more creative and efficient than national research and expansion of EU-funded research in the future would be a beneficial development.

Across the 27 EU countries, 61% of people are very or moderately interested in scientific discoveries and technological developments.[5] There is obviously a large variation between countries; on one hand, Luxembourg and France are best informed (79% and 77% respectively) and, on the other, Romania and Bulgaria the least (35%). Overall 57% of EU citizens agree that scientists do not put enough effort into informing the public about new developments in science and technology.

Significantly, the majority of European citizens – 63% of respondents at the EU27 average – feel that scientists working at a university or

---

[4] The 27 EU Member States, plus Iceland, Croatia, Norway, Switzerland and Turkey.
[5] See pages 8–18 of the report.

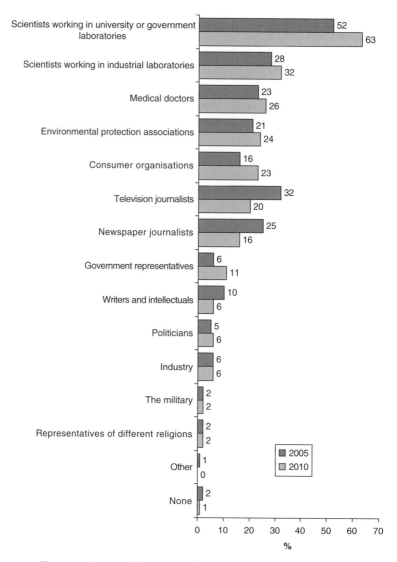

Figure 8.1 Best qualified to explain the impact of scientific and technological developments on society. From *Europeans, Science and Technology: Special Eurobarometer 340* (European Commission 2010).

government laboratories are the best qualified to explain scientific and technological developments and are the highest rated of all groups, as shown in Figure 8.1.[6]

---

[6] See pages 90–94 of the report.

Scientists working in industrial laboratories are considered the next best at 32% of respondents and above medical doctors at 26%. (A 2009 study by the Pew Research Center for the People and the Press also found that Americans have positive views of the scientific community (Pew Research Center 2009).) The confidence of scientists working in universities or government laboratories has increased from 52% of respondents in 2005 at the EU25 level to 63% of respondents at the EU27 level in 2010. The perceived role of newspaper journalists has diminished from 25% in 2005 to 16% in 2010, television journalists likewise have a reduced role, declining from 32% to 20%, while that of consumer organisations has increased from 16% to 23% and of environmental protection organisations from 21% to 24%.

The survey shows that people are generally not publicly active in science and technology. Europeans are most active in donating money to fundraising campaigns for medical research such as research into cancer where 39% of respondents did so. Only 13% of respondents engage in signing petitions or street demonstrations on matters of nuclear power, biotechnology or the environment and 86% of respondents never did this. Even fewer Europeans (9%) attend public meetings or debates about science and technology; 91% of respondents have never or hardly ever done so.

Regarding the behaviour of scientists and the integrity of science, one in two respondents supported the view that private funding of scientific and technologic research limits our ability to understand things fully – 58% of Europeans agree that scientists cannot be trusted to tell the truth about controversial scientific and technological issues because they increasingly depend on money from industry.[7]

Overall, the latest survey shows that European citizens are fairly optimistic about science and technology but there is a slight shift towards scepticism compared to the 2005 survey. Although it may bring benefits, Europeans do not have very high hopes that science and technology can solve all the world's problems. A clear majority of 54% is of the view that science and technology can play a role in improving the environment, but very few – 22% at EU27 level – think that science can solve all problems. Only 21% believe that science will lead to the world's natural resources being inexhaustible. This may point to a slight increase in scepticism, or to an overall increase in apathy, but may also point to a milder view where Europeans are more at ease and

---

[7] See pages 24–27 of the report.

are generally less concerned about the potential drawbacks of scientific and technological developments.

Regarding the interaction between science and society, most Europeans feel that decisions about science and technology should be made by scientists, engineers and politicians, and the public should be informed about these decisions (36%).[8] Only 29% claim for a more active role, in particular that the public should be consulted when making decisions about science and technology.

Europeans have a positive view of the effect of involvement with science on young people but feel that governments are not doing enough to stimulate wide interest.[9] More efforts by governments to stimulate women to be involved with science is seen as necessary and would, if successful, have a positive effect on development of the sciences in Europe.

With regards to EU research, 74% of citizens think that collaborative research across Europe and funding by the European Union will become more and more important.[10] Over six out of ten Europeans also believe collaborative research is more creative and efficient than national research. Joint collaboration between Member States is widely supported (72% of Europeans agree).

The Eurobarometer survey also shows that nearly 60% of Europeans think that scientists should put more effort into communicating about their work. In 2007, EURAB, the European Research Advisory Board of the European Commission, published a report which warned the scientific community about not paying enough attention to the dialogue with society:

> European publics are not questioning the scientific information as much as they are actually questioning the institutions generating it (a loss of confidence in business, government and academia). Research is seen to be good when it solves problems and is relevant to people's lives – when research is useful to society, and not just in an economic sense. Too often though, researchers are perceived to be addressing issues that the public may not necessarily consider as beneficial to society. Researchers work in systems that are rational and instrumental, and have a tendency to assume that society behaves likewise. But society does not always behave rationally, and in certain sensitive areas, researchers should keep in mind that their systems operate in a public context. (European Research Advisory Board 2007)

To avoid lost opportunities and suspicion about R&D in the future, the report urged more societal engagement and open dialogue on emerging research fields, such as nanotechnology and therapeutic food additives:

---

[8] See pages 85–87 of the report.   [9] See pages 95–106 of the report.
[10] See pages 116–135 of the report.

In Europe, GMOs, nuclear energy and crop protection science are examples where all research elements were in place but the societal concerns were misrepresented or not adequately considered, leading to a loss of public trust that has been detrimental to the innovation process. (European Research Advisory Board 2007)

'The most universal quality is diversity', said Montaigne.[11] This is certainly true in Europe where the European diversity adds to the difficulty of science communication itself. There are indeed some Europe-specific challenges to science communication. As the European Research Area linking national efforts becomes a reality, Europe is sorely lacking a genuine mechanism enabling it to draw full benefit from its 'home-grown' research activities. At present, there is no structured mechanism for informing the media in one Member State of scientific activities going on in another and giving the highest possible profile to European research. A survey carried out by ESO (European Southern Observatory) showed that the majority of the articles published in Germany on space and astronomy concerned US research. Although Europe has leading facilities in this field, US research still tends to dominate European media.[12]

IN PRACTICAL TERMS

In addition to FP7 contractual obligations, the European Commission's Research Directorate-General (DG) is actively involved in communicating the results of EU-funded research to the media and the general public. Support and help are provided to assist research project coordinators and team leaders to generate an effective flow of information and publicity about

- the objectives and results of their work,
- the contributions made to European knowledge and scientific excellence,
- the value of collaboration on a Europe-wide scale, and
- the benefits to EU citizens in general.

Some other initiatives have been taken by the European Commission to improve communication, outreach and dissemination of results from EU-funded research projects, and to facilitate the work of project contractors in this respect. Researchers involved in FP-funded projects are

---

[11] Montaigne, 1580; quoted in Tracy Novinger, *Intercultural Communication* (Austin: University of Texas Press, 2001).

[12] Claus Madsen, European Southern Observatory, personal communication.

encouraged to contact the Research DG's Communication Unit to co-operate and produce online news, press releases, articles in the *research°eu* magazine,[13] video clips etc.

The Commission also manages three major websites to provided information on EU programmes and initiatives, including projects funded and results obtained:

- The research pages under EUROPA, the official EU website,[14] which currently has some 30000 pages devoted to EU research that are looked at by over 300000 separate visitors each month, as well as pages of historical interest (e.g. FP5, FP4) which are less visited. EUROPA provides up-to-date information on the latest decisions and latest advances in European research. In 2009, there were nearly 9.5 million visits to this site leading to 18 million page views.
- CORDIS, the Community Research and Development Information Service, is run separately and is designed primarily for current and potential participants in the Framework Programmes. In addition to providing information on FP7, CORDIS is intended to enhance exploitation of research results and to promote the dissemination of knowledge.
- The so-called 'Participant Portal', which regroups all the information necessary to participate in FPs (calls for proposals, guide for proposers, participation rules etc.). The Participant Portal has been created to become a single entry point for the participants in the research programmes implemented by the European Commission. It aims to facilitate the monitoring and the management of proposals and EU-funded projects throughout their life cycle.

The European Commission does not impose any predetermined format or structure for the communication activities undertaken by FP7 projects. Rather, it draws the attention of participants in FP7-funded projects to the fact that they can no longer ignore the 'public communication' dimension of their activity. Exposing non-specialists to the

---

[13] *research°eu* aimed to broaden the discussion between science and society (the publication is currently interrupted). The magazine used to present and analyse European projects, results and initiatives with the aim of reinforcing and federating scientific and technological excellence in Europe. Published 10 times a year, *research°eu* is available in English, French, German and Spanish: http://ec.europa.eu/research/research-eu/index_en.html).

[14] http://ec.europa.eu/research/index.cfm

results of research work helps to improve their understanding of scientific and technological developments and stimulate public discussion of important issues, which not only meets a very real social need but also contributes to the success of a research policy, as Schiele put it: *'A science policy relies first and foremost on a science communication policy.'* (Schiele 1983)

At the same time, the communication of results and the announcement of exploitable developments are of direct value to the participants themselves. Suitably framed messages can help by:

- drawing the attention of national governments, regional authorities and other public and private funding sources to the needs and eventual benefits of the research;
- attracting the interest of potential partners and/or correspondents;
- encouraging talented students and scientists to join the partner institutes and enterprises;
- enhancing the reputation of participants, at local, national and international level;
- aiding, where appropriate, the search for financial backers, licensees or industrial implementers to exploit the results; and
- generating market demand for the developed products or services.

The European Commission's Research DG has published two practical guides and a dedicated website[15] to assist project coordinators and team leaders to generate an effective flow of information and publicity about the objectives and results of their work, the contributions made to European knowledge and scientific excellence, the value of collaboration on a Europe-wide scale and the benefits to EU citizens in general. Guidelines and best practices are provided to help project participants in communicating and disseminating their research results with the aim that they will be presented and discussed.

The guides available on the communication website particularly address relationships with the mass media (TV, radio and the written press), the workings of which are less familiar to scientific/academic partners. They also cover websites and other internally generated support such as print publications, CDs and video. They provide good practices that can be employed in:

---

[15] http://ec.europa.eu/research/science-society/science-communication/
index_en.htm

- defining key messages;
- establishing target audiences;
- selecting the appropriate modes of communication;
- tailoring information to the intended outlets;
- building good relationships with the media;
- evaluating results;
- maximising the exposure of messages; and
- tapping useful Commission and other external resources.

As well as providing sound advice on how best to proceed, the content includes examples of successful approaches that have been used to date.

The European Commission also organised the *Communicating European Research 2005* conference which took place in Brussels on 14 and 15 November 2005, showing the growing importance and recognition of public communication of science and technology.[16] In opening the conference, EU Commissioner Janez Potočnik, in charge of science and research at that time, said:

> *The objective of this conference is to explore how and why science needs to reach out and touch a wider audience. [. . .] It is quite an achievement to bring together close to 3 000 scientists, journalists and policy makers under the same roof, all of whom face the same challenge. This challenge is twofold: on the one hand we need to improve the ways in which we communicate research and on the other hand, we need to improve the image of science in society. [. . .] Therefore, communicating research and engaging with the public is more than a priority. It is an obligation.*

The conference, which was the first ever organised by the Commission on this issue, was a major success, as illustrated by the sheer number of participants and the feedback received from them.[17] During two days, participants including project coordinators, journalists and other communication professionals, press officers and representatives from research organisations met to promote mutual understanding of their respective roles, to share best practices and to define strategies to improve communication, outreach and dissemination of research results to the public and the press at a European level.

---

[16] More information on the conference, including the programme and speakers' presentations, is available on the website: http://ec.europa.eu/research/conferences/2005/cer2005/

[17] According to internal European Commission reports, participants who attended in order to exchange best communication practice considered the event overall as of high standard. The conference was rated as very good across all the different components.

Within FP7, some funded projects concern science communication. This is the case, for example, of ESConet Trainers organised by the European Science Communication network, which provides science communication training to scientists involved in a FP project.[18] The training aims at improving the ability of these scientists to interact with national and international media, for example how to present their work on TV and radio. It also includes training on how to use new media with the objective of establishing a better dialogue with society. A considerable number of other FP5, FP6 and FP7 projects have funded public communication training courses for scientists at all levels and other interested professionals.

In addition to communication and outreach activities undertaken at the level of the projects, the European Commission has also designed its own specific communication strategy for research which sets out the following main objectives:

> To communicate Europe as a leading and innovative place for doing and investing in research; show the results and benefits of European research to European citizens and hence foster understanding of research as a driver for European integration and for uniting people beyond the EU and provide first-class information on possibilities under FP7.[19]

EUROPEAN SCIENTISTS AND THE MEDIA

Because the EU is providing increasing funding to research and innovation, the Research DG has decided to gain a better understanding of the issues, variables and constraints faced by European researchers when communicating with wider audiences (European Commission 2007). To this end, in-depth telephone interviews were carried out in 2007 with a sample of 100 researchers who have participated in projects funded by FP6. Researchers from all Member States and representing a broad spectrum of scientific fields were interviewed in order to adequately reflect different subgroups.

Only 20% of scientists interviewed claimed to have an active relationship with the media, although most have been sporadically or very occasionally involved in some way in communicating to a wider audience. Those scientists said they were taking an active role because they believed it is their moral duty to do so. However, there appeared to

---

[18] http://www.esconet.org/ESConet/Welcome.html

[19] European Commission, internal document.

be a significant willingness to create dialogue and partnership with the media to achieve better coverage of science and hence to improve the public's perception of scientific culture and its benefits.

The survey also showed some misunderstanding between the media and the scientists. The great majority of scientists interviewed (just over 90%) recognised an obvious mismatch between what scientists want covered in the media and what media people regard as news-worthy. For many scientists, explaining science in general and the scientific method is more important than the short-term dissemination of the results of their work. Although groundbreaking research results are likely to interest the media, there is great potential for scientists to be the interpreters of the day-to-day events that affect people's everyday lives, but that potential does not seem to have been fully harnessed by either side.

Scientists understand that the media have the power to influence the public, but also believe that the media have a responsibility to educate the public rather than simply respond to popular interest areas. According to the survey, scientists show a clear lack of realism in their view that the media can perform a purely educational role; they tend to forget that media are commercial businesses that are not obliged to be responsive to the scientists' own interests, as other chapters in this book make very clear.

Many researchers reported that the fact that their work is funded by the EU generates little media interest, so they do not try hard to include the source of their funding in their communications. This situation is different in some of the smaller and newer Member States (in Eastern and Central Europe), where EU research funding is perceived as more newsworthy. In the older Member States, it is vital to adapt messages to the national context, for example by highlighting national benefits.

The survey showed no significant differences in the views of scientists by nationality. However, scientists who have been working in former communist countries, as well as the older generation of scientists (those around the age of 60+ years), were more distrustful of the media because they were very aware of its sensation-seeking behaviour. In contrast, younger generations seemed to be more open and were particularly aware of the force of the internet.

As a general remark, European scientists often claim that they are not well equipped to disseminate the results of their work more widely. According to a survey published in June 2006 by the Royal Society, 70% of UK scientists believe that *'funders of scientific research should help scientists to communicate with the non-specialist public'* and 46% of them do not *'feel well equipped to engage with the non-specialist public'* (Royal Society 2006). The goodwill shown by many is pushed to its limits by difficulties that to some extent stem from the lack of professional recognition for those scientists who are successful at communicating their work to the public. In a community that rewards specialist publications and does not emphasise the need for general communication, it is obvious that scientists lack funding to support specific communication measures and lack time to communicate.

THE ASSESSMENT SO FAR

There is not much information available regarding the public and media engagement activities undertaken by FP6 and FP7 projects. According to the Commission's internal data, 93% of FP6 projects did have a project website. The Second FP7 Monitoring Report[20] published by the European Commission in 2008 covers the implementation of FP7 and provides some data on communication and dissemination of results following a survey by National Contact Points, which helps the Commission in providing information and assistance related to the participation in FP7. The data show that 32.9% of the respondents find the communication and dissemination of FP7 project findings by the project consortia satisfactory (and 24.9% good), and by the Commission 33.2% satisfactory (and 32.2% good).

As regards the dissemination of project findings, it was acknowledged by those who commented that it was still very early in the programme to make definitive judgements, but there was some agreement that this had improved in FP7 and that knowledge transfer issues remain a challenge to research funding agencies across the board.

The most interesting result is the fact that scientific knowledge, as measured by the questions included in the Eurobarometer surveys,[21]

---

[20] http://ec.europa.eu/research/reports/2009/pdf/second_fp7_monitoring_en. pdf#view=fit&pagemode=none

[21] 1992, 2001, 2002 and 2005 Eurobarometers included the following questions on science and technology. *'Here is a little quiz. For each of the following statements, please tell me if it is true or false. If you don't know, say so, and we will go on to the next one. The Sun goes around the Earth; The centre of the Earth is very hot; The oxygen we breathe comes from plants; Radioactive milk can be made safe by boiling it; Electrons are smaller than atoms; The continents on which we live have been moving for millions of years and will continue to move in the future; It is the mother's genes that decide whether the baby is a boy or a girl; The earliest humans lived at the same time as the dinosaurs; Antibiotics kill viruses*

seems to have increased substantially in most European countries between 1992 and 2005. Over 15% increases in the percentages of correct answers have been observed in Luxembourg, Belgium, Greece, the Netherlands and Germany; among the new EU Member States, with the Czech Republic and Slovenia, showing a 10% increase in only three years. Sweden achieved the highest rates of correct answers. Further analysis of the Eurobarometer data confirmed the overall trend towards higher scientific literacy in all European countries (Claessens 2008). Interpretation of this trend remains unclear but it is likely that the increase of science festivals, science museums and science centres in Europe is part of the answer. Also, one may argue that media coverage of recent crises and controversies in Europe (climate change, nuclear energy, GMOs, avian flu, swine flu, mad cow disease, contaminated blood etc.) has brought many scientific and technological concepts and issues onto the public radar and has subsequently raised the overall public understanding of science in the EU countries. This is supported by the analysis of Shimizu (2007), who argues that the 1995 Kobe earthquake contributed to the public understanding of plate tectonics.

However, despite a growing number of public communication of science activities in Europe, and increasing support from the public authorities for them, there is still a large gap between science and society. Science is seen as a 'closed shop' with the public having no say in its development. Rarely do discussions and public debates accompany decisions about research issues and priorities. Europe still needs a genuine science communication culture, and because of this, the public is not in a position to anticipate scientific and technological crises, or deal with future developments. We need only to look at three examples – nuclear energy, GMOs and cloning – and think of the public concern, to see this is the case. In short, we are not there yet and issues such as scientific research and what should be done at EU level versus national level remain in the strictest sense of the word 'uncommunicated'.

This situation deeply handicaps science–society relationships and the public acceptance of advancements in science and technology. Furthermore, Europeans want to be consulted and involved in shaping the course of 'progress' and the decision-making process. How do we build public trust? How do we improve the dialogue between science and society?

as well as bacteria; Lasers work by focusing sound waves; All radioactivity is man-made; Human beings, as we know them today, developed from earlier species of animals; It takes one month for the Earth to go around the Sun.'

Scientists are encouraged or even obliged to inform audiences about what they are doing, but they also have an imperative to listen. Researchers these days must understand the social context within which they operate: what people worry about, what they expect or need from science, what they do not want in their lives. In short, the ivory tower is no longer an option.

One proposed solution is the systematic and even perhaps institutionalised organisation of public consensus conferences. These scientific 'grand juries' could stimulate communication and political decision-making in scientifically controversial areas. Used judiciously, they could offer a realistic answer to our society's inability to control and appreciate the development and the application of science and technology. Communicating is truly an imperative in a democracy, and this applies also to scientific research if one is to build trust and legitimacy for activities funded in great part by the public.

Key resources

Cheng, D., Claessens, M., Gascoigne, T., Metcalfe, J., Schiele, B. and Shunke, S. (eds.) (2008) *Communicating Science in Social Contexts*, New York: Springer.

Christensen, L.L. (2007) *The Hands-on Guide for Science Communicators*, New York: Springer.

Claessens, M. (2007) *Communicating European Research 2005*, New York: Springer.

Claessens, M. (2009) *Science et communication: pour le meilleur ou pour le pire ?*, Paris: Quae.

European Commission (2006) *Communicating Science: A Scientist's Survival Kit*, Brussels: European Commission, also available at http://ec.europa.eu/research/science-society/pdf/communicating-science_en.pdf

European Commission (2007) *European Research in the Media: The Researcher's Point of View*, Brussels: European Commission, also available at http://ec.europa.eu/research/conferences/2007/bcn2007/researchers_en.pdf

European Commission (2010) *Europeans, Science and Technology, Eurobarometer 340*, Brussels: European Commission, also available at http://ec.europa.eu/public_opinion/archives/ebs/ebs_340_en.pdf

European Research Advisory Board (2007) *Research and Societal Engagement, Final Report, 07.013*, Brussels: EURAB.

Royal Society (2006) *Science Communication: Survey of Factors Affecting Science Communication by Scientists and Engineers*, London: Royal Society, also available at http://royalsociety.org/uploadedFiles/Royal_Society_Content/Influencing_Policy/Themes_and_Projects/Themes/Governance/Final_Report_-_on_website_-_and_amended_by_SK.pdf

References

Claessens, M. (2008) European trends in science communication. In *Communicating Science in Social Contexts*, Cheng, D., Claessens, M., Gascoigne, T., Metcalfe, J., Schiele, B. and Shunke, S. (editors), Heidelberg: Springer, pp. 27–38.

European Commission (2007) *European Research in the Media: The Researcher's Point of View*, Brussels: European Commission, also available at http://ec.europa.eu/research/conferences/2007/bcn2007/researchers_en.pdf

European Commission (2010) *Europeans, Science and Technology: Eurobarometer 340*, also available at http://ec.europa.eu/public_opinion/archives/ebs/ebs_340_en.pdf.

European Research Advisory Board (2007) *Research and Societal Engagement, Final Report, 07.013*, Brussels: EURAB.

Eurostat 2008: http://epp.eurostat.ec.europa.eu/tgm/table.do?tab=table=init=1plugin=1&language=en=pcode=tsiir020

Pew Research Center (2009) *Public Praises Science; Scientists Fault Public, Media*, available at http://people-press.org/report/528/

Royal Society (2006) *Science Communication: Survey of Factors Affecting Science Communication by Scientists and Engineers*, London: Royal Society, also available at http://royalsociety.org/uploadedFiles/Royal_Society_Content/Influencing_Policy/Themes_and_Projects/Themes/Governance/Final_Report_-_on_website_-_and_amended_by_SK.pdf

Schiele, B. (1983) Enjeux cachés de la vulgarisation scientifique, *Communication–Information*, vol. V, n° 2–3.

Shimizu, K. (2007) *Japanese Survey of the Public Understanding of Science and Technology: Review of Results, Impact and Recent Secondary Analysis*. Communication at the International Indicators of Science and the Public meeting, Royal Society, 5–6 November 2007, London.

9

Tackling the climate communication challenge

Moments for scientists don't get much more dramatic than the scene in Paris on February 2, 2007, as lead authors of the 2007 report from the Intergovernmental Panel on Climate Change (I.P.C.C.) described evidence pointing to an increasingly human-heated planet.[1] This report, the fourth assessment of the causes and consequences of climate change in the nearly 20-year history of the panel, was the first to conclude with greater than 90 percent confidence that humans had become the main force driving warming and that centuries of rising temperatures and seas could be blunted only if emissions of heat-trapping gases were substantially reduced.

At the news conference following presentations, reporters pressed for the human element. One journalist asked Susan Solomon, one of the two supervising authors and an award-winning atmospheric scientist for the United States government, *"to sum up what kind of urgency this sort of report should convey to policy makers."* She gave the furthest thing from a convenient sound bite:

> *"I can only give you something that's going to disappoint you, sir, and that is that it's my personal scientific approach to say it's not my role to try to communicate what should be done . . . I believe that is a societal choice. I believe science is one input to that choice, and I also believe that science can best serve society by refraining from going beyond its expertise. In my view, that's what the I.P.C.C. also is all about, namely not trying to make policy-prescriptive statements, but policy-relevant statements.*[2]

---

[1] www.ipcc.ch/pdf/press-releases/pr-02february2007.pdf

[2] http://www.nytimes.com/2007/02/06/science/earth/06profile.html

Successful Science Communication, ed. D. J. Bennett and R. C. Jennings. Published by Cambridge University Press. © Cambridge University Press 2011.

Contrast her stance with the impassioned actions of James E. Hansen, the pre-eminent climatologist for the National Aeronautics and Space Administration of the United States, who in 2004 publicly criticized President George W. Bush and endorsed another candidate for President because of their stands on global warming and who would go on to get himself arrested outside the White House in 2010 and a coal company's offices in West Virginia the year before.[3]

In 2010, Hansen published a short essay on his Columbia University website explaining that his role as a grandparent fueled, and justified, his activism:

> Stabilizing climate is a moral issue, a matter of intergenerational justice. Young people, and older people who support the young and the other species on the planet, must unite in demanding an effective approach that preserves our planet.[4]

When I taught a graduate seminar at Bard College in 2007 on the role of communication in setting environmental policy, I split the class into "Hansenites and Solomonites" and had the students debate the strengths and pitfalls of each scientist's approach to climate communication. After the showdown, there was no clear winner, even though virtually the entire class had begun the exercise favoring Hansen.

Welcome to the rough-and-tumble interface of climate science, communication and society. It's a realm with no easy answers or simple menu of solutions, particularly these days as the world of communicating *anything*, let alone a complicated mix of science, ethics, and policy, is in a state of turbulent flux. Climate discourse is an arena in which leading scientists have taken starkly different stands on how to convey the broader meaning of their work, where environmental campaigners and like-minded politicians have been locked for more than a decade in pitched battles with a varied array of professional and amateur skeptics and contrarians, where the lay public – distracted by economic turmoil, constrained by what psychologists call peoples' "finite pool of worry" and buffeted by claims of catastrophe and hoax amplified by conflict-seeking media – has largely chosen to sit this issue out. I've sometimes compared shifting public attitudes on climate to water sloshing in a shallow pan. There's a lot of commotion, and tens of millions of dollars have been spent to try to turn opinion one way or another. But the depth of concern hasn't changed much in the quarter

---

[3] http://www.nytimes.com/2004/10/26/science/26climate.html; http://dotearth. blogs.nytimes.com/2009/06/23/hansen-of-nasa-arrested-in-coal-country/

[4] http://www.columbia.edu/~jeh1/mailings/2010/20100824_Activist.pdf

century I've been reporting on human-caused climate change, particularly if gauged by the ultimate metric – the relentless upward trend in greenhouse-gas emissions.

The din hit a particular crescendo late in 2009, when someone stole or liberated (choose a label depending on your politics; as of this writing the police have yet to call the incident a crime) a decade's worth of e-mail and files written by an international array of climate researchers. The batch of correspondence – presumed by the authors, perhaps naively, to have been private – was laced with attacks on intellectual antagonists and phrases hinting of data manipulation or other dicey behavior, providing red meat for critics of climate science and interest groups fighting restrictions on greenhouse gases. In the end, a series of inquiries concluded that some exchanges were unseemly and others may have violated British freedom of information laws, but there was scant evidence that the e-mails and other disclosed files undercut the broad, deep, and diverse body of research supporting greenhouse-driven warming.[5]

Around the same time, the intergovernmental climate panel faced its own challenges as some errors and sloppy patches were found in its 2007 reports. Inquiries by the InterAcademy Council and a Dutch government committee found plenty of problems, many having to do with how the science was summarized for the public and policymakers. But, again, there was no evidence that the revelations undercut the basic body of knowledge of climate change and its human component, and every sign that the I.P.C.C. could modify practices to boost accuracy, transparency, and credibility.[6]

In 2008, quoting a reader's comment about climate stasis, I posed an unsettling question in the headline of a post on climate and communication on my Dot Earth blog: *"Are We Stuck With 'Blah, Blah, Blah . . . Bang'?"* [7] I don't think so. Despite the troubles of late, there's plenty that can be done to improve the chances that climate information can *matter* – that the fruits of research on climate change, energy choices, and human reactions to environmental risk can meaningfully influence decisions by individuals, institutions, companies, and elected leaders in ways that reduce the odds that humans will dangerously disrupt climate and boost human resilience to climate-related hazards. In many ways, the failures so far, together with the explosively rapid changes in

---

[5] http://www.cce-review.org/

[6] http://reviewipcc.interacademycouncil.net/; http://www.bbc.co.uk/news/10506283

[7] http://dotearth.blogs.nytimes.com/2008/08/04/are-we-stuck-with-blah-blah-blah-bang/

how information on science flows between scientists and the public (and back again), create a great opportunity for fresh starts.

A first step in finding effective ways to convey climate findings is to recognize the hurdles to doing so. It would be hard to find an area of science that is more fraught with communication challenges than work on climate change. One challenge is simply the nature of the basic science. Evidence that greenhouse gases from human activities are warming the planet and likely to lead to disruptive environmental change doesn't come from a single finding, or a single field, for that matter. The science revealing rising risks of disruptive human-driven climate change has accumulated over 30 years like dots added to a pointillist painting. But the resulting image still lacks the memorable punch of an expressionist work like Edvard Munch's iconic "The Scream."

The result is what seems to be one of the great paradoxes of the early twenty-first century – a planet-scale risk that perpetually hides in plain sight. Parts of the picture of a human-warmed climate are revealed now in high resolution. There is no longer any reasonable way to explain recent changes in atmosphere and ocean temperatures without including a substantial contribution from accumulating human-generated greenhouse gases. But while the general picture of greenhouse warming is robust, the details that matter most to society – the pace at which seas rise, forecasts of how precipitation and temperatures change region by region, even the extent of warming from a given buildup of greenhouse gases – remain laden with persistent uncertainty. Any accurate depiction of the climate challenge must convey the uncertainty as well as what is known. In the meantime, audiences, whether elected officials or the general public, tend to demand "proof" of risk before ambitious actions are undertaken.

This means it's also vital, when discussing the amorphous concept called global warming or climate change, to be sure that one delineates which facet is being explored, and to define terms. Consider that the only conclusion of the I.P.C.C. that was "unequivocal" was that the climate had warmed. In the public discourse, though, that level of certainty often became conflated with the broad package of phenomena wrapped into the idea – that it all was certain. This kind of oversimplification then allowed those eager to perpetuate doubt to shout, legitimately, about overstatement.

There are other challenges in grasping the nature of the problem. As John D. Sterman, a professor of management at the Massachusetts Institute of Technology, has found, even a well-educated group like M.I.T.

graduate students has a hard time absorbing another facet of the climate problem – created by the long-lived nature of the most important human-generated emission, carbon dioxide. The gas accumulates like unpaid credit card debt or delayed homework assignments as long as emissions exceed the ability of forests, the oceans and other "sinks" to absorb the gas. As Sterman has put it, the atmosphere is like a bathtub with a partially opened drain. Carbon dioxide from burning fuels and forests is flowing in roughly twice as fast as it is being absorbed by plants and the ocean, and there's some evidence that the capacity of such systems to sop up the gas is not keeping up, meaning that the "drain" is, in essence, getting a bit clogged. At the same time, the decades-long useful life of new sources of emissions such as coal-burning power plants means that the "faucet" for carbon dioxide is getting cranked open just when it should be going in the opposite direction.

In a tub, this is a recipe for a flood. In the climate system, Sterman and many climate scientists say, this characteristic calls out for a prompt start in curbing and then cutting emissions to have a decent chance of avoiding dangerous thresholds. But few people seem capable of fully comprehending this kind of problem, he has found.[8] In one study that Sterman co-authored in 2007, after 212 M.I.T. graduate students were given a primer on the cumulative nature of carbon dioxide, when the participants were asked to draw a graph showing emission tracks that could stabilize the gas concentration, 84 percent instead drew curves that would result in concentrations continuing to climb.[9] This kind of research can be seen as utterly discouraging, or as yet more evidence of the need – and opportunity – for a lot of creative communication aimed at clarifying the situation.

I spent the first two decades of my journalistic exploration of global warming focused mainly on geophysical, biological, and technical questions related to sources of emissions, anticipated impacts of shifting temperature and precipitation patterns, and choices for policies and technologies that might limit emissions even as humanity's growth spurt peaks in coming decades. In all that work, I don't think anything unnerved me nearly as much as the reporting I've done more recently on the climate challenge within the human mind.[10]

[8] http://www.sciencemag.org/cgi/content/full/322/5901/532?ijkey=
ww8NhGSuSTLSw&keytype=ref&siteid=sci
[9] http://jsterman.scripts.mit.edu/On-Line_Publications.html#2007Understanding
[10] http://dotearth.blogs.nytimes.com/2009/08/05/is-the-climate-problem-in-our-heads/

To get just a hint of the internal hurdles potentially impeding an effective response, have a look at the following partial list of "psychological barriers" that could impede action, taken from the table of contents of *Psychology and Global Climate Change*, a 2009 report written by a task force of the American Psychological Association:[11]

> Ignorance
> Uncertainty
> Mistrust and reactance
> Denial
> Judgmental discounting
> Place attachment
> Habit
> Perceived behavioral control
> Perceived risks from behavioral change
> Tokenism and the rebound effect
> Social comparison, norms, conformity, and perceived equity
> Conflicting goals and aspirations
> Belief in solutions outside of human control

You get the idea. The parts of the human mind that judge risks and initiate responses, and the social institutions that provide a backstop, are not (yet, at least) well set up to deal with century-scale, globe-spanning, uncertainty-laden, incrementally building, feedback-laced, cumulative sources of risk. Deeply embedded human traits guarantee that even perfect communication of scientific insights pointing to certain kinds of threats hardly guarantees that people will absorb them, let alone change behaviors or policies as a result. People and communities still tend to focus primarily on the "near and now" and to use what some economists call "hyperbolic discounting" when weighing how much to invest to limit long-term threats. Rather than take up space with more specifics, I encourage anyone eager to learn more about the mental filters that affect how people absorb, or reject, climate findings to read the psychological association's report and another vital resource, *The Psychology of Climate Communication*, published in 2009 by the Columbia University Center for Research on Environmental Decisions.[12]

Further distortion of the traditional sense of environmental responsibility comes because populations generating the most heat-trapping emissions are mostly separated in space and time from the

---

[11] http://www.apa.org/science/about/publications/climate-change.aspx

[12] http://www.cred.columbia.edu/guide/

communities or ecosystems most exposed to potentially heightened risks of flooding, drought, and other climate-related hazards. In the meantime, the wealth created through processes that generate emissions – from burning coal to cutting forests – can insulate emitters from some climate-related risks.[13] On top of these factors, people, largely through the differences in deeply rooted values systems identified by academics and pollsters, have a wide range of views on how much they are obligated to invest to limit risks primarily facing communities in poor, distant places.

Can communication, using the best possible mix of words, imagery and other content, break through these barriers? Here's how David Ropeik, a consultant in risk communication on everything from nuclear power to car safety and the author of *How Risky Is It, Really*, explored this question:

> In order to be successful, any communication has to respect not just what the communicator wants to say, but what the audience wants and needs to know, and present the information at a length and in a language and form designed more to reach the audience than satisfy the communicator. Scientists too often fail to let go of their paradigm of "knowledge". . . detailed, nuanced, erudite . . . and as a result fail to take the audiences' needs and interests more to heart.
>
> Scientists communicating climate change must also accept what social sciences tell us, that no matter how clearly they communicate, the information will be interpreted through the subjective lenses of the reader's perceptions. Frustrating as it is, scientists communicating facts must understand that what seems like fact to them will only be one input among many that contributes to how people think and feel and act. This is particularly so with a contentious issue, and a risk issue. Both characteristics trigger powerful subconscious subjective information-filtering processes. The objective of communicating, then, is to add information to the tools people have for making up their minds, not to make them "get it," as in understanding things the way the scientist wants them to.

In other words, those diving in to help foster public awareness and response on climate change, and the actions that would be required to blunt climate risk, in part have to let go of the expectation that some single new explanation, future I.P.C.C. report, consensus statement by scientific academies, or prize-winning documentary will magically lead to traction. Deeper human traits, and feelings, are involved in how people react to something as profound as the idea that actions that have built today's prosperity – mainly the unfettered combustion of fossil fuels – are imperiling future prospects, both economic and

---

[13] http://www.nytimes.com/2007/04/03/science/earth/03clim.html

ecologic. Because of cultural filters, a more informed public can actually be a more *divided* public on an issue like global warming. In the United States, the *Six Americas* study of climate attitudes by researchers at Yale and George Mason University and periodic surveys by the Pew Research Center both have shown that more education tends to deepen opposing convictions of both climate skeptics and those very worried about warming.[14]

For all these reasons, and many more, some researchers – already familiar with a class of economic and social problems deemed "wicked" because of layers of potentially conflicting cause and effect and interests – have proposed calling the climate challenge "super wicked."[15] To me, it's not a stretch to say the challenge is "*beyond* super wicked."

Old models for explaining the challenges posed by climate change are clearly not up to the task, given the many levels of complexity and the profound divisions in society. The "woe is me" frame, epitomized by the 2006 Time Magazine cover proclaiming, *"Be Worried. Be Very Worried,"* was bound to fail, as some sociologists warned at the time.[16] The "shame on you" approach hasn't done much better. One long-standing vision of the "climate story" has been to cast it as a political battle between a scientifically enlightened left and economically motivated right. Mind you, there's been ample disinformation over the years, much of it financed by money from conservative philanthropists or companies dependent on fossil fuels for their profits. But it's far too simplistic, many social scientists have said, to think that if such efforts were exposed, if the scientific realities defining risks from human-driven warming were undistorted, the world would somehow magically move to abandon polluting energy choices. The epic scope of the climate challenge and the related energy challenge as humanity's numbers and appetites crest in coming decades will necessitate sustained engagement and communication on a host of fronts involving a wide range of audiences and a wide range of communicators.

While the conventional path of conducting a study or review, writing a paper or report, drafting a press release and then waiting for an experienced science reporter to call will persist for a while, it will

[14] http://environment.yale.edu/climate/news/global-warmings-six-americas-june-2010/; http://pewresearch.org/pubs/282/global-warming-a-divide-on-causes-and-solutions

[15] http://www.law.georgetown.edu/faculty/lazarus/docs/articles/Lazarus_SuperWickedProblems.pdf

[16] http://www.time.com/time/covers/0,16641,20060403,00.html; http://www.nytimes.com/2006/04/23/weekinreview/23revkin.html

never again be the norm. Conventional, and particularly specialized, media are a shrinking slice of the world's fast-expanding pie of communication portals. It would behoove anyone interested in making an impact to experiment with new media, to test boundaries, to interact with audiences of all kinds (making sure to listen as much as expound) and, in the end, to absorb fully that scientific knowledge of climate change is merely a starting point for progress – not a means in itself.

MANY CLIMATE CHALLENGES, MANY PATHS

In July 2010, as the leadership of the I.P.C.C. finished assembling the hundreds of authors for the chapters in its fifth climate assessment, the chairman, Rajenda K. Pachauri, sent a letter to the participating scientists admonishing them to *"keep a distance from the media."* The defensive tone of the letter was predictable, given the months of assaults on the integrity of the panel from commentators, politicians and groups trying to sustain status-quo energy policies.

But even strong supporters of the climate panel, including scientists who'd signed up to devote a substantial part of the next four years of their lives helping to write the fifth assessment, loudly complained. Edward R. Carr, one of the new panel authors and an associate professor of geography at the University of South Carolina, blogged that this line reflected the same *"bunker mentality"* that had created problems for the panel through the preceding year.

For the panel, and for anyone or any institution trying to communicate clearly and credibly on the state of the climate and choices facing the world's nations in seeking to limit risks, this is the time to engage, not hunker down. For too long, as Mike Hulme, a professor of climate change at the University of East Anglia has put it, there has been an artificial oversimplification of "global warming" or "climate change" into a single phenomenon, even a badge of identity for some. Hulme, the author of *Why We Disagree About Climate Change*, described the situation in an essay in the Royal Society Arts Journal in 2010:

> [C]limate change has come to signify far more than the physical ramifications of human disturbance to the composition of the Earth's atmosphere and its energy balance. Climate change has become as much a social phenomenon as it is a physical one. Arguments about the causes and consequences of climate change – and the solutions to it – have become nothing less than arguments about some of the most intractable social, ethical and political disputes of our era: the endurance of chronic poverty in a world of riches; the nature of the social contract between state and citizen; the cultural authority of scientific knowledge; and the role of

*technology in delivering social goods. Climate change has become a metaphor for
the imagined future of human life and civilisation on Earth.*[17]

The utter divergence in views of the climate challenge among people
with different interests and situations was vividly on display during
the two long weeks I spent covering the tumultuous round of treaty
negotiations in Copenhagen in December, 2009. There was barely any
overlap in positions as angry African delegates stormed through the
halls demanding money to help them avoid climate calamity, Chinese
diplomats coolly and flatly described their primary need for economic
growth, American officials stated flatly they could only offer what was
politically possible at home, and environmentalists unveiled a daily
"Fossil of the Day" award for countries seen as obstructing commitments to cut emissions.

To my mind, the first step in accurately, and potentially effectively,
conveying the science pointing to a rising human influence on the
climate system is to separate that body of understanding from the next
stages in the debate. These include discussions of the anticipated
impacts, along with the uncertainties, and of course how to respond –
both through boosting resilience to climate hazards and blunting the
rise in concentrations of greenhouse gases.

The next is to embrace the reality that science merely delineates
the choices facing societies, and often with very fuzzy – if not entirely
blurry – portions of the picture. This is where values come in, including
the values of scientists. Scientists happen to be human beings outside
their work, and many find themselves both frustrated with stasis and
passionate about doing whatever they can to prod society to act in ways
that can reduce the chances of big regrets down the line. So what is the
right path for a concerned scientist to take?

In a way, there is no best route – as can be seen in the variegated
set of paths chosen by Susan Solomon, James Hansen, and dozens of
other climate researchers who've decided to take the time and energy
required to come out of the computer laboratory or back from field
studies to testify at hearings, appear on television, develop blogs, or
write columns and books. But there are certainly basic principles that
can help scientists and their institutions shape their choices, choose
their medium and frame their messages.

Stephen H. Schneider, the Stanford University scientist who
passed away in 2010 after spending the better part of four decades

---

[17] http://www.thersa.org/fellowship/journal/archive/spring-2010/features/
heated-debate

studying both climate science and policy, always tried to stress the importance of delineating where data left off, expert judgment kicked in and – in the end – where personal values determined choices. He was a big fan of concerted action to cut emissions, but always acknowledged this was his personal view, not a matter of science. Here's how he put it in an e-mail message in 2006:

> To be risk averse is good policy in my value system – and we always must admit that how to take risks – with climate damages or costs of mitigation/adaptation – is not science but world views and risk aversion philosophy – and whether you fear more the type one error (wrong forecast so you wasted resources by acting on it) or type two error (right forecast but too uncertain so you didn't act and it happened and you really got hurt by not hedging) is a value tradeoff.

He also frequently stressed the importance of scientists, once familiar with the boundaries laid out above, getting engaged in public discourse. As he put it in the abstract for a talk on climate and communication at the 2010 annual meeting of the American Association for the Advancement of Science:

> Despite controversy, scientists should not be discouraged on principle to enter the public debate on policy issues (climate change in my case) either as scientist-advocates or as scientist-popularizers. If we do not enter the debates, then popularization of complex issues will occur without our direct input and will likely be more inaccurate.[18]

To provide a range of perspectives, I invited some scientists and specialists in science communication to provide some practical advice for those who do jump into the breach.

Susan Joy Hassol, a climate communication consultant and writer:

> We can convey the science both accurately and effectively by speaking in simple, plain language ("anthropogenic," for example, is not simple, plain language), leading with what we know, and placing new findings in the context of the core message that climate is warming and that human activities are the primary cause. It's also important to make clear that this conclusion is based on evidence, not opinion or belief. (The term "consensus" can sound like it's referring to opinion.)
>
> One thing to avoid is using words that have different meanings to the public than to scientists. For example, scientists frequently use the word "enhance" to mean increase, but to lay people it means to improve (as in "enhance your appearance"), so the "enhanced greenhouse effect" sounds like a good thing! Try "intensify" or "increase" instead . . . "Positive" connotes good and "negative" connotes bad to nonscientists. So "positive trends" and "positive feedbacks" sound like good things!

[18] http://aaas.confex.com/aaas/2010/webprogram/Paper2399.html

> To most laypeople, a "theory" is just an unsubstantiated hunch, opinion or
> conjecture, not what scientists mean at all. See my Eos article, "Improving How
> Scientists Communicate About Climate Change," for more examples and
> suggestions for alternatives.[19]

Randy Olson, a marine biologist turned filmmaker and, more recently,
author, sent a line from *Don't Be Such A Scientist: Talking Substance in an
Age of Style*, his book for scientists who want to be understood:

> The time has come, in our new media environment, which is so cluttered with
> information that it is often hard to tell fact from fiction, for new attention to be
> paid to "errors of boredom," in which the speaker fails to hold anyone's interest.

He then added this thought:

> Communication is about "voices." People listen to voices they like. They don't listen to
> voices they don't like. The bosses at BP figured this out the hard way last spring.
> Shortly after the Gulf spill they began running television commercials featuring
> BP CEO Tony Hayward and his British accent. Guess what. Within a month they
> wised up, dumped those spots, and came out with a whole series of commercials
> featuring working class Gulf of Mexico residents with their deep southern drawls.
> It's about voice. Al Gore is a very courageous man, but he speaks with the voice of
> an affluent, white, older, male Democrat. "An Inconvenient Truth" did an
> effective job of reaching the affluent, white, older, male Democrat crowd. Now it's
> time to radiate the message out to other ethnicities, income levels, and sexual
> persuasions. It's about voices.

Edward Maibach, the director of the Center for Climate Change Communication at George Mason University, speaks as often as he can about
the need for *"simple, clear messages, repeated often, by a variety of trusted
sources."* Here's more from him:

> This formula for public education/outreach has worked rather well for the public
> health community on a wide range of health issues, and it is also working rather
> well for the fossil fuel industry in their efforts to oppose climate legislation.
> Conversely, the community of climate scientists – like many communities of
> scientists – hasn't embraced this approach yet. Simplicity of the messages? Message
> repetition, again and again, at every possible opportunity? Engaging other
> communities of trusted professional in also stating these messages (again and
> again)? I don't mean to be harsh, but I think the community of climate scientists is
> batting 0 for 3 by this measure.

But I have to return to David Ropeik for one more reminder that the
most important, and possibly toughest, challenge for climate scientists

---

[19] http://www.climatecommunication.org/PDFs/Eos.pdf

engaging others on this issue is to remember that information is not meaning. Here's how he put it in a note he sent for my blog:

> *Alone, facts are lifeless stones on the ground. They only become the living walls of our perceptions and ideas based on our interpretations of how they fit together. It's exciting, and cause for hope, that we understand a lot about how this subjective information processing happens. So let's move past the rationalist pretense that there can ever be "perfect" knowledge, and use the rich evidence we have about the subjective ways people process information to help the species think past our instincts and truly grasp that we're living unsustainably in a finite biological system.*

With such awareness, scientists or others seeking to captivate and energize the public can dive into the astonishing menu of communication

Figure 9.1 Global air volume at sea-level pressure. Conceptual computer artwork of the total volume of air within the Earth's atmosphere, seen as a sphere, centred over Europe. It dramatically shows how finite the available air supply actually is. The sphere measures 1999 kilometres across and weighs 5140 trillion tonnes. (© Adam Nieman/Science Photo Library.) See colour plate section.

pathways to test ways to make information work. For some this may be through a blog like Realclimate.org, a comic strip like the Throbgoblins climate cartoons drawn by Marc Roberts, an eye-opening illustration like Adam Nieman's depiction of the volume of the Earth's atmosphere as a sphere that, when placed alongside the Earth, is not big enough to hide western Europe (Figure 9.1). For others, it may be as simple, and important, as visiting local schools or writing a column for the local paper. There is always the option of doing the work, writing a press release, and waiting for a phone call. But I wouldn't count on that changing the world.

10

Dealings with the media

Let's get rid of what still remains a myth – scientists and journalists are not opposing forces, they are on the same side. Scientists want to make their research and findings available to the widest possible audience. And journalists want stories that their readers, listeners and viewers will find interesting and engaging. Journalists are not multi-headed beasts out to trap you, trivialise your story and/or make things up. Their only currency is 'a story' and you are the one with the story. So, joint mutual working is the order of the day. But to do that it is incumbent on us, the sciency end of the equation, to learn and understand a little of the world of the media.

The media today comes in a myriad of forms. We still have all the traditional types: newspapers; radio; and television – at all levels – international, national, regional and local. Magazines, from the generic to the out-and-out esoteric, published weekly or monthly. It is said that if you can think of any human (or in-human) activity then there is a magazine for it – from apple-growing to astrology, from philately to picture restoring to physics, and from yachting to yoghurt – all 'life' is here.

But the major new player is the web. Every traditional part of the media has its own website to provide instant updates and extra stories that print or broadcast cannot run due to lack of space or time, or because stories have broken after a crucial internal deadline has past. Apart from these adjuncts to the 'old' media, new websites are springing up every day to cater for ever more specialist audiences, rather like magazines online. Add to these the bloggers, 'citizen journalists', podcasters and social networkers and we have more opportunities to disseminate our stories than ever before. And it really doesn't stop

Successful Science Communication, ed. D. J. Bennett and R. C. Jennings. Published by Cambridge University Press. © Cambridge University Press 2011.

there; all our organisations – universities, research units, research councils, funding bodies, learned and professional associations, research charities – have their own web presence – all run news stories, all want to be noticed, all want a share of the worldwide electronic audience.

At the turn of this century I would have advised any scientist who wanted to reach the public to have used and stuck to the old media, but today that advice has to change – both old and new media have to be exploited if we want to get our stories noticed. On every media/science communication training course I teach, I ask a simple question of the participants: 'Where do you get your news from?' From my extremely non-scientific survey the answers appear to shift over time and according to age. Almost everyone under 30 uses the web, whilst those over 30 do read newspapers and listen to the radio and watch television, but they also use the web for a quick catch-up, the lunch-time dip into BBC News online for the breaking story or the update; and with the BBC site receiving over 200,000 hits a day it has a truly massive, international lay audience.

So, if that, in brief, is today's media then how do we, as scientists and researchers, exploit the opportunities and try to get our stories out there?

I've used this term 'story' already and I'm aware that for many scientists the word is equated with 'fiction', but in the media context it is simply a short form for a piece of news that a journalist, and his or her editors, believes will interest their audience. And the key word is 'news'. But what is 'news'? Can it be defined? Not really. But news really should be new, or at least new to that audience. News is arbitrary, whimsical, ever changing. What makes a brilliant news story one day might be confined to the trash bin the next, because it is all about the judgement of a very few human beings and is dependent on all the other things that are going on in the world on that day. A bomb explodes, an earthquake happens, a(nother) footballer is caught with his pants down, a new treatment is discovered for cancer, more job losses, the FTSE goes wildly up or down – it's all potentially news – something has happened, someone has done something to someone else, something has been discovered. So, news is about action(s).

There are some pointers to help us think about what might make a news story. Does the story involve/affect people, and preferably a large number of people (i.e. that particular media outlet's audience)? Does the story involve controversy, especially these days where others can take the moral high ground? There is also a journalistic acronym that can help – FOB – First, Only, Biggest (or Best). Is this the first time something has happened, is it the only time it has happened, is it the biggest or the best? There is also something called the 'CFM effect', which may or may not be apocryphal. In the bad old days before the web and email, stories from around the world used to come into newsrooms on 'tickertape' machines. They would be printed out onto very long narrow strips of paper and a man would permanently sit by the machine and rip off these strips of paper and hand them to the relevant journalist or editor. One particular man, or so the story goes, would say: 'Cor F**k Me', to indicate that the story he had just read was great – and CFM was born.

All the above go into the judgemental mix when decisions are being made about whether to run the story or not, but perhaps the most important question ever asked within journalism is: '*So what?*' This can be damning. You've discovered/invented/created a new nanoparticle, or you've managed to elucidate the genome of a rare bacteria, or you've found out that two different parts of the brain 'fire' when we watch sport on TV – so what? What do any of these important and worthy stories in science mean for the media's mass audience – the proverbial 'man on the Clapham omnibus' (now there's a phrase that needs bringing up to date, perhaps it should be – the 'man on the Northern Line with his free copy of Metro'?). The key to unlock all or any story, for the non-specialist, is to consider the implications and applications, even if you do have to speculate, extend the logic, or the timescale.

So, the stories above could perhaps answer the 'so what' question by adding the implication or application:

> '*. . . a new nanoparticle potentially able to deliver chemotherapy drugs only to cancer cells has been created . . .*'
> '*. . . the reading of the genome of a humble bacteria could allow scientists to interfere with the genetic make-up of* E. coli, *the bug that kills XXXX people in the world every day . . .*'
> '*. . . finding out which parts of your brain work when we watch sport on TV could mean new treatments for people with severe brain injury . . .*'.

I'd read any of these. None of the above detracts from, or trivialises, the original or basic science, but what it does is allows the audience to engage with the story, it brings it within their everyday knowledge, it makes it real, and it allows them a glimpse into an unfamiliar world. But why all this emphasis on news? Well, everything that you read, see or listen to in the media has started its life as a piece of news. The feature articles, the columnists perorations, the editorials, the radio series, the TV documentaries, the blogs all have their beginnings as news. So, my thesis is if we can get the news 'right', then all that follows will also be 'right'.

BECKHAM'S ACHILLES

Back in the cold spring of 2010 when the England football team were gearing up for the World Cup to be played in South Africa that summer attention turned, not for the first time, to David Beckham. He ruptured his Achilles tendon playing for AC Milan, and therefore his chances to play for England in the World Cup had gone. Now whether you like, or even care about, football and the health affairs of an individual player this microsecond episode gives an insight into how the news event – the rupture of the tendon – spawned a whole raft of material.

Features over the next few days followed about Beckham's history in football; his quasi-inconographic status within sport and modern culture; and how the fans were reacting. But it also allowed medical specialists, sports scientists and behavioural researchers to become part of the story with features about the Achilles tendon and how it can be repaired, and material on how his loss to the team could affect the team's performance. These real-world events happen every day and therefore every day the scientific community has opportunities to add value and specialist knowledge to whatever is going on – whether it's Beckham's Achilles, or the plate tectonics of the 2010 Chilean and Haitian earthquakes, or why spring will be early/late this year. If we want science and evidence-based knowledge to be an equal partner and contributor to the daily life of the public worldwide, then we all have to take a level of responsibility in proactively and opportunistically engaging with the media on the stories of the day. These stories and events may seem tangential to our daily scientific endeavour, but look around you – just about everything has an element of science, engineering or technology about it, and I bet that it wouldn't take longer than half an hour to find an expert who can and should engage and comment.

BUT WHAT ABOUT YOUR STORY?

The above is responsive, it's science muscling-in on the events and news of the day, but what about when you have a story of your own, when you have discovered something, or added to the accretional knowledge about the world we inhabit, what do you do then?

Step 1. The first thing to do is to test whether what you have is actually a story, whether an audience beyond the three other people in the world doing similar research would care. In other words see if you can get it past the 'so what' test. To do this you have to find a representative of the lay public and tell him or her your story and see if they first, can understand it and then whether they find it interesting, engaging, exciting. When I started doing this kind of work I was working in an academic environment and used to take my stories to the staff in the canteen (my institution didn't have a refectory) – they became my touchstone for whether I had passed the 'so what'.

Step 2. OK, so you've passed the test, what next? Now, you have to write your story as if it were a news story in a newspaper. This piece of copy can be called a 'news release', or a 'media release'. This is not as hard as it sounds because all around us we have well-crafted examples of how to do this – look at the news pages of a newspaper or look at news websites – all you have to do is copy the style, the format, the language, but perhaps a few hints and tips will help.

The news release, a maximum of one web screen or one side of A4, should aim to imitate a news story, in essence it is a precis of the main findings of a research study or conference paper. The first paragraph, roughly 30 words, must capture the newest and most important points in a way that will make the reader want to read on to find out more.

The news release, just like the news story, is a complete structural reversal of the learned journal paper. In journals the usual order is: the background is fully laid out; the methodology is described in agonising detail; the results are itemized one by one; and only at the end are the significant results mentioned, along with the conclusions, discussion and implications. Invariably the last paragraph(s) of the journal paper can become the first paragraph of your release. A scientific writing formula is normally: '$a+b=c$'; but what we, the audience, want is: 'c because of $a+b$'.

News has a very simple shape and is the same in all media – an inverted triangle. The key findings go right at the top and the information cascades down in a descending order of priority or importance. So the key is: from the most important at the top, to the least important at the bottom, this means that there is no such thing as chronology within this form of writing. It may seem logical, for instance, in a court report to read first the charges, then what each side of barristers said, then the witnesses and the defendant and then, and only then be told the verdict and sentence. But as the audience we want the news first – the verdict – that to us is the most important point and that is why news reporting comes in this form. Compare these two intros to a story and decide which you would rather read?:

> 'At a world conference symposium held today at the University of Knighton the chair thanked the sponsors, the Dalek Time Travel and Health Corporation, for their generosity in bringing together four of the foremost world experts on nanotechnology.'
>
> 'Scientists have created minute nanoparticles that can cause cancer cells to commit suicide. This was just one of the results announced today at the first world conference on Cancer and Nanotechnology.'

The first paragraph, first 30-odd words, is the most important sentence or two that you will write – if your reader hasn't been hooked by then they will likely hit the back button, the delete key or turn the proverbial page. Journalists are trained to answer what is called the 5 Ws in that first paragraph – What?, Who?, Why?, When? and Where? This is excellent guidance, but sometimes it can be hard to manage in 30 words. Concentrate on answering the question What? because that equates to the news – what's been found out, what's been discovered, what's new. Depending on context answering the question Why? comes next, as this can introduce a problem that your research has solved, or bring in the implications and applications.

Things that you can dump from your release are both the methodology and the theory, unless, of course, that is the story – you've invented a new and better methodology, or cast significant doubt on a long-standing theory. You can dump your methods for two very good reasons. The first is that even if you do include them it is very unlikely that we, the reader, will really get a good understanding of the 'kit' you use every day. And secondly, because we trust you. You are the professional researcher and therefore we implicitly believe that you will have used the correct methods to carry out your research.

Language is often a problem, especially for novice news release writers, on two fronts – jargon and technical terms, and getting the tone and level right. It should be obvious that writing for a lay audience means that jargon – your in-house, in-laboratory speak – should be cut out, as it cannot be assumed that readers will understand what to them could be seen as a foreign language. But invariably within science we have to use technical terms, so explain them in a simple and clear way perhaps using an analogy, metaphor or simile to allow your reader to 'see' what you mean. Have a look at this:

'In order for cancer cells to undergo metastasis they have to bind to a protein–protein signalling cascade.'

or:

'When individual cancer cells break away from the primary tumour to set up secondaries in other parts of the body this is called metastasis. This happens when a series of messages is delivered from elsewhere in the body – rather like you receiving a court summons delivered by your local postman.'

This may be a bit longer, but it attempts to unpack a lot of technical terms.

The tone and level of language used is often inappropriate for the audience. Copy is often packed with polysyllabic words, which can get in the way of the reader actually grasping what to them will be new information. A colleague, who used to work for the *Guardian* newspaper, once commented: 'even on the Guardian we did not "endeavour to ascertain", "we tried to find out"'. But why? Well, the media carry out a great deal of research with their readers, listeners and viewers and part of that research is about language – what words and phrases people can and cannot understand. Generally the longer the word the more likely it is that the audience cannot give you a dictionary definition. These long words are nearly always Latin or Greek in origin, but we readers of English much prefer it when the roots of our words are Anglo-Saxon. So don't write 'erroneous', 'facilitate' or 'necessitate' when you could and should use 'wrong/false', 'help' or 'need/require'. Another small trick to stop you using these rather formal, flowery and pompous words is to say them out loud, preferably to someone else. The words will sound odd and wrong. Try always to find the conversational form and write those words down, it will always come across as friendlier and more appealing.

Whilst on the subject of reader research the media also conduct research about what their audiences want to see, hear and read. What is striking about all the research results that I have seen is that science, health and medicine always appear in the top 10 list of subjects that audiences want; strangely, perhaps, politics is usually listed somewhere in the teens.

Again to ape the news story use 'simple' sentences – *Two people joined the department yesterday.'* Or 'compound' sentences – *Two people joined the department yesterday and raised the total number of staff to 31.'* Why? Because as readers we prefer these sentence types and they are easier to understand. The sentence that winds on line-after-line with innumerable subordinate clauses is always going to test the reader's comprehension and energy levels. The goal should be – one idea per sentence.

Also because news is about action then you must write in the active voice, as opposed to the passive. So rather than *'Jones was arrested by the police'*, please can we have *'Police arrested Jones'* – this is not only active it is also shorter, meaning that you can pack more into your one side of A4. Again because it is news we want to know what did happen rather than what didn't happen. So this means trying to eliminate negatives from your writing and using positive verbs. I would rather have *'The experiment failed'*, than *'The experiment was not successful.'* The first is both positive and again shorter.

You must also remember that news stories contain quotes from the person who has carried out the research – you – so your release must include them. I would always think very carefully about these words as they may be seen and read by hundreds of thousands of people and those words may be the only way that the readers make a judgement about you.

And just a final thought on the writing/drafting – these days many organisations and institutions have professional press officers who can and should help, and they certainly can cast a non-scientific specialist eye over your copy. So, if you are a novice, or even if you are quite experienced at drafting this type of communication, then seek out the professionals in your organisation and be humble enough to accept that there is no such thing as a perfect piece of writing and that any draft can be improved.

Step 3. So well done, you have a story and you've drafted your release in a media- and audience-friendly form, the next step is distribution – how do you get it to those key journalists? Even five years ago I would have said that printing out your release and sending it in the post to named science correspondents and editors was the best method. The journalists used to love the daily postbag because they felt that people like us had taken the care, effort and trouble to ensure that they got our story. But today email is king and finding the email addresses of the journalists you want to reach is, as with so much else, only a Google search away.

As with the writing and drafting above, if your institution has a press office then ask them about distribution, this really is their technical area. Often scientists will say *'I only want my story covered in a good quality national newspaper/TV/radio.'* Mistake. Because of the enormous amount of competing demands and inputs on the national newspapers your story has to be very strong to get a look-in. The local and regional media have fewer demands and are therefore more likely to cover your piece, and this layer of the media is being constantly monitored by the nationals (and indeed internationals) so your story once published locally has a good chance of being picked up and used by other parts of the media.

Another key route to the media is via press agencies. These bodies act like newspapers, they have their own specialist, general and, indeed, regional reporters and they go out and about collecting and writing stories, but they don't actually publish any of this material themselves – they sell it, on subscription, to the rest of the media. The main national agency in the UK is the Press Association, but you will find mini versions in many cities around the country, and similarly in many other countries, so don't forget to add them to any distribution list. Additionally, for a few years now we have had a specialist science distribution agency called AlphaGalileo. This has been funded by all sorts of science organisations both in the UK and right across Europe – its mission is to distribute 'science stories' to science reporters and editors around the world, and that is exactly what it does. 'AlphaG' works on the basis that you can't upload stories onto their online distribution system unless you pay a subscription, so whilst this network is an excellent way to get to just the right target audience in terms of the right journalists you will have to get your institution to pay up and buy a subscription – it won't break the bank.

I could go on at inordinate length about the subject of distribution because it is so key to getting any story actually covered by the media but it would be quite boring except for the aficionados, suffice it to say that the question of when you send your story out is quite crucial – a story embargoed for 00.01 hours Monday has more chance of being published than trying to compete with the busiest news days of the week – Tuesday, Wednesday and Thursday. Much has been written, debated and argued in relation to embargoes – this is the system by which we can send our releases to the media, but they cannot publish the story until the time and date that we set (the embargo), i.e. the time and date when the journal paper is published, or the conference paper is actually given. This helps the journalists as they know that there is a level playing field and gives them time to do some research, if that is necessary. I have always been very clear within my own organisations that no release should ever leave the office without an embargo – it is simply just good professional practice.

And finally, once your story is out there please, please make sure that you are around so that the poor hapless journalists can find you and talk to you. There is nothing worse from the journalist's point of view than to get a story that they want to cover and then find that you have gone off to some conference in foreign parts, without your mobile.

DO THINGS GO WRONG?

I've painted a positive picture so far – that the media and the public want your stories and that the media will work collaboratively with you to make your story accessible to their audience; that there are more outlets and opportunities for your story than ever before; and that science has a part to play in bringing its knowledge to bear on everyday (non-science) stories. But, of course, things can and do go wrong.

The world of media communication is inherently imperfect – how could it be anything else given the number of human judgements and decisions made every hour of every day? The surprise is actually that the media get so little wrong. If you consider the average daily newspaper in the UK, it may have roughly a quarter of a million words, put together by a bunch of journalists, subeditors and editors over a period of about six to eight hours. That scenario to most people would be a recipe for endless mistakes and factual errors, but the converse is the truth – the mistakes and error rate is tiny. And my own experience of acting as an intermediary between scientists, applied scientists and the media over the last 25-plus years backs this lack of error rate. In all that time, and before, I can count on the fingers of a couple of badly mutilated hands the number of times that things have gone badly wrong. The majority of those occurrences can be laid at the door of inexperienced or over-excited scientists who have said things in public, and to a journalist, that they wished they hadn't and then tried to deny saying it. I remember one incident where a group of scientists were explaining a whole new training programme for the police, and almost as an aside one of them said: 'I suppose the down side of our work is that we will end up with a load of socially skilled bastards.' Very luckily for him the journalists present all got together and agreed not to use the quote, although they could have done and the effect would have been to call into question years of research and applied work. There have been a couple of howling journalistic goofs, where the reporter either totally misreported the evidence, without checking with the researcher, or seemingly deliberately added in a result or two that were not part of the original paper. There has also been the odd run-in with a columnist, as opposed to a news reporter, who wanted to add in implications and speculations of their own, because of their own campaigning or political position. However, having listed these rare errors they all provided even more opportunities to refer to the science, to the story, and to get corrections published.

But, as we all know there have been some science stories that have not been exactly positive – GM foods, the MMR vaccine, and perhaps most recently 'Climategate', as it has been dubbed.

Much has been written, researched and analysed about all three, and at much greater length and by people who are more expert than I. But both GM foods and MMR seem to be clear examples of twin phenomena – a science story that leaks over into a political story; and stories where the real scientific experts kept their collective heads well below the parapet thus allowing either non-experts or vested interest to take centre stage, and the consequences have been huge.

On the GM front Europe is almost the only place on the planet without a well-managed and safe GM agricultural programme, which is helping to feed local populations. On MMR the silence led to totally unnecessary deaths of children from measles because the number of children immunised went below the critical number and allowed the disease to erupt again and reach out its fatal fingers.

The other side of both of these stories is the political, in that both moved from initially being dealt with by science and medicine specialists to being written by political correspondents – the argument being that both matters concerned national policy, respectively agriculture and health. This changed the game-plan overnight, it shifted from any discussion of the scientific merits and evidence into a 'let's bash the establishment and the government'. With the benefit of 20:20 hindsight it is easy to see what should have happened – the scientific establishment, the Royal Society and the appropriate Research Councils should have cried 'stop and foul' long and loud, but given the furore at the time it is also easy to see and understand why those with the knowledge and evidence decided not to join in with the media's feeding frenzy. But let us hope that the next time, and there will be a next time, science will have learnt its lessons, grown up a bit and got a lot more confident, and that scientists will put their expert heads up to be listened to and counted.

A fairly constant debate within science and indeed certain parts of the media is whether only journalists with a scientific background or training should (be allowed to) write science stories. My initial thought is: what would a journalist trained as an astrophysicist know about palaeobotany, and how would his or her background help unlock these other branches of science for the lay reader? I'll leave you to ponder that thought. But, my mind goes back to when I started working within the scientific milieu in 1985. I had come from a background far removed from science – art, design, trade unionism and public relations. So, I thought I'd better do a bit of mugging up, sorry, research. Given that I knew that much of my new job was to act as an intermediary between scientists and the media I invited myself to spend some days with a random sample of science and medicine editors and correspondents on national newspapers. I wanted to find out what they did, how they did it and what they wanted from someone like me. Many things struck me about those very well spent days and about the characters I met – to a person they were friendly, helpful and welcoming (I think they were rather surprised that anyone was interested), they had prodigious memories, especially for scientific contacts (remember that this was years before the web and Google), they were highly skilled writers (as you would expect), they listened intently, they asked only key and relevant questions of their interviewees and, to a person, not one of them had any scientific or medical training or background, and they rarely got anything wrong. They were professional journalists who happened to specialise in science and a lesson I learnt was that their lack of knowledge helped enormously. Their thesis was that if the scientist could explain it to them so that they understood the story, then they could explain it to their readers (listeners and viewers). After all the media is in business to communicate its content to its audience in a form and manner that every 'reader' can understand every story.

But does this small historical observation contribute to the debate? Of course I would love to see every journalist have a much greater knowledge and appreciation of science, but there again I would love to see every journalist have a greater knowledge of the law, economics, education and why not gardening and cookery. In fact I would love it if we all knew a whole heap more about everything – but will we, can we? – I doubt it. On the other side I would love it if more and more scientists took to their keyboards to write for the media, but of course only if they could actually write in audience-friendly ways, in other words the way that the media produces copy every single day. But in reality I don't want too much of this, because I want those scientists to get on with their science, to increase our knowledge of the universe and the world around us, and the people and organisms that inhabit our planet. So I want scientists to do science and journalists to do journalism – the essential bit is in the middle where the two professions meet each other for mutual benefit. So, perhaps we can put aside this rather arcane debate and just get on with doing our respective jobs, respecting each other's professionalism and accepting that sometimes journalists, like scientists, will get something wrong.

In the last 25 years since Sir Walter Bodmer published his report and COPUS, the Royal Society's Committee on the Public Understanding of Science, was formed the whole territory and, more importantly, the attitudes of science and scientists have changed dramatically. I started running media training courses for my organisation at the same time as the Bodmer Report came out, and I can clearly remember in those early days that great slabs of what should have been skills training time was taken up with often vitriolic attacks on the media by my 'students'. The accusations were usually on the basis of trivialisation, inaccurate quotations, not including all the facts and detail, or getting the facts wrong. The events recounted, at length, were overwhelmingly second-hand – they had allegedly happened to someone else. I often wondered whether these attendees actually wanted to improve their own skills in dealing with the media, or whether they had simply turned up for a senior common room (for they were mainly academics) boxing match – a good old rant. But over time and in an exemplary Darwinian way the great number of delegates have evolved – although there is of course always the odd throwback. Today they want to interact with the media, they want to know how to go about it more effectively and efficiently, many have ambitions and aspirations to become programme presenters, or the regularly called-upon expert to sit on TV sofas. They clearly understand that science and its implications and applications should be, and are, part of the lives we all live. They seem to understand that trivialisation is the pejorative term for making things accessible and interesting to the lay audience. They realise that a 300- or 400-word news story can never contain, nor should it, all the statistics, meta-detail and caveats found in the 5000-word peer-reviewed scientific journal paper. They seem to get the rather obvious idea that if you don't want to be quoted by a journalist then don't say it, and, even better, anticipate the questions you might be asked and think very carefully so that you can prepare some well-chosen and apparently impromptu quotes. And quotes that have colour, imagery and resonate with the audience.

They also understand the idea that a journalist has neither the time nor the specialist knowledge to read and comprehend the full journal paper. Therefore, it is up to the scientist to ensure that the journalist understands the data, the facts, the results, the implications and applications.

I have ruminated on why this evolutionary change has come about, and again my very non-scientific analysis has thrown up a whole raft of independent and non-independent variables:

- a lot of the old academic ivory tower dinosaurs have retired and/or died taking with them their anti-popular-communication and insularity with them;
- in almost every academic department there are now role models of colleagues who regularly and happily interact with the media – and that activity has not hurt the academic credibility or career prospects of those individuals;
- there are numerous examples where a well-placed news story has led to extra research funding and collaborations with researchers from another discipline and often another country;
- more and more journals, and especially the high-impact ones, are issuing regular media/news releases in the hope of getting increased coverage for the science and increased profile for the journal – inevitably this has involved the author of the paper;
- the major funding bodies and especially the research charities have entered the media process, again both to increase the profile of the science and the organisation, often as part of a fundraising programme;
- just about every university and higher education institution wants to increase its profile with the public, and especially potential students, by telling the world via the media about its excellent research outputs;
- there is an increasing general acceptance that as much research is carried out by monies from the public purse, then the public have a right to know the results; and,
- communicating with the public via the media is now an acceptable activity as it increases the public profile and awareness of the specific scientific discipline and by extension all science.

The last 25 years have also seen the development of 'science communi-cation' as an evolving scientific sub-discipline and as a specific and acceptable career pathway. We now have international and national conferences and journals devoted to the subject as well as professional associations and email discussion fora. We now have international and national programmes of research funding, from major research char-ities, from research councils and from the EU Framework Programme. We now have Chairs – professorships – in the public understanding, awareness, appreciation, communication, engagement, etc. – perm any one from many – of science. We now have annual prizes and lectures that recognise excellence in science communication. We even have government committees and regular reports devoted to the exhortation and promotion of science to the lay public. Many newspapers have specialist science supplements or pages, although these do wax and wane on the back of rises and falls in advertising revenue. Newspapers and magazines sponsor and run science writing competitions. The BBC has its 'years of science', where extra commissioning and programme resources are brought to bear to increase science output across all its channels.

25 PB

So, after the first 25 years PB – post-Bodmer – public understanding, public awareness, public engagement and dialogue have become not just acceptable, but almost a part of the individual responsibility of every researcher and scientist, and using the media to reach tens or hundreds of thousands of people is seen to be both efficient and effective. And the media, as ever in responsive mode to this increasing mass, have played their part and covered more science. Overall it's all been rather a success.

Key resources

The copy below has been taken from the home pages of various organisations. These are sites that I regularly visit and find useful:

Psci-com (www.intute.ac.uk/pscicom) is a gateway to evaluated, high-quality Internet resources relating to public communication of science, public engagement with science and the impact of science on society. It is aimed at science promotion practitioners, scientists wishing to communicate their science to lay audiences, researchers, science educators and anyone with an interest in science and society. In addition, Psci-com provides a bibliographic database called *Psci-comLit* of references to books, reports, journal and newspaper articles.

AlphaGalileo (www.alphagalileo.org) is Europe's leading online service for the best of news releases and other information from science, health, technology, the arts, humanities, social sciences and, recently, business. The news service, which is moderated, is provided by the independent not-for-profit organisation, AlphaGalileo Foundation Ltd. *We only occasionally originate news material or write releases. We act as bridge between the research community and the media. We receive science news from prominent scientific organisations and disseminate it on their behalf to the world's media. We provide 24/7 access to press releases,* *event details, publications, multimedia items and broadcast media, reporting on the recent developments in research.*

Science Media Centre (www.sciencemediacentre.org) is an independent venture working to promote the voices, stories and views of the scientific community to the national news media when science is in the headlines.

ABSW (www.absw.org.uk) *For over 60 years, the Association of British Science Writers (ABSW) has helped those who write about science and technology. Our members are journalists, broadcasters and science-based communications professionals.*

STEMPRA (www.stempra.org.uk) is an informal network set up to bring together people working in science communication. *We offer the opportunity for people to get together and share information and expertise – events, a newsletter and email discussion list.* (STEMPRA stands for Science, Technology, Engineering, Medicine Public Relations Association.)

11

Dealings with the U.S. media

When I train young U.S. scientists in communication, I begin by laying out some sobering facts about the state of science coverage in the American media today. It's a marvel most don't just give up right there.

Science journalism, as a press specialty in the U.S., has been decimated by technologically and economically impelled changes in the media industry. Perhaps most notably, and as documented by Cristine Russell of the Harvard Kennedy School, the number of specialized U.S. newspaper science sections has shrunken by more than two-thirds over the past two decades – from 95 in 1989 to 31 in 2009 [1]. This dismaying saga was capped in 2009 when the *Boston Globe*, located in a city that is a Mecca of the biotech industry, cut its Monday Health/ Science section.

And not only are entire science sections disappearing. According to Russell's study, those that remain are shifting their coverage to softer topics, like consumer health and fitness. It all reflects a broad judgment, on the part of newspaper editors and owners, that more serious science coverage just doesn't pull in enough profit. With newspapers struggling, rather than boasting the huge margins of previous decades, the science beat can no longer be subsidized by the shrinking revenues drawn in by other parts of the paper [2]. More generally, as the remaining science coverage shifts online, and to lower-paying venues like blogs, science writers are having an increasingly difficult time piecing together a career.

Science news on television, too, appears to be getting worse. In late 2008, CNN cut its entire science, space, and technology unit. The most prominent departure: Miles O'Brien, who covered the 2003 space

Successful Science Communication, ed. D. J. Bennett and R. C. Jennings. Published by Cambridge University Press. © Cambridge University Press 2011.

shuttle *Columbia* disaster for the network. CNN's move, once again, hints at a broader trend. Just one minute out of every 300 on U.S. cable news is now devoted to science and technology.

Faced with such facts, it is very difficult to convince American scientists not to give up – that they mustn't abandon communication efforts, but should instead redouble them. But that's precisely what I argue. To put forward the case for this "once more unto the breach" philosophy, I make the following observations:

First, though the media may be falling down on the job, science is in fact more relevant to public policy and decision-making than ever. So if the press can no longer explain that relevance, the crucial task necessarily falls to scientists themselves. There is simply no one else to do the job.

Second, when it comes to the media we must be careful of idealism and wishful thinking, and instead embrace a sober realism. As Matthew Nisbet of American University has often put it, you have to deal with the media you have, rather than the media you would wish to have.

Third, while the media is hardly living up to its responsibility for covering science, the truth is that fault lies on both sides of the divide. As a group, American scientists have not exactly been media friendly over the years. From the snubbing of Carl Sagan by his peers (some of whom considered the great communicator not a great enough scientist), to the continuing failure to reward successful communication in academia, the scientific community has often acted – either directly or indirectly – to discourage greater media outreach in its ranks.

So if the media has failed in its job, scientists haven't made things any easier. Indeed, there has been a longstanding arms-length relationship with both the press and the U.S. public, one reflected in surveys of U.S. scientists showing they overwhelmingly distrust both. I won't soon forget the headline from a 2009 Pew Research Center survey underscoring this fact: *"Public Praises Science; Scientists Fault Public, Media."*

If scientists desire better relations with the remainder of the traditional U.S. media – now denuded of many of its science journalists – I advise them to first try to get inside the mindset of a general-interest journalist. The exercise can be very valuable, but it requires a serious and open attempt to see the world through a truly alien intellectual framework.

In my experience, it helps if scientists can try to envision the divide between themselves and general-interest journalists as a kind of "two cultures" rift, of the sort made famous by the British novelist and scientist C.P. Snow. It is a rift in which two smart and talented groups of people, both devoted to the search for "truth" in its broadest sense, nevertheless often fail to communicate or understand one another due to their very different sets of norms, assumptions, and practices.

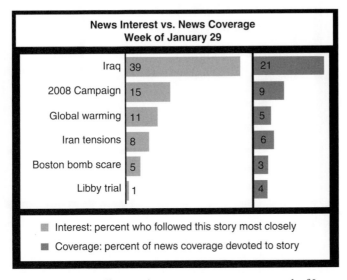

Figure 11.1 U.S. media news interest vs. news coverage, week of January 29, 2007. Used with permission from "Too Much Anna Nicole, But the Saga Attracts an Audience," *Weekly News Interest Index*, February 16, 2007, Pew Research Center For the People and the Press, a project of the Pew Research Center.

To see these "two cultures" in action, just time warp back to the week of January 29, 2007 (Figure 11.1). For science in the news, it was a very significant time: This was the week that the United Nations' Intergovernmental Panel on Climate Change (IPCC) released its *Fourth Assessment Report* – a once-in-five-years event in which the IPCC provides a new and definitive update on our scientific understanding of this most urgent of problems. And indeed, according to the Pew Research Center for People and the Press [3], the U.S. media dedicated roughly 5 percent of its news coverage to climate change that week. Not exactly generous, but not awful, either. Other leading topics that week: The Iraq war (21%), the 2008 presidential campaign (with the election still well over a year away, 9%), and the Scooter Libby trial (4%).

However, global warming is not a story that goes away in a week. Especially when the science only gets definitively updated once every half decade, you might think journalists would dig in and provide some depth and sustained coverage. Enter the "two cultures": by the next week,

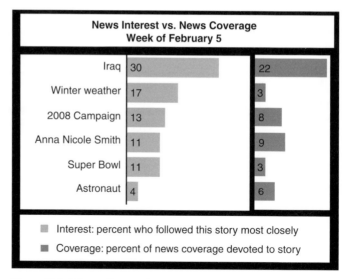

Figure 11.2 U.S. media news interest vs. news coverage, week of February 5, 2007. Used with permission from "Too Much Anna Nicole, But the Saga Attracts an Audience," *Weekly News Interest Index*, February 16, 2007, Pew Research Center For the People and the Press, a project of the Pew Research Center.

global warming had vanished from the leading news stories entirely (Figure 11.2). It was supplanted by, among other topics, the Super Bowl (3%), the death of supermodel and reality TV personality Anna Nicole Smith (9%), and the bizarre tabloid story of an astronaut love triangle (6%).

This small snapshot of the difference between scientific and journalistic priorities can help us begin to understand why these two ships too often pass in the night. Their mandates are vastly different. So are their views of the world – and of each other.

Indeed, one major factor driving the divide is that in the U.S., both scientists and journalists tend to have negative, stereotyped opinions of those in the other camp.

On the journalist side, there is much derision of wonky, nerdy scientists. According to a 1997 *Freedom Forum* report, 62 percent of the U.S. journalists surveyed considered scientists "*so intellectual and immersed in their own jargon that they can't communicate with journalists or the public*" [4]. The disdain was well captured in a 2008 *Newsweek* article by journalist Malcolm Jones, who wrote of Charles Darwin: "*[He] was hardly even a scientist in the sense that we understand the term – a highly trained specialist whose professional vocabulary is so arcane that he or she can talk only to other scientists*" [5].

But – voila the "two cultures" – scientists often think no better of journalists. In the aforementioned 2009 Pew survey, 76 percent of U.S. scientists considered it a *major problem* that the news media did not distinguish between findings that are *well-founded* and those that aren't; and 83 percent ranked TV news coverage of science as *"fair or poor"* [6]. Griping about the press today qualifies as a time-honored scientific pastime. Some scientists, scorched by a negative media encounter, will simply refuse to engage again or to return a journalist's call.

Why is there such negativity, occurring on both sides of the divide? The reason, I believe, is that journalistic and scientific values are extremely different – a situation that tends to generate vast misunderstandings (as well as, at times, sweeping denunciations).

In particular, the professional norms of journalists are often hard to square with scientific priorities. As seen in the January 29 vs. February 5, 2007 media pattern above, press coverage is often episodic and event-driven – always in search of the dramatic and the new. Science, in contrast, is a *process* of sustained inquiry. So if scoop-chasing journalists seize upon a few isolated scientific publications or events, and ignore this underlying hum of activity, they will very likely misrepresent or oversimplify what is really going on.

Indeed, this unhealthy approach to covering science sets the stage for what has been called "whiplash journalism" [7]. The phenomenon occurs when reporters pounce upon one study with a striking implication; then drop it; and then later pounce on another study with an opposite or even directly contradictory finding. Whiplash journalism is a particular problem in the coverage of medical research [8] (*Drink coffee! Oops, never mind, don't drink coffee!* [9]) but it also bedevils coverage of controversial subjects like human cloning (a sheep cloned [1997]! A human cloned [2002]! Oops, never mind [2002, a few hours later]!).

And that's just a small sampling of the different assumptions driving scientists and journalists. Among scientific complaints about the media, perhaps none causes more wall-punching and hair-tearing than the problem of unthinking "balance."

The ideal of objectivity is a central norm in the news business, and in the abstract, quite an admirable one. In practice, however, what "objectivity" often means is that in their coverage, journalists refuse to take sides in an ongoing political or public debate. Rather, they employ "balance." They give both sides an equal say.

Alas, such an approach can lead to big problems when it comes to the coverage of science. If journalists naively apply a "balanced" story

model when covering topics like evolution or climate change–
where there really aren't two valid "sides" of the issue – then they are
virtually guaranteed to mislead their readers. These aren't actually
scientific "debates." Covering them as such amounts to printing
misinformation [10].

Scientists' gripes about journalistic coverage have much substantive basis, then. But – the "two cultures" again – many scientists also
have unrealistic expectations of journalists. Consider: a 2001 survey of
Dutch scientists [11] found that nearly 80 percent thought journalists
should comprehensively present the results of scientific research – but
media time and space considerations make this simply impossible.
Ninety percent of the scientists, meanwhile, felt journalists should let
scientists review their articles prior to publication (a condition few
journalists would submit to, as it calls into question their integrity
and independence from their sources, as well as likely interfering with
deadline constraints). Furthermore, 50 percent of the scientists thought
journalists should be *obliged* or *required* to make the changes that the
scientist reviewer required to their copy. No self-respecting journalist
would submit to this arrangement.

The scientists in this Dutch survey – and in my experience, many
U.S. scientists share a similar perspective – seem to think journalism
should undergo something akin to scientific peer review. Alas, anyone
holding such views is making a huge category error. Journalism isn't
science, shouldn't be, and indeed, can't be. If scientists set their expectations unreasonably high, they will continually be disappointed, and
their media encounters will be unsuccessful or worse.

And so – to use another of C.P. Snow's famous phrases – we must
move away from a situation of *"mutual incomprehension"* between scientists and journalists. That's especially the case in light of the present-day
disappearance of science journalists from the traditional media. If any
group stood well positioned to bridge the "two cultures" gap between
scientists and journalists, it was they. Now that they're vanishing, we
are all going to need a lot more understanding, and a lot more humility.

So what should scientists – once they grasp this "two cultures"
analysis, and have tried to look upon the world as a journalist might –
do to promote better media encounters, both for themselves and for
the journalists involved?

The first critical step for a scientist who expects or seeks media
encounters is preparation. Or to continue the Shakespearean invoca-
tions, *"the readiness is all."* Not only can preparedness help ensure
that inquiring journalists get what they're looking for in scientist

interviews. It can also ensure that scientists themselves are protected from occasional bouts of reportorial irresponsibility, or what I have called *"drive-by"* media encounters.

Sadly, the phrase is apt. While they're hardly the norm, there are certainly irresponsible journalists in the world who will burn a scientist and never look back. If anything, such journalists are probably more likely to be encountered by scientists today, thanks to the demise of science journalism.

But there are also many techniques for detecting and avoiding these hack reporters, or at least handling them very carefully. An essay like this one can hardly do a comprehensive job covering all of these techniques; entire books, like Cornelia Dean's *Am I Making Myself Clear?* [12], or the Union of Concerned Scientists' *A Scientist's Guide to Talking with the Media* [13], have been written to help scientists deal with reporters. The points below are broadly consistent with these more in-depth treatments – and I've been much influenced by them – but are no substitute for reading such texts in their entirety.

The first aspect of readiness involves knowing what type of journalist you're dealing with. The differences between a telephone interview for a long lead-time magazine story, and an in-studio TV interview for a program airing later that afternoon, are vast. Here is my rather cynical take on some of the differences across media, just to help you set your expectations low (in the hope of being pleasantly surprised):

- *TV/Documentary*: Be filmed for an hour, and find your words reduced to a 20-second sound bite.
- *Newspaper/Magazine*: Talk for an hour and help educate a very smart, capable journalist, only to find the story takes months to run or never appears. Or when it appears, you're not even quoted at all.
- *Radio Talk Show*: Talk for half an hour, and then wait for other smart people (and conspiracy theorists) to join in by phone.

And when it comes to media preparedness, you mustn't merely determine what medium the interview will be for. You also need to know something about the different *types* of journalists working within a particular medium. As an example, take newspapers. Just within this single branch of the media, there are a number of different press personalities you may encounter, either directly or indirectly. Once again, my cynical take:

- *Editors:* Often don't know much about the details of the topic, but will try to sex things up, insert lots of pop culture references. May also write sensational headlines and captions.
- *Political Writers:* Want to know who's ahead, who's behind, and where there's conflict. May never talk to you again.
- *Science Writers:* A struggling breed who care about the details of your work and know something about research norms and processes.

In light of this complexity, it greatly behooves a scientist who is expecting media calls, and feels some trepidation about the matter, to gather background information on any journalist who makes an inquiry *before* agreeing to a formal interview. I like to call this the *"IRS Principle,"* in reference to the U.S. tax collecting agency, the Internal Revenue Service.

Consider: if the IRS is calling you (and this story assumes you have caller ID) you probably don't want to pick up the phone and start gabbing right away. Rather, you will let the phone ring and the IRS can leave a message. That way you can figure out what the inquiry is about, gather your thoughts and any appropriate documents, and only *then* phone back.

It's the same with journalists (although they are considerably less intimidating!). Here are some things you might want to know before agreeing to a media interview:

- *What type of journalist has contacted you? What has he/she written on before? How much does he/she already know about the subject?*
- *What angle will the story take? Is it decided yet? Who else is being interviewed?*
- *Has this journalist had a long career? Been involved in any controversies?*

How to gather such information? Well, a Quick Lexis–Nexis [14] search should find most previous stories, and perhaps any previous controversies. From such a search, you can learn about the length of the journalist's career, the kinds of subjects he or she has covered, and also whether his or her stories have drawn many complaints. For instance, Lexis–Nexis archives story corrections, and letter exchanges occasioned by published articles. If those have occurred, you can find them.

Many of the other questions can be put directly to the journalist by your institution's public affairs officer (assuming you have one). Use this officer to gather background information about the interview before setting it up formally. Or, if you're feeling confident enough, you can also ask a journalist these questions yourself by phone. Then, once you're satisfied you know what you need to know, you can ask for a little time to collect your thoughts (this is a smart idea that Cornelia Dean suggests in *Am I Making Myself Clear?* [12]) and then get back in touch.

If the journalist makes first contact by email rather than by phone – a practice that is increasingly common these days, especially when the writer is not on a tight deadline – the same principles apply. You can call back to gather more background information before consenting to the interview, or have a public affairs officer do this intermediary work for you. Or, you can email back, provisionally consenting to the interview but asking for more information first.

Note: As you gather information about the reporter and his or her story, don't make it look as though you are trying to protect yourself. Don't appear timid or defensive. Rather, explain your requests by observing that the more you know about what the reporter is looking for and how much background he or she has in the subject, the more helpful you can be.

Throughout all of this, bear in mind that it is very important not to put a journalist off for too long. From the very start, you should know the reporter's deadline and plan to make yourself available in a timely way. If there is a very tight deadline (like, say, three hours), you may have to make a judgment call about whether you can really gather much background on the reporter and still help him or her. But for the vast majority of media encounters, there's no reason you should have to go in blind or unprepared.

Finally, let me add that scientists who are more experienced with the press can and will skip many of these steps. They simply won't need them, as media interactions become more of a normal affair, and instincts develop that can substitute for stepwise preparation. But if you're just starting out in dealing with the press, and feel any anxiety about the matter, I would advise that you don't cut corners – at least not until you've found a real comfort zone.

The next thing to bear in mind, once you're ready for a media encounter, is what kinds of behaviors you should and shouldn't engage in when talking with a journalist. In short, some media "dos and don'ts."

Once again, book-length treatments go into much more depth. But let's do what we can, beginning with the "don'ts":

- *Don't Get Angry:* You're making yourself – not the science – into the story.
- *Don't Blast Fax or Email Spam Journalists:* You're making yourself an annoyance.

- *Don't Be a Publicity Hound:* It makes reporters highly skeptical of you.
- *Don't Talk Down to Journalists:* Rather, treat them like smart students.
- *Don't Be Pedantic or Nitpicky:* It's not helping anybody. If you don't like a journalist's analogy, give a better one. Journalists *need* analogies.
- *Don't Linger on One Bad Story:* "It's fish and chips," as the British expression goes. Or, by the time you read it in the paper and get upset about it, that same newspaper is being used to wrap fish and chips all across London.

There are some common themes here, of course. You should aim to be helpful, but not cloying. You should aim to be available, but not demanding. You should aim to be flexible, and not rigid. You should aim to be likeable, but not defensive. And so on.

Applying the same principles, there are also many things you should feel entirely comfortable doing in media encounters – like the following:

- *Do Offer to Read Passages for Accuracy:* Just passages, not the whole article. And just offer, don't demand.
- *Do Cultivate Relationships:* Journalists are very busy people. So never overload them. But you can send them email FYIs, especially to the *right* journalist, one who will find it relevant.
- *Do Complain about Bad Coverage and Point out Mistakes*: Make your argument cogently and seriously, and without attacks or insults. Most journalists will listen.
- *Do Admit It When You Don't Know Something, or Are Out of Your Expertise*: It is no scandal. It just makes you human.

Once our increasingly media-savvy scientists have learned about the journalistic mindset, about how to screen journalists, and about basic rules for interacting with them – in short, the basic content above – they've probably gone about 50 percent of the way towards being really effective.

Alas, the remainder of the media odyssey is harder, because it requires considerable thought and creativity. Not all scientists will be equally adept at this stage. Some will excel, some will hesitate.

The next task, you see, involves figuring out what it is you actually want to *say* to a journalist. It involves designing your media "message," a critical device in helping you to stay on topic, avoid comments you'll later regret, and just generally convey what *you* want to get across, rather than what the journalist considers to be amusing, entertaining, sexy, or whatever else.

First, let's begin with some attributes that your "message" should have, before getting into more detail about how to design it. It should feature the following characteristics:

- *Brevity:* Whatever it is that you want to say, can you say it succinctly? Can you explain your research or your story in 150 words? At a cocktail party? In an elevator? To your 80-year-old grandmother?
- *De-Jargonization:* Have you made sure you aren't using any words that don't easily bridge the science–journalist culture gap – like "theory"? Like "mouse models"? Like "probability distribution function"?
- *Personalization:* Have you thought of a way to make your story relevant to broad audiences, or to particular journalists, rather than just to your fellow scientists? Why would someone who isn't one of your research peers actually *care*?

In designing your message, and preparing to deliver it, you should also be conversant with at least three important communication "technologies," or techniques, that all of the pros understand (albeit only intuitively in many cases). As usual, there are actually far more techniques than these (read those books cited above and below!), but I consider these to be the most essential.

The first such technology is "framing." The term itself refers to a vast body of research [15] – and a vast debate – that can hardly be done justice here. But let's engage in some "framing" ourselves, and pare down that complexity into a manageable format.

The core point is that when you design your media message, you should be aware that you can't possibly say everything about your particular topic, and wouldn't want to. Not only is there too much information, but that information has the potential to be organized into multiple different *kinds* of stories (or narratives, or frames) that you might tell about your research.

Each story reduces the complexity to a more manageable format – but that's not all. In addition, different types of stories have very different impacts on different audiences. Indeed, different stories have different appeal, and will affect the size of audience that you'll be able to reach.

What this means is that when communicating about science, not every storyline ought to be: *"I have a new study out that shows X."* Such a scientific, or technical, frame can limit the amount of interest in what you have to say.

In contrast, oftentimes stories about science can also be told employing economic, political, or moral frames, rather than purely scientific ones. So for instance, if you watch Carl Sagan's *Cosmos*, you will immediately see that Sagan did not frame his story as a technical one about the intricacies of astronomy or astrophysics. While technical details are sometimes included, Sagan *framed* his story as being about something vastly larger – our place in the universe, and what studying it reveals about ourselves and the meaning of human existence. No wonder *Cosmos* was ultimately seen by 500 million people around the world!

Granted, moving beyond the realm of the purely scientific can be a delicate matter for a researcher. It can be uncomfortable. But it is critical to realize that this move often greatly broadens a message's appeal and its potential audience.

The second important technique or technology is called "bridging." It is particularly critical for television and radio interviews, because it allows a communicator to remain on message essentially no matter what the interviewer asks.

At the outset, it is crucial to emphasize that bridging has absolutely nothing to do with dodging an interviewer's questions or failing to answer them. As a rule, dodging questions is a risky media strategy that can lead to hectoring cross-examination and extreme embarrassment. My advice: *Just don't do it* – ever!

In contrast, deft "bridging" involves directly addressing whatever question you are being asked, but then quickly transitioning back to what it is that *you* want to talk about. So some examples of bridges might be, *"That's an intriguing point, but I see it a bit differently . . ."* or *"I completely hear you on that, but I think it's really important to emphasize . . ."*

The final technology is the so-called "sound bite," a short, pithy, striking statement that underscores your core message and – crucially – remains fundamentally accurate on a scientific level. So for instance, *"This is the smoking gun"* is certainly a sound bite, but not one you should use unless you really mean it and can defend it. The same goes for *"We've never seen anything like it . . .," "This could revolutionize our understanding . . .,"* and so on. Sound bites must be handled carefully.

The theory behind using sound bites is simple and pretty incontrovertible. For television interviews, and also for many radio programs, media time constraints are often very dramatic. So journalists film or record lengthy interviews with their sources, but they only wind up using a small snippet of the interview – and that snippet is often the best, most memorable sound bite.

Given this media reality, the failure to master sound bites can be tantamount to ensuring that your voice simply won't be heard. Indeed, if you don't deliver any sound bites, it's quite possible your entire interview will end up on the cutting room floor.

To see examples of effective "sound bites," I would advise watching science-related segments that appear in the mass television media. A report on ABC's *"Good Morning America"* entitled *"Science Rocks!"*, which originally aired on June 1, 2008 and can be watched online provides an excellent example [16].

In this very positive three minute and twenty-one second segment, the program (viewed by well over a million people) reported on the World Science Festival – an initiative seeking, as the show put it, to turn *"geek chic."* In obeisance to this storyline, the sound bites that made it into the segment largely involved commentary on how to make science fun, interesting, and have broader appeal, and included the following:

- Film director Doug Liman: *"I actually think that scientists are the new sexy."*
- MIT robotics engineer Cynthia Breazeal: *"I think the stereotype is kind of the older, engineer, Dilbert kind of persona. And if you're a girl in high school looking at that, it's like, are you going to think about engineering or computer science as a career?"*
- NASA planetary researcher Chris McKay: *"There's two fields that always seem to attract kids and lure them into science, even if they don't end up in it. One is dinosaurs, the other is space programs. So I'm saying, let's talk about sending dinosaurs to Mars!"*

Hopefully, it will be apparent why these sound bites were striking and effective. In the case of the last one, it was by far the most memorable part of the segment, because it caused the ABC interviewer to laugh and play along. The result was not only good television, but an overwhelming impression of NASA's McKay as a likeable, entertaining, *fun* scientist – which is pretty much the best image one can project on a general-interest program like *"Good Morning America."*

I am well aware some of these communication techniques may make some researchers feel uncomfortable. There is even a view held by some in the scientific community that strategically packaging one's research, in order to broaden its appeal and make it more communicable, represents a form of corruption or dishonesty.

I strongly disagree. To me, none of the techniques described here involve putting out skewed information or misinformation. All communications from scientists to the public should be rigorously accurate and honest – but that doesn't mean they can't also be humorous, insightful, gripping, or entertaining.

Another criticism – and the *"Good Morning America"* sound bites seem sure to trigger this one – is that to communicate in this way is tantamount to "dumbing down" the science. And indeed, there's a sense in which it's true. The *"Good Morning America"* segment did not contain a lot of technical detail about scientific findings. It was not an educational program.

However, the segment did convey a very positive image of scientific research to a broad, general audience. And I would argue that when you get to audiences numbering in the millions, something like "dumbing down" is simply unavoidable, and not to be lamented – because audiences this large simply can't be captivated by scientific detail and nuance in the way that more specialized audiences can be. Or at least, so the programs' producers assume.

That's an assumption scientists would do well to recognize – and they should work with the journalists involved, rather than embracing an unhelpful purism. Different segments of the public require different communication approaches, and some viewers who enjoyed or were intrigued by the *"Good Morning America"* segment will be inspired and motivated to learn more on their own – including by attending an event like the World Science Festival, for which the segment provided excellent publicity. Once again, that's an overwhelmingly positive outcome – and the scientists quoted above were able to be part of it because they spoke memorably, on camera, in sound bites.

When it comes to learning how to effectively communicate science through the media, there is vastly more that might be said. One could go into added detail about how to design media messages, how to frame scientific information, or even how to dress to appear on camera (and what kinds of body language ticks to avoid). This chapter makes no pretension to cover this vast amount of ground. However, it clearly underscores how important it is that scientists begin to understand the media, to think like journalists, and to prepare themselves for press encounters. In the end, a more scientifically informed public – and a more publically attuned scientific community – will be the desirable, and indeed magnificent, result.

References

1 Cristine Russell, "Covering Controversial Science: Improving Reporting on Science and Public Policy." Working Paper, Spring 2006. Data updated after personal communication with the author.

2 For the best account of this trend in the newspaper industry see Alex Jones, *Losing the News: The Future of the News that Feeds Democracy*, Oxford University Press, 2009.

3 Pew Research Center, "Too Much Anna Nicole, But the Saga Attracts an Audience," February 16, 2007, available online at http://pewresearch.org/pubs/413/too-much-anna-nicole-but-the-saga-attracts-an-audience

4 Jim Hartz and Rick Chappell, "Worlds Apart: How the Distance Between Science and Journalism Threatens America's Future," First Amendment Center, Freedom Forum, 1997.

5 Malcolm Jones, "Who Was More Important: Lincoln or Darwin?" *Newsweek*, July 7–14, 2008.

6 Pew Research Center, "Public Praises Science; Scientists Fault Media, Public," July 9, 2009, available online at http://people-press.org/report/528/

7 Andrew Revkin, "Climate Experts Tussle over Details: Public Gets Whiplash," *New York Times*, July 29, 2008.

8 Susan Dentzer, "Communicating Medical News – Pitfalls of Health Care Journalism," *The New England Journal of Medicine*, 360 (2009), 1–3.

9 Nicholas Bakalar, "Coffee as a Health Drink? Studies Find Some Benefits," *New York Times*, August 15, 2006.

10 For a further deconstruction of media "balance," see Chris Mooney, "Blinded by Science: How 'Balanced' Coverage Lets the Scientific Fringe Hijack Reality," *Columbia Journalism Review* (November–December 2004), 43, issue 4.

11 Jaap Willems, "Bringing Down the Barriers: Public Communication Should Be Part of Common Scientific Practice," *Nature*, 422 (2003), 470.

12 Cornelia Dean, *Am I Making Myself Clear?*, Harvard University Press, 2009.

13 Richard Hayes and Daniel Grossman, *A Scientist's Guide to Talking with the Media: Practical Advice from the Union of Concerned Scientists*, Rutgers University Press, 2006.

14 A widely used, searchable web-based archive of content from newspapers, magazines, legal documents and other printed sources.

15 Matthew C. Nisbet and Chris Mooney, "Science and Society: Framing Science," *Science*, 316 (2007), 56.

16 At http://abcnews.go.com/video/playerIndex?id=4973238

12
_____

Relations with public interest organisations: consumers

INTRODUCTION

Consumer organisations act as an important interface between the public and scientific developments and innovations. Our independent approach helps people to assess the implications of developments in a clear and simple way. Surveys have regularly put consumer organisations, along with other public interest organisations, among the most trusted sources of information and advice.

We therefore have an important role in communicating scientific issues and their implications to the public, as well as acting on their behalf in order to try and influence scientific and technological developments and the controls that oversee them in the consumer interest.

A BRIEF HISTORY

The consumer movement dates back to the 1950s when there was an explosion in consumer goods coming on to the market. *Which?* was established in the UK in 1957, filling a void where the public was poorly protected from unscrupulous traders and overwhelmed by the choices available. Based on the model of Consumers Union in the United States, *Which?* was set up to be independent of government and industry and this remains the case today.

Which? exists to make people as powerful as the organisations they have to deal with in their everyday lives. This includes ensuring that services are provided in the way that consumers want, whether that is financial services or healthcare. As a research-based registered charity

Successful Science Communication, ed. D. J. Bennett and R. C. Jennings. Published by Cambridge University Press. © Cambridge University Press 2011.

funded through the sale of our range of magazines and other consumer information, our not-for-profit status means that the information we provide to consumers also provides the funding for our broader policy and campaigns work on behalf of all consumers.

Science communication is fundamental to what we do. Every issue of our magazine will contain numerous product tests rating the quality, performance and value of a broad range of products. In the last year, for example, this has included such diverse reports as laser eye surgery, child car seats and weight loss products. In this way, as envisaged when we were first established, we help consumers to make sense of complex markets and make sure that they are able to buy consumer products that are safe and meet their needs.

IDENTIFYING EMERGING ISSUES

We also play an important role in alerting our members to emerging issues and through them and the media enable the wider public to keep abreast of developments that are in the pipeline. This includes distinguishing those that may offer benefits as well as those we think are a waste of time or even dangerous. There have been many examples of issues that we have reported on before they have become mainstream. We first reported on potential risks and benefits of genetically modified (GM) foods in 1989, for example, the marketing of genetic testing in 2001 and the potential impact of nanotechnologies in 2007.

Famous for our *Which?* 'best buys', we have more recently introduced 'don't buys' and now allow manufacturers to apply for a licence to use the *Which?* Best Buy icon in their advertising. This, together with our annual *Which?* Awards, recognises manufacturers who have come out best in our independent tests and analysis and helps encourage others to improve.

INFLUENCING GOVERNMENT POLICY

But *Which?* also has a much broader role. We have been behind much of the UK consumer protection legislation that we take for granted today, such as the Competition Act in 1980, Sale of Goods Act in 1979 and Toy (Safety) Regulations in 1967, tightening standards and banning the use of lead paint. In 1975, a government-funded consumer body, the National Consumer Council, now Consumer Focus, was established with which we work closely.

Through our policy and advocacy work we can sustain action on important issues, identifying areas of consumer detriment, developing policy solutions and campaigning for government and industry to address them. We work to ensure responsible development and the right level of oversight so that consumers can benefit without being put at unnecessary risk. This will often require a longer-term approach to achieve the necessary change, particularly as it is increasingly the European Union that is responsible for regulation.

As well as influencing government, we work closely with industry, trade associations and other stakeholders. We are asked for our advice and input in order to help shape the approach that companies take. Where we feel that self-regulation will achieve change more quickly and cost-effectively and the buy-in of the majority of the sector responsible can be achieved, we will support and work towards more effective industry codes. This may be particularly valuable in fast-moving areas while more formal regulation struggles to keep pace with technological development.

We will call for government regulation where we feel this is the best way to ensure consumers are properly protected, whether from unsafe products or misleading claims or advertising. We were for example involved in the development of the Responsible Nano Code which aimed to provide a clearer framework for responsible development of the technology in the absence of legislation, while also recognising that in such a diverse and fast-moving industry, consumers also need legal protection and assurance that all companies will comply. Co-regulation, a combination of the two approaches, may also be appropriate in some situations, such as controls over some forms of advertising.

IMPACT OF GLOBALISATION

The global nature of risks, regulation and the companies that consumers interact with has also meant that we increasingly have to look beyond the UK to ensure adequate levels of consumer protection and we have sister organisations in many countries. In 1960, recognising the importance of trying to co-ordinate our research, testing and advocacy work, *Which?* helped to establish the International Organisation of Consumer Unions, now Consumers International (CI), and in 1962, BEUC, the European Consumer Organisation. It is through CI, which now has over 220 members in 115 countries from all regions, that *Which?* has representation at key global decision-making bodies, such as the World Health Organization, World Trade Organization and Organisation for Economic Co-operation and Development (OECD).

It is increasingly the case that these bodies will determine the level of protection that UK consumers can expect and set the framework for risk governance. CI develops its positions in consultation with all of its membership which means that both the interests of consumers in developed and developing countries need to be reflected, although there is a lot of consensus around the key issues for consumers.

Similarly, at European level, it is BEUC, the European Consumer Organisation, that acts as the umbrella body to facilitate policy development and co-ordinated lobbying among European consumer organisations to help us ensure that EU legislation and broader policy work in the consumer interest. Current ongoing work includes trying to ensure a more robust regulatory framework for nanotechnologies by influencing reviews and implementation of relevant legislation such as the General Product Safety Directive (GPSD), the Cosmetics Regulation and the Novel Foods Regulation.

Two other important bodies help us to work more closely with consumer organisations in other countries in order to make most use of our resources and enable us to have a greater impact. International Consumer Research and Testing (ICRT) exists to co-ordinate joint testing between consumer organisations. This includes testing of a diverse range of products, including car and tyre safety. The Transatlantic Consumer Dialogue (TACD) is a more recent organisation, established to feed into EU and US discussions about policy such as the Transatlantic Economic Council, along with the Transatlantic Business Dialogue. This facilitates the development of joint policy positions which are discussed with relevant government officials from both administrations. Inevitably, the different approaches adopted by the EU and US in their regulation of new technologies such as cloning, growth hormones and genetically modified foods have been key issues for TACD. TACD policy committees are currently focused on food, intellectual property, information society, nanotechnologies, climate change and financial services.

In terms of standardisation, we work with ANEC, the European consumer voice in standards setting, which in turn works to influence European (CEN) and International Standards Organisation (ISO) standards. Our testing work is often based on the applicable ISO or British Standards Institute (BSI) standard, but our product testing can sometimes flag up areas where improvements are needed, such as in the case of energy efficiency testing of washing machines to reflect real use.

TWO-WAY RISK COMMUNICATION

Risk communication is a fundamental part of our work and of consumer organisations in general. We need to be able to communicate complex scientific issues to consumers in a balanced way that sets out the main issues (often in the space of a two-page article). But we also have an important role ensuring that communication is two-way, so that consumer attitudes and concerns are also taken into account by industry and regulators. We therefore conduct research in order to understand public reactions to developments so that we can ensure that our policy and associated advocacy work addresses and represents consumer interests.

Our campaigning work also focuses on ensuring that decision-makers listen to consumers and conduct meaningful public engagement to ensure that the consumer benefits of scientific innovations are realised and adequate safeguards are put in place at the right time.

To be effective, we need to engage at a range of levels. This may include commenting on very specific product developments or working to ensure that the relevant governance framework and institutions are sufficiently consumer-focused and that key principles such as transparency, effective consumer representation, independence and precaution underpin risk regulation. One example of this was our role in establishing an independent food agency following government failure to protect consumer interests, brought to the fore with the bovine spongiform encephalopathy (BSE) crisis (Davies and Todd, 1996). The Food Standards Agency was therefore set up in 2000 to put the consumer first, to operate transparently and to be evidence-based and overseen by an independent board.

THE CONSUMER PRINCIPLES

When analysing issues from a consumer perspective we will draw on our own internal expertise, whether that is expertise in understanding consumer trends, conducting market analysis and consumer research, or specific subject expertise, as well as working with external experts and laboratories.

When assessing the benefits and risks of new issues for consumers, we rely on a set of consumer principles originating from the 1960s, but still applicable today. In 1962 on 15 March (now recognised as World Consumer Rights Day), President John F. Kennedy made a speech about consumer protection and established four basic consumer rights: the right to safety; the right to be informed; the right to choose; and the right to be heard (Hilton, 2003). These have since been supplemented by a further four principles: access, quality, redress and value for money.

These principles help form the questions most people are going to ask about the implications of scientific and other developments that affect them. Sometimes they may conflict and need to be traded off against each other. Providing choice may be at odds with ensuring safety, for example, and so issues need to be looked at on a case-by-case basis.

A recent issue we have been working on, nano cosmetics, is an example of this. Our approach has had to balance the potential for a wider choice of new products with claimed benefits, such as anti-ageing properties, against potential safety concerns. We are also looking at the validity of the claims that are made and whether the claimed technological advancements are really worth paying more for. Although there is no explicit hierarchy of the principles, safety will inevitably take priority. The level of response required to address the principles may also differ, for example, aspects of quality are often left up to consumer choice and competition, whereas safety will generally be subject to regulation in some form.

These are termed the 'consumer principles' and sometimes people's interests as consumers may be different to their interests as citizens. But this distinction is becoming increasingly blurred as people want to act on broader societal concerns, whether ethical or environmental issues for example, as well as more immediate needs when buying or using consumer products.

The Consumer Principles

Access
Choice
Consumer influence and representation
Quality
Information and education
Redress
Safety
Value for money

REPRESENTATION IN POLICY DISCUSSIONS

As well as fulfilling our role representing consumer interests through our campaigning, magazines and in the media, we frequently represent consumer interests in government and industry working groups and policy committees. We will be able to provide an informed consumer perspective drawing on our research, expertise and consumer insight work.

However, broader consumer representation and engagement is also needed to ensure that scientific developments move forward in line with consumers' expectations. If the principle of consumer choice is looked at in its broader sense as well as consumers' right to be heard, people should be able to express their views about which types of developments are likely to bring benefits for them, which they could be open to under the right circumstances, and which they think are unnecessary or even threatening in some way. Decisions about how to proceed require the risks and the benefits to be assessed so that a socially acceptable level of risk and innovation can be achieved. If the public is not consulted at an early stage in the development of a new technology, its potential for consumers may never be realised or it may be pursued in a way that is of little interest, or even concern, to many consumers. Effective public engagement is also fundamental in order to gain public trust and support.

MOVING BEYOND THE THEORY

Despite a lot having been said about the importance of public engagement in recent years – for example in the UK from the House of Lords report on Science and Society (House of Lords, 2000) to the more recent work commissioned for Science for All (BIS, 2010), it is rarely done in a meaningful way. This has particularly been seen with major innovations with a broad reach and range of potential applications, such as biotechnology, nanotechnologies and, crossing both of these, synthetic biology. These types of innovations raise a complex mix of issues for science, as well as broader social and ethical issues. These all need to be understood and addressed, but often become confused.

Experience with the handling of genetic modification (GM), for example, showed that failing to involve the public at an early stage can lead to a complete breakdown in confidence and large-scale rejection of a technology. Public concern was motivated by fears of tampering with nature, together with concern that not enough was known about the long-term safety and environmental consequences, a mix of science and ethics. A failure to see any tangible benefits, compounded by an initial inability to make an informed choice due to the mixing of GM and conventional varieties, meant that many people were not prepared to accept any risk and wanted to avoid GM products in food. In contrast, people have been much more open to the use of the technology in the medical area where the benefits were more obvious and made any potential risk more acceptable.

The UK Department of Health's 'Fright Factors' (Department of Health, 1997) although developed several years ago, still help explain why GM foods have been controversial and how perceptions of safety can be closely intertwined with other considerations.

The Department of Health's Fright Factors

Risks are generally more worrying (and less acceptable) if perceived:
— to be **involuntary** rather than voluntary
— as **inequitably distributed**
— as **inescapable** by taking personal precautions
— to arise from an **unfamiliar or novel** source
— to result from **man-made, rather than natural** sources
— to cause **hidden and irreversible** damage
— to pose some particular danger to **small children or pregnant women** or more generally to **future generations**
— to threaten a form of death (or illness/injury) arousing **particular dread**
— to damage **identifiable rather than anonymous victims**
— to be **poorly understood by science**
— as subject to **contradictory statements** from responsible sources

---

Despite this experience, the same mistakes seem to be regularly repeated. Regulation frequently fails to keep pace with developments and scepticism remains about the value of public engagement.

SHAPING INNOVATION

From our experience, public engagement has to be early in the process but grounded in concrete examples to the extent that is possible, rather than discussed in the abstract. Involvement at the research stage is therefore critical. This helps to ensure that people's views can help to shape the direction of innovations and any conflicts or areas of significant concern can be identified early enough to be dealt with.

A wide range of methods and tools are now available that enable this to be done well, whatever the background people come from or their initial level of interest, such as citizens' panels and other deliberative fora. The Engineering and Physical Sciences Research Council (EPSRC) 'Grand Challenge' on nanotechnology and healthcare discussed by Professor Richard Jones in the first chapter of this book is a good example of how these can be used, as it organised a public dialogue exercise which fed directly into research prioritisation (EPSRC, 2008).

The complexity of supply chains can make it difficult to determine where and when engagement should take place. It will be too late to take account of the public's concerns by the time a product is ready to go to market, but those who are responsible for the initial development, as with carbon nanotubes that have a broad range of applications for example, may also find it difficult to assess the acceptability and implications of applications possible at a later stage. The GM example also illustrates this as, while in the mid-1990s UK retailers were talking to stakeholders about how to openly introduce and label GM foods and indeed did so successfully, US producers further up the supply chain were already mixing GM commodity crops with conventional varieties without any distinction.

INVOLVEMENT IN DECISION-MAKING

As well as feeding into discussions about the direction of scientific developments, it is also crucial to have effective public input into the policy and decision-making stages that determine the nature of developments and conditions for what is allowed onto the market. This applies to government regulatory frameworks, but also to self-regulatory approaches.

Again, this needs to begin at an early stage and in some cases, where the implications and issues raised by a particular area of research may not be immediately obvious, strategic, multi-stakeholder fora can sometimes be a useful way of identifying areas to be addressed. The Human Genetics Commission and Agriculture and Environment Biotechnology Commission in the UK set up in order to consider biotechnology developments are good examples of how this can work, bringing together a mix of interested parties to provide advice to government and try and reach agreement on contentious issues.

RISK ANALYSIS

As consumer organisations, it is our role to set out and advocate the issues we think need to be addressed within the framework legislation for the regulation of particular scientific developments in order to help get the balance right between precaution and innovation – whether at national, European or international level.

The risk analysis that determines the nature of government or industry controls is generally recognised as having three incremental but iterative stages: risk assessment, risk management and risk communication. Risk communication is about explaining the decision openly, but should also be about ensuring that there is effective public engagement throughout the whole decision-making process.

RISK ASSESSMENT

Risk assessment is where any risks are characterised and the reality of any harm resulting in practice assessed and, where possible, quantified. In order to have confidence in the ultimate decision, it is essential that risk assessment is conducted independently and transparently. In the UK and EU more broadly, it is usually the responsibility of expert scientific committees.

Input from consumers and consumer representatives is important at this scientific stage in order to ensure that the risk assessment draws on public attitudes and concerns and ensures that they are addressed. *The Government Chief Scientific Adviser's Guidelines on the Use of Scientific and Engineering Advice in Policy Making*, for example (HM Government, 2010), emphasise that *'where possible, there should be public involvement in framing the questions that experts and policy makers need to address'*.

There is also a recommendation in these Guidelines that departments and committees should consider the potential benefits that consumer or lay representatives can bring to the clear communication and transparency of the scientific advice that is provided by committees. This advice recognises that public interest or consumer representatives can provide valuable input and ensure that the questions that lay people are likely to ask are addressed, resulting in greater openness and making sure that the conclusions of the committee and any assumptions they have been made are clearly communicated.

The UK government's scientific committees that provide advice on food issues are a good example of this. As a result of a breakdown in confidence in advice that the committees gave after BSE, there was a large overhaul of their operation in order to make them more transparent and relevant. The Food Standards Agency (FSA) has issued guidance requiring its committees to hold their meetings in public and to appoint two public interest representatives, one of which should be an expert consumer representative and the other should be a lay person. Despite some initial resistance, this approach is seen to work well, helping to enhance the quality of the advice and ensure a greater degree of trust.

Wherever possible, public consultation should also be a part of the risk assessment, with draft opinions published where practical in order to ensure that there is an opportunity for all stakeholders to comment. This would include *Which?*, where we have relevant research and expertise.

RISK MANAGEMENT

Risk management includes a much more explicit consideration of consumer interests, alongside the results of the risk assessment. It is essential that policy-makers have a meaningful understanding of the public's concerns which may be safety related or could be about other ethical, social or economic considerations.

Public engagement is therefore essential in order to understand people's attitudes and help determine the advantages and disadvantages of particular risk management options. It is here that many of the consumer principles that have been outlined will need to be balanced and traded off with other economic and commercial interests, for example whether people's concerns can be dealt with by labelling or whether limits or restrictions are necessary.

Consumer organisations can have an important role at this stage, helping to set out the issues from a consumer point of view and advocating the type of approach that is necessary. This may be in the form of stakeholder groups to input into policy or more ad hoc consultation. We can help to set out the potential risks and benefits of different interventions and promote what we consider will work best for consumers based on our consumer research and understanding.

In the case of GM foods and nanotechnologies, for example, *Which?* organised in-depth citizens' panels held over a succession of days in order to provide an opportunity to set out the issues in detail from a range of perspectives and understand consumer reactions. In the case of the *Which?* nano panel (*Which?*, 2008), people became very engaged with the technology and were open to benefits, although expected adequate safeguards to be in place. Applications in medicines and healthcare were seen as most exciting, with greater concern over the safety of food and cosmetic uses. In order to ensure that we had properly assessed people's likely reaction to the use of animal cloning in food which can have ethical and welfare implications, we conducted a survey to understand people's attitudes.

A PRECAUTIONARY APPROACH

We advocate that a precautionary approach is applied to the use of new technologies and how they are regulated. This requires openness, transparency and public involvement throughout the decision-making process in order to ensure that uncertainties are made explicit and adequately addressed.

The 'precautionary principle' has formed the basis of much of the legislation that we rely on to protect public health, from tackling cholera in the nineteenth century (EEA, 2001) to ensuring chemical safety in the twenty-first century (EC, 2006), but has unfortunately become highly politicised in recent years. It is sometimes viewed as anti-innovation or anti-science since the term can be wrongly interpreted as a call for zero risk. But failure to apply precaution is likely to be far more damaging in the longer term.

Precaution is about being clear about uncertainties, carefully balancing the risks and benefits of a particular innovation or product and making sure that effective action is taken early enough to ensure that the public is protected when all of the implications may not be fully understood. Precautionary measures may take various forms such as limiting levels of a particular chemical, requiring a label or warning, not permitting a product onto the market or requiring post-market monitoring, for example.

REMIT OF REGULATION

Risk communication as the third stage of the risk analysis is, therefore, as much about effective public involvement and engagement as it is about explaining scientific developments and the policy linked to them to people.

Even when public engagement is recognised and carried out by policy-makers, it can often fail to feed into the actual policy decisions. This may be because other factors are seen to carry more weight, economically or politically, and will also depend on the extent to which the regulatory framework allows broader consumer concerns to be taken into account.

Some scientific developments may require specific cross-cutting legislation; others may be addressed by updating relevant sector-specific legislation. For some types of consumer products, government will be responsible for their close regulation. Many aspects of food production, from the use of additives to food contact materials for example, are subject to pre-market approval on a case-by-case basis based on an EU-wide risk assessment by the European Food Safety Authority. Other consumer products, such as cosmetics, are subject to general requirements that they have to be safe before they go on the market and the manufacturer will have to demonstrate how this has been ensured only if challenged.

The extent to which the risk assessment, i.e. science alone, will determine the final policy or other considerations are relevant to the decision can also vary. This again reinforces the importance of ensuring that the overarching regulatory framework recognises broader consumer interests. There is, for example, a general requirement cutting across all food legislation to take account of 'other legitimate factors' as well as the risk assessment (EC, 2002) but it has not been clear how this possibility of taking into account broader social and ethical issues will be applied in practice – particularly where the risk assessment indicates that there is no or a very low level of risk, but there may be significant ethical issues raised. The European Commission Directorate-General for Health and Consumers (DG SANCO) has, however, recently indicated that it wants a more explicit consideration of the benefits as well as the risks of innovation as part of the regulatory process (Dalli, 2010).

The international dimension is also important in this respect. Even if there is scope to take account of broader consumer issues at EU or national level, they could be open to challenge unless also reflected within international standards and trade agreements. It is therefore important that consumer interests are effectively promoted through these international bodies and their decision-making processes.

CONCLUSION

Consumer organisations therefore have an important role to play in science and risk communication and in a variety of ways. Although we are perhaps most widely recognised for the information that we provide to consumers on scientific issues, we also represent consumer interests more broadly in scientific developments.

This work can take us into a broad range of areas, from tackling issues related to specific products and specific companies to engaging with a wide range of policy-makers in order to shape the regulatory frameworks and processes that will help determine the nature of scientific developments and their oversight.

References

BIS (2010) *Science for All,* Report and Action Plan from the Science for All Expert Group, February 2010. London: Department for Business, Innovation and Skills.

Dalli, J. (2010) Innovation needs to be in tune with the broad values of society. Speech by John Dalli, Commissioner for Health and Consumer Policy, European Commission Speech/10/43, 30 March 2010. http://europa.eu/rapid/press-ReleasesAction.do?reference=SPEECH/10/143&format=HTML&aged=0&language=EN&guiLanguage=en

Davies, S. and Todd, S. (1996) The need for an independent food agency. *Consumer Policy Review,* **6,** Number 3, May/June 1996.

Department of Health (1997) *Communicating about Risks to Public Health: Pointers to Good Practice.* London: HMSO.

EC (2002) Regulation (EC) 178/2002 of the European Parliament and of the Council of 28 January 2002 laying down the general principles and requirements of food law, establishing the European Food Safety Authority and laying down procedures in matters of food safety.

EC (2006) Regulation (EC) 1907/2006 of the European Parliament and of the Council of 18 December 2006 concerning the Registration, Evaluation, Authorisation and Restriction of Chemicals (REACH).

EEA (2001) *Late Lessons from Early Warnings: The Precautionary Principle 1896–2000,* Environment Issue Report No. 22. Copenhagen: European Environment Agency.

EPSRC (2008) *Nanotechnology for Healthcare,* report prepared for the Engineering and Physical Sciences Research Council. London: EPSRC.

Hilton, M. (2003) *Consumerism in Twentieth Century Britain.* Cambridge: Cambridge University Press.

House of Lords (2000) *Science and Society.* 14 March 2000, House of Lords Science and Technology Committee, Third Report, Session 1999–2000, HL38.

House of Lords (2010) *Nanotechnologies and Food.* 8 January 2010, House of Lords Science and Technology Committee, First Report, Session 2009–2010, HL22.

HM Government (2010) *The Government Chief Scientific Adviser's Guidelines on the Use of Scientific and Engineering Advice in Policy Making, 2005.* London: HMSO.

Which? (2008) Report on the Citizens' Panel Examining Nanotechnologies Prepared by Opinion Leader, *Which?,* 2008.

13

Relations with public interest organisations: patients and families

INTRODUCTION

There have been enormous advances in scientific understanding of our basic biology, and the relationships between genetics, physiology and the ultimate appearance of diseases. Yet modern medicine still has little to offer that will alter the natural history of most diseases which cause chronic ill health, increasing disability and premature death. While an increasing number of diseases are becoming treatable, few are curable. In some cases, we even see the resurgence of diseases such as TB and polio which many thought were conquered through the development of antibiotics, vaccinations and other interventions.

Patients and families affected by, or at risk from, life-limiting diseases have a special relationship with the biomedical research community. Without a sustained commitment to high-quality research and development the conditions that affect them will continue to exert a toll on both the length and quality of their lives. This will have an impact not only on those affected today, but also on future generations. This is particularly the case when the diseases in question have a genetic cause or for which there is a substantial genetic predisposition. For patients and families in this position, research offers hope for the future. It means that, just because things are as they are today, this will not necessarily be the case in the future. Circumstances may change for the better – if not for them then for their children or for other families in this position.

Indeed the majority of patients and their families are very supportive of biomedical research. They are anxious to see its outputs translated quickly and affordably into safe effective interventions that

Successful Science Communication, ed. D. J. Bennett and R. C. Jennings. Published by Cambridge University Press. © Cambridge University Press 2011.

will address the diseases and disorders that trouble them. Supporting research can take a variety of forms. Patients worldwide raise substantial sums of money to fund academic and medical research. Often they can be the major source of funding for particular diseases, especially when these are rare and deemed to be of little interest to public or private sector funding streams. In addition, patients and relevant family members are often willing to participate in research projects directly. This can be as subjects, donating samples and providing data or, increasingly, as partners with their academic and clinical colleagues. They help to phrase the research questions, plan the investigations and recruit volunteers willing to participate in projects and clinical trials. Supporting and participating in research often benefits patients and families by giving a sense of taking control over their disease rather than being controlled by it. This can improve their psychological and emotional well-being, even if it does not substantially change their physical condition or longer-term prospects.

GETTING THE MESSAGE ACROSS

While patients and families might historically have been prepared to accept what scientists did on trust, believing that it was too difficult or too specialised to understand, this is no longer the case. Increasingly patients and families want to engage with the research community, to understand what is going on, to shape it and to help convey the message about its importance to the wider world. The emergence of partnerships between scientists and patients has been invaluable in generating public understanding of and support for investment and participation in research and development. Properly handled, this partnership can add value through the creation of synergy. Scientists can be seen as having a vested interest in a particular line of enquiry. It is, after all, their career. Patients and families, while not uninterested in the outcomes, are generally disinterested in the specifics. What they want is to be sure that resources (both human and financial) are being used to best advantage, and will produce the biggest possible 'bang' for every 'buck' invested. Given the opportunity, patients will often be eager to develop their own expertise in order to communicate the importance of biomedical research and development more effectively to a wider public as well as for their own satisfaction. How can we develop tools and strategies that will ensure that patients and families have a realistic appreciation of what is known in areas of interest to them? How can they help efforts to increase public understanding in a broader community and promote appropriate progress towards increasing that knowledge and their likelihood of being able to benefit from it?

A CLEAN SLATE?

Though it can be tempting to assume that science communication starts from scratch, and patients are empty vessels waiting to be filled, this is never the case. Although the formal science education of most citizens (patients included) may be slight, and have taken place many years ago, science and medicine have a substantial media presence, and are seen as good tools for selling newspapers and getting people to watch TV channels. However, the media agenda, with (necessarily) its emphasis on entertainment, tends to focus on a black-and-white approach which can be substantially less nuanced then we might wish. Advances in medical research are often presented as 'breakthroughs' or 'miracle cures' if they are deemed to be positive, or 'the thin end of the wedge' or 'a slippery slope' if they are not. As a result many patients will engage from a starting position that sees science as more definitive than is actually the case. After all, if the forensic use of DNA can tell with (apparent) absolute certainty whether an individual is guilty of a crime or not, surely it can do the same with regard to the future health or disease status of a person? If we can clone a sheep, we can clone a person – remember *The Boys from Brazil*, Ira Levin's 1978 novel that subsequently became a highly successful film? Getting round this can be difficult, but it's not impossible. It requires a strategy and the investment of time, energy and resources, but properly carried through this will yield a significant dividend.

CAN IT REALLY BE DONE?

When patients and patient organisations started to expect a greater effort from scientists to communicate with them about their research, some members of the scientific and clinical community feared that the message would be too complex for lay understanding. When research funding charities started putting patient representatives on scientific review panels or even setting up parallel committees to look at research proposals and determine whether or not they should be funded, there was considerable unease about the anticipated outcomes of such developments. Patients, it was assumed, would not be able to understand the complexities. Nor would they be interested in basic research, preferring to concentrate on 'near-patient' interventions and improvements in service delivery. In practice this has not been the case. Patients want good clinical services and their diseases treated as effectively as possible when no complete cure exists. But they would much rather be in a position where this was not needed because the underlying problems had been cracked by good basic research. Indeed, placing a requirement on scientists to explain to lay panels what they want to do, why it is important, how it will advance knowledge and how it relates to their experience of disease has often improved the quality of proposals. In some cases it has even increased the commitment of the applicants because they relish the challenge of justifying their ideas to the ultimate 'end-users' of their efforts. Poorly thought-out proposals can no longer be hidden in the scientific long grass! To put this partnership in place successfully requires a commitment to transparency and honesty from both parties. It needs to recognise the reality of likely achievements and the timescale to achieving them. The partnership needs to be able to resist the temptation to hope on the one hand, and to hype on the other.

SIX STEPS TOWARDS A GOAL

Patients and researchers share a common goal – the development of interventions that will treat, prevent or cure their disease. This goal can seem tantalisingly close. But like the next peak in a mountain range which on a clear day can almost seem near enough to touch, the journey from where we are to where we want to be is often long, tortuous and full of false turnings and unexpected obstacles. Sustaining the effort requires the development of shared understanding and a true partnership.

There are a number of steps that scientists can take that will succour this partnership, and help sustain the engagement of patients and families in supporting their work.

The starting point is to recognise that the patient already knows a lot about their disease. They know how they feel, and they know how their condition limits them. They know which aspects they find frustrating, or painful, or distressing even if they do not know why or how these manifestations are brought about by the failures in their underlying biology. So, the basis of effective communication between scientists and patients with the disease they wish to investigate is:

(a) State what the problem is that you wish to address. How does this fit into the bigger picture that the disease creates in the patient? Which aspect of the condition are you targeting, and how does this relate to those features which patients and families deem to be important?

(b) Be clear about what you hope to find out. Although patients may hope for breakthroughs they are generally realistic, and know that things that sound too good to be true usually are. Over-promising generates cynicism and can result in a breakdown of trust. Of course a highly competitive research funding environment (whether in the public or the private sector) creates pressure to hype but in the long run this is counter-productive and undermines the sustainability of research.

(c) If the work involves human subjects, be honest about what you want to do to your volunteers and how often you need to do it. Be straightforward about possibly painful procedures and about risks that you can anticipate (and what you can do about them if they happen). Patients appreciate that research carries uncertainties with it – otherwise it would be treatment, but try and be clear (especially with first in human work or early stage clinical trials) that the knowledge gained may not benefit them personally through any tangible amelioration of their condition. Recognise and acknowledge the disruption to family life that participation in research necessitates and negotiate ways of working that minimise this. For example, the beginning and end of the school day can be difficult times for parents, whilst older people may not want to travel until they can use their bus passes, so recognise these factors and plan for them and people will be more likely to engage with you.

(d) Pay attention to the content and the layout of any written materials. Use plain language. Write short sentences. Avoid jargon. Pay attention to the layout. Pages of densely typed script on institutional headed paper are intimidating. Patients (and families) are usually under a degree of stress due to their condition. In this situation, they are less well able to appreciate complex ideas that, under normal circumstances, they could assimilate with ease. Layout, clear spaces between blocks of text, and the use of illustrations all help to boost effective communication.

(e) Test things out before you use them in earnest. Many patient organisations will allow you to 'dry run' your communications with a 'readers' panel'. If their explanation of what the meaning is coincides with your own understanding then go ahead, but if their interpretation differs from what you think you have said then there is a problem that needs to be rectified. After all, is it easier to understand *'sibling allogenic haematopoetic stem cell transplants for haematological malignancies'* (a real example taken from a consent form) or *'taking stem cells from one brother or sister and using them for the other if they will lead to a treatment for the cancer in the blood'?*

(f) Think about the onward journey of your interaction and communication with patients. Patients will discuss the research they are involved in with their family, their friends and the wider community. They can be influential in raising the profile of the work you are doing, boosting a wider public appreciation of its significance, and helping to ensure its sustainability over the longer term. Patients want you to succeed, and they can have a significant role in helping you to achieve this – directly through their participation, and indirectly by their advocacy on your behalf.

CONCLUSION

While some scientists are natural communicators, able effortlessly to convey complex ideas in ways that non-expert listeners are able to understand and appreciate, most (like most people from other walks of life too) are not talented in this way. However with planning, a bit of training and a degree of effort, significant improvements can be made in the quality of the interactions between scientists, patients and their families. This can result in substantial gain in patients' participation in research and their cooperation with the programme protocol. It can also generate realistic expectations as to when, and what, the outcomes are likely to be. This shared understanding can boost public acceptance of the nature of scientific endeavour. It can foster a more realistic appreciation of the limits and possibilities that innovative research targeted and unmet medical needs can achieve. It can move us all on from miracle cures and slippery slopes to a more nuanced and realistic appreciation of where we are, and where we still need to go to reach our goal.

USEFUL RESOURCES/EXAMPLES OF GOOD PRACTICE

(1) For examples of literature developed by patients and professionals together on, for example, clinical trials, biobanks etc. visit www.biomedinvo4all.com/en/publications. These are a result of a joint venture by EGAN, The Patient Network for Medical Research and Roche, the global pharmaceutical company.

(2) A wide range of leaflets in most European languages developed by patients, academics and clinicians working together to explain complex genetic topics are available at www.eurogentest.org, go to 'Patient Leaflets'. These have been produced by Eurogentest, an EU-funded Network of Excellence.

(3) The Genetic Alliance UK website (www.geneticalliance.org.uk) contains samples of teaching materials, literature and other useful tools for developing accessible communications with patients, including a protocol for translating information into other languages without loss of clarify of meaning.

(4) The Science Media Centre (www.sciencemediacentre.org) runs short courses for scientists and doctors wishing to improve their ability to communicate effectively with the media and with lay audiences.

(5) Sense About Science provides information and support for clear communication on complex topics, and helps challenge misconceptions about scientific and medical topics in the media and elsewhere: visit www.senseaboutscience.org.uk. (See Chapter 6: *The common language of research*, by Tracey Brown, Managing Director, Sense About Science)

(6) PatientPartner(www.patientpartner-europe.eu) is an EU-funded project creating ways of making clinical trials more patient-friendly by developing structures and strategies that will boost understanding and engagement.

(7) Patient support groups for specific disease usually have a lot of user-friendly information for lay readers on their websites or available on request. For information on how to reach specific organisations contact the national umbrella body for the country, for example the Genetic Interest Group in the UK or VSOP (The Dutch Genetic Alliance) in the Netherlands.

Alternatively the European Patients Forum (www.europeanpatientsforum.org) or the International Alliance of Patients (www.patientsorganizations.org) should be able to guide you to the relevant contact information.

14

Relations with environmental
organisations: a very personal story

STUDENT YEARS

I was born in the Netherlands at the end of the 1950s in a society when
many people were working hard to rebuild a society destroyed by war
and fascism. As a future citizen I grew up in a world dominated by a 'cold
war' between capitalism in the West and communism in the East. While
in the 1960s they agreed a 'peaceful coexistence', liberation wars raged
in former colonies of industrial nations, which later became generally
known as 'developing countries', often characterised by hunger and
violence. But our own society was affluent. Even the sky was not the
limit, as I saw men walking on the moon for the first time. In the 1970s
I went to secondary school where I discovered that I liked biology,
physics, chemistry and history. I was also eager to learn foreign languages
such as English, German, French and Spanish. I further remember reading
a pocket book from my parents' shelves; the report from the Club of
Rome on the future depletion of Planet Earth's resources of raw materials (Meadows *et al.* 1972). For the first time, because of the environment,
there seemed to be limits to (economic) growth. Although the Club of
Rome report has often been reviled because of some of its incorrect
predictions, its gloomy message was largely supported by the Millennium Ecosystem Assessment launched by the United Nations in 2001
(Millennium Ecosystem Assessment 2005).

At the end of the 1970s I left my home town and started my
studies at the Agricultural University in Wageningen in the Netherlands. There I was trained and examined in the prevailing technoscientific paradigm for 'modern' agriculture and food production. More

Successful Science Communication, ed. D. J. Bennett and R. C. Jennings. Published by
Cambridge University Press. © Cambridge University Press 2011.

specifically, I studied the biological orientation of molecular sciences with courses like genetics, microbiology, plant physiology, biochemistry and molecular biology. But, in contrast to most fellow students in molecular sciences, I also followed many courses in philosophy of science, and science and society. Moreover, I could not avoid being influenced by alternative streams in society such as environmental, peace, women's, Third World and squatting movements. These movements held emancipation and democracy in high regard. The ideal of people who are autonomous in creating their own lifestyle, as well as solidarity with people who are less well off, appealed to me. I also wished to be 'critical' and participated in many debates about world hunger, alternative agriculture and criticism of technocracy. In the 1980s I saw how a neo-conservative restoration was shaped through neoliberal 'no nonsense' politics aimed at the privatisation of many public utility services. In that period political governance and decision-making started moving more and more to the European Commission and the European Parliament in Brussels and Strasbourg, while international trade agreements started having increasing impacts.

ACTIVIST YEARS

In the mid 1980s I finished my studies in Wageningen. Unlike most of my fellow graduates in molecular sciences who started pursuing academic research careers, I had no clue about what to do with my studies until somebody from the environmental movement handed over a report on biotechnology by the Organisation for Economic Co-operation and Development (OECD): four hundred pages that he had somehow managed to photocopy – a lot of work in those days for a rather obscure but nonetheless very interesting report. This was a report on how industrial countries around the globe could foster the research and development of biotechnology and its applications in areas such as healthcare, agriculture, food production and environmental remediation. Mind you, those were the days without the Internet for easy, cheap and wide dissemination of emails, newsletters and electronic copies of (official) publications and reports. That OECD report inspired me to team up with two other graduates from the agricultural university: one had studied agronomy and planning, and the other non-Western rural sociology.

Soon we began to hear companies, governments and researchers starting to use the term 'modern biotechnology'. On the one hand it was 'modern' because new scientific knowledge was being applied. On the other hand it was not so new because, since prehistoric times, humans had bred crops and cattle and made bread, cheese, wine and beer, all examples of so-called 'traditional biotechnology' based on experience and craftsmanship. It was further claimed that modern biotechnology could help to resolve world hunger and clean up the environment. As engineers we were fascinated by the technological opportunities, but we also had our doubts. Since the development of biotechnology and genetic engineering was generally justified as indispensable for cleaning up environmental pollution caused by chemical agricultural and industrial practices, we considered it to be a grand technological attempt to reconcile economics and ecology.

We further saw how research institutions were increasingly forced to get research contracts from commercial organisations, to apply for patents on inventions and to start companies. And we became concerned about the fact that so few people were controlling so much research. We therefore started informing and persuading civil society groups to think about this technology. We ourselves wrote, printed, published and distributed a magazine called *Bio-Text* and a booklet with the title *Harvest from the Laboratory*. We also organised meetings with many public groups, gave lectures at universities and, as a result, we were often approached by journalists from newspapers and TV and radio stations for a 'critical' perspective. By the end of the 1980s we tried to push major consumer, environmental, farmer, animal protection, rural women, and Third World organisations to campaign for a broad public debate on biotechnology. The campaigning issues we suggested were: (1) genetically engineered bovine growth hormone, (2) ecological risks of environmental releases of genetically engineered organisms, (3) patents on biotechnological inventions, and (4) social–economic consequences for developing countries. But it should also be noted that despite the subject of genetically manipulated organisms (GMOs) and connotations like 'playing God', we were wary of discussing the 'ethics' of biotechnology in those days. Our fear was that this would lead to committees of ethicists and philosophers that would soothe the conscience of the genetic engineers and at the same time de-politicise the societal debate.

In the beginning of the 1990s I left Wageningen and went to Brussels where I started working for the environmental organisation, Friends of the Earth Europe. With money from the European Commission, I began the Clearinghouse on Biotechnology with the aim of informing national Friends of the Earth groups as well as other civil society organisations in Europe about discussions on EU policies and regulations on biotechnology between representatives from the

European Commission, the European Parliament and European associations of biotechnology and food industries. I also had to lobby European Parliamentarians and European Commission representatives about the viewpoints and positions from my constituencies. In fact, they had hardly developed any views on biotechnology in those days, probably because they regarded biotechnology as something in the future. Yet, genetically engineered bovine growth hormone was about to be approved for the European market and the first field trials with genetically engineered plants were being conducted. And in the European Parliament, the Greens seemed to be the only political party with serious views on biotechnology, albeit with a fully confrontational and opposed attitude. Other political parties mostly seemed to hold the rather simplistic view that 'science and technology meant progress'.

My attempts to achieve a collaboration with other environmental organisations in Brussels, such as Greenpeace, the European Environmental Bureau and the World Wildlife Fund, in working together on biotechnology were without success. Even the field testing of genetically engineered plants with resistance to chemical herbicides did not persuade these environmental organisations to start thinking about campaigning. As a consequence, it was far more difficult for me to move other environmental organisations at the European and national level into public debates and campaigns on biotechnology than to participate at meetings and conferences organised by the European Commission and the biotechnology and food companies.

After a couple of years I left Brussels. Partly for personal reasons but also because I felt increasingly forced to defend a blanket opposition against agro-food biotechnology. My own constituency had started to take the issue a bit more seriously but seemed not yet able to differentiate between desirable and undesirable applications. For me, that was not workable, as I had (and still have) the view that we should assess, on a case-by-case basis, the potential benefits and risks of applications of biotechnology compared to those of alternative solutions.

PROFESSIONAL APPRENTICE YEARS

Back in the Netherlands I was hired by an environmental consultancy whose main client at that time was the Ministry of Environment, more specifically, the unit for regulating 'dangerous substances', such as radioactive materials, chemicals and GMOs. This unit had commissioned the consultancy to design and make operational an information technology-based (IT) system for administrative processing of notifications and applications for permit activities with chemicals and GMOs. The consultancy was further commissioned to assist this Ministry's unit in building capacity for risk assessment and risk management of GMOs in several south-eastern African and central and eastern European countries. The work at this consultancy was technically interesting, while it was also very instructive about how governmental institutions and scientific advisory bodies interact. Nonetheless, at a certain moment, my work field felt too limited, as it only concerned the 'biosafety' of GMOs.

Then I was approached by a consultancy in public communication in The Hague that had just been set up by a former publicly well-known representative of a major consumer organisation. This new consultancy had started as a spin-off from a major marketing communication consultancy in the Netherlands and its view on societal communication appealed to me. So, I accepted joining a trip to the US in the summer of 1995, together with a delegation composed of representatives of major international Netherlands-based food and retail firms. On that trip we were taught all we should know about the genetically modified Roundup Ready soybean which had been developed by Monsanto as it would soon be introduced on the European market. We were told that in conventional soybean cultivation weeds were controlled by so-called 'selective' herbicides that were applied several times before they emerged and at some specific stages during crop growth. Now, with the Roundup Ready soybean it was possible to control weeds after they had emerged by applying the 'non-selective' herbicide glyphosate. This would not damage the crop because of its built-in resistance to glyphosate. According to Monsanto, this would provide flexibility in weed control and facilitate no-till agriculture which would help to mitigate soil erosion. Moreover, compared to commonly used selective herbicides in conventional soybean cultivation, the environmental impact caused by glyphosate would be negligible.

After that trip to the US, I accepted the job and became the very first employee at this consultancy for public communication. I knew that Monsanto would be my first account. My work was to support a 'soft landing' of its Roundup Ready soybean on the Dutch market, for which a communication strategy had to be designed and implemented. In this communication strategy the Product Board for margarines, fats and oils, a public body for implementation of certain trade rules and promotion of the interests of operators in the agro-food chain of vegetable oils and fats, would play a pivotal role, whereas the media profile of Monsanto would be kept low.

Concerning content, the technical information about this GM soybean, the way it was being cultivated in the US, its potential risks and benefits to agriculture and the environment, the widespread use of soya ingredients in many processed consumer food products and animal feedstuffs, all that had to be comprehended and verified as much as possible. For this purpose, we commissioned a study of Monsanto's GM soybean by the Centre for Agriculture and Environment, a private research organisation highly esteemed by the Dutch environmental movement for its independence. The general objective was to evaluate the potential of the GM soybean to contribute to sustainable soybean cultivation in the US. The researchers reached a twofold conclusion. First, cultivation of this glyphosate-resistant GM soybean could lead to a 10 to 30 per cent decrease of the amount of active ingredients applied per hectare compared to conventional soybean cultivation. And second, according to the environmental yardstick previously developed by this organisation for policy debates on reduction of the environmental burden of pesticides' usage in agriculture, glyphosate's environmental profile was more favourable than that of the herbicides commonly used by conventional soybean growers.

After the verification of all the technical information, it had to be translated into information comprehensible by the (non-technical) representatives of interested target-groups such as those operating in the soya agro-food chain, i.e. the constituency of the Product Board, including major (international) grain traders and food companies. This information also had to be transferred further to representatives of major retail firms, key government officials and a few well-known scientists with views supportive of the use of GM crops in agriculture. The Dutch press was informed by means of a meeting at which the results of the study were presented. So, at the time when the first shipments of GM soya arrived at Dutch harbours in 1996, the whole soy agro-food chain in the Netherlands, the government and the press were more or less aware that this could become a 'media event'.

Ironically, it was Greenpeace, after it had showed no interest in campaigning on genetically manipulated herbicide-resistant crops a few years before, that now managed to raise massive public attention. Obviously, the organisation used its well-established media-genic practice of rubber vessels fighting against large ships like David and Goliath.

For me, this media event initiated more than two years of daily supporting 'societal communication' of the ins and outs of Monsanto's Roundup Ready soybean to many public and private individuals and organisations such as government officials and advisors, biotechnology and food industries, researchers, journalists and representatives of various civil society organisations. From a commercial business point of view, it was a great account for this consultancy, no doubt about it! But personally I felt that I was not doing the right thing. I wished to be independent. So, I quit my job and started my own consultancy in biotechnology which I continue to run.

PROFESSIONAL YEARS

Meanwhile, just before the beginning of the new millennium, I was in my early forties and on my own. I hired an office, bought up-to-date computer hardware and software and got connected to communicate by phone and the Internet. Then I informed my network about my new professional status. This time, my first account was Greenpeace with a request to find out at which locations fields trials with GM crops were taking place in the Netherlands. In those days this meant travelling to The Hague and visiting the public library of the Ministry of Environment where the files with permit applications, risk assessments, field trial locations and decision-making documents were, and still are, publicly available. Since I knew my way around the library and these complicated files and permit application procedures, I managed to deliver a report on the field trial locations. I further concluded that in many cases the files in the Ministry's library were not complete and did not comply with provisions for public information as laid down in Dutch legislation. For Greenpeace, this report fed their suspicion about the alleged secrecy of field trials with GM crops in the Netherlands. It also attracted considerable media attention and led to critical questions from Members of Parliament to the Minister of Environment. This probably helped to make all files at the Ministry's library complete and accessible a month or two later.

Soon afterwards, I worked on Monsanto's GM soybean, again, as my consultancy got another client. This time it was the Product Board that commissioned me and the Centre for Agriculture and Environment to compare the agronomic and environmental effects of the cultivation of the Roundup Ready soybean in the US over the last three years to those of conventional soybean cultivation. Notably, this time the steering committee for this study was not only composed of representatives from soya agro-food chain operators. Representatives of a major consumer organisation and two environmental organisations, one of them Greenpeace, were also on board. This may or may not be typically Dutch but it was certainly an example of the Dutch so-called 'Polder model' of deliberation between parties with conflicting interests and opposing views – a model which originally focussed on negotiating practical measures for water distribution and management on which the Netherlands of course depends. Anyway, before we started the study, the steering committee convened a kick-off meeting to discuss and agree on a set of research questions. At the end of the meeting, all parties agreed on the research questions and the research methodology, and all parties would also provide relevant literature and reports that we as researchers had to address in the study. It was also agreed that only after the study's completion would the parties comment in public on its findings.

In this setting, we began our process of collecting, scrutinising and analysing data and information from a wide variety of sources. Thanks to the further expansion of the Internet, it had in the meantime become far easier to get scientific papers and technical reports and studies from different kinds of research institutions in many parts of the world than ten years ago. After a while we delivered our interim report to the steering committee. Our preliminary conclusions that had been substantiated empirically as far as possible were, depending on one's interests, comforting or upsetting. We reported a modest decrease of up to 10 per cent of the use of herbicides in the cultivation of Monsanto's GM soybean compared to that in conventional soybean cultivation. Moreover, we could establish neither an increase nor a decrease in yield associated with Monsanto's GM soybean.

Unsurprisingly, with these (preliminary) conclusions Greenpeace could not live. At the steering committee's interim meeting, its representative suddenly waved a report that had just been released by an independent consultant in the US. This consultant concluded that over the last three years herbicide usage had increased, while yields of the GM soybean had decreased compared to conventional soybean. As a consequence, we, the researchers, were requested by the steering committee to address these findings in our final report. So, we looked at the data and the methodology in this report, compared them to ours and corresponded with its author about the interpretation of the data. But in the end we felt we could not support his conclusions because of differences of views on his statistical treatment of the data.

Greenpeace had however already communicated its findings to the media, notably, before the final meeting of the steering committee at which we presented our conclusions. Unfortunately, we were not able to resolve the dispute on statistics with the representatives of Greenpeace and the other environmental organisation at that final meeting. Moreover, the other members of the steering committee considered Greenpeace's premature communication to the media foul play. Nonetheless, from a public communication point of view, our report probably gained a far more friendly reception by the Dutch media than the other report.

Following the first arrivals of GM soybeans from the US in Europe in 1996 and a few years of massive media interest and intense public debates in the Netherlands and many other European countries, there was a reduction in public interest at the beginning of this century. Sometimes civil society organisations still managed to focus some public attention on imports of animal feed ingredients from GM soy and GM maize imported from North and South America. But the general public mostly remained unaware that in the EU only one GM crop was approved for commercial cultivation and that its adoption by farmers was very modest. While at the national level the dynamics and outcomes of public and political debates differed significantly between EU Member States, at the EU level serious disputes over marketing approvals of other GM crops between the European Commission and EU Member States remained largely unresolved. At least that was one of my main conclusions from a technical evaluation of one of the EU key directives on GMOs, in which I was involved as one of the experts. While three years earlier I had done a more general evaluation together with a UK-based consultancy, this time the evaluation had to be particularly focussed on the conditions for market approval of cultivation of GM crops. Its results showed again a wide divergence of views and interests between European Commission services and advisory bodies, national authorities, biotechnology companies and civil society organisations on how to do an environmental risk assessment of the cultivation of GM crops in Europe and what to monitor when they are grown on a commercial scale.

Moreover, times have been a-changing. In the first decade after the new millennium environmental issues in general went down on the public agenda, including biotechnology. Moreover, in the eyes of proponents of so-called 'green' biotechnology because of agricultural applications such as GM crops, several established environmental (and development) organisations lost some of their credibility. And for the mainstream media, their total opposition was hardly newsworthy any more. At the same time, further industrial and governmental support to research programmes in life sciences, genomics and synthetic biology opened novel possibilities for numerous technological innovations with totally new opportunities for exploitation, management and conservation of Planet Earth's natural resources.

For me and one of my old buddies from Wageningen, who had worked for many years for Dutch and European consumer organisations before he also became a private consultant, it was high time for us to revisit our twenty-year-old 'activist' booklet *Harvest from the Laboratory* (Schenkelaars and De Vriend 2008). We knew in advance that writing *Harvest from the Laboratory – Revisited* would require a lot of work. And it would result in a book for only a very limited market. Yet, we wished to share our experience with the public debate on biotechnology in the Netherlands and Europe. Over the years we heard many times that the public debate on GM crops had failed in Europe, usually from industry and government representatives and researchers. We also heard developers and promoters of other new emerging technologies frequently suggesting drawing lessons from this public debate, mostly with a rather defensive view to shield off societal interference that might endanger further development and commercialisation. We actively participated in consumer lobbies in Brussels and in the Dutch government's public debate *"Eating and Genes"* in 2001, and we followed what the government did with its recommendations. We played a role in (international) discussions on risk assessment of GM crops and GM food. And we experienced what drives researchers in gene technology and how differently parties may interpret scientific information and data underpinning a risk evaluation.

Frequently, we were stunned. Extensive research programmes for ethical, legal and societal aspects of biotechnology were set up and implemented, but the results were hardly used. Regularly, there were political debates in the Dutch and European Parliaments but most politicians jumped on their pet topics without discussing their underlying visions on (un)desirable futures of agriculture and food production. To public research institutions and civil society organisations, we proposed a research plan to compare the sustainability of agricultural systems with GM crops to that of conventional and organic crops. But none of the parties seemed to be interested in this sort of knowledge that we thought to be relevant.

With these experiences in mind, but still fascinated by the growth of scientific knowledge and the pace of technological advancements, we started reviewing our twenty-year-old analysis again. We saw that concentration in the agro-food biotechnology, food-processing industries and retail sectors had further increased. Moreover, ties between industries, governments and research institutions had grown closer and biotechnology's toolkit had become more sophisticated due to expansion of scientific knowledge at the biomolecular level. We also saw that public debates had polarised strongly and how governments responded by revising regulations and organising public dialogues. We further saw that genomics research and synthetic biology were leading to new scientific, ethical, political and social–economic questions that, at least in our view, should be on the public agenda. We also felt that there still was a role to be played by civil society organisations in democratising research and technology development, particularly concerning the public–private distribution of investments in research and innovation. We looked again at the issues of world food supply and the potential role of gene technology therein. This time we also analysed the meaning of images of nature in ethical and political viewpoints on gene technology. And since we had heard simplistic slogans both from proponents and opponents too often, we concluded our analysis of twenty years of experiences with public debates on biotechnology in Brussels and The Hague by a call to all parties to operate in a socially responsible way that pays due respect to the complexity of living systems and societal issues.

Together with our publisher and because of financial support from Wageningen University Fund and the Association of Rural Women, we managed to keep the price of the book low and we also knew how to raise attention for our new book from major newspapers and radio stations. We also gave several presentations at universities and at meetings set up by farmers' organisations. But, admittedly, sales were modest and the book did not lead to a new turn in the public debate on agro-food biotechnology in the Netherlands.

Now at the end of the first decade of the twenty-first century, a series of global crises have emerged into the public eye, especially in areas like food, energy and finance, which seem to provide a new political and economical context for developments in biotechnology. In this new political–economical–environmental context, proponents of biotechnology launched the concept of a 'bio-based economy'; an economy based on the production and use of renewable biomass instead of an economy based on the exploitation of fossil resources. For instance, at the Climate Summit in Copenhagen in 2009, the European biotechnology industry organisation called upon negotiators to consider biotechnology as *the* toolkit for addressing climate problems. For companies, bio-based production processes could be of interest if they reduced the costs of energy, water and greenhouse gas emissions leading to economically more efficient production. For governments fostering a bio-based economy could strengthen industrial competitiveness, support regional and rural (re)development and decrease reliance on imports of fossil oil from 'politically unstable' regions.

It should however be noted that the OECD was again one of the main international organisations that had already started developing and promoting the concept of a bio-based economy more than ten years ago. And again, most environmental organisations in the Netherlands and Europe were hardly interested in looking beyond the environmental consequences of first-generation biofuels produced from annual crops like maize, soybean, sugar cane, sugar beet and wheat, or from palm oil or coconut oil. But in contrast to twenty years before, promoters of a bio-based economy now showed interest in a public dialogue with environmental and other civil society organisations. Among many other initiatives, I was commissioned by a government-sponsored research initiative in genomics to organise a stakeholder dialogue on white biotechnology, i.e. the use of (GM) microorganisms in industrial production processes. The dialogue process was based on an attempt to align the supply side of white biotechnology with the demand side as expressed by European, Dutch and UK environmental organisations in their campaigns on chemicals, hazardous waste and energy. Yet, the dialogue could not be called a success, largely because of the lack of interest from these civil society organisations. Moreover, a critical article on the lack of interest of most environmental organisations in the issue of a bio-based economy, written by my old buddy and me a few years later and published in the magazine of one of the major environmental organisations in the Netherlands (De Vriend and Schenkelaars 2010), still did not lead to any serious response!

So far, I have gained twelve years of experience as an 'independent' consultant in biotechnology and managed to work for different kinds of clients in the Netherlands and Europe, coming from all sides of the debate on technical, regulatory or sustainability aspects of this societally still controversial technology. However, my basic drive to engage in contributing to socially responsible biotechnology developments has not changed radically since I finished my studies and started as an activist; that is, my drive to supply interested parties with high-quality information that is based on science to the extent possible, tailored to their needs as much as possible and communicated as comprehensibly as possible.

REFLECTIONS

When I started my studies at Wageningen University, I considered science to be a superior source of knowledge as it was based on hard and empirical facts, and not on unverifiable beliefs and dogmas. One of the things I learned to understand was scientific thinking and how to use scientific language when I had to write reports on laboratory experiments and papers on different kinds of research subjects. I further learned that most scientists learn to do science by training without an explicit need to reflect (philosophically) on science as one source of rational knowledge among numerous other sources of human knowledge and wisdom. Notions such as 'objective', 'value-free', 'freedom of scientific enquiry' and 'fundamental versus applied science' were therefore used rather easily.

At the end of my studies, I chose to write two papers on philosophy of science instead of doing another six months of laboratory research, as I already had done more than fifteen months of laboratory research in molecular biology, biochemistry and physical chemistry. My fellow students in molecular sciences considered this choice to be a bit awkward and not really helpful if you wished to pursue a research career. Nonetheless, I enjoyed studying and writing about the origin of molecular biology in the 1930s initiated by quantum physicists who had moved from questions in their field to questions about genetics in the field of biology; while their application of physical and chemical research methods to questions in biology was deliberately promoted by the first science manager in the history of science with substantial funding from the Rockefeller Foundation in the US.

I also enjoyed writing a paper on the double-helix model of DNA, in which I analysed a hardly noticed scientific controversy over the correct representation of the three-dimensional structure of this iconic molecule in the 1970s. It was instructive to see how a group of stereochemists from India and a electrical engineer from New Zealand had arrived at similar alternative three-dimensional models for the DNA molecule, in which the two single strands are not wound into a double helix as two Nobel Prize winners had suggested in 1953, but side by side as in a 'warped zipper', so that for its replication the DNA molecule does not need to unwind at high speed with the aid of specific postulated enzymes. However, these researchers were not allowed to publish their alternative side-by-side models in a prestigious scientific journal, in fact they published in rather obscure scientific journals. By contrast, one of the two Nobel Prize winners was given extensive space in *Nature*, one of the foremost scientific journals in the world, to defend 'his' double helix and refute these alternative models without serious examination.

In my activist years I kept studying the science driving biotechnology, because I also needed a better understanding of living systems at other than molecular levels, given the potential risks of genetically engineered organisms. This meant that I had to gain better knowledge of scientific disciplines like ecology and population genetics. But because of their application in agriculture and food production, I also had to learn more about the lessons of the Green Revolution of the twentieth century which had promoted agricultural systems in developing countries that were based on crop varieties bred for a high yield under conditions of irrigation, nitrogen fertilisation and chemical pest management. However, most of the work was focussed on understanding how vested interests were shaping developments in biotechnology at that moment, in order to organise countervailing power and engage major civil society organisations in democratising (bio)technology research and development.

With that objective in mind, complicated scientific information and policy papers needed to be translated into a format understandable and attractive for many different civil society organisations, such as consumer, environmental, farmer, rural women, animal welfare, development, trade union and church groups. The challenge was not to fall back into scientific writing but to write in a more journalistic manner without sacrificing scientific nuances too much. I also learned hard lessons in practice about speaking on biotechnology in layperson's language and discussing it with very different audiences, ranging from researchers, policy-makers and journalists to environmentalists, farmers and rural women groups.

When I worked in Brussels for an European environmental organisation, I had to understand how policy-makers at different European Commission institutions, politicians and lobbyists from industry were dealing with each other to shape conditions for desirable biotechnology developments. Since there was and still is a widespread tendency to substantiate positions and arguments with 'science-based' information, I soon became familiar with the practice of 'shopping for science', where the authority of science is abused by commercial or ideological interests, often through transgressing the boundaries between scientific knowledge, uncertainty and ignorance.

It was peculiar to note that studies on agronomic and environmental consequences of growing GM crops that were sponsored by industry led to positive conclusions about their benefits. Similar studies commissioned by environmental organisations led to opposite conclusions. It was also peculiar to become confronted again with the question 'what is science?' An answer to that question, like 'everything that is published in a peer-reviewed scientific journal' seemed to be too simple.

There was a series of incidents following publications in scientific journals that suggested risks of GM crops to the environment or humans and animals. The authors of these publications were fiercely attacked by other scientists because of allegedly flawed research methodologies. These 'scientific' controversies even led to headlines in many newspapers around the world, while they also raised my doubts about the system of peer-review for the quality assurance of scientific knowledge.

It was also interesting to learn how science was used by scientific risk assessors and regulatory authorities in decision-making on activities with GMOs outside laboratories and in the fields. Sometimes I was amazed by what decision-makers counted as valid scientific proof or not. Frequently, I also contributed to regulatory debates on the issue of defining 'environmental risk' or 'environmental harm'. As in my view science is only able to predict the likelihood of the occurrence of a certain effect on the environment, I suggested that science cannot establish whether an environmental effect should be considered 'risky' or 'harmful'; in the end this can only be negotiated normatively.

So, more than twenty-five years of experiences in biotechnology and science communication left me to draw two conclusions: (1) Science is not a superhuman but a human activity, and (2) Communication is useless without an open mind.

Key resources

Friends of the Earth Europe: www.foeeurope.org/GMOs/Index.htm
Greenpeace International: www.greenpeace.org/international/en/campaigns/agriculture/problem/genetic-engineering/
GeneWatch UK: www.genewatch.org/index-396405
TestBiotech Germany: www.testbiotech.org/en
Save Our Seeds: www.saveourseeds.org/en.html
The ETC Group: www.etcgroup.org/en
Union of Concerned Scientists: www.ucsusa.org/about/
Scientists for Global Responsibility: www.sgr.org.uk/
EcoNexus: www.econexus.info/index.html
Gen-Ethisches Netzwerk: www.gen-ethisches-netzwerk.de/
Genetic Resources Action International Network: www.grain.org/front/

References

De Vriend, H. and Schenkelaars, P. (2010) 'Biotechnologie: Duur of Duurzaam?' ('Biotechnology: Duration and Durable?'). *Milieudefensie Magazine* 39: 2, 12–14, February 2010.

Meadows, D. H., Meadows, D. L., Randers, J. and Behrens, W. W. III (1972) *Limits to Growth*. New York: Universe Books.

Millennium Ecosystem Assessment (2005) *Ecosystems and Human Well-Being: A Framework for Assessment*. Washington, DC: Island Press. www.millenniumassessment. org/en/Framework.aspx

Schenkelaars, P. and De Vriend, H. (2008) *Oogst uit het Lab (Harvest from the Laboratory)*. Utrecht: Jan van Arkel. www.oogsuithetlab.nl

Part III What you can do and how
to do it

DAVID J. BENNETT

15

Building relations with the various groups

WHY BUILD RELATIONS?

I always remember the story about the then director of what is nowadays a major medical research centre – although both shall better remain nameless! He was faced with a great deal of very vocal opposition from the surrounding community to planned building extensions. And this was for medical research when you would normally expect support and encouragement. But the locals were up in arms about the land that would be taken and which could otherwise be used for much-needed local housing, disruption caused by the building works, subsequent increased traffic, and so on – the 'NIMBY – not in my back yard' syndrome if ever there was! He was asked what he had done about inviting the local people, journalists and politicians into the centre and showing them what was going on and why. Looking at his inquisitor with a rather baffled expression, he answered with words to the effect that *'Oh, I never thought of anything like that and I would have been too busy anyway what with all the building planning work as well as running and developing the centre.'* The story does have a happy ending however because he took the message on board and acted on it immediately so that later it developed into a major medical research centre of world standing and of which the neighbouring community is now, and has been for some time, rightly proud.

That was a long time ago and nowadays many scientists do put a great deal of effort into building relations and communicating about their science personally.[1] There must be very few universities and companies that do not have open days, schools outreach programmes and some of the

---

[1] Possibly one of the most renowned has been Richard Feynman, physicist at Caltech, bongo-drum player, juggler and safe-cracker, pioneer of the quantum

Successful Science Communication, ed. D. J. Bennett and R. C. Jennings. Published by Cambridge University Press. © Cambridge University Press 2011.

223

other very broad range of things that can be done in building and maintaining effective relations with the different local and more distant key groups of people. This may well be so, but you may still ask *'Why should I put time and effort into these kinds of things rather than just doing the research which I'm paid for and which my career depends on?'* and *'It would take a lot of time out from my research and I don't get any recognition or reward for doing it'* or *'Even if I feel I should do something, I really don't know what to do or how to do it, and isn't the PR department supposed to do it anyway?'* These and similar are very good questions so let's have a look at them before we go on.

As Professor Richard Jones says in his Introduction to this book and James Shepherd in his Chapter 23 about The Triple Helix run by science undergraduates illustrates perfectly, the sheer desire to share one's enthusiasm for science is one of the main motivations for becoming involved in building relations and engaging with the wider community. But there are as many others as there are scientists so involved, as Richard Jones also points out.

Many researchers are recognising that there are distinct benefits in building relations and communicating their work more widely, both for them and for those who therefore become aware of it and would otherwise not be. A research paper in a prestigious journal, even *Nature* for example, may only be read and cited by a relatively small number of other people in the same research community. Spending some time with a journalist, for instance, means that you reach a far larger and wider audience. I remember a couple of hours over lunch with a charming and very professional lady which led to a seriously good three-page article in a women's magazine with a circulation of hundreds of thousands and countless interested reactions as a result. True, it must also be said, I have also been selectively, and hence distortedly, quoted once in two leading newspapers in the UK which did cause a problem, but that's another story. One scientist told me it was a 'no-brainer' to be doing this kind of thing since he now has new interest in his work from people and places he could never have reached through research journals. On the other hand it does not suit every researcher and some are probably better sticking to their work and not forcing themselves, or being forced, into it. Then again, while talking to school children might not be your *forte* you may be able to give an excellent

computing field and joint Nobel Prize winner for the discovery of quantum electrodynamics, developer of Feynman diagrams fundamental to string theory, originator of the concept of nanotechnology, and much else as well as being a superb communicator.

after-dinner talk to a business club or discuss your research with a specifically related patients' organisation or charitable foundation. On the time factor, when departments do look at their research areas, think about the different activities possible and then match the interested and appropriate staff to them, they are able to do much more in total without affecting the overall research output as more people share the load. Indeed, many universities are progressively embedding this kind of approach into their practices, as Maarten van der Sanden and Patricia Osseweijer discuss in their Chapter 27. Recognition and reward for one's efforts, at least in tangible form, still remains an issue although this is improving as universities and funding bodies in some countries are already including these kinds of activities in their assessment procedures.[2] Of course this all means time, although reduced when shared, experience, which may be helped by training and advice, not a little risk, even though this is often overestimated, and sometimes opprobrium from colleagues, but most scientists say they feel they should be doing it and increasing numbers are, as in fact is shown by various surveys (MORI & Wellcome Trust 2001; Royal Society 2006).

Some reasons for doing it are quite personal. For example, it helps you to understand your subject better. There is nothing like talking with people who do not share the things which you take for granted for seeing the gaps in your own thinking that you did not even realise were there before. The classic is the child's asking 'But why?', and then when you give an answer, 'But why?' comes again and again until you arrive at the point when you cannot easily reply and have to think hard about it. Working out the ways to respond to the usual party opener 'So what do you do?' in a way that encourages conversation rather than closing it off is a real test. For many subjects talking with the wider world can open up new research questions and new slants on your research and teaching, especially when you do it early in the planning, and help to adapt and improve them later. The character of the student population is changing rapidly so interacting with the public can help to ensure your teaching materials remain appropriate and contemporary. And, what's more, talking to other people about your subject can often remind you just how interesting it actually is when you are feeling overworked and a bit downhearted.

[2] For example, the Higher Education Funding Council for England (HEFCE) has recommended that public engagement be included in research assessment as part of the new Research Excellence Framework which will come into effect from 2014 based on a pilot in 29 UK higher education institutions which confirmed the feasibility of the approach (HEFCE, 2010).

Some of the reasons are to do with the present climate that science finds itself in. Put bluntly – and every scientist knows this in their heart of hearts – relations between scientists and the wider public have changed dramatically during the last fifty or so years, and the ivory tower is long gone. The upside, and quite contrary to what many scientists believe and are often astounded to hear, is that they routinely come out top of the list in European public opinion polls as those most trusted to explain the impact of science on society. This is so whether they work in university, government or industry labs as Michel Claessens for example shows from the Europe-wide Eurobarometer survey in his Chapter 8, Figure 8.1 (European Commission 2010). They also have a favourable image in the USA, as shown in Table 15.1 here, although the military score highest (while the military are among the lowest groups in Europe) with teachers next and then scientists (Pew Research Center 2009).

Table 15.1. *USA scientists' image*

How much do each contribute to well-being of society?

	A lot (%)	Some (%)	Not much/nothing (%)
Members of the military	84	11	4
Teachers	77	17	4
Scientists	**70**	**23**	**5**
Medical doctors	69	24	5
Engineers	64	25	6
Clergy	40	37	15
Journalists	38	41	17
Artists	31	43	22
Lawyers	23	46	27
Business executives	21	43	31

Source: Pew Research Center (2009) *Public Praises Science; Scientists Fault Public, Media*, p. 2. http://people-press.org/2009/07/09/section-1-public-views-of-science-and-scientists

In the UK the series of surveys carried out by the Research Councils and Ipsos MORI show that, overall, public attitudes to science are positive and interest in science has increased since 2000 (United Kingdom Research Councils 2008 and Ipsos MORI 2011).[3] Scientists are often very pleasantly

---

[3] Responses to United Kingdom Research Council questions: '*I am amazed by the achievements of science*' – 82% in 2008 from 75% in 2000; '*Science is such a big part of our lives we should all take an interest*' – 79% in 2008 from 74% in 2000. According to Ipsos MORI, nine in ten of the UK public (88%) think 'scientists make a valuable contribution to society', while eight in ten (82%) think they 'want to make life better for the average person'.

surprised at the reception they get during laboratory open days for instance when one of the main problems is dealing with the mums fighting to ensure that their young Jane or Johnny gets a turn at the experiment! On the other hand, as we all know very well, their standing has been damaged by very publicly aired controversies over such issues as climate change and vaccination, long-running debates such as about nuclear energy and genetic modification (GM), and the key difference in approach from politicians and public who seek definitive answers and reassurance, and are most unhappy with uncertainty while science is based on it, as John Adams discusses in his Chapter 6 on risk perception and communication.

Be that as it may, some may be spurred by just such outside enquiry. People in general, journalists, politicians, company personnel all want to hear from and speak with scientists directly in person as the experts on their particular field of science. They do not want to be side-tracked by intermediaries such as public relations – PR – departments, offices or agencies – and are often suspicious and resistant when attempts are made to make them do so. It is real, live scientists and their doings that people want to see on TV, hear about on the radio or read about in newspapers and magazines; that industrialists, politicians, lawyers, investors, teachers and other professionals want to get advice from; and that journalists want to interview. Public relations companies or such offices in universities and companies can be of great help because they have professional expertise, contacts, networks and experience. However their main job is in communication and marketing aimed to publicise and promote the organisation or science in a one-way, 'deficit model' manner rather than helping with relations between scientist and outside world. Unfortunately they can also hinder or even block direct contact from the outside with their scientists, either because it is university or company policy, misguided though it may be, or simply in the attempt to protect their own fiefdoms. Their task is to provide the expertise and smooth the path between scientist and the outside world, and vice versa, as Richard Hayhurst illustrates in his Chapter 17.

Direct contact is crucial. It is an oft-repeated truism, for example, that both inter-specialty and interdisciplinary collaboration between colleagues and technology transfer from lab to company work best 'when carried out on foot' – that is when people are in close proximity and contact, and building and maintaining relations are easy. Not for nothing has the clustering of hi-tech companies close to centres of research in Silicon Valley and around MIT in the USA and Cambridge University in the UK as well as elsewhere around the world been so successful.[4] The same is also very true for relations in the much broader sense. 'Science communication' is not to be seen as something only to be done with 'the general public'. It also needs doing within the department and between departments in universities. Importantly it needs doing with their Vice-Chancellors, Presidents, Rectors so they understand what is going on in their universities and is to be represented by them. And just as importantly, it also needs doing with local industry and business exchanges so they know about the research and technology potential in their neighbourhood, and to local politicians and journalists for similar reasons, as well as with the wider public. Every channel that can needs to be used to build relations and help ensure that research is understood beyond the lab and specialist community and in the wider social context, and, equally significantly, that those in the former understand the latter's responses to it.

Another pressing reason for becoming involved in the public debate as a scientist is the situation in which many of the forms of variously called and structured public consultations, consensus conferences, citizen's courts and so on find themselves. There is a high level of scepticism about such public consultation events, as was shown for example at least in the UK by the United Kingdom Research Councils' public opinion survey in 2008 illustrated in Table 15.2 (United Kingdom Research Councils 2008). Its report concluded: *'The results suggest that people like the idea of public consultation in theory but are comparatively less interested or willing to be personally involved in it.'* An earlier survey in 2005 had revealed a lack of awareness of what public consultation was with 88% of respondents saying they knew not very much or nothing at all about public consultation in science (MORI/OST 2005). Little has changed for in 2011 only 2% said that they were already actively engaged in public consultations on science issues and 50% said they would like to know that the public was being consulted but didn't want to get involved personally (Ipsos MORI 2011).

[4] For example, an evaluation of the Higher Education Funding Council for England (HEFCE) third stream funding (see below) concluded that community-based interactions *'represent in many cases the most fruitful way that universities can foster the development, through informal and people exchange activities, of a rich set of interactions which may lead to further and deeper patterns of collaborative research and teaching based activity'* (http://www.cbr.cam.ac.uk/pdf/AcademicSurveyReport.pdf, p. 22).

Third stream funding can be defined as *'the generation, use, application and exploitation of knowledge and other university capabilities outside academic environments. In other words, the Third Stream is about the interaction between universities and the rest of society.'* Molas-Gallart, J. et al. (2002) *Measuring Third Stream Funding*, Science and Technology Policy Research (SPRU), University of Sussex http://www.lse.ac.uk/collections/CCPN/pdf/russell_report_thirdStream.pdf, pp. III–IV.

Table 15.2. *Attitudes towards public consultation – motives and values*

	Agree (%)	Neither (%)	Disagree (%)
What people like me think will make no difference to the government	61	17	23
Public consultation events are just public relations activities and don't make any difference to policy	49	35	16
Public consultation events are unrepresentative of public opinion	47	35	18
Base: All respondents (2137)			

Source: United Kingdom Research Councils (2008) *UK Public Attitudes to Science, 2008: A Survey*, p. 23. http://www.rcuk.ac.uk/documents/scisoc/pas08.pdf.

The experience from these kinds of exercises has shown that they suffer from two major unfortunate disadvantages. One is that they tend to attract as participants mainly those who are interested in the topic beforehand and already committed in their views, whether positively or negatively, and then polarise them even further in their already pre-formed opinions.[5] The problem then of course is that those who were not previously interested, or sufficiently so to attend, which is often the

---

[5] For example, the UK Government's final report of the country-wide *GM Nation?* public debate in 2003 costing £650,000 concluded that '*Broadly speaking, it reflects the views of people who are regularly engaged in politics and current affairs. Such people are far more likely to be uncertain, suspicious or hostile towards GM and to have made up their minds about it.*' (Department of Trade and Industry 2003). Similarly, Cass Sunstein, a Harvard constitutional law professor, in his book *Going to Extremes: How Like Minds Unite and Divide* (2009), finds that deliberation does not necessarily lead to compromise or to convergence of opinions. Groups tend to polarise in the direction of whatever bias they had to begin with. Doctors deciding collectively, for example, are more likely to support 'extreme' strategies to save terminally ill patents than the average individual doctor. Juries tend to vote for more 'extreme' financial awards than the average individual juror among them would award. Interestingly, he also pointed out in *Republic.com 2.0* (Sunstein 2007) that while newspapers present people with all kinds of material they did not ask for, the internet allows them to look for only what they agree with, thus refuting claims that it opens people to new ways of looking at things. In practice, it lets people isolate themselves in informational micro-environments of their own choice: it makes them not more cosmopolitan but more parochial. His central insight is that deliberation and the internet, far from bringing people together, can drive them to extremes. Well-intentioned campaigns of public information and 'dialogue' therefore risk doing more harm than good, as the *GM Nation?* public debate possibly illustrates.

majority of people, do not participate and so their opinions are not heard nor do they contribute to any recommendations, decisions or whatever that may ensue. The other downside, especially from the experience of more recent such events in some countries, is that some have been taken over, hi-jacked if you like, by activists who have interrupted or blocked discussion with demonstrations, having recognised that these events provide already organised and publicised opportunities for them to get media attention and coverage, publicity and hence political influence together with additional memberships and membership income.[6] It is for both reasons that these kinds of activities, even though seemingly desirable for good open democratic governance reasons, have become less frequent as these lessons have been learned and spread. As much as we may like to believe in public consultation, the reality, at least up to now, is different. So, while these kinds of events may provide useful experiences, their limitations mean that the debate devolves back onto the shoulders of scientists themselves and their building relations. Significantly, the proportion of people in the United Kingdom Research Councils' survey cited above agreeing that *'In general scientists want to make life better for the average person'* is high and rose from 67% to 76% between 2000 and 2008 (United Kingdom Research Councils 2008).

A further argument for scientists' interaction with the wider public is heard more and more frequently, at least in Europe, where science has come under challenge because it has to compete for financing in the public, political, media and activist arena with other pressing priorities and conflicting interests. This is that scientists have a special position in this critical situation because, while innovation, specialisation and institutionalisation have made science ever more complex, distant from and less understood by the majority of people, scientists alone remain expert and knowledgeable about their science, its technological applications and our dependence upon them. Scientists, it is argued, therefore have a special responsibility to explain their science and its import for the general good. They need to listen to and understand the concerns which other people may have about their work and its effects, take them on board and respond to them. They also need to act for their own good as public-sector scientists because via taxes and government policies they are paid to do it by the rest of the population to whom they therefore also need to provide account.

---

[6] See for example: Andrew Schneider (2010) *Why Nanotech Hasn't (Yet) Triggered "the Yuck Factor,"* AOL News. http://www.aolnews.com/nanotech/article/why-nanotech-hasnt-yet-triggered-the-yuck-factor/19401419

Whether they actually view it in these kinds of ways or not, most scientists see the need to communicate and engage with the public. Some do it very well but many are hesitant or held back for the readily understandable reasons of priority of research, publication and career, lack of training and confidence, and lack of tangible rewards. The answer would seem to be to concentrate on building relations for the wide range of public communication and engagement activities which experience shows do have significant genuine effect and which are possible within the given circumstances. The chapters in this section of the book give accounts of a series of very varied examples in fair detail written by the people who are actually doing them on a day-to-day basis. Hopefully they will provide illustrations and practical leads with useful ideas and know-how as guides or bases from which further ideas may grow.

GOING ABOUT BUILDING RELATIONS

'Let a thousand flowers bloom', Chairman Mao's slogan,[7] applies to many things, not least to science communication. There is no 'single' or 'best' way of doing it, the only limitations being human ingenuity coupled with enthusiasm, know-how, time and, as usual, money. This chapter now concentrates on the many ways scientists, at whatever level or in whatever kind of organisation, can build relations with their local and more distant communities. Remember that for those people who do not make science their career, all that remains from their school science lessons are vague memories and unless they have specific interest – a cystic fibrosis child, amateur astronomy or what effect pesticides may have on their food – when they become experts, their knowledge comes from what is garnered from the television or newspapers, or, as Cass Sunstein has argued, selectively from the internet. Science pervades every aspect of modern life and it can be brought closer to the lives of people, and theirs closer to it. This is valuable for the fundamental reasons of improving human understanding and condition which Alfred Nordmann speaks about in Chapter 7. It is also valuable for the quite pragmatic reasons of establishing and maintaining good relations between people, whether they be local, academic, student, staff, business, political, media, interest organisation or whatever. Good relations

---

[7] This is a common misquotation. What Mao Tse-Tung actually said in Beijing in 1957 translated was 'Let a hundred flowers blossom and a hundred schools of thought contend.'

may also reveal problems if they are not taken care of and problems are to be ignored at one's peril!

Family, friends and people one meets every day

People are inquisitive. It is one characteristic we all share, evolutionarily selected and highly adaptive, according to human biologists. We all want to know what other people do. Sometimes we ask directly and sometimes when sensitivities preclude the direct question, we try to assess from other signals. It comes as a pleasant surprise to many scientists to find that most people are genuinely interested in what they do. Only when the explanation becomes too detailed, too obscure and too difficult for the other person to understand, connect with and respond to, does the glazed expression appear and the conversation drop. The moral, obviously, is to try initially to anticipate the level needed, listen and ask to try to understand the other's particular interests and feelings, and the reasons for them, and to carry the conversation on accordingly. Much easier said than done – it needs working at! Some people are more gregarious than others and find it easy, others may tend not too. If you're one of the latter then try it and work on it. You'll find it gets progressively easier and you'll be agreeably surprised. The standard advice, and it bears repeating, is to try it first with the people who love you! They'll understand what you want and be patient – at least for a time! – and they'll be honest and you'll trust them enough so you'll get really good at it after a few goes. Then chat with the people you meet in the pub or on the train or plane – I've learned more, I'm sure, in just this kind of way than probably any other.

If you haven't tried it, this is very seriously meant. First think especially hard about how you would explain what you do to people who know very little or anything about it. Then sit down with your girl or boy friend, mum or dad, wife or husband, kids, aunt or uncle, grandparents, whoever over a cup or glass of whatever when they have a few minutes. Explain what you want to do and that you need their help. They'll probably look at you as if they think you've gone mad, laugh but then understand and enter into it. Get them to ask 'Well, what do you do then?' and off you go, trying of course to pitch it at what you think is their level. Keep it short to begin with and stop to ask whether they understand and what they think about what you're saying. You'll undoubtedly get some surprises – both pleasant and otherwise! Listen very well to what they say, brace yourself, smile and try again. Repeat until everybody collapses in laughter, congratulates you and says *'Let's try that again tomorrow or whenever we can.'*

Remember, crucially, that people are most interested in, and influenced by, what affects themselves and their close families, friends and colleagues personally. We may have been semi-joking about the NIMBY, 'not in my backyard', syndrome at the beginning of this chapter as a deterrent but the converse as a positive force is vital. Think of the way in which you view and react to things outside your own research and work interests, think of other people viewing and reacting to yours in similar sorts of ways, and you won't go far wrong!

Open days, science festivals and science museums

The next step after family, friends and people one meets every day is of course to invite them into the laboratory and, as said at the outset, there must be very few universities and research institutes now that do not have an open day every year and many companies too. And hugely successful they usually are. They take enthusiasm, ideas, time, planning and organisation, and not a little interruption to normal life. Again they are not for everyone but they are probably the most effective and successful way of building relations with local people of all ages and walks of life. The initiative can come either from the top – the head of the laboratory – or the bottom – the undergraduates and postgraduate students, but it has to be a meeting of the minds – and of the efforts. Probably the best way to go about it first is to get the good advice from people who have organised these kinds of events before. They will know what kinds of things work and what don't, how to set them up, what precautions to take about safety, how to advertise the event before-hand, to manage the queues and channel the crowds around the corri-dors, and, importantly, to get the local journalists in to spread the message. Rikke Kjærgaard shows how important visual communication is in such contexts in her Chapter 22. Get your group together, pool ideas, select what you think is feasible and will be attractive, draw up a plan of who's going to do what with whom, where and, vitally, by when. And, importantly, don't forget to build in the means to evaluate your event as Laura Grant shows in her Chapter 26 so you can improve it for next year. You will then have very successful events drawing in the families out for the day, school teachers bringing their groups, and the people who are just interested in having a look at what you are doing.

Other very good ways of opening up your research and your laboratory to the wider world are to join in a science festival or even take some of your research and experimental equipment into a science museum. Nicola Buckley and Sue Hordijenko show how this can be done in their Chapter 21 on science festivals and Paul Hix and Wolfgang Heckl describe their open laboratory at the Deutsches Museum in Munich in Chapter 24.

Local schools, young people and teachers

Like most other people, for the majority of teachers their science is where they left it after their university days, updated possibly from their own interests and occasional in-service updating course. Like other people they are overburdened with the day-to-day tasks, among which, and perforce towards the bottom of priorities, is keeping up with changes in the curriculum. So it is no small wonder that they welcome help from the scientists at the neighbouring university or company. Some are already giving talks or demonstration lessons but if you are not one of them, then consider doing so. These often begin because of a chance conversation between scientist and teacher as friends or neighbours, at parents' evenings or in the pub and grow into more formalised relations and long-term activities such as when a university department or company partners with a particular school. Patricia Osseweijer and Tanja Klop show in their Chapter 25 how such relations can develop into something like *Imagine* – a long-running initiative of scientists working with high-school students on projects in developing countries. Teachers are often hesitant about approaching a university or company but if the initiative is taken and the offer made and discussed with them, it will usually be taken up with alacrity and the relationship will build.

Local and national print, radio and TV journalists

There are several other chapters in this book dealing with the various aspects of journalism by the practising professionals and I, although very much interested in it and having learned a little along the way from good friends and colleagues in the profession, will therefore leave it largely to Stephen White, Chris Mooney, Peter Evans and Richard Hayhurst in their Chapters 10, 11, 16 and 17. Suffice it to say that journalism tends to be a much-maligned profession by many scientists, and countless stories abound in the community of their mis- or selective reporting, distortions of what the scientist considers 'the truth' and downright mistakes. On the other hand, many scientists have learned that it can be hugely valuable to establish good working relations with journalists and many would like to do so but are still hesitant. And if you are one of the latter then there are several caveats to be remembered.

One is that they have their job to do, which is to sell newspapers and to get people to watch TV or read their piece on the internet in a highly pressured and competitive, ratings-driven profession – and it is a very different job from yours. A second is that journalists should never be viewed as a 'channel' whose purpose is to publicise your research – their 'purpose' is to report, according to their professional experience, judgement and expertise, what they consider to be 'news'. A standard press release simply describing in rather stilted fashion what may seem important to you but is not what the journalist is interested in covering that day will just join the many others in the email 'Deleted' folder. Save your time, keep an eye out for likely trends and issues, and when you have something you judge will make an attention-grabbing, perhaps controversial, contribution, then that is the time for a well-crafted press release. Well-crafted not only for attractiveness and readability but also for busy journalists to cut-and-paste from. Your name, phone and email address will be at the bottom as the contact so make sure you really are available to take the incoming telephone calls and reply to the emails immediately. If when they ring up the journalist gets told 'She or he's in a meeting' or 'She or he's away at such-and-such a conference' then they will simply go on to the next person on their list and you've lost the opportunity. The easier you make it for them, the more likely it is you will find your 'news' is taken up, your view quoted, you will be interviewed, on a radio or TV panel or whatever.

On the question of mis-reporting and 'mistakes' – no journalist likes to make mistakes. As when one makes them oneself, they cause problems – for the journalist who has to deal with the complaint, with his sub-editor or editor who may also get drawn in and have her or him 'on the carpet' and, to be avoided at all costs if possible, to have to publish an apology or face a court charge. So, despite what you may think, journalists do their best not to make them. If there is sufficient time before the deadline you will have the opportunity to check their copy, and if you are not offered, then ask – the journalist will be grateful for helping to ensure there are no mistakes. If on the other hand, the deadline is in a couple of hours' time or a real-time radio talk show or blogging and twittering is involved, then don't expect to be able to check.

The incredible pressure and sheer pace of the media nowadays means that when a journalist finds a reliable, authoritative source who responds quickly, positively and helpfully in these kinds of ways, they will come back to that source in the future when they have to cover a similar topic. If you do wish to get involved with the media, the message is very clear – try to understand how the media works and then do your best to initiate, build and maintain relations with its members.

Business, women's, trade union, special interest and similar groups

As with teachers, these groups welcome talks from scientists from the local university or company on topics which are of interest to them – and that may be a surprising range. Again, as with teachers, the initiative may come from chance meetings but if not, then it should be taken and contact made with the organiser of the group. There are usually many in the neighbourhood and it just means deciding to set up this kind of programme, looking them up and contacting them. Such talks work best when they are accompanied by a good, well-designed Powerpoint presentation although you may need to take your own equipment and, if appropriate, demonstrations of materials, experiments, etc. Start off with a good joke, encourage questions and discussion in a friendly, open atmosphere and you will be thanked very sincerely, invited again and the word will be spread to other similar organisations. This is an excellent way of building relations with the opinion leaders in your local community and through them with their members.

Special interest groups and organisations are perhaps in a different category precisely because they have their special interests and your research may relate to their interests in quite specific ways. The many patients' organisations are concerned with the individual conditions of their members and their carers, as Alastair Kent, director of an alliance of these organisations, discusses in Chapter 13. Sue Davies describes the approach taken by a major consumer organisation, *Which?*, as its policy advisor in Chapter 12 and Piet Schenkelaars, that from his experiences in the environmental movement and Friends of the Earth in Chapter 14. Lise Kingo and Susanne Stormer illustrate how a leading international company using biotechnology, Novo Nordisk, has dealt with its dilemmas and societal expectations in Chapter 20.

Local, national and international politicians and policy-makers

Typically these are highly pressured people who have to deal with a wide range of continually changing topics in real time. Their life is a continuing struggle to brief themselves in preparation for the next meeting or debate on a particular topic in the face of often conflicting advice and lobbying. The key to opening and building relations with them is in following the political and policy-linked trends in your field so you can anticipate the topics and the times when they will be of interest in the political calendar, and in presenting your material in an assimilatable and useful manner. Then it will have a good chance of being picked up and used. This is where your institution's or company's public relations department can be very helpful, as can that of your academic society or trade association. Their job is to follow the trends, they will often already have contacts that open doors and they will be able to advise you on timing and material. Having made the initial opening, then like journalists, if they have found you helpful and useful politicians and policy-makers will be likely to return to you for further advice on related topics when they occur and relations will build.

The web: Twitter, YouTube, Facebook, etc.

And finally, arguably the greatest relation-builder of them all is the internet – certainly among younger people and ever-increasingly among the not-so-young. Hayley Birch explains how the internet can be practically useful in her Chapter 19 on *The social web in science communication*' and Chris Smith demonstrates in his Chapter 18 on *The Naked Scientists*'[8] online science radio show and podcasts, to both of which I warmly recommend you in conclusion.

Key resources

Bubela, T. *et al.* (2009) Science communication reconsidered. *Nature Biotechnology*, **27**(6), 514–18. http://www.law.ualberta.ca/centres/hli/userfiles/file/publications/ CM_nbt0609_Caulfield.pdf

Wellcome Trust *Communicating Your Research* website:

- Schools and young people – inspire the next generation of researchers.
- Broadcast – reach large audiences through the use of audiovisual media.
- News and media – become a spokesperson for your field and help set the news agenda.

---

[8] http://www.thenakedscientists.com/

- Government and science policy – interact with and influence decision-makers.
- Arts – stimulate new ways of thinking.
- Festivals – showcase your work to new audiences.
- Patient groups – interact with the people affected by your research.
- Public meetings.

http://www.wellcome.ac.uk/Education-resources/Communicating-your-research/index.htm

Research Councils UK, *Schools and Young People*. Brochures: *Engaging Young People with Cutting Edge Research: A Guide for Researchers and Teachers* and *Resources for Schools*. http://www.rcuk.ac.uk/documents/scisoc/SchoolsPolicy,pdf

American Association for the Advancement of Science, *Communicating Science: Tools for Scientists and Engineers*: online resources include webinars, how-to tips for media interviews, strategies for identifying public outreach opportunities, and more. http://communicatingscience.aaas.org/Pages/newmain.aspx

SciDev.Net Practical Guides:

- Explaining controversial issues to the media and the public. http://www.scidev.net/en/science-communication/practical-guides/explaining-controversial-issues-to-the-media-and-t.html
- How do I become media savvy? http://www.scidev.net/en/science-communication/practical-guides/how-do-i-become-media-savvy-.html
- How do I write a press release? http://www.scidev.net/en/science-communication/practical-guides/how-do-i-write-a-press-release-.html

Fenichel, M. & Schweingruber, H.A. (2010) *Surrounded by Science: Learning Science in Informal Environments*. Washington, DC: National Academies Press.

References

Department of Trade and Industry (2003). *GM Nation? The Findings of the Public Debate* (Para 140). http://webarchive.nationalarchives.gov.uk/20100419143351/http://www2.aebc.gov.uk/aebc/reports/gm_nation_report_final.pdf

Department of Trade and Industry (2005) *Science in Society: Findings from Qualitative and Quantitative Research*. Office of Science and Technology, Department of Trade and Industry. http://www.bis.gov.uk/files/file14950.pdf

European Commission (2010) *Europeans, Science and Technology*, Eurobarometer **340**, pp. 90–94. http://ec.europa.eu/public_opinion/archives/ebs/ebs_340_en.pdf.

Higher Education Funding Council for England (2010) *Research Excellence Framework Impact Pilot Exercise: Findings of the Expert Panels*. http://www.hefce.ac.uk/research/ref/pubs/other/re01_10/re01_10.doc

Ipsos MORI (2011) *Public Attitudes to Science 2011*. London: Ipsos MORI Social Research Institute & Department for Business Innovation and Skills. http://www.ipsos-mori.com/Assets/Docs/Polls/sri-pas-2011-main-report.pdf

MORI & Wellcome Trust (2001) *The Role of Scientists in Public Debate: Full Report.* London: MORI & The Wellcome Trust. http://www.wellcome.ac.uk/stellent/ groups/corporatesite/@msh_peda/documents/web_document/wtd003425.pdf

MORI/OST (2005) *Science in Society: Findings from Qualitative and Quantitative Research.* London: Market & Opinion Research International and Office of Science and Technology,

Pew Research Center (2009) *Public Praises Science; Scientists Fault Public, Media.* Washington, DC: Pew Research Center, p. 2. http://people-press.org/2009/07/ 09/public-praises-science-scientists-fault-public-media

Royal Society (2006) *Factors Affecting Science Communication: A Survey of Scientists and Engineers.* London: Royal Society. http://royalsociety.org/uploadedFiles/ Royal_Society_Content/Influencing_Policy/Themes_and_Projects/Themes/ Governance/Final_Report_-_on_website_-_and_amended_by_SK.pdf

Sunstein, C. (2007) *Republic.com 2.0.* Princeton, NJ: Princeton University Press.

Sunstein, C. (2009) *Going to Extremes: How Like Minds Unite and Divide.* New York: Oxford University Press.

United Kingdom Research Councils (2008) *UK Public Attitudes to Science, 2008: A Survey.* Swindon: RCUK. http://www.rcuk.ac.uk/documents/scisoc/pas08.pdf.

16

Finding the right words: how to shine in radio and television interviews

Before the eye-opening Bodmer Report activated the whole PUS movement, many (if not most) researchers tended to think of the media as a foreign country about which they knew or cared little. Its inhabitants were largely considered hostile, sensation-seeking and probably deeply unintelligent. Its outputs – be they in printed or electronic form – were frequently dismissed as superficial, unhelpful and often plain inaccurate.

These attitudes did not change overnight with the publication of the 1985 Report. Indeed, in some isolated corners, they still persist. But Bodmer did put in train some key, ecumenical ideas, namely:

(1) The need to understand the importance of the media in making public what goes on behind the laboratory door, and which would otherwise remain unseen and unheard.
(2) Urging researchers to get to know this hitherto alien culture, to learn its strange language, practices and behaviour.
(3) Stressing that interacting with the media represents an opportunity to reach a far wider audience about scientific achievements, not an automatic threat to academic integrity.

IMPACT IN THE REAL WORLD OF BROADCASTING

These ideas had two practical repercussions for those who work in the media – editors, journalists, broadcasters, producers and so on. Firstly, at an organisational level, research institutes, university departments and other science-based agencies became more proactive in their

Successful Science Communication, ed. D. J. Bennett and R. C. Jennings. Published by Cambridge University Press. © Cambridge University Press 2011.

dealings with journalists. Instead of waiting passively for the media to find the stories that researchers had to tell, they started to try to make it far easier for the media to discover what was new and exciting.

Secondly, individual researchers began to express a need to learn more about the media and to be trained in how to interact with reporters. Increasingly, they would now come to a radio or television studio primed and informed as to what was wanted from them and eager to ensure that they delivered it. In short, the two cultures, at the everyday, operational level, started to come closer.

What follows here represents the fruits of several decades of devising and delivering media courses to scientists, clinicians and engineers from every imaginable discipline and sub-discipline and all levels of seniority – from Nobel Prize winners to humble MSc students in their first term. And it starts by stressing the importance of understanding just how the media works.

THE MEDIA CULTURE

The media, for the most part, is all about making money by providing entertainment. Of course, it can operate at many intellectual levels and vary enormously in the information content it bears. But, crudely, it is essentially a means of diversion: popular, ephemeral and seductively packaged. It is not a substitute for education. It cannot in the space of a 3-minute radio interview plug every gap in an audience's scientific knowledge.

That said, however, the media – radio, television, newspapers, magazines, web pages, the blogosphere and so on – are the way in which most people find out about science. In recent years, scientific stories have become increasingly sought after – and people able to translate research ideas into the everyday language of mass audiences are a valuable commodity.

But, for all the interest shown in science by the media, one has to bear in mind that this is a fierce marketplace. Science-based organisations are constantly trying to 'sell' stories to the media while, internally, reporters and producers have to sell ideas to their editor. Science has to compete with all the other events taking place – be it the outbreak of war, an erupting volcano or a political scandal.

In order that a story can compete it must have strong news characteristics. What is news? Well, it is anything that is new, original, novel, unique, engaging, intriguing, counter-intuitive, funny, tragic – the list of adjectives is endless but they all amount to one basic quality – relevance to the reading/listening/viewing public. There is also another important consideration. News is anything that an editor thinks it is. There are really no formulae. It is all very subjective, even whimsical.

This is true right across all the various branches of the media – from local, low-budget television or radio stations to national, high-profile, prime time news and current affairs programmes. Some programmes specialise in scientific research. The reporter or interviewer may be a dedicated science correspondent. More often, though, journalists are generalists – people who cover a wide range of subjects – one day an experimental psychology story, the next crop failure among farmers. Their audiences too will vary from committed, educated individuals who like science (and may even be trained in it) to ordinary folk, as Americans might say, 'Joe Sixpack', who know little, if anything, about science.

RELEVANCE AND COLOUR

In fact, these two sorts of reporters – the specialist and generalist – are not so different as they might first appear. They both want scientists to make their story *relevant* to their audience, to bring research down to a basic level. Remember, even someone trained in one area of research knows usually very little about a different sphere of expertise. Everyone has gaps in their knowledge.

If relevance to the audience is important so too is 'colour' – drama, conflict, even disaster. The film *Apollo 13* shows how the US public was bored with NASA's Moon missions until a tragedy loomed. As audiences we like drama. No newscaster would get much attention with the headline *'Ocean Liner Remains Afloat'*. The international monetary system is very dull unless and until some computer whizz kid manages to swindle it out of billions of euros. A flood, an air crash – these are the stuff of news.

Whatever the circumstances, however, all media interactions represent an *opportunity* for scientists to tell their story. Normally, the procedure is proactive. An organisation may issue a press release telling the world that something new has happened. Occasionally an organisation and its researchers need to be reactive – 'fire fighting' as it is sometimes called. On the surface it seems as if the two scenarios are different. In practice, interviewees can ensure that they are quite similar – turning what seems to be a damage limitation exercise into a vehicle for conveying positive messages.

The reason for this may surprise you. Most people believe – wrongly – that a media interview is driven exclusively by the reporter or interviewer. It is not. The expert, the person with important and interesting things to say, can steer the interview. The interviewer, far from being a puppet-master, is really only taking his or her cues from the interviewee.

WHAT AN INTERVIEWER REALLY WANTS

Interviewers, then, want a powerful story to seduce their audiences. They want this from the lips of a well-informed and committed individual who appears keen to impart information in an entertaining way. What interviewers do not want is: an excess of methodology or theory; all-inclusive technical explanations; academic or esoteric asides. You will find, constantly, that you will be asked 'Why is this important?' – the critical 'So what?' question.

Interviewers will try always to get researchers to relate what they are talking about to their readers/listeners/viewers. The more you know about these audiences, therefore, the easier you will find it to convey your messages. So listen and look carefully at the treatment of science stories in the media. Note the kinds of questions asked and think about what answers the interviewer is trying to elicit.

Almost invariably you will find – another surprise perhaps – that the interviewer wants to be on the same side as the interviewee. Many believe that the purpose of an interview is to maximise the discomfort of the interviewee and distort his or her messages. Nothing could be further from the truth. With the exception of political or 'issues'-based interviews that are intended to challenge the interviewee on behalf of the public, the media believe that alienation makes for a bad interview. If there is conflict and discomfort, then there will not be that smooth exchange of entertaining information that audiences want. Instead there is confusion.

PREPARING FOR INTERVIEWS

If a broadcaster approaches a scientist with a request for an interview, he or she should ask some key questions in order to prepare.

- *What is the programme* in which my contribution will appear? What can you tell me about your audience – their scientific sophistication, age range, demographics etc.?
- *What format* is the programme? News, magazine or documentary? How will you use my contribution? Will it be

edited and set alongside other material? If so, where does that material come from?

- *What ground are we covering?* This is vital. You must agree on the areas of your work that you will be asked about. Many difficulties arise simply because an interviewee believes that he or she will be asked about Topic A whereas the journalist wants to talk about Topic B or C or even X.

- *Is the interview live or pre-recorded?* Many inexperienced interviewees prefer recorded interviews because they feel – quite rightly – that if they make a mistake, get tongue-tied or simply dry up it is not a disaster. You stop the recording machine and start again. Others prefer live interviews because, in truth, you can say exactly what you like. If you have good, strong, clear messages you can state them and repeat them and no one can do much about it! You can see why politicians like to take part in live broadcasts!

- *Am I on my own* or are you interviewing others at the same time in a discussion format? Who are the other contributors? You can readily see the importance of knowing this. A nuclear engineer may be asked, for example, to argue his or her case against an environmental activist, a hostile politician, a concerned taxpayer worried about the health risks from radiation etc. The more you know, the better you can prepare your case – if advocacy is required.

- *Where and how* will the interview take place? Face to face in a studio? On location? In my office? Down a studio-to-studio line? On the telephone? Novice interviewees prefer face-to-face interactions that enable them to respond to non-verbal cues. Studio-to-studio line interviews can be disconcerting if you are not accustomed to doing them. You may feel happier, too, if a reporter or film crew comes to your lab or office where you are on 'home ground' rather than in the strange surroundings of a studio. Again this is usually a matter of experience.

One word of warning about giving telephone interviews. The telephone is a familiar instrument, used every day to chat, discuss, share confidences and so on. It is quite easy to say more than you intended to over the phone, and to regret it afterwards. So, imagine, when you are giving your interview, that your head of department, supervisor, manager, team or project leader is standing right behind you.

One final matter to raise about a prospective interview might be *'What questions will you ask me?'* Certainly *'What is your first question?'* is useful. The big problem with asking for *all* the questions in advance is that there is no guarantee that the reporter will adhere faithfully to them. Interviewers are, if nothing else, good listeners. If in the course of your answer you say things that seem particularly interesting, you will usually be asked to clarify or amplify. In other words the interviewer may, in the interests of the audience, depart from a strict sequence of questions. There has to be flexibility.

Once you have asked the broadcaster these preparatory questions and received satisfactory answers, you can proceed with the interview. If the answers are not satisfactory you may wish to think again about agreeing to take part.

SELECTING YOUR MATERIAL

The average interview on radio or television lasts around 3 minutes. You have just 180 seconds to get your messages across. So, what are the two or three key things that you want to say? Make sure you have them fixed firmly in your mind. You will not be able to speak clearly and briefly unless you are sure about them. Make sure too that you have relevant facts and figures readily to hand – how small, how big, how fast etc. Do you also have good examples, anecdotes or images well in mind?

In framing your answers remember the *'So what?'* imperative. Remember that the general public cannot be expected automatically to be interested in all aspects of your research for their own sake. You need to give them a reason to be involved. Few of us are fascinated, for example, in macroeconomic theory or fiscal niceties. But we are very interested indeed in rates of personal taxation or the health of the world's stock markets because these topics bear directly on our everyday lives. You have to make the same bridges of relevance for your work. For some researchers – working on cancer biology or climate change for example – this is usually not at all difficult. But, for some areas of research, you may need to work a bit harder at 'hooking' your audience.

COMMON PROBLEMS

Sometimes – not as often as you might think, but often enough – an interviewee ends the interview without having conveyed a clear message at all.

One barrier is straightforward jargon or technicality. Very few people know what 'polymorphisms' or 'clades' are, let alone the other techno-speak that you use in your everyday conversation. 'A bell-shaped Gaussian distribution' and 'nuclear receptors' may well form part of your *lingua franca*, but try using those phrases on the cafeteria staff or a taxi driver and you know what look of incomprehension will spread across your listeners' faces. Yet those people are exactly the audience you have to keep in mind all the time you communicate your science through the media.

Research often relies on numbers – size, distance, proportion and so on. But numbers cause people difficulty. People prefer 'about 1 in 6' to '17%'. They are uncomfortable with 'nanoseconds', '10 to the minus 7', etc. Again, think of people in general and find ways of converting numerical ideas into more accessible language. Better than 'one part per 100 billion' is 'one drop of water in an Olympic swimming pool'. Be careful too if you are putting numbers on risk (a difficult area for the media as other chapters in this book make clear). 'One in a million' or 'An 80% chance . . .' mean nothing to ordinary folk. Better to set these estimates in a telling context. 'There is less chance of an accident than seeing a UFO/winning the Lottery/ finding gold in your garden.'

It is easy to assume that other people know the same things as you do, even quite mundane items of knowledge such as the basic structure of the cell. Researchers from all disciplines tend to make this assumption, by the way. A palaeontologist, for example, will talk unthinkingly about 'the late Cretaceous' or 'adaptive traits' while the physicist will blithely discuss 'electrons', 'neutrons' and 'protons'. Whether it concerns protons, proteins or protozoa, basic scientific knowledge is simply not in everyone's heads. In an interview you may have to put it there or try to limit the amount of information you discuss.

CONVERSATIONAL STYLE

Alongside errors of judgement about the intellectual or linguistic ability of the audience come a range of more cosmetic errors: not what the interviewee says but how he or she says it.

Do not forget that an interview is a social interaction, not a lecture or monologue. Allow your interviewer to react to what you are saying, especially if it is particularly exciting or novel. *'We have, almost by accident you could say, happened upon an event unlike any we have seen before'* needs a pause to allow the audience to take it in and the reporter to ask

'*What is it and why is it important, do you think?*' You can underline your message by asking your interviewer a question '*We found a particular kind of phenomenon – and I wonder if you can guess why we were so excited?*' simply begs for the reporter to say '*Tell me!*'

Tone and style are important in interviews. A dull monotone is not the way to talk about exciting, valuable research findings. People are not enthused by the lecturer's declamatory style. Think instead of the interview as a social chat on which listeners or viewers are eavesdropping. Here, for example, is Ken Caldeira at the Lawrence Livermore Laboratory explaining to a radio audience the basic chemistry behind the acidification of the oceans by atmospheric carbon dioxide.

> *I was vacationing on the beach last summer and it happened to be in Mexico where the sand is made of calcium carbonate. And as a demonstration to my kid I squeezed some lemon juice on this calcium carbonate sand and it all fizzed up, and the sand started dissolving. And carbon dioxide in the ocean forms a weak acid, it's called carbonic acid, and this carbonic acid attacks the shells of many marine organisms – the organisms that make their shells out of calcium carbonate. These include coral reefs, molluscs, and tiny single celled plants that live on the surface of the ocean. All these organisms build their shells or skeletons out of calcium carbonate, but the carbonic acid is corrosive to this carbonate mineral and it makes it more difficult for these organisms to grow their shells. If these organisms can't exist then the entire food chain will be modified and that will have consequences up the food chain, possibly even including affecting the whales and so on.* (BBC Frontiers 27.4.2005)

A friendly, non-argumentative voice comes across far better than a tetchy 'boffin'. Say, for example, an interviewer were to broach the subject of possible health risks in certain common products. It would be inappropriate for a scientist to laugh it off scornfully. Better to recognise the questioner's concerns and anxieties. One could go one step further and remind the interviewer that you too are as concerned as anyone with safe, healthy foods.

Inexperienced interviewees understandably can become anxious and, when they do, they often make their answers too long. They try to fill the silence in the studio by chattering on long after they have made their point. Remember it is the interviewer's job – not yours – to keep the interview moving along. If you finish your answer – even if it is a simple '*Yes*' or '*No*' – then be quiet until the next question comes. You may lose your thread altogether, but that too is the interviewer's problem, not yours.

As a rule, long answers are usually boring too.

All branches of the media – broadcast or print – deal in *pictures*, both real visuals but more importantly images created in the minds of the audience. As an interviewee you should fuel this need for graphic representation because pictures:

- Allow you better to convey the complexities of your subject matter
- Reduce the psychological distance between you and your audience
- Leave something that resonates in the mind – a mnemonic for your messages.
- Entertain people.

In a BBC radio documentary on the origins of our Moon, Robin Canup from the South West Research Institute in Colorado sat in front of his computer simulation and evoked this description of a planet the size of Mars colliding with the early Earth.

> *It's just sort of grazing into the side of the Earth. During the first few hours what happens is the impacting planet comes in, it grazes into the proto-Earth and is effectively sheared apart into a long bar of material that extends out from the proto-Earth oh by maybe a few Earth radii. So, whereas you started with this spherical impacting planet, the effect of the grazing collision has stripped it into a long bar of material.* (BBC Frontiers 27.4.2004)

Now to another example of graphic narrative, this time in the biological domain, from a programme on the mechanism of inflammation. The researcher is John Saville at Edinburgh University's Centre for Inflammation Research.

> *So what might happen classically if you prick your finger with a rose thorn in the garden is passage from the blood vessels (which become dilated and therefore the area looks red), passage from those blood vessels of white blood cells which are armed and dangerous and ... capable of killing bacteria and other microorganism. But they're also capable of inflicting friendly fire injury on tissue and damaging tissue. So this response has always been a trade-off. We all know an acute inflammatory response is painful, but generally it's beneficial and it resolves completely and the damage heals up.* (BBC Frontiers 20.10.2004)

Here are some of the ways in which one can create verbal pictures.

Anthropomorphism is a useful strategy. The late Peter Medawar once entertained an audience by suggesting that the cosmos may have been 'too reticent' to begin with a Big Bang. Primo Levi, industrial chemist-turned-author of *The Periodic Table* described stannous chloride as *'aggressive but also delicate, like certain unpleasant sports characters who whine when they lose'* – thereby introducing a neat simile as well into his explanation. One of the classic pieces of anthropomorphism is that of Richard Feynman in a public lecture on neutrinos. *'These particular objects,'* said Feynman, *'do practically nothing at all except exist. You can use your son-in-law as a prototype!'*

The following example comes from David Fedson, an expert on the genetic complexities of the influenza virus, in a radio documentary assessing the prospects for a future lethal flu pandemic. Here it is the virus that is anthropomorphised. Indeed, it is also, initially, even compared to a leopard!

> *The influenza virus has the capacity to change its spots. It has a very 'plastic' genome, meaning that the . . . eight genes that comprise the influenza virus particle are changing all the time. And they're changing because this is the way the virus manages to escape the immunity in a population that would otherwise suppress its existence. So, in order to continue to thrive, continue to spread, to go from year to year, the virus has to change and it's always seeking ways to escape the defences of whatever the host might be – whether it's a bird or a human.* (BBC Frontiers 24.11.2004)

Similes can be telling. *'The surface is thick and sticky like marmalade'*, *'The vehicle hops along like a pole vaulter'* or *'Trying to communicate with them is like talking to a coffee cup'*. These all capture the essence of the idea in – the crucial point – images that everyone immediately understands. Faced with the challenge of bringing the arcane features of string theories to a general audience, John Barrow – Professor of Mathematical Sciences in Cambridge – had recourse to this homely image.

> *Imagine that your Theory of Everything is a rather unusual shaped vase or something like that, so a three-dimensional thing, and if you shone a light on it in different directions it would cast a funny looking shadow on each of the walls of your room, and each of those shadows would look a bit different. And so these string theories were rather like that – they were shadows of the theory that we've not found.* (BBC Frontiers 11.05.2005)

Comparisons likewise stir our imagination. In his book *The Mysterious Universe* the British astronomer James Jeans captured the vastness of space by estimating that there are as many stars in the sky as there are grains of sand on all the world's beaches. Now he may not be strictly accurate in this. Indeed, one modern astronomer estimates that he is orders of magnitude in error. But that is really not the point. The sheer mind-boggling size of the number – which anyone can contemplate – gives the impression that the writer wanted to convey. Likewise one might compare the atomic nucleus to an orange inside the Millennium Dome – or Chartres Cathedral or the Rome Colosseum etc.

At the Madison Dynamo Laboratory, Cary Forrest works with a machine that simulates the activity of the hot, flowing material at the Earth's core. To capture these complex swirls in language suitable for radio, he hit on the idea of the twisting in a bullet as it leaves the barrel of a gun. For good measure he also brought in the idea of air movement in a tornado.

> It's producing flows that have a special property, we think about as 'helicity'. Now helicity is the idea that a flow as it moves might also be twisting, a kind of a rifling action – a bullet as it moves through the air is spinning and the flows that we have here are basically that same type – they're both moving in a certain direction and they're twisting about that same direction. So, we have two big helical vortices of flow inside the sphere. And that property of helicity is a common ingredient in solar and geo-dynamos, which is a result simply of the fact that we have buoyant hot material from the centre of the Earth moving outward and, as it moves outward, just like air moving upward in a tornado produce a twisting helical flow, you get these same types of helical eddies coming out in the Earth's core. (BBC Frontiers 6.4.2005)

Metaphor is a scientist's prime ally in the battle to explain research to a lay audience. Biologists have long exploited metaphor. Cell biologists have constructed a whole drama in which proteins act as workers, supervisors and managers in the cellular factory, taking their coded instructions from head office where genes direct operations. Immunology too has a superb, overarching military metaphor: immune cells acting as a defence force against invaders. In this microscopic battleground you will even find the biochemical equivalents of uniforms, flags and communication lines.

But physical scientists too can draw on metaphor, sometimes with quite astonishing power. Here is one particularly eloquent exponent of radio science interviews, theoretical physicist and writer Michio Kaku, in full flight for a documentary on the search for a Theory of Everything.

> If we had a super microscope and you could peer into an electron you would see a rubber band, we think, a tiny rubber band. And if you kick it, it changes frequency and it turns into a neutrino, you kick it again and it turns into a graviton, you kick it again it turns into a photon. So why do we have this ocean of subatomic particles? It's nothing but musical notes. Chemistry therefore is

nothing but the melodies you can play on these little rubber bands, these little strings. Physics is nothing but the laws of harmony. The universe would be a symphony of these vibrating strings and then the mind of God, that Einstein wrote about, the mind of God would be cosmic music . . . resonating through 10 dimensional hyperspace. (BBC Frontiers 11.5.2005)

Of course, a metaphor is only a graphic approximation. It is not the real thing. Remember, when trying to devise metaphors to explain your own research, that they are to aid communication to a lay audience not to explain science to your peers.

Try using *anecdote and storytelling*. Research is a human activity and, as such, will inevitably generate interesting human stories. Everyone remembers, albeit in a mutilated form, the story of Fleming's discovery of the action of penicillin on his contaminated dish. But, every day of the year in some lab around the world, something surprising, unexpected, foolish or dramatic happens. Serendipity plays a larger part in science than most people imagine – Pasteur, Roentgen and Becquerel were just three of its beneficiaries – and that sort of occurrence makes for good listening and viewing.

Michael Black at Brown University is one of a team of neuroscientists and technologists working on brain–machine interaction with a view to developing devices to aid injured patients to move their limbs again. His narrative comes to life for listeners by moving temporarily out of the lab and into fiction.

It certainly has the feeling of science fiction at times, what we're doing. There was an interesting book and somewhat poor B movie that was made called Donovan's Brain and in it was a mad scientist and he finds a brain, puts it in an aquarium, keeps it alive and sticks electrodes in it. And he notices that there's this pattern of activity that he's recording from the brain and he says 'If I could find a code which translates the relation between these electrical outputs he's got and the mental image then the brain could communicate with me.' And in that sentence Curt Siodmak, who wrote the book, summarises what we're trying to do – we're trying to understand the code, that is how does the brain represent information? If we can do that, we can come up with algorithms to translate it and, fundamentally, this is about communication or restoring people's ability to communicate. (BBC Frontiers 13.4.2005)

If you can set your research within some anecdotal framework it will help both to make it memorable and to 'humanise' you, the scientist.

Humour too is entertaining and useful. If your work has an amusing element in it, exploit that in your interview. Some research on novel materials with 'memory' would almost certainly have gone unreported without the scientist saying, during a press conference, that this would allow underwear manufacturers to create a bra that would 'remember' the exact shape of the breasts of its wearer and model itself accordingly. The world's media had a wonderful time with that!

Pictures then are valuable to you in interviews. So too is a certain amount of reflexivity. Bring yourself and your feelings into the interview if appropriate. When discussing possible environmental hazards, for example, it strengthens a researcher's case if he or she says things like: '*I have children/ a partner/ a pet too and I'm worried about it*' or '*You've every right to ask that question. I would too in your place*' and so on. In other words, be yourself.

THE WORST QUESTIONS IN THE WORLD

You know better than anyone what is in your own Orwellian 'Room 101' so far as difficult questions are concerned. Make a list of these and work out your answers. But bear in mind that, however threatening or aggressive a question may be, you can – if you have your material ready to use – always come back with your positive message.

Use deflection. Politicians do it all the time when they say '*That's a good question and I'll answer it in a moment but, before I do, let me tell you . . .*'. Not only do they get across the points they wanted to make, but they gain valuable thinking time. With luck of course, especially in a live interview, the interviewer may never have time to bring you back to the hard question if you carry on talking for long enough.

If you do not know the answer to a question, say so. It is better to offer to find out an answer than to lie or appear evasive. Ask the interviewer to rephrase the question if you do not understand it. (Even if you do understand it, this will again give you thinking time, if you need it.) Never use a phrase such as '*No comment*'. To journalists and probably to the public at large, this means '*I am guilty/ lying/ have something to hide/ not to be trusted.*'

DEMANDS OF TELEVISION

So far, what we have been discussing relates to all branches of the electronic media. An interview on television though is a bit different from a radio encounter in that you are visually as well as verbally exposed. Your appearance and manner matter, just as much as what you say. The surly, unshaven Richard Nixon lost the presidential TV battle with the handsomely packaged J.F. Kennedy before either of them uttered a word.

So far as your physical appearance is concerned, you should not get too paranoid. Everyone initially hates their appearance (just as they hate the sound of their own voice). Given that you are not going to have extensive and dramatic cosmetic surgery to 'improve' yourself, here are a few tips:

- Dress quietly – suit or dress – without too many strong colours and patterns.
- Avoid tinted lenses if you can. Television makes you look shifty if you wear them.
- Accept the offer of a change of tie/sweater/blouse from the director as he or she knows best. The same is true of make-up.
- Above all, feel comfortable in your clothes and choose them to convey the image you feel appropriate – be this busy researcher or calm administrator.

More important than the minutiae of clothing is your body language. Sit forward on chair or sofa. Leaning back looks defensive, as if you want to escape. Look at the interviewer – not cameras or crew – and use your normal non-verbal language – nodding the head, hand gestures, smiles, frowns. If this causes a problem with say the camera alignment, this is for the director to resolve not you.

PRACTICE PAYS

There may well be an 'interview gene', but everyone can (and does) improve with practice. You can arrange this for yourself. Interview yourself in your own head. Ask the sorts of questions you think appropriate and think of ways of answering them. Try alternative explanations if you get dragged down by technicality. Alternatively find someone from a totally different area of research or, better still, from someone outside science altogether and try out your explanations. It is all a bit like an actor thinking himself into an unfamiliar role. You have one big advantage over the actor, though. The lines you speak are your own.

EDITING, VETTING AND OTHER MATTERS

Pre-recorded interviews – like newspaper interviews – are invariably edited. For three reasons: to bring them to the required length; to eliminate boring, repetitive and extraneous material such as stops and starts or coughs and sneezes; and to select the segment needed for the particular purpose of the interview. Anything you say may be used which is a good reason for not saying anything you do not want to be broadcast. Most editing is purely cosmetic – cleaning up the messy bits.

It is unreasonable to ask a broadcaster to let you hear or see the 'edited version' of the interview. There usually is not enough time for this in the programme maker's fairly frenetic schedule. If something changes in the news agenda – a bomb explodes in a city or a stock market crashes – then your 3-minute interview may be rapidly cut to 90 seconds or less. All this happens in real time – so there is simply no opportunity for you to review your contribution.

To put it another way, if an interviewer, especially a news journalist, says to you with the best will in the world: *'You'll be able to hear the piece before it goes out'*, do not believe him. No one can guarantee you a preview. There are exceptions to this, but relatively few.

The good news is that, on the whole, misrepresentation is rare. Reporters do like to make their stories accurate and fair. It would be quite foolhardy for them to incur the wrath and suspicion of key organisations such as universities and research institutes that represent a constant source of major stories.

In sum, symbiosis rather than parasitism is the relationship you should expect. Both sides should benefit from the interaction.

AN INTERVIEW CHECKLIST

Finally, here is brief checklist for any intending interviewee about to sit in front of a microphone (or camera) for the first time.

(1) *Attitude is crucial.* Remember throughout the interview that the journalist is asking the questions he or she believes the audience wants answered. Be friendly and courteous – and expect your interviewer to be the same. This is a chat, an exchange of ideas – not a battleground.

(2) *Answer the question.* That means listening to it, acknowledging it and giving some sort of reply – even if you want to go off at a tangent with your own, positive points.

(3) *Slow down and sit still.* Too much movement of the body or too rapid speech can be tiresome for audiences. If your ideas are complicated you may lose them altogether.

(4) *Don't try to fill the silence.* The interviewer is paid to do that.

(5) *Use verbal pictures* to explain concepts, emphasise important points and entice your listeners.

(6) *Avoid technicality, jargon, theory, methodology.*

(7) Bring in *storytelling and humour* if appropriate.

(8) Be *enthusiastic*. If you are not, you cannot expect anyone else to be remotely interested in what you are saying. Enthusiasm and commitment act as a powerful incentive to audiences to stick with technical explanations, even when these are at the very limits of their understanding.

(9) *Never argue with your interviewer*. By all means correct a wrong impression or fact but do not create a confrontation. You will always lose, however strong your arguments.

(10) Afterwards, thank your interviewer and ask the producer or reporter to let you have *a copy of the interview* as broadcast so that you can review your performance.

Key resources

(1) Programme material

BBC website (bbc.co.uk). Access a huge range of BBC audio and visual material, especially the archive for the documentary radio series *'Frontiers'* which can be heard via the *'Listen Again'* facility.

(2) Media skills

In truth, there is alarmingly little literature available (apart from this volume) on the practicalities of being interviewed. However, the following does contain some relevant material: *Hitting the Headlines*, Stephen White, Peter Evans, Chris Mihill and Maryon Tysoe, BPS Books.

(3) Science communication in general

These titles offer valuable insights and background – and have the added merit of readability! *Communicating Science: Professional, Popular, Literary*, Nicholas Russell, Cambridge; *Science in Public*, Jane Gregory and Steve Miller, Basic Books; *Social Scientists Meet the Media*, Edited by Cheryl Haslam and Alan Bryman, Routledge.

17

Nanotechnology and the media: front page or no story?

In the mid 90s, the combination of Prince Charles' fears about 'grey goo' and Michael Crichton's novel *The Swarm* served to increase fears that nanotechnology would be the latest in a series of late twenti-eth-century science scares that would hinder if not completely delay development and application of the needed technology. The fact that science communication was still in its infancy and that many of the limited pool of practitioners had been involved in the nuclear and GM debates added to an air of near fatalism. It was feared that only one incident of, for example, toxic nanoparticle release would suffice to push public opinion decisively and irreversibly against the technology. In this chapter, drawing on my experience as a public relations practitioner rather than an academic, I will investigate the reality of the situation and come to the conclusion that this is far too simplistic a view and furthermore, that nanotechnology has had a fairly easy ride in the media and is far from top of the agenda for even specialist journalists. This avoidance of scandal has enabled nanotechnology to put down such strong roots and already deliver such tangible benefits that I believe its future is secure. Any future problems will be viewed by the media on a case-by-case basis and not lead to condemnation of the technology *per se*. The chapter is based on a series of situation reviews presented by the author to the European Commission-funded NanoBio-RAISE and Nanomed Round Table projects during the 2005–2010 period.

The first issue seems to be that those involved in 'protecting' the image of nanotechnology have failed to see the 'bigger' picture. Natur-ally they believe that nanotechnology is one of the main issues in science and thus of major importance to the media. Nothing could be

Successful Science Communication, ed. D. J. Bennett and R. C. Jennings. Published by Cambridge University Press. © Cambridge University Press 2011.

further from the truth. In one of the greatest eras of scientific advance, nanotechnology is competing for 'share of voice' with topics such as cloning, the Human Genome Project, HIV research, general medical advances, particle physics and more recently global warming and climate change.

Competing is indeed the operative word, since if we look at the media world, science is only one of a number of topics covered by the media. Domestic news, foreign affairs, politics, business, lifestyle, health, entertainment and sport predominate. Furthermore, the increasing fight for circulation, and thus the other lifeblood of the media, advertising revenue, means that editors put pressure on journalists to 'sex up' stories, believing a diet of scandal and controversy sells more issues than balanced debate. In the UK, in a trend being followed by other countries, there is an increasing tendency for all stories to be celebrity-led or at least have a human angle.

In general, staff journalists, let alone the vast army of freelancers who depend on 'selling' in ideas, find this pressure hard to resist. Many a balanced thoughtful overview has suffered from the modern equivalent of the editor's red pen – the delete button. When it comes to specialist science writers, the pressure is often unbearable.

At this juncture it is worth looking at the development of science reporting over the last 20–30 years, again focussing on the UK since developments here were on the whole mirrored elsewhere. The 'science' correspondent/editor was originally a highly respected position with their submitted copy being published unedited because of its specialist content. Many of the correspondents had science degrees themselves and came to the position through work on peer-review publications such as *Nature*. In the broadsheets, there also seemed to be the assumption that the reader was fairly well educated and that there was nothing wrong with challenging them with difficult concepts. Accompanying illustrations were either extremely complex or amateurish in the extreme. This situation carried on through the GM crisis during which agriculture and political correspondents took the lead.

The real turning point for science reporting came with Dolly the Sheep. In my opinion the reason for this was that for the first time there was a specialist public relations agency involved in 'launching' Dolly to the world. This in turn stemmed from the foresight of the Roslin Institute and PPL Therapeutics scientific team and De Facto Communications led by Sue Charles who took the conscious decision to prewarn science correspondents in the first instance about the successful cloning of sheep embryos by the Roslin Institute. Anticipating widespread public interest, a great deal of effort was put into producing understandable briefing packs, question-and-answer sheets and simplified graphics. Unheard of at the time for a science story, a 'situation' room was set up at the agency to deal with enquiries. However, no one could have foreseen the impact the story would have, as witnessed by the almost simultaneous arrival on the Sunday night of faxes from the Vatican and the White House asking for briefing notes!

Science correspondents were in demand to say the least – feted and given top place at the editorial table. Print journalists found themselves giving radio and TV comment. However they were also overwhelmed by the physical demands of the ongoing media circus and had to enlist the help of colleagues from other desks. And this opened a Pandora's Box. Firstly Dolly, her high profile and the interesting 'unstuffy' way in which she was reported inspired a whole new generation of science communicators. Soon every research institute in the country had a communications team and the whole business of science communication became almost self-replicating as universities fell over themselves to introduce science communications modules if not whole degrees. Interestingly at the same time, the discovery of DNA fingerprinting added a new dimension to crime fighting and inspired a whole new series of crime TV shows such as the CSI TV programme franchise in the USA and BBC TV's *"Waking the Dead"* which in turn have ironically led to the current glut of forensic science graduates!

However the media did not rush to hire this new generation. Instead existing journalists were emboldened to tackle science issues and in fact many took the attitude of *'Why shouldn't I write about science – the most important consideration is that I am a trained journalist.'*

In short, forced to simplify the science for their colleagues, specialist science journalists lost their position as ultimate gatekeepers. Science as popular entertainment became a general trend. Government concern about standards of science teaching in schools also gave a major boost to children's programmes and science centres. Lovely, cuddly Dolly proved a perfect role model.

Furthermore, the frank open reporting about Dolly paved the way for the next major scientific advance – the Human Genome Project. This had all the classic ingredients of an adventure to capture the public's imagination: the race between the 'goodies' at the Sanger and the 'baddy' Craig Venter – and the promise of untold treasures for mankind in the form of healthcare breakthroughs. The fact that it was billed as the Human Genome rather than just the Genome Project and could be steered initially towards safe areas such as incurable diseases meant that the politicians again could embrace the project. Sensing votes by being able to promise rapid healthcare paybacks for relatively small investments they became enthusiastic backers on both sides of the Atlantic and beyond. Genome research centres sprang up like mushrooms as each country sought to play a role including China, then opening up, which came in towards the end and did 1% of the sequence.

In addition, the world economy was going through a boom period and again the politicians sensed that one of the main ways – in the UK it seemed even above lowering taxes – was to invest in healthcare provision. And the scientists rapidly learned to play the game – perhaps too well, since what was essentially a blue sky breakthrough was portrayed in the media as the gateway to vast short-term gains in the form of personalised medicine.

Coupled with the rapid technological innovation in the fields of computing and telecommunications and science was becoming an all-round good thing! People were seeing for themselves personal benefits from scientific advances. Antagonism and suspicion were largely banished. GM seemed dead and buried, as was nuclear power. True not that many kids were going into science, but Europe and the US still seemed to think that scientific innovation could be a key strength of their future economies. As did the EU which was looking for areas in which to form its own policy.

It was against this background that nanotechnology arrived on the scene. The EU immediately saw an opportunity to use nanotechnology as an example of a pan-European enabling technology that could benefit the economies of both individual states and the EU as a whole. By creating the regulatory and other environments deemed necessary for successful development of nanotechnology research and applications, the EU could demonstrate its worth in framing science/economic policy.

For a combination of factors, the EU also regarded public opinion and acceptance as key to successful uptake of nanotechnologies. Partly this was a result of new awareness of the 'power of PR' and partly because many of those involved in framing science policy remembered beyond the Genome Project back to the GM fiasco.

To this end the EU started to commission a series of projects looking at all aspects of nanotechnology – regulatory, safety, economic impact, ethics and communications. The question was whether the economic benefits – if proven – were going to outweigh potential safety and ethical concerns. The main approach taken by these projects was to gather expert groups to investigate these topics individually and then together.

My interest began with one of these groups NanoBio-RAISE where I was invited because of my background as director of a leading science PR agency and thus supposed wealth of front-line experience of communicating controversial science issues such as stem cells, cloning, agriscience and fertility. My role was fourfold:

— to explain the workings of modern science media
— to report on the current state of nanotechnology reporting and image
— to advise on how the perceived issues related to nanotechnology might play out in the media
— to suggest how nanotechnology could be 'promoted' in a responsible way to enable informed public opinion to appear.

In explaining the workings of science media, I stressed many of the points already covered.

Looking at that moment in time, science reporting was almost becoming a victim of its own success. There were so many press releases being issued on a daily basis by researchers, companies and institutions around the world that rather than substantial in-depth pieces, coverage was being reduced to snippets with bolder and bolder headlines – *"Cure for Cancer", "New Gene Holds Key to Autism"*, etc. This in turn prevented consistency and context-building in the reader's mind.

Such was the demand for science content that I emphasised that science reporting was no longer the preserve of specialists. You could find news, social affairs, economic, industrial, business, environmental, political, lifestyle and even religious correspondents writing 'expert' or 'opinion' pieces. Furthermore, this observation was based on experience close to home. My wife was at that time a health and beauty editor for the leading women's magazine, *Grazia*, and despite her non-science background saw no reason why she should not write about nanotechnology – one story doing the rounds at that time was the use of nanoparticles to make suncreams smoother and more effective – along with other controversial topics such as DNA, gene expression, etc.

Again speaking to an audience who were used to honing and refining manuscripts over a long period, I thought it also worth explaining the time pressures journalists worked under. Staff journalists work to daily deadlines, only having a few hours to research and write. Naturally they turn to the internet since they know information is there waiting to be mined. However, when it comes to digging further, time becomes a real issue – no matter how extensive their contact book is, there is always a fair chance that nobody will be available. Freelancers work in two ways – either being commissioned to follow up an existing story with a definite deadline or to write up an idea they have pitched. Either way they still have major time pressures – if only to be able to pay the bills they need to get work in on time if not sooner. So the rather naïve belief that a freelancer puts his/her all into a piece and you perhaps get more than from a staff writer does not in my experience hold true. They do exactly what they have to – not a word or phone call more. So in essence the 'accuracy' of the piece depends on availability of information/spokespeople at any given time.

On top of this I pointed out that whilst stories in their original form might contain balanced opinions and detailed research, this could change dramatically when placed in front of an editor. Whole paragraphs could be cut, introductions and conclusions changed and attention-grabbing headlines inserted. At least in that situation there was a chance of a warning. A still worse situation often arose when a story has had last-minute changes from a sub-editor – and it appears upon further investigation just for the fun of it! Many a time my own agency has had to explain to a client why a story the original journalist had checked with them appeared in a far more sensationalist form. And of course there is even less control over what a picture editor decides to provide from stock libraries usually to add further colour to a piece.

Incredulity grew even further amongst my fellow project members whose dealings with the press were in the main restricted to peer-reviewed journals when I went on to explain the time pressures most journalists work under. Whereas submitting a peer-reviewed article can take months, even years, to publication, national press work to punishing deadlines with often only a few hours to research and write a piece. This is bearing in mind that although my original presentation was only a few years ago I would now have to rewrite that section with the advent of blogging and twittering to say many journalists comment and write in real-time! Which of course opens up a whole new can of worms.

However my final point was too much for some. Rather than second-guess, I thought it would be instructive for my colleagues to know what journalists were actually taught to look for in a story. I boiled this down to three ingredients, which could be present in any combination –

- Sex
- Scandal
- Celebrity

Even though by sex I meant excitement, this was taken too literally and one member actually commented that why should we have to communicate with journalists and by default the public at all if they were so ignorant! On the whole though my observation was noted and accepted, if not approved. I also backed it up by looking at the current situation of science reporting which on balance seemed positive as the following table shows.

Sex – Genome Project, cloning, forensics
Scandal – GM, BSE, blood transfusions
Personality – Dolly, CSI, Venter, Winston, Greenfield

The next step was to present a snapshot of nanotechnology reporting to date. I chose to approach this as if I was a journalist looking into nanotechnology and if there was potential for a hard-hitting story with any of the above-mentioned ingredients. There were four main tools we would use in such a situation –

(1) Google searching
(2) A journalistic tool called Lexis–Nexis which tracks coverage in leading publications worldwide
(3) Websites of key publications in main European countries – France, Germany, UK
(4) Journalist survey.

In order to get a sense of perspective I repeated the exercise for GM.

Google was chosen because it was just starting to come into its own as a tool for journalists – although it is established as their No. 1 source nowadays. In the words of one respected science journalist: *'I start with a press release, then read the full paper and get a feel for what else has gone on in the area by searching on Google, as well as speaking to a couple of different sources if they are available.'*

The results were illuminating to say the least. On Google there was a relatively high number of hits for both nanotechnology– some 18 million. But more importantly and illustrated by a comparison with 'Googling' GM, there was little controversy. The first page of entries – beyond which journalists would rarely stray – was dominated by research institutes, guides to nanotechnology and Wikipedia. No sign of Prince Charles's fears about grey goo or Crichton's scary prophecies having found devotees. Contrast this to the first page of Google searching for GM which resembled a bloody battlefield with corporations trying to silence NGOs – the stuff of dreams for an investigative journalist. No, a journalist looking for scandal or even sex as the basis for a nanotech story would probably give up at the first hurdle. You would wonder what all the fuss was about – and only get a hint if you could be bothered to plough your way through to the end of the Wikipedia entry which merely stated:

- *There is some speculation about doomsday scenarios which have led to a debate amongst advocacy groups and governments on whether special regulation is warranted.*
- *The Centre for Responsible Nanotechnology suggests that new developments could result, among other things, in untraceable weapons of mass destruction, networked cameras for use by the government, and weapons developments fast enough to destabilize arms races ("Nanotechnology Basics").*
- *Alternatively exacerbate the wealth gap between developed and developing nations.*
- *Researchers have discovered that silver nanoparticles used in socks to reduce foot odour are being released in the wash with possible negative consequences*
- *A major study published more recently in* Nature Nanotechnology *suggests some forms of carbon annotates – a poster child for the "nanotechnology revolution" – could be as harmful as asbestos if inhaled in sufficient quantities*

However, I felt that these potential risk stories were balanced by the number of serious prestigious institutes associated with nanotechnology. Surely any journalist would think *'Why would they be involved if there is a risk? There's no story here.'*

In addition, and again in contrast with GM, the nanotechnology images and videos on offer were in the main positive.

Nanomedicine was a bit more promising – with hints of new cures and treatments. But again, nothing earth shattering compared for example to a search on the Human Genome.

The next step was to look at Lexis–Nexis which for years was the primary research tool used by journalists since it was able to provide electronic summaries and cuttings of articles appearing in the world's press for a fee. Using the same search terms, 'nanotechnology' and 'nanomedicine', only revealed a handful of articles – 716 mentions over the previous 6 months compared to 675 on the hottest topic at that time – body cleanses – in 1 week.

Lexis–Nexis as with all cutting services was not, however, 100% reliable, and so I also looked at some of the key European quality press in Germany, UK and France. I deliberately chose titles that I knew had a reputation for science coverage. If they were not writing about nano-technology nobody would be. These included *Le Soir*, *Sciences et Avenir* and *La Recherche* in France, *Der Spiegel*, *Die Welt* and *Focus* in Germany and *The Times*, *The Economist* and *New Scientist* in the UK. On top of this I also looked at the BBC.

The results were sparse to say the least – only a handful of stories. In France concentrating on the wonders of nanotechnology and potential in treating CNS disorders in particular, in Germany on Nanorobots and in the UK on nanomaterials and nanomedicines and a little on human enhancement. However no scandalous headlines and hardly anything to suggest that nanotech was a subject that would feature heavily in the future.

Finally I phoned round a number of leading science journalists in the UK, drawing the response that they were highly unlikely to proactively write about nanotechnology unless there was a major scandal and in general they were unaware of any major issues, having dismissed Prince Charles's and Crichton's claims. One or two were aware of some potential problems with nanoparticles in suncreams but saw this as an isolated incident and were not drawing general conclusions about health risks. They had plenty of other issues to deal with and little time to look into the subject.

Science freelancer: *No, I don't think it will be like GM – I think we've already seen much more positive press on nanotech, mainly because of the medical benefits.*
The main negative stuff has been the 'carbon nanotubes are as toxic as asbestos' thing. And there's been a lot of concern about the effect of nanoparticles on the environment.
But I think the biggest problem is that a lot of people still don't really understand what it is, or they just switch off when they hear about it. That's just my take on it though!

Science/health TV reporter: *I don't think you can say nanotech has blown over. Seem to remember that* Which? *came out with some negative comments a few months ago.*
All depends whether *The Mail* decides it wants to start another health scare.
Think GM food and MMR vaccine . . . they took on a life of their own without any good science showing there was a reason to be concerned!

Leading international science journal: *My view is that nano will become a major issue, but not in the same way as GM.*
The 'very small' concept isn't as intuitively scary as 'shuffling' genes, so it will take some nasty findings in the 'nano' field before people sit up and realise there needs to be some regulation – and some safety research.

Leading broadsheet journalist: *I wish I could foresee the future. I suspect not, unless there was some sort of health scare over it. But anything is possible.*

Overall I reported that nanotechnology was not really on the media's radar – even for the specialist press. Therefore there was a breathing space to clarify the risks buried in Wikipedia and how they could be reported in the future – and possible counter-arguments.

The other experts in the project then duly proceeded to come up with a range of issues that certainly had all the ingredients of headline-grabbing stories! Two seemed to have particular potential for creating bad headlines.

Toxicity – the size of the particles and their ability to filter through cell walls – the very property that made them ironically so useful for use as medicines and imaging agents – could be magnified into a health risk on the scale of asbestos and anthrax. As to how this could come about, scenarios were conjured up, the favourite being an explosion at a nano factory causing a cloud of nanoparticles to be released over the neighbouring town!

Human enhancement – whilst initial discussions on nanomedicine focussed on the potential for regenerative medicine, they soon moved on to the idea of human enhancement. Nanotechnology was seen as a potential key to creating superhumans. Again I could see a storm being whipped up leading to a potential call for a moratorium on research.

However, this had to balanced against applications of nanotechnology where there were no obvious risks, only advantages:

Medicine – a journalist I had briefed concluded that nanomedicine provides a new paradigm in medicine. By enabling improved imaging and diagnosis of disease as well as more effective delivery of therapeutics, nanomedicine also held the key to reducing healthcare costs.

Materials – smart materials would be welcomed by the public with for example temperature-sensitive coatings. As would stronger light car components reducing fuel consumption.

Fuels – nano additives could again increase fuel efficiency and reduce pollution.

Food – could be a problem because of the bizarre public attitudes to food science. On the one hand they wanted fresh natural food sourced organically even, on the other they wanted uniformity of shape, preservatives to increase storage life and were not adverse to superfoods with additives such as omega-3 and other vitamins. Also the food companies seemed to be extremely reluctant to admit any nanotechnology research.

Consumer goods – of course the iPod Nano led the way, but constantly improving and more powerful phones, laptops, etc. would be welcomed as empowering.

My gut instinct at the time was therefore that there could/ probably would be isolated problems, but nanotechnology *per se* would not automatically be seen as 'bad'. Therefore I concluded that the way to proceed was to anticipate and prepare.

By this I meant providing information in an open and transparent way, with up-to-date websites, newsletters, briefings, etc. spearheaded by respected research institutions rather than government or industry. Of course the press were not naïve enough to think that all research institutes were completely independent but were at least often prepared to give them a chance to put their case as opposed to industry or government spokespeople.

That was the situation some five years ago in 2005. Doing a similar analysis today in mid-2010 at the time of writing, I find that nanotechnology has advanced as a science without too much of a fuss in the media. Again if I was to start out to write a sensationalist story I would probably be disappointed. Amazingly the first page of a Google Search has remained almost unchanged: Wikipedia and a series of informative, in truth rather 'geeky' and almost generic, 'guide to nanotechnology' and 'nanotechnology' research institute sites. Nor are the upfront images even vaguely disturbing.

Lexis–Nexis as a searchable archive is pretty redundant these days such is the power of Google and the new favourite of journalists, YouTube. Yes, the majority of users are probably looking for the latest weird home video stunt, but YouTube came second in a survey of top research tools used by journalists. It is widely used by NGOs and companies to post informative video content and since many journalists are nowadays tasked to provide copy for both printed and on-line editions, they naturally gravitate there.

What then does a YouTube search on nanotechnology reveal? Some 5000 hits and this time, believe it or not, a series of videos on the first page giving the image that nanotechnology is cool. Hip presenters in science centres take us on nano tours and then there is the wonderful 'nano' song that deserves a far wider audience!

So no scandal there and a look at leading websites again fails to excite the scandal hunt. For example, the BBC has only some educational pieces – with only Woman's Hour of all places hinting at a need to ask questions on where it might all lead.

Even if I was to cheat with my inside knowledge and combine the search terms nanotechnology and toxicity I would be disappointed. The entries date from several years back, talking rather tamely about the need for some research – little calls for moratoriums or prophecies of doom. In addition the fact that the entries are old automatically kills the story in a journalist's mind. *'Must be under control'* is probably the automatic reaction.

Going back to the journalists, most of whom are still in place, I got similar responses. Nothing much has happened, they assume the toxicity issue is under control and human enhancement fears are too fanciful. They continue to be swamped by stories on healthcare discoveries, while some of them have been diverted almost full-time to the current big thing – climate change. And since the world is looking to science to solve this problem (as well as trying to make our iPod Nanos even smaller and smarter), science is getting a pretty good press just now. Nanotechnology is not an issue. And even if it was, some of the nano bioethicists are coming up with some radical thoughts – surprise surprise, just as all journalists think they can write about science, it appears increasingly that the public can understand that science involves risks and that their presence alone is no reason to halt research. Which in the long run might be good for journalism in that the public start to look for balanced investigative pieces rather than sensationalist snippets. Some hope.

Key resources

European Science Foundation (2005) *ESF Forward Look on Nanomedicine 2005.* www.nanopharmaceuticals.org/files/nanomedicine.pdf

Azonano (2005) *Survey Shows Print Media Shuns Nanotechnology*, posted 15 Dec 2005. www.azonano.com/news.asp?newsID=1728 -

New Scientist (2005) After the hype – what Dolly the Sheep really did for us, *New Scientist*, Magazine issue 2558, 3 July 2006. www.newscientist.com/. . ./mg19125582.900-after-the-hype-what-dolly-the-sheep-really-did-for-us.html

Project on Emerging Technologies (2005) *Nanotechnology and the Media: Realities and Risk*, 14 Dec 2005. www.nanotechproject.org/events/archive/new_page/-

Project on Emerging Technologies (2007) *Nanotechnology and the Media: The Inside Story*, 18 Dec 2007. www.wilsoncenter.org/index.cfm?topic_id=166192&fuseaction=topics.event_summary&event_id=343009

Nanopublic (2008) *Germany: Positive Image of Nanotechnology in the Media*, 14 Nov 2008. http://nanopublic.blogspot.com/2008/11/germany-positive-image-of.html

Frank Swain (2010) The dangers of nanotech, *Wired*, 14 Sept 2010. http://scienceblogs.com/sciencepunk/2010/09/the_dangers_of_nanotech.php

18

The power of the podcast: the *Naked Scientists'* story

PODCAST – *distribute (multimedia files) over the Internet for playback on a mobile device or a personal computer.*

In 2010, the *Naked Scientists* project entered its tenth year of operations, celebrating in the process more than 14 million downloads of its programmes internationally. From humble beginnings on a small-scale commercial radio station it now ranks amongst the world's most downloaded science shows with a loyal following in almost every country. This transition occurred through a communication revolution that swept across the Internet in the early 'noughties': the podcast. By making available to all, on demand, content that would previously have been accessible only to a small number of people, the *Naked Scientists* used the true power of the web – the ability to scale at very low cost.

Rather than lecture the reader on the pros, cons and general power of podcasting, I have chosen to chart the route that the *Naked Scientists* venture has taken. Hopefully our experiences as we have grown from what began as a spare-bedroom-based weekend hobby for one, into a unique university-based international multimedia multi-million-audience enterprise with five staff, two interns (currently) and a PhD student will help to encourage others to communicate science in even more imaginative ways of their own. . .

BACKGROUND TO THE NAKED SCIENTISTS

What do you get if you take an onion, chop it finely, add water, half a pint of washing-up liquid (lemon-scented variety optional), a handful of

Successful Science Communication, ed. D. J. Bennett and R. C. Jennings. Published by Cambridge University Press. © Cambridge University Press 2011.

salt and simmer at 60°C (140°F) for 10–20 minutes before pouring through a coffee filter, collecting the juice, adding some fresh pineapple juice, incubating at body temperature for 10 minutes and then adding some ice-cold aftershave?

The answer is: a glutinous blob not dissimilar to 'snot'.

Contrary to what you might be thinking, the recipe above is actually a technique for extracting large amounts of DNA from an onion using simple ingredients you can find at home. More importantly, it's also the recipe that got the *Naked Scientists* started on the radio.

I've always been very keen on science, and particularly on talking to people about it, so when someone emailed me asking if I would be willing to help out at Cambridge University's annual Science Festival, by giving a talk or demonstrating something suitably scientific, I jumped at the chance.

It was early 1999, I was half way through my medical degree and PhD, and the GM food debacle was in full swing. But, from talking to people, it was pretty clear that most hadn't got the faintest idea what DNA actually is or even what it looks like, let alone how it works, so this seemed like the perfect opportunity to show them.

In front of an assembled audience who had packed into one of the university's lecture theatres, I set up the onion DNA demonstration a bit like a cooking programme, inviting members of the audience to 'come on down' and help with the procedure.

The end result was a spectacular handful of onion DNA, a rapt audience for whom I was able to debunk many of the inflammatory molecular myths being peddled by the mass media and, even more exciting, a phone call from a local commercial radio station inviting me for an interview the following Thursday.

For moral support, I took along a public-spirited scientific colleague, Shibley Rahman, who is extremely funny and very articulate. Initially we appeared as guests on someone else's show but, quite quickly, it became clear that to realise the true potential of what we wanted to do, we were going to need our own show. As luck would have it, at around the same time one of the UK's mainstream scientific funding bodies, the Biotechnology and Biological Sciences Research Council (BBSRC), unveiled a new scheme to promote the 'public understanding of science' – by getting scientists talking about their subjects – and they were looking for applicants.

Thinking 'in for a penny, in for a pound,' I immediately launched into negotiations with the radio station to attempt to buy a year's worth of airtime in order to set up a dedicated one-hour weekly science programme that would be broadcast live on a Sunday evening. After some very lengthy discussions we eventually had a deal, and after a hurried bid for funding from the BBSRC, in January 2000 we heard we'd been successful in our bid, and the show, which was initially christened *ScienceWorld*, was on the road. I signed up another 'sciencey' colleague from Cambridge University, Catherine Hawkins, as a co-presenter alongside Shibley. Together, on 20 February 2000, we took the plunge.

I'm sure we sounded terrible to begin with. The transition from guest to show host is a difficult one. That said, we improved rapidly and before long it was really starting to hang together. We turned the show into a light-hearted look at what was happening each week in the world of science, technology and medicine, and interspersed the chat with popular chart music.

One of the things we had realised during the first series of the show was that, with a live radio programme, if someone missed the show or lived too far away to tune in, they missed out and there was no prospect of being able to catch up on the content again later. The solution, I felt, was to make use of something that was beginning to transform the way we communicate the whole world over: the Internet. This, I knew, had the potential to deliver a truly global audience, and at very low cost.

At the time, virtually no one was doing anything like this, and certainly not for science radio programming, so I wrote another grant application to the BBSRC asking for support for a further series and funding to develop a website to act as an online companion to the radio show. The idea was to maximise the reach and educational potential of the material being generated for each show by archiving it in text and audio formats on the web so that anyone, anywhere, anytime, could listen to it, or read it.

I also realised we needed a sexier name, and, while I was trying to write a particularly challenging part of my thesis, the name 'Naked Scientists' drifted into my head. It seemed like the perfect choice – it was slightly naughty, it made people laugh, it clearly said 'geek-free', and best of all, the domain name was unclaimed on the Internet!

The BBSRC were kind enough to grant us another year's support so, after my medical finals, armed with an idiot's guide to HTML, a very large jar of coffee and some very late nights, I taught myself how to code webpages and set up www.thenakedscientists.com during the two weeks of 'holiday' I had before my new job as a medical doctor began in the late summer of 2001. As a result, when the new *Naked Scientists* radio show hit the airwaves shortly afterwards it also went live across the Internet, becoming in the process one of world's first science podcasts.

The BBC called up mid-series to invite me over for a 'chat', which culminated in an offer to move the next series of the show to BBC Radio Cambridgeshire. This would see us grow from talking to a few thousand people around the city and outlying villages, to talking to a whole county. By this time it was obvious that we were on to something and that what we were doing had the potential to be much bigger. But having never had any formal training in radio or science communication, I couldn't help thinking that I lacked the experience and credibility required to drive a project like this forward to reach greater heights, and bigger audiences.

Having drawn a blank in my search for some help achieving the necessary training and experience in the UK, I decided to look *down under* – to Australia, not least because I'd heard that the weather was a lot nicer there! By luck rather than judgement I found my way onto the website of the Australian Broadcasting Corporation (ABC), and from there came across the work of someone who I later realised is undeniably one of the best science radio presenters in the business, Robyn Williams.

At the time I had no idea who this person was, so I wrote a brief email introducing myself and explaining what I was trying to do but didn't really expect to hear anything back. You can imagine my surprise then when, one Friday evening someone from Australia called saying that Robyn Williams was in London for a conference and was willing to meet me.

What ensued was a two-hour conversation, over several cups of coffee, about the creation of the *Naked Scientists* and the fact that I felt, to take it further, that I really needed some training in how to do things the 'right' way. Robyn immediately offered to arrange for me to go to Sydney to join the ABC Radio National Science Unit for a spell in 2004. The only thing missing was the minor matter of money and sponsorship. Fortunately, there is a wonderful organisation called the Winston Churchill Memorial Trust (www.wcmt.org.uk), which was established as a living memory to Winston Churchill and offers 'the opportunity of a lifetime' to successful applicants who want to do something 'life-changing'.

So, in late 2002, I applied to the Churchill Trust, and after a month or two, and an intense interview, I received a letter saying that I had been awarded a prestigious Churchill Fellowship. Being the only person from my home county (Essex)[1] to win one of the Fellowships that year, the press release of successful applicants published by the Trust

---

[1] UK county to the north-east of London endowed(?) with a characteristic culture(?) much envied(?) by people from elsewhere.

was picked up by BBC Essex, who invited me along to take part in *Tea at 3, with Steve*, one of their afternoon talk programmes. I went along to tell them what I'd been up to and what I had planned, but while I was there I also took the opportunity to play some of our previous *Naked Scientists* shows to the BBC Essex director of programming, Tim Gillett. Two days later he phoned to say that, when the new series of the *Naked Scientists* started on the BBC in Cambridge, they would also like to broadcast it simultaneously on BBC Essex, potentially tripling our audience. Furthermore, he wondered whether, in the meantime, I would like to make some special two-hour-long Bank Holiday programmes for them?

The prospect of running a two-hour live science show, on an untried audience, at peak time, at a radio station I'd visited only once and using equipment I didn't have the foggiest idea how to operate, was trouser-soilingly scary. But then there's always been a part of me that just cannot resist a challenge so, terrified as I was, I heard myself saying 'That'll be wonderful, thank you.'

Mercifully, my fears evaporated when those shows were broadcast live at peak time in May and August 2003. They drew an enormous audience response; people of all ages from nine to ninety phoned in with questions like 'How many pieces of toast can you make with the energy in a lightning bolt?', 'Why does my car do 8 miles to the gallon more with an air filter full of mothballs?', and 'How many organs can I donate and still remain alive?'

They were certainly one of the most enjoyable experiences I've ever had with this project, mainly because I suddenly realised what the show could achieve. Another major benefit of our success on BBC Essex was that the managing editor, a wonderful lady called Margaret Hyde, was sufficiently impressed by what we were doing that she then persuaded all of the other BBC radio stations in the surrounding region, with a potential audience of 6 million, to take the new series of the *Naked Scientists* when it launched the following autumn, in September 2003.

With the BBC relaunch we introduced a few changes. The major change we made was to switch the programme to an all-talk format. We ditched the music and began to focus heavily on science news items, answering more listeners' questions and featuring interviews with live studio guests who had interesting scientific stories to tell. The results were spectacular; we picked up listeners all over the world including people in Australia, Canada, California, and even Japan.

After six months we took a break while I headed off to Sydney to join the ABC in early 2004. At the ABC they threw me in at the deep end. I began making reports for Robyn Williams' *Science Show*, including an interview with the Danish developers of a strain of landmine-locating GM cress plants that turned red when they grew on top of buried ordnance.

Compiling these pieces was a tremendous learning experience. Thankfully, I did improve quite quickly and things began to take hours rather than weeks to complete. It was at this point that Robyn pointed me down the hall in the direction of Radio National's *Breakfast* programme, an extremely popular and hard-hitting news-based talk show broadcast across Australia every weekday morning.

As I was chatting with the production team I looked over their content schedules for the forthcoming week and noticed that there was no coverage of anything remotely connected to science. 'Who's your science reporter?' I asked. 'We don't have anyone,' came the reply. Live radio and commenting on science being something I felt I knew a bit about, I asked if they'd let me step in. 'Sure, let's give it a go,' they said.

So, out of that wander down the hall came a weekly seven-minute science slot on Radio National *Breakfast*. Each week I would trawl through the journals and pick out the highest impact discoveries and breakthroughs and then go into the studio to talk about them live on air with the presenter. What it taught me was how to spot strong stories, distil the key points from the scientific paper and then convey those points in the space of just a few minutes of airtime.

Tough as it was to start with, this new science slot quickly became quite popular to the extent that, when I came to leave Australia in mid-2004, the *Breakfast* team asked me to continue to contribute each week from a studio in the UK. I'm really delighted and honoured that the science segment we started in 2004 continues on the ABC, all these years later.

I finally left Australia, with something of a heavy heart (because I knew the weather back home wouldn't be a patch on Sydney sunshine!), in July 2004. Arriving home, I regrouped the *Naked Scientists* presenting team and we set about getting the show back on the road.

One of the things I learned at the ABC is that doing these things well takes teamwork, but up until that time, when it came to the nuts and bolts of actually producing programmes, identifying and booking guests, publishing podcasts and writing webpages, I was pretty much a team of one. And realising that my working pattern was probably not compatible with life much beyond the age of forty, I set about looking for a way to get some help.

Thankfully, the Wellcome Trust came to my rescue. I wrote an application to the Wellcome asking them for some serious funding to take on some staff and to launch the *Naked Scientists* properly, with a major radio and web presence. Daring (and pricey) as that bid was, the Wellcome went for it and agreed to help out. The result was that finally I could take on some professional staff.

It was as we were gearing up to do this in 2005 that Apple's iTunes platform announced that they were going to be opening up their online music store to include podcasts. Realising that this could have a huge impact on our ability to reach a wider, global audience, I took a day off work and sat in my living room, working out how to rewrite the RSS feeds that served up our podcasts to the world so that they would be iTunes compatible. Looking back, that day arguably ranks as one of the best spent and most important things I ever did in the history of the *Naked Scientists*.

In fact, things went so well as a result that the ensuing demand for our content actually blew the top off the processor in our webserver! It happened because, literally overnight, we went from seeing a few thousand web downloads of our programmes every month to receiving tens of thousands of download requests per *day*. The bills for the Internet bandwidth were eye-watering, but it was money well spent because, whilst most people were struggling to find their feet in this new audio-arena and were making one or two shows a month, we were pumping out several studio-quality programmes per week. Consequently, and aided by being one of the few science podcasts around at that time, we secured a huge swathe of loyal listeners, who in turn spread the word and helped us to sign up even bigger audiences, internationally.

We ended up topping the charts in the iTunes stores of most countries worldwide. Suddenly, what had been a small-scale local radio programme from one tiny corner of the UK now had a global following with listeners in all four corners of the Earth. With it came an inbox-busting torrent of emails from listeners far and wide containing ideas for programme topics, feedback, interesting science stories and questions on every subject under the sun.

One listener, a teacher, said he was frequently setting our programmes as 'homework' for his class, and it was this particular communication that got me wondering whether we could take the *Naked Scientists* a step further than being just a radio programme. What if we were to introduce a practical, hands-on experimental component to the broadcast? Could this be the way to produce a programme with simultaneous appeal to both adults and younger people? The answer, it turned out, was 'yes', which is how *Kitchen Science* was born.

The idea was to design a series of experiments that audience members all over the world could try out at home whilst listening to the show; these experiments would make use of simple ingredients and apparatus, which could be located with only a modest amount of cupboard-emptying or larder-raiding. And, most importantly, by making the experiments relevant to the subject matter of each programme, I felt we could add a visual component to the traditionally non-visual medium of radio, making it much easier to convey some of the more complex concepts we wanted to communicate.

Each week we researched, designed and built a suitable hands-on activity that we would include in the show and then ask listeners to attempt to replicate, inviting them to call in live with their 'results', which we broadcast. It was an instant sensation and people loved it. We had listeners everywhere making their own butter, producing clouds in drink bottles, making fireworks from crisp packets and even measuring the speed of light in their microwaves.

But it wasn't all just hard work and physics. Recognising that tea breaks are important too, we decided to carry out the world's first objective, scientific appraisal of the acclaimed uselessness of a chocolate teapot, which, in fact, turns out to be a *myth*: a chocolate teapot, we found, can actually produce a pretty pleasant brew!

To make the teapot, we first needed to know what thickness of chocolate would be required. To find out, we filled sections of Perspex drain pipe with different depths of molten chocolate. Once it had set into a hard plug, we added boiling water and timed how long it took before the chocolate melted out. These experiments showed that a layer of chocolate about an inch thick could withstand the effects of the boiling water without melting through. This meant that, to make an actual teapot, we were going to need nearly 2 kilograms of 'Bournville Dark'. This was obtained by emptying the entire shelf of chocolate in our local shop, the proprietor of which then asked if we wanted any insulin as well, pointing out that there was a chemist next door!

The chocolate was melted and then cast using two glass bowls, one placed inside the other as a mould. A hole was drilled in one side and a spout was assembled and attached, producing a slightly rough, but nonetheless functional teapot, capable, we proved, of brewing a perfectly palatable, albeit slightly sweet, cup of Earl Grey for the *Naked Scientists* team. An added bonus was that, incredibly, it also didn't drip when poured!

Experiments like these helped to reinforce the 'science with a sense of humour' motto we were keen to convey with the *Naked Scientists*; it also helped to attract legions of loyal fans to the radio programmes, podcasts and website.

In the meantime we've also diversified what we do on the radio quite considerably. A chance encounter with a producer from South Africa's hugely popular Johannesburg-based *Talk Radio 702* led to the creation of a *Naked Scientists* weekly slot on the station every Friday morning, featuring me appearing from my living-room studio. The programme runs as a phone-in, giving listeners the opportunity to call up and ask questions about any aspect of science, medicine or technology that's on their minds. The reaction has been huge and it draws a phone-jammingly-large response every week.

Partly as a result of the success of this show, our entire *Naked Scientists* team was invited to take part in the 2009 SciFest, South Africa's annual science festival, which takes place in Grahamstown, the home of Rhodes University on the Eastern Cape, north of Port Elizabeth. What they were after was a series of one-hour science-based stage shows that would entertain and educate young people.

Pulling a few all-nighters, Dave Ansell built a gherkinator – literally an electric chair for gherkins – so we could plug pickles into the mains to make them glow orange; we developed a way to make polycarbonate bottles spectacularly explode when filled with liquid nitrogen; we turned a vacuum cleaner into a bazooka; used a toaster to power a hot-air balloon; and I came up with a few experiments involving hydrogen-powered rockets and methane-filled snakes.

We had just one day to rig up and rehearse after we arrived so this was going to be tight. Nonetheless, the house was packed and the roar from the crowd of 10–13-year-olds when we walked on nearly blew us over. But not quite as nearly as one of the experiments . . .

We were demonstrating how gases burn by igniting balloons filled with hydrogen, which make a satisfying 'boom' when they ignite. But because we figured it was a large auditorium and the audience wanted to see some exciting stuff, I also rigged up a balloon containing a mixture of hydrogen *and* oxygen. When this mixture is lit, it *should* detonate with a much louder bang, because the reaction happens much more quickly. So you can imagine my disappointment when, having talked this up before an expectant audience, I held a lit taper up to the balloon and it just went 'pop'.

What had actually happened is that the taper went out just before it got to the balloon, so all that happened was that the sharp end of the extinguished taper just burst the balloon. Realising this is what had happened, Ben Valsler, the other co-presenter in our team, moved on to another experiment whilst I went backstage to rig up another balloon.

I'm not really sure how I did it, but this time I must have got the mixture of gases absolutely right for the reaction to work perfectly. I was probably also a bit more generous with the amounts I put in too. Anyway, I went back on the stage, apologising for the previous mis-fire, and re-cued the audience; as I donned my ear-defenders I warned them that it might be a bit noisy . . . which actually turned out to be the understatement of the century.

To say that the ensuing blast was devastatingly loud would be like calling a nuclear weapon a small firework. The shockwave literally blew me backwards, destroyed several, normal air-filled balloons that were sitting on a table a yard or two away and filled the air in front of the stage with the dusty remnants of a balloon that appeared to have been ripped apart at the molecular level, quite possibly also creating a simultaneous rift in the space–time continuum.

The audience were momentarily stunned into silence and, for a few seconds, the loud cheering and clapping that had pervaded the rest of the show was replaced by a strange serenity, punctuated only by a cloud descending from the ceiling of the theatre as decades of accumulated dust, dislodged by the blast, began to drift floor-wards. Then everyone went wild, making a noise almost as loud as the blast, crying 'Do it again . . .'

And do it again we did, five times in Grahamstown followed by another four shows in Cape Town. It was both exhilarating and, at the same time, a truly humbling experience to meet young people who had, in some cases, travelled for more than thirteen hours in a minibus to come to see our shows. Somehow, after all that, we made it home in one piece and then, in 2010, we celebrated the tenth year of this project. And almost perfectly on cue, we notched up the ten-millionth podcast download earlier that year (and now, in 2011, we've passed 18 million downloads).

TO SUM UP

Clearly, as this story shows, translating what began as a terrestrial radio show with a few thousand listeners to the Internet has enabled us to expand to reach a global audience in the millions, but with very high efficiency and low overall cost. However, a pertinent question is whether podcasting is therefore merely as easy as taking the formats and production values that apply to radio, and re-packaging content produced this way for Internet-based consumption? And who are the people who listen to podcasts, and are they the same crowd that listen to traditional radio shows? The answer is, at the moment, we don't know, which is why we have initiated a PhD project to find out how consumers interact with the 'new media'.

So far, we've run two very large surveys (gathering approximately 1000 responses to each) amongst our podcast audiences, gathering data about educational level, age, sex and social demographic, interest in different science disciplines and listening behaviour. What's emerged from the initial analysis of this data is that our podcast audience tend to be younger, aged on average 35, half of the audience have no qualifications in science with one-third of them stopping formal science at age 16, whilst the other half of the audience have a science degree qualification or higher. In fact, we were shocked to learn that 25% of our audience have a Masters and one person in ten has a science PhD. This intriguing dichotomy, with highly scientifically literate listeners enjoying the programme alongside non-scientists, defies the traditional 'rules' of broadcasting which claim that most programmes preach to the converted. We've also tried to ensure throughout the project that we maintain an even balance of male and female presences on the programme. Perhaps as a reflection of this, we have been gratified to see a relatively high proportion – at 34% – of female listeners, which is significantly higher than that reported by other competing science podcasts; the *Astronomy Cast*, for instance, found that only about 10% of their audience were female.

Another interesting feature to emerge from our analysis has been the finding that listeners clearly utilise podcasts quite differently to traditional radio programmes. Programme directors at radio stations will talk about their audiences 'making an appointment' to listen to a certain show or a certain presenter at a certain time. Doubtless some people do do this, but our data show that we also have a significant number of listeners with the electronic equivalent of bulimia; they'll binge on our programme back-catalogue, taking away several hundred hours of programmes, which they'll listen to over a space of time, before returning later to refuel their iPods with another slug of freshly served-up science. Consequently we frequently receive emails from listeners who have exhausted their supply of archived shows and are now imploring us to step up our output to fill the void in their day!

From my perspective, I'm still incredulous and delighted that something that started out over ten years ago as a fun DNA-based demonstration for a science festival has turned into a global sensation that has now won seven national and international communication and broadcasting awards. But, more importantly, none of it would have been possible without the incredible and loyal team of people who have been part of it and supported it over the years including Dave Ansell, Ben Valsler, Meera Senthilingam, Diana O'Carroll, Helen Scales and Kat Arney; in my view, the best bunch of broadcasters there is!

Key resources

The Naked Scientists website – http://www.thenakedscientists.com
The Naked Scientists science discussion forum – http://www.thenakedscientists.com/forum (for the answers to all the science questions you could ever dream up).
Wikipedia article about the Naked Scientists – http://en.wikipedia.org/wiki/The_Naked_Scientists
Wikipedia article on the history of podcasting – http://en.wikipedia.org/wiki/History_of_podcasting

19

The social web in science communication

INTRODUCTION

Two arguments are always made by the proponents of Twitter, You-
Tube, Facebook and the like. Both, I think, are ill-conceived if they are
aimed at persuading the uninitiated to dip a casual toe into the rising
sea of social media networks and tools. The first is that no one can
afford not to do it. Now, this kind of talk never fails to raise a few
hackles – no one likes being told what they can and cannot do. The
second is that to really understand social media, you have to just get
stuck in, which is another way of saying that it's too difficult to explain.
It is unsurprising then that people, and especially scientists, want
better reasons for using social media. People, and *especially* scientists,
want evidence that it works.

The problem is that most of us who are regular users – those of us
who are already sharing videos of our pets on YouTube and uploading
our holiday snaps to Facebook while we are still in the airport – have
probably never thought too hard about it. We found ourselves drawn to
social media in much the same way as the spider is drawn to the plughole. All we know now is we cannot get out. For the younger generation,
particularly, it is hard to remember a time when YouTube did not exist; it
is inconceivable to think of a world where friends could not be reached
instantaneously by a tweet or Facebook message. And if *'I'll Facebook you'*
was the last decade's *'I'll email you'*, what comes next? Social media are
evolving so quickly that every website and application mentioned in this
chapter may be extinct within the next five years – and thus what can
indeed be difficult, is keeping up with the pace of change.

Successful Science Communication, ed. D. J. Bennett and R. C. Jennings. Published by
Cambridge University Press. © Cambridge University Press 2011.

Of course, the purpose of this chapter is not to explain social media *per se*, but to explain how they can be practically useful to us as scientists and science communicators. So, besides practically useful definitions, I will not indulge in any long-winded descriptions of specific tools. And assuming that some of you are users since the womb and others social media sceptics, I will not try to campaign for or against the application of Twitter and Facebook, or their descendants, in science communication projects. Or try to suggest that anyone is a fossil because they have not heard of AudioBoo.[1] What I will do is consider what can be achieved by using tools such as these in science communication, and what the advantages and disadvantages are. I will also provide some case studies. For while it is true that social media cannot be ignored and should be experimented with, there are pitfalls, especially when it comes to communicating an area as tricky as science, and therefore it cannot do any harm to go in well prepared.

DEFINING SOCIAL MEDIA

Given what has already been hinted at about the ever-changing landscape of social media, it may come as no surprise to hear that any 'definition' is a work in progress. As such, I refer to the oracle of the internet; the collaboratively authored and continuously edited people's encyclopaedia, Wikipedia. Ordinarily, scientific publications would stray away from citing Wikipedia as a source, but in this case, it might just be the most accurate.

> Social media is a term used to describe the type of media that is based on conversation and interaction between people online. Social media . . . support the democratization of knowledge and information and transform people from content consumers to content producers.
> (Wikipedia, retrieved 4 May 2010.)

This, of course, is what Wikipedia itself does. Every entry is the product of several or potentially thousands of different people's work. Users might not be directly conversing, but they are pooling knowledge and publishing it in a collaborative way such that it can be described as a social activity. With other social media, the social aspect might be based on dialogue rather than information-sharing – the most obvious example being Facebook, which allows users to exchange messages

---

[1] AudioBoo is an audio blogging platform that allows users to publish short pieces of audio on the internet direct from recording on their mobile phones.

publicly on the internet or comment on messages that other users have written. Already, without too much of a leap, it is possible to see how social media could fit into the current dialogue model espoused in science communication by presenting opportunities to engage in direct two-way conversation with target audiences via the web.

		Social presence/media richness		
		Low	Medium	High
Self-presentation/ Self-disclosure	High	Blogs	Social networking sites (e.g., Facebook)	Virtual social worlds (e.g., Second Life)
	Low	Collaborative projects (e.g., Wikipedia)	Content communities (e.g., YouTube)	Virtual game worlds (e.g., World of Warcraft)

Figure 19.1 Types of social media. (Reprinted from Kaplan, A.M. and Haenlein, M. (2010) Users of the world, unite! The challenges and opportunities of social media.

In 2010, Andreas Kaplan and Michael Haenlein outlined a classification system for social media to help separate collaborative projects such as Wikipedia from social networking sites such as Facebook (see Figure 19.1).[2] Their system is based on differences in self-presentation (the degree of control a user has over what impression they create of themself) and social presence/media richness (a measure combining factors including intimacy, immediacy and the amount of information that can be shared). As such, collaborative projects focused on information-sharing are classified as low self-presentation, whereas social networking sites like Facebook that allow the user to customise a profile page are classified as high self-presentation. Meanwhile, video- and music-sharing communities occupy a low self-presentation category but are considered of a similar social presence level to Facebook, presumably because of their immediacy and substantial content-sharing capabilities.

In reality, social presence/media richness and self-presentation are sliding scales and every community, network or project occupies its own very precisely positioned niche in the social media landscape. It is also worth remembering that many of the principles of social media – such as those of interaction and democracy – are shared across the board. YouTube, for example, is not just a platform for sharing of

[2] A. M. Kaplan, and M. Haenlein (2010). Users of the world, unite! The challenges and opportunities of Social Media. *Business Horizons*, **53**, 59–68.

content; it also provides an opportunity for users to respond to videos with comments, to discuss their responses with other users, and, like some blogs, to highlight comments they agree with via a democratic thumbs up/thumbs down system. Voting systems akin to the 'thumb' system are similarly used by news-sharing networks like Digg, where users share web links to stories that interest them.

THE YOUTUBE GENERATION

A couple of years ago I attended a talk at which Bob Eggington, the man who set up BBC News Online, was talking. Despite thinking of himself very much as a technologist, Bob admitted he still did not understand Facebook in the same way as his daughter. His argument was essentially that those who have not grown up using these kinds of technologies are not in the same 'state of mind', and that state of mind, he said, is very difficult to fake. Yet audiences appear to be changing. In 2009, a year after Bob gave his talk, the marketing agency 123 Social Media reported a trend towards uptake of social media by slightly older users – social media networks, it claimed, are not solely the domain of teenagers and 20-somethings any more.[3] Similarly, a 2010 report on social networking trends by comScore showed a small but noticeable increase of around 6 per cent in the number of Facebook users aged 25–49 compared to the previous year. Conversely, Twitter gained users in the younger age groups, but this may be a reflection of its already more mature audience – only 9 per cent of its users in 2008 were between 18 and 24.

Is the reason for this shift simply that the first generation of social media users is starting to move into an older age bracket? Or is it that older web users are starting to get dragged down the plughole with the rest? Who knows? But one thing we can be certain of is that the number of individuals born into this ultra-connected, web-savvy society can only go up. Social media use is rising – fast. Facebook reported 400 million active users in March 2010, each posting an average of 25 comments a month and spending more than 55 minutes a day on the network. Regardless of what your opinion of Facebook might be, this is a quite staggering number of users and surprising degree of engagement. And perhaps the reason for this is that it is becoming the means by which not just online social interaction but a significant proportion of all

[3] 123 Social Media (2009). *Social Media Demographics and Analytics 2008–2009*. 123 Social Media, online: http://123socialmedia.com/2009/01/01/social-media-demographics-and-analytics-2008–2009/

social interaction takes place today. I have a couple of friends who obstinately refuse to register with Facebook, on the basis of what they perceive to be the weak social interactions that it fosters. But to find out what their friends are doing, they are forced to persuade their girlfriends to check their Facebook accounts for messages and event notifications. Even my mother, who has never sent an email in her life, reluctantly asks my brother to log on to Facebook so that she can look at my holiday photos. Thus by resisting change, by viewing Facebook and Twitter as the preserve of the younger generation or as threats to traditional offline social interaction, people cut themselves off from what is swiftly becoming *the* new means of communication (Figure 19.2).

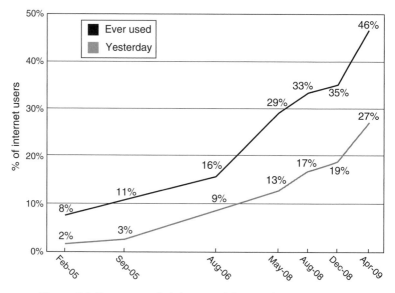

Figure 19.2 Percentage of adults on social networking sites including Facebook, MySpace and LinkedIn, 2005–2009. (*Source:* Pew Research Center's Internet and American Life Project.)

Faced with its new audience of frequent and social web users, old media have been forced to embrace change and you will see evidence of this on any of the major UK newspaper websites, which allow readers to comment on articles and share them via a multitude of different social networks – not just Twitter and Facebook, but Digg, Reddit, Stumbleupon, Buzz, LinkedIn, Windows Live, the list is endless. And everyone, it seems, is jumping on the bandwagon, as celebrities, charities, political parties, universities and even my local bakery compete for friends and followers on the various networks.

Scientists, being perhaps more technically minded than the majority of the population, have not been slow on the uptake and the large number of scientific bloggers and tweeters regularly sharing information and opinions about new research and upcoming science-related events are evidence of this. Marcus du Sautoy, Oxford University's Simonyi Professor for the Public Understanding of Science, regularly shares mathematical brainteasers and photographs of places linked to the history of science with his followers on Twitter. And it is possible to observe a community of practising scientists all tweeting about the frustrations and triumphs of their laboratory lives in real time.

NEW OPPORTUNITIES

Now that we have considered the audiences for social media, let us address some of the reasons for using it in the first place. One of the greatest advantages of social media, aside from the fact that it is largely free to use, is that control over when, what and how to publish is placed directly in the hands of the user, who need not have any in-depth knowledge of web publishing. As we will see, this level of control, combined with the immediacy of the format, can have its pitfalls, but used intelligently, social media can be a remarkably effective way to communicate with a potentially large audience, rapidly, and on a level playing field. Lord Drayson, the UK's Science Minister until 2010, is well known for being an active user of the social network Twitter, conversing directly with his 'followers' on matters of science policy. Thus, social media can give members of the public opportunities to put their questions directly to policy-makers; in Drayson's case, aspects of an online debate about blue skies research also culminated, in 2009, in a physical (offline) debate on the same subject.[4] Similarly, there are opportunities for interactions with scientists – even high-profile ones. The Nobel Prize website's Ask a Nobel Laureate project (2009) invited contributors to upload videos to YouTube of themselves posing questions to Nobel Prize winners. In return, the laureates, including American astronomer John Mather who won the Nobel Prize for Physics in 2006, posted videos of themselves answering the questions. In Mather's case, questions ranged from 'What [are] your opinions on string theory and whether it is provable or not?' to 'How large would we be if we were made up just of our nuclei and not the rest of our atoms?'

---

[4] 'Blue Skies Ahead? The Future of UK Science' was held on 30 November 2009 at the Wellcome Collection in London. See http://www.colinstuart.net/twitter/drayson-debate for more details.

In terms of its reach, one crucial aspect of content published via social media is its portability around the web – videos originally from YouTube can easily be embedded into blogs and the profiles of Facebook users, and tagged by social bookmarking applications such as StumbleUpon, which randomly generates links to pages that users as a whole found interesting. Many people perceive this portability to be a problem, since it means that content can be copied, repurposed and potentially misused. But if the quality of the content is high, the ripple effect that ensues can bring benefits in terms of web traffic and feedback to the publisher. Thus, the fact that a video from the Ask a Nobel Laureate project was incorporated into the website of popular science author Richard Dawkins, and described as 'cool' can only be considered a publicity benefit from the point of view of NobelPrize.org.

Another powerful argument for using social media is connectedness where it would not have otherwise been feasible. This is taken to the extreme in the virtual world Second Life, which allows users from completely opposite sides of the world to interact with virtual representations of each other (avatars). As such, it is even possible to host online conferences, or virtual components of real-life conferences in the virtual world. In 2009, the Science Online conference, which took place offline in London, opened its doors to delegates attending virtually – an entry fee of £10 ($15) could be paid to gain access to the Elucian Islands in Second Life, where the event was being broadcast live. Virtual delegates could communicate with speakers via a go-between who was simultaneously attending the event in London and online in Second Life.

NEW CHALLENGES

The key challenge in communicating science on the web is the immediacy of the online format. As a writer, I am constantly asked to meet tough deadlines for science magazines that once published weekly or even monthly in print format but now push their in-house staff and freelancers to keep their websites updated on a daily basis. The rise of social media has led web users to seek even more rapid reactions to emerging news stories. Increasingly, media organisations and their employees are actually breaking stories on social media networks; commentators are even offering up quotes via Twitter. But while the latter may mean easy pickings for journalists, there is no doubt that such rapid fire communications present risks. In a world where immediacy is so highly prized, it is tempting to rush out a blog post or an opinion before it has been properly formed. This, combined with the public visibility of certain networks, and copy-and-paste culture among users, catches out even experienced social media scribes.

Thus, it is advisable to think carefully about any professional persona you want to protect, even when you are 'off-duty'. Unfortunately, this is complicated by the fact that the various networks have different privacy settings. Whereas on Facebook, individuals can choose exactly what kind of personal information and messages they want to be available to whom, on Twitter, it is possible to view all the recent 'tweets' (140 character messages) that a person has published without logging in – they are completely in the public domain. Yet it seems it is easy to forget this, even for individuals with a reputation to uphold. Kristine Lowe, a freelance journalist in the UK, recalls on her blog[5] an incident where Milo Yiannopoulos, then a technology blogger at *The Daily Telegraph*, used Twitter to attack protesters at the G20 summit in London in 2009, as well as other tweeters who disagreed with his views. He later deleted his aggressive tweets – in itself, an action often frowned upon within the 'twittersphere'. Lowe's guidelines for journalists on Twitter boil down to good old common sense and decency, and thinking before you act (or tweet). And they apply to science journalists just as they do to the media at large. Only recently I noticed the news team for the highbrow scientific journal *Nature* tweet about an article that they called 'Rouge radio signals sully soil satellite's sensing'. Their mistake – the first word should, of course, have read 'Rogue' not 'Rouge' – was quickly spotted and the team joked that the person responsible had 'been shot'. In this instance, the consequences were probably minor, but consistently illiterate posting could certainly be damaging to *Nature*'s reputation.

Not only does using social networks require lightning reactions and careful judgement, it requires time and effort invested in learning the subtle differences between the various networks – in the way information is shared and commented upon, and in the way users interact with each other. Disrespecting or misunderstanding the (sometimes unwritten) rules of the community can mean that people fail to take you seriously or, worse, that the message you are trying to convey becomes twisted. But getting acquainted with all of these new social spheres might seem intimidating to someone who has never heard of them, which raises the question: can you just hire someone better acquainted to do it on your behalf? The answer is yes, but only if you trust them to represent the views and expertise of your organisation as

[5] http://kristinelowe.blogs.com/

a whole. If time is limited, it certainly may be more cost-effective to hire someone who is a seasoned social media user than to let a 'newbie' struggle on in vain. However, you must weigh up the advantages of knowing the format versus knowing the content. Think also about consistency: it is easier to avoid churning out conflicting or confusing messages if one person is responsible for coordinating communication efforts across all social networks associated with a certain project or campaign.

Mastering the necessary tools is crucial, but being able to use them does not guarantee success. Whether the aim is simply to reach a wide audience or whether it is to engage meaningfully with a smaller audience, success depends on employing the same principles that are applied universally by those working in science communication – namely knowing and respecting your audience, producing timely, accurate and engaging content, and evaluating honestly and appropriately. Get it right, and the potential arises for some very smart, cost-effective engagement and dialogue.

THE SAME RULES APPLY

If we have learned anything in the last 25 years, it is that the public is far more discerning than it is given credit for. Communication models that previously painted the public as a homogeneous, sponge-like mass, ready to absorb whatever pool of information it was exposed to, have shifted towards two-way communication models, with diverse publics being capable of making valuable contributions towards societal debate. A recent Scientists on Public Engagement (SCoPE) report concludes that scientists now increasingly understand what were viewed as scientifically 'deficient' publics as 'intelligent, supportive and scientifically capable' publics.[6] Still, particularly for those who are unfamiliar with social media norms, it can be easy to dismiss or underestimate internet users on the basis of fickleness and apparently unsophisticated language. In a 2007 article that has been cited in science communication texts, the German journalist Ulrich von Rauchhaupt blamed what he perceived to be the randomness, idiosyncrasy and redundancy of Web 2.0 on the fact that discussion via this medium is conducted increasingly by *'anyone capable of operating a browser'*.

---

[6] K. Burchell, S. Franklin and K. Holden, (2009). *Public Culture as Professional Science.* BIOS, London School of Economics and Political Science, online: http://www.lse.ac. uk/collections/BIOS/scope/scope.htm

While I agree that there is much on the internet to be ignored, there is also much that is of value. During my own research on online discussions about science, I sifted through hundreds if not thousands of well-informed, focused and often thought-provoking comments posted on blogs associated with science podcasts. Similarly, the online comments sections of, for example, *The Times* newspaper in the UK or *Washington Post* in the USA, often contain deftly argued points made by people who are passionate about science and the impact that policy decisions related to it may have. But the key is 'people who are passionate about science' – much of the discussion is clearly going on between people who already have a strong interest in the subject. If I post a link to an article about science policy on my Facebook profile, I can guarantee that the people who respond to it will be colleagues or acquaintances whose work in some way involves science. Twitter seems to be even more tunnel-visioned; people make connections based on common interests rather than their real-life friendship groups. Online, then, as offline, we have to consider to what extent we are 'preaching to the converted'. If one of the arguments for involving the public in discussions about science is the incorporation of broad-based social perspectives as well as highly specialised technical knowledge, then it is not enough to canvass for opinions in a way that is only going to attract the already science literate (if we can even agree on what 'literate' means).

And what about the rest of the internet? The YouTubes and the MySpaces of the web can hardly be described as places where important scientific discussion goes on – can they? Perhaps the movement towards dialogue and debate has got us hung up on dialogue and discussion, which are not always the aim. Science communication also has a remit to embed science in culture; we could count it as a success, could we not, if we reached a point where a ten-minute video clip of a science show was attracting as many viewers and as many comments as contestants on *The X Factor* or a gorilla drumming to the beat of Phil Collins' 'In the Air Tonight'?[7] There may be examples where YouTube videos have provoked real, open debate on issues of a scientific nature, but in the end we arrive at the old problem of assessing the long-term impact of such interactions. How can we tell what influence a few scribblings on the internet may have had on a teenager's decision to study physics at university? Will someone who joins a Facebook group for their local science centre be inspired to visit more often as a result? These are

[7] Since its release in 2007, Cadbury's Dairy Milk advert featuring the drumming gorilla has attracted over 4 million hits on YouTube.

questions that are as difficult to answer as whether any traditional science activity, such as a lecture or a hands-on demonstration, influences a person's attitudes to science.

It is never as simple as saying 'this method works' or 'this method doesn't'. Practically, however, using social media should not require a change in best practice of science communication more generally. Here are some examples:

- **Upstream engagement:** It is not for you to decide what your followers/fans want or need – ask them what they think about your project and let them shape its development.
- **Know your audience:** As always, market research and good audience targeting are key. It is easy to think that creating a Facebook page works in every instance, but would a specialist patient support website be a better way to target people with Crohn's disease?
- **Content is king:** Web audiences suffer from information overload, so content has to be high quality and original to stand out. Also, consider the fact that everyone is into social media these days, so simply using it brings nothing new or innovative to the table – use it creatively.
- **Evaluate – and not just with numbers:** It is not enough to count the number of times an article or video has been shared or commented on. In-depth qualitative evaluation reveals so much more.

CASE STUDIES

These are not intended to be in-depth case studies, but an introduction to ways in which social media can be utilised in science communication.

Why Science?

Collaborative blogging is a way of creating co-authored diaries or commentaries in an online format, usually incorporating the social media tradition of allowing readers to add their own comments. *Why Science?* was a 2009 collaborative blog coordinated by science teacher Alom Shaha, aimed primarily at answering the question 'Why is science important?' as part of a film production project of the same name. Video and text contributions from prominent scientists and science communicators were added to the blog, using YouTube and Vimeo as publishing platforms for contributors' short films, which were then embedded in the site itself. The contributions formed part of a longer documentary produced by Shaha. *Why Science?* is therefore an interesting example of a science communication project that utilises social media platforms as a means of achieving what is otherwise a straightforward piece of media production. In fact, the audience for the individual films on YouTube was low – in the tens of thousands – compared to, say, the 'Large Hadron Collider rap' (around 6 million views since July 2008), but the final impression is one of a participatory project that has generated some high-quality discussion.[8]

#COP15

Certain key attributes of Twitter lend themselves to coverage of real-life events and incorporation into mainstream media output. One of the most important is the so-called hashtag system, which allows users to align all 'tweets' on a specific topic. During the 2009 Copenhagen climate negotiations, major publications like the *Guardian* exploited this system to create a live stream of comments about the talks, all tagged with the #COP15 hashtag, on their own websites. Within Twitter itself, #COP15 provided a way to identify others on the network tweeting about Copenhagen, promoting discussion and connections between people with similar interests. It also allowed those attending the conference to publish updates on the proceedings faster than any of the more traditional forms of media, bar live radio or television, could have achieved.

Other events covered via the hashtag system:

- #meteorwatch: launched by the Newbury Astronomical Society to highlight the occurrence of the Perseids meteor shower, the topic attracted more than 10 000 tweets.
- #ten23: a tag used by campaigners against homeopathic remedies, who planned a mass overdose of homeopathic medicines on 30 January 2010.

Richard Wiseman

One growing use of social media by scientists and science communicators is as marketing tools for a personality – as opposed to a project. Psychologist and author Professor Richard Wiseman, for example,

---

[8] http://www.whyscience.co.uk

maintains an active presence on Facebook, where he has more than 6000 fans, on Twitter, where he has over 84 000 followers, and on his blog, where he incorporates videos and live comment streams from other relevant social media platforms. He is not just Richard Wiseman; he is the brand 'Richard Wiseman', and the web is a way to sell books and talks as much as a way of engaging directly with an audience. Others including Ed Yong (author of *Discover* magazine's 'Not Exactly Rocket Science' blog) and Ben Goldacre (the *Guardian*'s 'Bad Science' columnist) employ social media to market themselves, inadvertently or not, as much on the basis of their personalities as on their science communication.

The *Tree of Life* web project

Under Kaplan and Haenlein's scheme for classifying social media, collaborative online projects are a class all of their own. Strictly speaking, however, some of the best examples of science-based collaborative projects do not directly incorporate any of the tools that one comes to expect of social media projects – comment functions, social bookmarking, sharing options, open content editing and so on. One example is the *Tree of Life* project, hosted at the University of Arizona, which seeks to document all living species by pulling together text and image contributions from experts all over the world. To maintain a high standard of scientific content and accuracy, the owners have chosen an editorial approach incorporating a rigorous online review process. Pages can be authored and submitted online, but must be reviewed by experts before they are published – as contrasted to the Wikipedia approach, in which the community as a whole is entrusted with the responsibility for creating accurate content and sifting out errors. While some may argue the review process goes against the spirit of the social web, the *Tree of Life* team evidently consider the results to be of greater value in the terms of a resource for schools and the scientific community.[9]

Other projects:

- Galaxy Zoo: users characterise galaxies as part of a mass participation research project.
- Be a Martian: an online space exploration game, in which players count craters for NASA.

---

[9] http://tolweb.org

IMPACT

As regards the real engagement potential of social networks, many questions remain. Is the world smaller than ever before or are we just replacing strong, real-life connections with weaker, more fleeting connections online? Can these connections really form the basis for lasting networks – online as well as offline? How can we evaluate the effects of engagement in these realms, given that many users remain anonymous? And while the tech-savvy bunch is tweeting happily away, does anyone else really care? Research on social media is a young field, and social media research as it applies to science communication is almost nonexistent. Therefore, we must use what we know about science communication more generally to determine how best to incorporate social media into our science communication endeavours. We know that the potential for public dialogue and engagement exists, but we must use our judgement to decide, on a project-by-project basis, whether social networks are the best medium. As I was told recently by a science learning facilitator, when it comes to inspiring children to choose science, there is no substitute for putting them in front of a real-life scientist. So we should never underestimate the impact of face-to-face communications, but that does not mean social media do not have a role to play.

Key resources

Birch, H. and Weitkamp, E. (2010). Podologues: conversations created by science podcasts. *New Media & Society*, **12**, 1–21.

ComScore (2010). The 2009 Digital Year in Review. *ComScore*, February 2010, 1–16.

Jenkins, J. (2006) *Convergence Culture: Where Old and New Media Collide*. New York: New York University Press.

Lowe, K. (2009). Twitter mishaps and netiquette for journalists. *Kristine Lowe: Notes on the changing media landscape*, 25 November 2009, online: http://kristinelowe.blogs. com/kristine_lowe/2009/11/twitter-mishaps-and-netiquette-for-journalists.html

Maddison, D. R., Schulz, K.-S. and Maddison, W.P. (2007). The Tree of Life Web Project. *Zootaxa*, **1668**, 19–40.

Morten (2009). Science Online London 2009 – Second Life, online outreach, blogging and the future of science communication. *Biomedicine on Display*, 18 September, online: http://www.corporeality.net/museion/2009/09/18/ science-online-london-2009-%E2%80%93-second-life-online-outreach-blogging- and-the-future-of-science-communication/

Otto, S. (2009). Perseids 'meteor watch' knocks Disney star Miley Cyrus off Twitter top spot. *Daily Telegraph*, 12 August, online: http://www.telegraph. co.uk/technology/twitter/6016550/Perseids-meteor-watch-knocks-Disney-star- Miley-Cyrus-off-Twitter-top-spot.html

Vance, K. and Howe, W. (2009). Social internet sites as a source of public health information. *Dermatologic Clinics*, **27**, 133–136.

20

Dealing with dilemmas and societal expectations: a company's response

SETTING THE SCENE

Novo Nordisk is a focused biotech healthcare company founded in 1923. Novo Nordisk combines drug discovery with technology to turn science into solutions for people with diabetes, men and boys with haemophilia, people with growth hormone deficiency and women experiencing the symptoms of menopause. Headquartered in Denmark, Novo Nordisk employs around 30000 people in 76 countries and markets its products in 179 countries.

The backdrop to Novo Nordisk's operations – and to this chapter – can be provided by a brief analysis of the pharmaceutical industry as a whole. Medicines developed by pharmaceutical companies have greatly contributed to the increase in life expectancy, to the improvement of quality of life and to the eradication of diseases that were previously life-threatening. Key figures indicate that the pharmaceutical industry is a major asset in the economies of Europe, the USA and Japan (e.g. European Federation of Pharmaceutical Industries and Associations, 2010). Given the nature of its products and the fact that they are most often paid for by public funds, the industry is highly dependent on public trust and customer confidence that it is truly dedicated to saving lives and improving well-being, and that it does not operate just to make profits. However, surveys indicate that public trust in the sector is low relative to other sectors (e.g. Harris Interactive, 2010).

This chapter aims to provide insight into Novo Nordisk's commitment to an innovative, proactive model of stakeholder engagement in order better to understand and respond to societal concerns and

Successful Science Communication, ed. D. J. Bennett and R. C. Jennings. Published by Cambridge University Press. © Cambridge University Press 2011.

expectations, and to enhance stakeholders' mutual understanding. To illustrate Novo Nordisk's approach, two recent initiatives are presented in detail: the company's efforts towards changing diabetes care, and its project to facilitate stakeholder understanding of basic ethics and to assist sound decision-making on ethical issues.

NOVO NORDISK AND THE TRIPLE BOTTOM LINE

The company's founders put great emphasis on respect and care for the patient as a person, for employees' well-being and for concern for the environment – in short, the elements of what today constitutes 'good corporate citizenship'. Building on this, in the early 1990s, when the term 'Triple Bottom Line' was first coined, Novo Nordisk committed itself to implement this principle: to operate in a manner that strives to ensure that decisions are based on a balanced consideration to be financially, environmentally and socially responsible. The philosophy behind the Triple Bottom Line is that it will help safeguard the company's long-term success and profitability, and at the same time reflect Novo Nordisk's contribution to sustainable development and balanced growth through its focus on global, societal goals. The term 'sustainable development' is referred to here as it was first defined in the 1987 Brundtland Report: 'development that meets the needs of the present world without compromising the ability of future generations to meet their own needs' (World Commission on Environment and Development, 1987).

The Triple Bottom Line principle has been anchored in Novo Nordisk's by-laws – the Articles of Association – since 2004. With the Triple Bottom Line now being a broad business principle, the commitment to sustainable development has been built into the company's corporate governance structures, management tools, reward scheme and individual performance assessments. It is the responsibility of the Board and of Executive Management to ensure consistent performance and continued improvement, but equally importantly it is the task of every single Novo Nordisk employee to bring the Triple Bottom Line principle into action.

A BUSINESS APPROACH IN TRANSIT: NOVO NORDISK'S JOURNEY

Reputation and trust are built on the basis of how well stakeholders buy into the individual company's overall meaning, as its leaders express it. However, to understand, analyse or even manage wider changes, such as the erosion of trust in the pharmaceutical industry, for example, we need to look beyond the single company and industry in isolation. Such changes are not a result of any one actor in society, but rather happen in the interplay of policy-makers, academic institutions, media, non-governmental organisations (NGOs), opinion leaders, companies and their stakeholders.

The evolution of the sustainable development agenda can be traced through a number of significant clusters of events that served as change agents and impacted upon multinational companies. From around 1900 to the beginning of the 1960s, the expansion of industrial production saw the focus placed on labour relations, and health and safety at work. The nascent environmental consciousness of the early 1960s gained momentum in the late 1980s, and was joined by the emerging social and human rights concerns that seized the agenda in the 1990s. Today, the challenges of globalisation are aptly linked to the notion of corporate sustainability and good governance.

The history of how corporate responsibility has evolved in the case of Novo Nordisk reflects the societal developments described above. A series of changes that were catalysed by external events stand out as defining moments for the company, with implications for how Novo Nordisk manages and organises its response to societal issues, and accounts for its actions.

The first turning point concerned the company's products, industrial enzymes, which have since been spun off. In the late 1960s cases of allergies were seen among British factory workers who had inhaled concentrated enzyme dust. The cases were reported in a medical journal, and after the article was picked up in the USA, a consumer movement effectively called for boycotts of all detergents with enzymes, making allegations that they posed a health hazard to consumers. As a result, enzyme sales plummeted and the company was forced to fire employees. An expert panel was asked to analyse the issue and concluded that there was no risk associated with use of the detergents; however by then the consumers' verdict had been made, and it took some time to rebuild confidence in the products. The main lesson learnt from this case was the imperative of staying attuned to stakeholder concerns, even if they may be groups that a company is not directly engaged with. Another outcome was that the company developed dust-free enzyme preparations to mitigate the risks to workers.

Two decades later, questions were again raised about the safety of the company's products, specifically the use of genetically modified organisms (GMOs) which were – and still are – applied in Novo Nordisk's production process. Having learnt from past experience, the company's management invited the most vocal NGOs to visit the factory and to discuss the issue with them. At the time, this was a most unusual step, but in hindsight it appears to have been a wise choice: listening to opponents opened up an exchange of viewpoints and a mutual acknowledgement that agreement is not always possible, nor, perhaps, an end in itself, but that both parties would learn from the process. The meeting was to become the first in a series of dialogues between Novo Nordisk and NGOs, and marked the beginning of a proactive stakeholder engagement strategy that the company has pursued ever since to learn *with* stakeholders.

Effectively managing stakeholder relations became a strategic tool for Novo Nordisk better to understand their perspectives, and to be able to adapt to changing societal expectations. Over time this has secured the company a valuable 'trust capital'. However, when in 2001 the company found itself under siege in the access to health debate sparked by the so-called South African court case over patent rights, together with some 40 other pharmaceutical companies, its reputation for listening to stakeholder concerns was severely challenged. While Novo Nordisk joined the lawsuit to defend the principle of patent rights that is at the core of the pharmaceutical business model, in the eyes of the public it was seen as an accomplice in preventing poor people from having access to life-saving medicines. The event became a turning point for how the company views its role as an actor in society.

DEALING WITH DILEMMAS AND SOCIETAL CONCERNS: A NEW STAKEHOLDER ENGAGEMENT MODEL

Novo Nordisk's experience in the 2001 South African court case signalled a paradigm shift from stakeholder engagement as a management discipline to a more reflective view: recognising that the company is not at centre stage, but merely one actor in a complex global community (see Figure 20.1).

The shift in approach reflects a change in the public perception of the role of business in society: today there is an expectation that business should assume responsibilities for contributing to solving general social problems (Grunig & Hunt, 1984). The implications of this transition are the change from a mindset of 'managing' stakeholders' expectations to one of 'respecting' their positions and the concerns they may voice on behalf of people and communities or the natural environment – not just passively, but by taking action – and also the

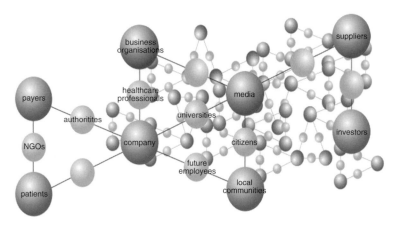

Figure 20.1 Novo Nordisk stakeholder engagement map.
(Source: Novo Nordisk.)

change from a prejudiced mindset to one that seeks to understand and learn. This makes reconciling different world-views – 'dealing with dilemmas' – and committing to contribute to resolving societal concerns core activities for the executive management.

In parallel, there is a change from a responsive risk management approach – complying with regulation, reacting to explicit stakeholder voices in a 'going-by-the-book' manner that demonstrates effective management – to a responsible growth approach. This means adopting corporate responsibility as a business principle, seeking to exceed expectations, trying to understand the motives for the deeper concerns of stakeholders and acting on the opportunities that arise, in a manner that demonstrates true leadership. Due to the rise in societal expectations of companies, corporate responsibility as risk management has effectively become the minimum requirement for companies to maintain their 'licence to operate'. Significantly however, if companies wish to gain an advantage by adopting a responsible growth approach they can also secure a licence to *innovate*.

The Global Business Initiative on Human Rights, which was launched in June 2009, provides a strong example of the approach described above. Led by a core group of companies including Novo Nordisk, and supported by civil society groups, human rights experts, the United Nations and the Swiss Government, the initiative provides a platform for companies to demonstrate leadership in integrating human rights into the management of their business and in operating in a socially sustainable way (Global Business Initiative on Human Rights, 2009).

For Novo Nordisk, maintaining a licence to innovate also means staying attuned to societal expectations, and being open not only to what stakeholders' positions may be, but also what those positions may mean for the company. Over the years, Novo Nordisk has developed an approach to dealing with emergent issues on the sustainability agenda based on a learning process: from trend-spotting and issue identification, to external review, stakeholder dialogue, and integration into management, and, as this matures, to strategy revision and continuous improvement. Over time, early topics move further up the 'learning curve', whilst new issues appear at the bottom of the curve (see Figure 20.2).

Figure 20.2 The Novo Nordisk 'learning curve', showing the company's Triple Bottom Line agenda at the time of writing. (Source: Novo Nordisk.)

Novo Nordisk's Triple Bottom Line approach enables the company to take informed decisions as to which emergent issues to respond to, and is the means of making decisions that lead towards sustainability. With the Triple Bottom Line as a business principle, Novo Nordisk takes a holistic view, seeking to balance concerns for all stakeholder groups with considerations for the environment and a view to long-term profitability. In the company's interactions with stakeholders and its approach to addressing global issues, particular focus is given to the people whose healthcare needs the company serves. Throughout the value chain stakeholders are involved in developing more sustainable solutions: the organisation works with NGOs and the public sector in partnerships, learning with stakeholders.

Novo Nordisk's approach to stakeholder engagement is exemplified by two recent initiatives: the company's efforts towards changing diabetes care, and its project to increase stakeholder understanding of ethics and to foster sound decision-making on ethical issues.

STAKEHOLDER INNOVATION: CHANGING DIABETES

Providing care for people with diabetes is the focus for Novo Nordisk's strategic business development and for how the company approaches the sustainability agenda. The aspiration of 'defeating diabetes' is explicitly stated in the company vision and Way of Management – Novo Nordisk's basic management principles – together with the commitment to engage actively with stakeholders for more sustainable solutions that benefit both the company and society.

Changing Diabetes® is the umbrella for Novo Nordisk's efforts not only to improve treatment and care for those people who have diabetes, but also to help prevent diabetes, which has become a pandemic and is recognised as a major global risk to human health and development. Diabetes kills almost as many people as HIV/AIDS, disables millions of people and is already causing damage to the global economy. Today, 285 million people have diabetes, but by 2030 this number is projected to increase to 438 million (International Diabetes Federation, 2009). This significant increase is largely due to lifestyle changes and presents a growing socioeconomic burden particularly in emerging economies where diabetes incidence is increasing at an alarming rate. National economies are faced with a double burden: not only because chronic care is a cost to the healthcare system, but also because people who have diabetes often develop severe complications such as kidney failure, heart diseases, blindness and need for amputations, so that they cannot work and sustain their families.

That is why health is a driver of economic prosperity: early prevention, early diagnosis and optimal treatment will improve the health of people with diabetes, which in turn helps alleviate the global public health problem of the unfolding burden of diabetes.

As a world leader in diabetes care Novo Nordisk has the potential and a responsibility to make a difference for people with diabetes and those at risk, facilitating change in addition to providing innovative treatments. Changing Diabetes® includes programmes and engagement at global, regional and national levels to improve prevention, diagnosis and treatment of diabetes.

By taking such an approach, it has been possible to pursue Triple Bottom Line strategies in a way that increasingly gets at the heart of core business processes, in the markets, as well as in the corporate functions and governance mechanisms. The approach is shaped through extensive stakeholder engagement followed by embedding in organisational behaviour and business operations.

Learning with stakeholders to improve diabetes care

One initiative that makes a particularly strong example of the value of the approach described above is the DAWN™ (Diabetes Attitudes, Wishes and Needs) programme; the largest ever global study aimed at uncovering the psychosocial aspects of diabetes. DAWN™ was initiated by Novo Nordisk in 2001 to increase understanding of how people perceived their diabetes, in order to develop better outcomes for treatment. Conducted in collaboration with the International Diabetes Federation and an international expert advisory board, the study involved more than 5400 people with diabetes and more than 3800 healthcare professionals from 13 countries (Novo Nordisk, 2009).

A key conclusion from the DAWN™ study was that despite today's effective diabetes therapies, the majority of people with diabetes do not achieve full health and quality of life. While the study found that many healthcare professionals focused mainly on the medical aspects of the treatment and the physical complications, it became apparent that the patients also needed self-management education and motivational guidance empowering them to take charge of their own health. By focusing on the person with diabetes as just that – a person, not a patient – the DAWN™ study made clear that a key to improved treatment lay in providing more integrated care dealing with both the medical and psychosocial challenges of living with diabetes.

Today DAWN™ has evolved as a programme calling for concerted action to improve diabetes care. National DAWN™ programmes involving academic research, educational programmes and new approaches to treatment at hospitals and clinics demonstrate that learning with stakeholders can be converted into valuable knowledge, dialogue and initiatives.

Multi-stakeholder engagement in the fight against diabetes

Using the lessons from the DAWN™ programme, it could be argued that the benefits of multi-stakeholder engagement are apparent: if all stakeholders in today's healthcare industry were to engage in new forms of interactive knowledge-sharing we would see solutions in partnerships for improved care (Amidon, 2004). Such innovation in public health promotion activities would help effectively reduce the burden of diseases such as diabetes (Skovlund, 2004). This aim forms the core of Novo Nordisk's Changing Diabetes® corporate programme, which includes the four initiatives outlined below: the DAWN™ advocacy initiative for national guidelines on psychosocial diabetes care, the Changing Diabetes® Leadership Forums, the Changing Diabetes® Barometer, and the Changing Diabetes® World Tour.

DAWN™ advocacy initiative for national guidelines on psychosocial diabetes care

The competing healthcare agendas and contrasting social and economic priorities with which governments are faced represent a major challenge for effecting change in the provision of diabetes care to incorporate patient-centred and psychosocial dimensions. Recognising that political support and investment in resources are essential factors in realising change, the DAWN™ programme features an ongoing advocacy initiative to call on more countries to introduce national guidelines on psychosocial aspects of diabetes care. This initiative began with a mapping study at national level in more than 20 countries, which revealed that only a small number of countries have national guidelines with clear recommendations on educational and psychosocial support for people with diabetes, and even where such guidelines are in place it cannot be assumed that practice reflects theory.

Findings from the DAWN™ programme presented governments with new insights into how management of diabetes and prevention of complications can be achieved cost-efficiently by taking a patient-focused and holistic approach. The challenge, however, lay in utilising these findings to engender real change at a national level. At the third international DAWN™ Summit in 2006, the approach was taken of equipping participants from more than 60 countries with the materials, networks and tools required to take appropriate action at a local level. A practical profile-raising framework was set out to assist participants in clearly defining the urgency of the problem, in demonstrating a feasible, valid policy solution, and in scanning the broad political environment to effectively address the politics of the issue.

The involvement of all stakeholders through a common vision, new actionable knowledge, and a profile-raising framework, has helped to stimulate international discourse on the elements that are required for sustainable patient-centred, evidence-based national guidelines on psychosocial diabetes care. The global treatment guidelines for diabetes have been revised to include the findings from the DAWN™ initiative and efforts are continuing around the world to revise and implement improved guidelines for psychosocial diabetes care in countries such as Germany, UK, Taiwan, the Netherlands and Japan. It is hoped that the ongoing promotion of dialogue between all stakeholders involved in diabetes care will continue to help embed the new approach to diabetes care at a national level.

Changing Diabetes® Leadership Forums

As part of its efforts to change the course of diabetes and improve treatment outcomes, Novo Nordisk is also working to put diabetes on public health agendas. Through Changing Diabetes® Leadership Forums, which form part of its commitment to call for a worldwide change in diabetes care, the company has engaged key stakeholders at a global level. The aim of the forums is to unite all key stakeholders in setting an agenda for change – including national diabetes strategies, early detection, improved diabetes prevention, access to diabetes care and quality of care for people with diabetes – as well as to commit stakeholders around national targets for improved diabetes care.

Since 2007, Novo Nordisk has sponsored and co-organised Global Leadership Forums in New York, Moscow, Beijing, Johannesburg and Dubai, each event gathering policy-makers, government officials, international organisations, patient organisations, healthcare professionals, people with diabetes and the media. The Global Leadership Forums have resulted in commitments including the launch of Novo Nordisk's Changing Diabetes® Barometer (see below), the adoption of the Russian Diabetes Resolution, including suggestions for screening and improved quality of care, a large-scale Changing Diabetes® Barometer project in China in cooperation with the Chinese Ministry of Health, and the Dubai Declaration on Diabetes and Chronic Non-Communicable Diseases in the Middle East and Northern Africa Region.

Through the Global Leadership Forums as well as National and Regional Changing Diabetes® Leadership Forums Novo Nordisk has engaged with over 7500 stakeholders in more than 77 countries. The National and Regional Forums are intended to address specific issues faced by the country or region, and have enabled Novo Nordisk to build strong national partnerships and to reach agreements on initiatives such as a national Barometer Goal and the monitoring of data in Australia, and the establishment of several pilot projects for monitoring quality data in Italy.

Changing Diabetes® Barometer

It seems reasonable to suppose that the impact of awareness-raising activities and stakeholder engagement is likely to be greater if the actual situation can be set in context against potential outcomes. Launched in November 2007, Novo Nordisk's Changing Diabetes® Barometer takes such an approach, by measuring progress in the fight against diabetes. A web-based project conducted in collaboration with the International Diabetes Federation's *Diabetes Atlas*, the Barometer provides an overview of the diabetes state of each nation and a projection of the future diabetes burden if no action is taken to curb it.

By increasing transparency and highlighting areas where improvements are possible, the Barometer provides healthcare professionals, patient organisations, politicians, institutions and the media with valuable information on outcomes in diabetes care. It aims to inspire national stakeholders to measure the impact of their efforts and to learn from international best-practice examples, in order to improve care delivery, improve quality of life for people with diabetes, reduce costs and ultimately save lives (Novo Nordisk, 2007).

The Barometer monitors progress across countries to encourage constructive competition, and creates an international baseline on the prevention, treatment and progress of diabetes as shown in future trends. At national levels, the Barometer seeks to stimulate informed dialogue on the necessity of measuring the progress of treatment and quality of care, as well as encouraging re-examination of the breadth and scope of existing national diabetes strategies. In short, the Barometer will enable healthcare providers to benchmark their practices with those achieving better results, and help both payers and policy-makers to optimise the use of available healthcare resources and achieve value-based outcomes in diabetes care that result in improved quality of life (Novo Nordisk, 2007).

Some national stakeholders have already utilised the Barometer to guide public policy, for example in Italy, where data collection has been improved through workshops and regional pilot projects. In 2009, a Memorandum of Understanding on the Changing Diabetes® Barometer project was signed by Novo Nordisk, the Italian Diabetes Association and the Parliamentary Association for the Protection and Promotion of the Right to Prevention.

The future success of the Changing Diabetes® Barometer will depend upon ongoing partnerships and collaborations with a range of stakeholders: payers and policy-makers, patient organisations, opinion leaders, people with diabetes and the media. The progress of this initiative is guided by bringing these stakeholders together to identify, discuss and reach agreement on actions aimed at improving the overall delivery of diabetes care and patient outcomes.

Communicating with the public on changing diabetes

Communicating with the wider public is an intrinsic part of Novo Nordisk's approach of understanding societal concerns at the earliest possible stage; this approach is also fundamental in order to earn and sustain stakeholders' trust, and as with many healthcare issues that affect a large number of people, raising public awareness can be an integral aspect of enabling positive change. As part of its Changing Diabetes® programme, Novo Nordisk has chosen to implement some innovative public communications initiatives, two of which are outlined in further detail below: the Changing Diabetes® World Tour and the Novo Nordisk Media Prize.

Changing Diabetes® World Tour

Since 2006, the Changing Diabetes® World Tour – also known as the Changing Diabetes® Bus – has travelled across five continents to raise awareness of diabetes and its social, humanitarian and economic consequences as part of an ambitious communications effort, 'A Global Drive to Change Diabetes'. Targeting the broader public, people with diabetes, healthcare professionals and politicians, the Changing Diabetes® World Tour has called for global change in diabetes prevention and care, and played a role in the adoption and implementation of the United Nations Resolution on diabetes. In addition, more than 260 000 people have visited the bus – an 18-metre mobile showroom – and learned about risk factors, symptoms and prevention of diabetes, through unique and interactive multimedia exhibits, designed to educate both adults and children. Visitors to the bus can also receive free health screenings.

Since the beginning of 2010, the Changing Diabetes® World Tour has given the general public access to a broader range of high-quality diabetes screening, whilst continuing to drive diabetes awareness by focusing on the benefits of detecting and treating diabetes earlier. The screening data will be collected and, it is hoped, will contribute to the further understanding of diabetes in the countries and regions visited. By assessing the association between known risk factors for diabetes and the presence of undiagnosed diabetes through the screening, Novo Nordisk also hopes to provide insight and recommendations for local screening strategies for diabetes.

Novo Nordisk Media Prize

With the prevalence of diabetes increasing throughout the world, there is a great need to provide the public with information about the various aspects of the condition and to share information on how better to prevent and manage the different types of diabetes. The media plays a crucial role in disseminating such information and raising awareness.

Founded in 2003, the Novo Nordisk Media Prize is an international award given to the best print article, best online article or the best TV feature about diabetes, published in lay media. Over the years, entries have increased steadily in number – for the 2010 award, entries were received from 22 countries worldwide – and have consistently addressed key messages such as the importance of healthy lifestyles to prevent diabetes and the potential risk of complications associated with the condition.

In addition to the Media Prize, Novo Nordisk regularly invites journalists to take part in a range of diabetes-related events, such as the 2009 DAWN™ workshop on diabetes and stigma issues, which was attended by over 50 journalists. Inclusion of the media in such events contributes to an ongoing process of helping journalists to enhance their understanding of the challenges that diabetes presents for individuals and for society.

ETHICS DILEMMAS: ENHANCING STAKEHOLDERS' MUTUAL UNDERSTANDING

Novo Nordisk and bioethics

As a healthcare company whose production is based on biotechnology, Novo Nordisk faces a number of complex bioethical issues. It was among the first companies to communicate openly about the dilemmas entailed and voluntarily report on bioethics issues, and today more than 100 Novo Nordisk employees are dedicated to addressing the bioethical dilemmas encountered by the company. This virtual, cross-functional team prepares and suggests new initiatives, develops and implements new policies and guidelines, and supervises the company's handling of bioethical issues worldwide.

Novo Nordisk's Bioethics Policy and general operational guidelines, together with the Changing Diabetes® programme, are embedded in the company's Way of Management. In common with Novo Nordisk's diabetes initiatives, its Bioethics Policy is also consistent with the company's Triple Bottom Line objective: to strive to be economically viable, socially responsible and environmentally sound by considering each of these three elements when making business decisions.

The ethics e-learning initiative

Novo Nordisk recognises that the very nature of bioethical issues means that there will always be differing views on what is right and what is wrong. For Novo Nordisk this means that the company must stay alert and seek to reconcile the inevitable dilemmas that arise as technology offers new opportunities in research and development and as societal attitudes and norms change. Often, however, there are 'grey zones' where there is no obvious right or wrong.

In May 2010, Novo Nordisk and the University of Copenhagen launched an online e-learning resource (http://www.ethics-e-learning.com) which aims to support users in navigating such grey zones, by facilitating a better understanding of basic ethics and providing practical guidance on how to make sound ethical decisions (Novo Nordisk, 2010). From its interaction with the bioethics division of the United Nations Educational, Scientific and Cultural Organization (UNESCO) and its role on an advisory group to BioLogue – a Danish knowledge network for medicines research and development – it had become apparent to Novo Nordisk that multiple stakeholders had a need for a training tool of this type.

A global advisory board was engaged at several levels of the tool development process with representatives from NGOs, universities and industry. Consequently, the particular strength of the e-learning tools, which are publicly available and free of charge to use, lies in their combination of academic knowledge with 'hands-on' experience from business and other practitioners. The tools are not specifically designed for pharmaceutical companies or indeed for business only, they are also applicable within academic teaching, and inter-governmental organisations, and are therefore targeted at employees and managers in companies, as well as students and organisations worldwide.

How it works: learning through questions and games

The interactive e-learning resource comprises two innovative tools: the 'Ethics Dilemma' and the 'Ethics Decision-Making Tool', which provide, respectively, a basic understanding of different ethical viewpoints and an operational tool to assist and enhance decision-making on ethical issues.

The Ethics Dilemma presents five ethical standpoints: contractarian, consequentialist, ethics of rights, relational, and virtue ethics. Through a simple questionnaire, users are able to enhance their understanding of their own ethical standpoint by responding to questions on, for example, what they would do if theirs was the only kidney that could save a distant relative they had only met once. The tool subsequently helps users to increase their knowledge of other possible ethical standpoints and how these may influence decisions in a number of hypothetical scenarios. One scenario, for example, places the user in the role of a hospital consultant. The user has to consider which standpoint to take in the case of a young father, for whom several cancer treatments have failed, but whom the consultant could refer for an experimental treatment abroad; the state, however, would be highly unlikely to provide financial assistance for the treatment.

Following the introduction to basic ethics provided by Ethics Dilemma, the second e-learning tool, Ethics Decision-Making, enables more detailed consideration of ethical dilemmas. The tool commences with an innovative checklist (see Figure 20.3) which helps the user to analyse an ethical dilemma and consider the pros and cons by posing nine questions under the headlines: 'Is it compliant', 'Is it responsible', and 'Is it generally acceptable'.

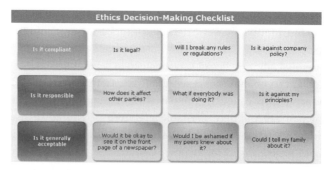

Figure 20.3 Ethics decision-making checklist, as featured in the ethics e-learning tools. (Source: Novo Nordisk.)

The second part of the tool is a healthcare-related business example of how a chain of decisions in a grey zone results in unintended consequences. The scene is set with the introduction of two employees of a pharmaceutical company, 'Pharma Co.'. One employee enters into an unethical arrangement with a hospital consultant that is subsequently reported in the media. Four further stakeholders are then introduced – shareholders, new management, sales manager and sales representative – and the user is invited to explore the stakeholders' responsibility for this situation, using the ethics decision-making checklist (compliance/responsibility/acceptability). The third and final part of the tool is an online board game that, with rolls of an electronic dice, enables users to play as one of five characters from a company and a hospital, and use the checklist before making decisions in a series of grey zone dilemmas.

At the time of writing the e-learning tools were still relatively new; however, it is hoped that in future, by enabling users to test their ethics decision-making skills and to better understand their personal ethics profiles, the resource will help to enhance mutual appreciation and fruitful dialogue between stakeholders from a broad range of backgrounds. The tools are being used internally in Novo Nordisk's business ethics training programme.

WHERE TO NEXT?

Being accountable to stakeholders has been a core element of Novo Nordisk's business activity for some time: it was among the first companies to report voluntarily on environmental and bioethics issues, and in 1994 became the first company in Denmark to publish an environmental report. In 2004 it made a bold move to integrate sustainability reporting into the annual financial report, and today contributes actively in the development of a new international framework for integrated reporting that aims to reflect more accurately a company's performance (International Integrated Reporting Committee, 2010). However, as this chapter has illustrated, external catalysts enabled the company to learn to *engage* – and subsequently learn – with stakeholders. Since then, Novo Nordisk has played a leading role in making societal changes through new engagement models for the industry. Through the DAWN™ programme, for example, the company has helped to change the paradigm about how diabetes care is delivered. Together with other innovative initiatives such as the ethics e-learning tool, DAWN™ counts as a 'game changer' in stakeholder engagement. By demonstrating leadership, however, a company effectively sets an example for others to follow suit; this gives rise to a fresh challenge.

For the pharmaceutical industry, stakeholder dialogue and new engagement models are essential for companies to understand and act on the sustainable development agenda, to continue to rebuild public trust, and to secure a licence to operate and innovate. The sector is rising to the challenge and in some cases is showing real leadership. Maintaining good relationships with stakeholders – including patients, general practitioners, dispensing chemists, healthcare providers, suppliers, universities, the media, NGOs, communities, governments and investors – has become an important strategic tool for most pharmaceutical companies. Many have adopted the concept of corporate responsibility, integrating social and environmental concerns in their business operations. This is illustrated by the fact that today most of the big pharmaceutical companies are listed in the Dow Jones Sustainability Index, in which Novo Nordisk has consistently been rated in the top rank as a sustainability leader in the healthcare sector. The real test, however, lies in how communication with stakeholders works in practice at all levels of a company's corporate activity. This situation represents opportunities for pharmaceutical companies; those companies that are best able to engage with – and address the concerns of – patients, healthcare providers, regulators and investors will be able to build a sustainable competitive advantage.

For other industry sectors, too, understanding the role of business in society may provide the platform for successfully utilising the dynamics of societal changes in ways that are both responsible and profitable. It is not a matter of sound risk management and contingency planning to secure the licence to operate, but rather the application of a radically different business principle that anticipates changes in the social environment, turns them into opportunities and enables the organisation, led by its management, to prosper and grow – to the benefit of the business and the society of which it forms part. In short, a model of corporate sustainability that successfully harnesses the power to innovate. By investing in society, a company will sustain the trust of its stakeholders and build awareness and profitable business growth. Ultimately, that is how the business of sustainability will become a sustainable business.

Key resources

Changing Diabetes initiatives – http://changingdiabetes.novonordisk.com
Ethics e-learning tools – http://www.ethics-e-learning.com
Global Business Initiative on Human Rights – http://www.global-business-initiative.org

Eccles, R. & Krzus, M. (2010). *One Report: Integrated Reporting for a Sustainable Strategy*. Hoboken, NJ: John Wiley & Sons, Inc.

International Diabetes Federation (2004). Putting people at the centre of care: DAWN in action. *Diabetes Voice*, 49 (Special Issue), 1–49.

Peyrot, M., Rubin, R., Lauritzen, T. *et al.* (2006). Patient and provider perceptions of care for diabetes: results of the cross-national DAWN study. *Diabetologia*, 49(2), 279–288.

Hatch, M. J. & Schultz, M. (2008). *Taking Brand Initiative*. San Francisco, CA: Jossey-Bass.

Skovlund, S. & Peyrot, M. (2005). The Diabetes Attitudes, Wishes, and Needs (DAWN) program: a new approach to improving outcomes of diabetes care. *Diabetes Spectrum*, 18(3), 136–142.

Wroe, J. (2006). The 3rd International DAWN Summit: from research and practice to large-scale implementation. *Practical Diabetes International*, 23(7), 313–316.

Hopwood, A., Unerman, J. & Fries, J. (eds.) (2010). *Accounting for Sustainability*. London: Earthscan.

World Health Organization (2009). *Fact Sheet 312 on Diabetes*. [Online] Available at: http://www.who.int/mediacentre/factsheets/fs312/en/index.html [Accessed 3 September 2010].

References

Amidon, D. M. (2004). *Innovationsmotorvejen*. Copenhagen: Børsens Forlag.

European Federation of Pharmaceutical Industries and Associations (2010). *The Pharmaceutical Industry in Figures – 2010 Edition*. [Online] Available at: http://www.efpia.eu/content/default.asp?PageID=559&DocID=9158 [Accessed 26 July 2010].

Global Business Initiative on Human Rights (2009). *Global Business Initiative on Human Rights Briefing Note*. [Online] Available at: http://www.global-business-initiative.org/ABOUT/assets/Briefing%20Note.pdf [Accessed 18 August 2010].

Grunig, J. E. and Hunt, T. (1984). *Managing Public Relations*. New York: Holt, Rinehart and Winston.

Harris Interactive (2010). *The Annual Reputation Quotient 2009 Summary Report*. [Online] Available at: http://www.harrisinteractive.com/vault/2009%20Annual%20Reputation%20Quotient%20Media%20Summary%20Report_public.pdf [Accessed 26 July 2010].

International Diabetes Federation (2009). *IDF Diabetes Atlas*, 4th edn. Brussels: International Diabetes Federation.

International Integrated Reporting Committee (2010). *Formation of the International Integrated Reporting Committee*. [Online] Available at: http://www.integratedreporting.org/node/18 [Accessed 3 September 2010].

Novo Nordisk (2007). *Changing Diabetes Barometer, First Report*. Bagsværd, Denmark: Novo Nordisk.

Novo Nordisk (2009). *Annual Report 2008*. Bagsværd, Denmark: Novo Nordisk.

Novo Nordisk (2010). *Ethics e-learning tools launched by Novo Nordisk and the University of Copenhagen*. [Online] Available at: http://www.novonordisk.com/sustainability/news/2010-05-ethics-decision-making-tool-launched.asp [Accessed 26 July 2010].

Skovlund, S. (2004). DAWN of a new era. *KM Magazine*, 8(3), 23–35.

World Commission on Environment and Development (1987). *Our Common Future*. Oxford: Oxford University Press.

21

Science festivals

WHAT ARE SCIENCE FESTIVALS? – THEIR SPECIAL CHARACTERISTICS

A 'festival' is a day or period of celebration (historically usually for religious reasons), or an organised series of cultural events, such as concerts or films. Over the last decade the UK has seen a huge surge in the number of festivals celebrating science.[1] This is concurrent with the increase in music festivals over a similar period – it would seem the British are a festival-loving nation. Science festivals generally focus their activity around a town or a city, often using multiple locations and frequently bringing science-related activities to places where these would not usually take place, such as pubs, bookshops, railway stations and in the case of the British Science Festival in 2006 and 2007, Norwich Cathedral and York Minster. They are invaluable opportunities for the host cities's universities to showcase their research and their researchers, and for local science-based industries to throw their doors open and let festival-goers see what takes place inside. What makes science festivals unique among other types of public engagement activity is the fact that they bring hundreds of thousands of people into direct face-to-face contact with scientists and engineers every year in a rich and diverse mix of activities.

The UK's science festivals embrace all of the scientific disciplines and all seek to explore the role that science plays within today's society.

---

[1] Most science festivals call themselves festivals of 'science' but in practice include events in engineering, technology, mathematics, medicine, and much more – including social sciences and arts. We use 'science' in this chapter to talk about the varied topics covered by science festivals.

Successful Science Communication, ed. D. J. Bennett and R. C. Jennings. Published by Cambridge University Press. © Cambridge University Press 2011.

Festival events take on a wide variety of formats. Many have family-focussed days which bring together a broad range of hands-on activities in one area. The Edinburgh International Science Festival has a daily event at the City Art Centre which it describes as *'seven floors of fantastic fun for all the family'*. Within its daily programme a visitor can typically find a range of workshops, shows, hands-on activities and exhibitions all aiming to engage with and inspire young people about science (Edinburgh International Science Festival, 2010). The Cambridge Science Festival bases many of its events within university laboratories and lecture theatres, inviting members of the public in to try hands-on experiments and attend talks and discussions for all ages (Cambridge Science Festival, 2010). All of the UK's science festivals include a programme of schools-specific activities within their schedules (Figure 21.1). This may involve having school parties attend Festival events but also includes outreach activities. For example, TechFest, Aberdeen and the north-east of Scotland's annual science festival, has a large secondary schools' programme which takes place entirely as an outreach activity locating around 40 scientists, engineers and science communicators out in the region's secondary schools (TechFest, 2010).

Figure 21.1 Young people getting hands-on at the British Science Festival.

As with any type of festival, the programme content will be diverse to attract as broad a range of individuals as possible. Any science festival might typically include performance elements such as stand-up comedy, theatre, dance, poetry, films, walking tours of scientific sites, book readings, music events, arts and crafts activities – all with a science-inspired focus – as well as hands-on activities for all ages and the more traditional talks, debates, interviews and discussions. Many science festivals are also taking up opportunities presented through new media: putting talks and discussions online as video or audio, producing podcasts from festivals, using Facebook and Twitter to connect and converse with their audiences and speakers, and using social media as part of particular events.

As part of the 2009 Manchester Science Festival, the organisation FutureEverything teamed up with the Manchester Beacon on a project called *Comixed: Enhanced – Remixing the Conversation*. In this event, three speakers from various backgrounds such as science, ethics, arts or a community group each gives a five-minute overview of their angle on a particular topic including something provocative to promote questions and discussion. The audience sits around in a circle surrounding the speaker so it is quite intimate and open. Some of the audience are 'curated', so that individuals who have knowledge about the topic, such as local community groups, get specific invites, as well as the event being open to the general public. The event is documented in real time via Twitter, live blogging, video. Young people are invited to contribute to a 'mash-up' session at the end of the event – using footage taken at the event to create their own interpretation and video of the event and its subject matter. The tweeting and blogging allows people to be involved online, so increasing the reach of the Festival event. This allows them to contribute virtually to the event as a form of documentation (Comixed, 2010).

PURPOSES OF SCIENCE FESTIVALS

While science festivals do function as celebrations of science, if science is to be truly part of culture then festivals also have a role of questioning and probing applications of science and its governance. Science festivals encapsulate many of the varied purposes and motivations for public engagement (Holliman and Jensen, 2009). Scientists and organisations become involved in public engagement with a range of purposes in mind: from winning support for science, to developing the learning of young people, to playing a part in opening up the practice of science, ensuring it can be ethical, accountable and transparent (Science for All Expert Group, 2010, p. 7). As well as inspiring young people, and promoting appreciation of science as part of culture for all ages, the UK's science festivals are tackling increasingly more and more topical and often contentious issues. This is important if science festivals are to be perceived by audiences as not just 'cheerleaders' for science, but also places where debate is central to the experience.

For example, in 2008 while MPs were preparing to debate a Bill updating the law on embryo research, an event at the Cheltenham Science Festival tackled the complex issues. Analysing issues raised by the Bill in the *Daily Telegraph* at the time, Roger Highfield wrote:

> These are profound issues in terms of science, law and morality – and this is why the Human Fertilisation and Embryology Bill, due to be debated this month in Parliament, is among the most divisive to have come before MPs. Indeed, it is so controversial that the Prime Minister has been forced to allow a free vote on the most contentious elements. (Highfield, 2008)

The issues are profound in terms of what was raised by the Bill and Cheltenham Science Festival confronted the issues head on by hosting an event involving a lawyer and lecturer in law and medicine, James Lawford Davies, Lyle Armstrong who had been granted a licence to create human–animal embryos for research, and ethicist Lord Harries of Pentregarth. Cheltenham Science Festival Director Sharon Bishop outlines the importance of this type of activity saying:

> Science festivals provide a public forum for debate and discussion, and must be prepared to tackle controversial topics. They offer the public a rare opportunity to come face-to-face with scientists and policy-makers: to question, criticise and comment on the issues that matter to them and their families. But, just as importantly, festivals offer the scientists and policy-makers a chance to take the temperature of public opinion, explain and defend their arguments, and explore the wider societal implications of their work. (S. Bishop, personal communication, 2010)

The 2008 British Science Festival, which was held in Liverpool as the city celebrated its year as European Capital of Culture, was replete with contentious issues aired through the media from start to finish. The Festival coincided with the switch-on of the CERN Large Hadron Collider. The then President of the British Science Association, the former UK Chief Scientist, Professor Sir David King, used his presidential address at the Festival to call for a gear-change among innovative thinkers to put more effort into pressing global issues such as climate change and suggesting that less time and money be spent on endeavours such as space exploration and particle physics. This suggestion was picked up widely by the media and generated an abundance of comment and opinion pieces culminating in a heated interview with King and Professor Brian Cox, particle physicist and the UK's leading CERN spokesperson (BBC News, 2008).

Science festivals could act more often as a space for more formal kinds of public engagement and consultation on topical and contentious issues. To date, most science festivals, like science centres, have facilitated more informal dialogue (also see Davies, 2009). The British Science Association experimented with a community x-change format in the run-up to the British Science Festival in Norwich in 2006 and Liverpool in 2007. These brought together members of the public, invited through the electoral roll, with scientists, community activists and councillors to discuss issues of local concern including the environment and climate change. This was still a process that did not have a planned way to feed into local policy, although it opened up discussion between different groups in society (Eady et al., 2008). There are numerous Government departments, regulatory bodies and scientific associations that do seek the views of the public – increasingly at an 'upstream' point in the process of scientific research (Wilsdon and Willis, 2004; Sciencewise, 2010). With joint working, there is the potential to use science festivals for more structured forms of public engagement with science feeding into policy.

RECENT DEVELOPMENTS IN SCIENCE FESTIVALS
AND CONTEMPORARY OVERVIEW

Science festivals have become increasingly prevalent over the last decade or so. A European Science Events Association survey described science festivals as a 'relatively new' phenomenon (EUSCEA, 2005, p. 5). A worldwide survey in 2008 found that 27 out of 52 science festivals which responded had started in the period 2006–2008, with only five starting prior to 1995 (Bultitude, 2009). The UK currently has a comparatively 'vibrant' science festival scene (Department of Innovation, Universities and Skills, 2008), with around 11 large science festivals taking place each year (Office of Science and Technology, 2004; Wellcome Trust, 2010). Hundreds of thousands of members of the public attend these UK science festivals each year (Technopolis Group, 2008, p. 57).

The history of UK science festivals could be traced back to the Royal Institution in London's Albermarle Street founded in 1799 by the Society for Bettering the Conditions and Improving the Comforts of the Poor with its annual Christmas Lecture since 1825, Michael Faraday's lecture in 1856 being shown as the frontispiece of this book, and the British Association for the Advancement of Science's annual meeting, founded in 1831 to encourage discussion between scientists and other learned individuals to promote scientific progress (British Science Association, 2009a). The annual meeting was renamed a Festival of Science in the 1980s and is now the British Science Festival. Other events which have shared the theme of 'celebration of science and technology' include the 1851 Great Exhibition at the Crystal Palace in London and other World Fairs, international Expos and the 1951 Festival of Britain. Contemporary science festivals tend not to have such high capital budgets, however, and instead bring together temporary exhibits, museum activities, scientists, school pupils and publics to create a time-limited special event.

There have been a number of types of impetus behind the foundation of a science festival. The Edinburgh International Science Festival was founded in part to complement the popularity of the numerous other cultural festivals in that city (Gribbin and Gribbin, 1989). The UK Government launched a National Science Week (now called National Science and Engineering Week) in 1994, which takes place each March. Co-ordinated by the British Science Association, it aims to engage and inspire people of all ages with science and technology and their implications. During the week, thousands of events are organised by a wide range of organisations. National Science and Engineering Week has been the occasion for the foundation of several science festivals, including those in Cambridge and Newcastle.

ORGANISATIONAL STRUCTURES

Science festivals may be managed by different types of organisations: science museums and centres, universities, independent charities, research councils, local government or Government-funded agencies (EUSCEA, 2005, p. 13). The organisational structure influences certain features of the festival, including the number of scientific researchers and students who help to deliver engagement activities. Key tasks for the staff employed to run science festivals include fund-raising, soliciting event ideas from contributors and programming key events, organising venues, producing promotional material including event schedules and websites, marketing the festival to schools and the general public, media liaison, health and safety management, meeting booking requirements by the public, and dealing with event logistics during the festival itself.

Science festivals typically draw their funding from numerous sources: corporate sponsorship, science research funding specifically for public communication, university funding, charitable trust donations, local government grants and income from ticket sales. This mix of funding can be helpful in ensuring that no one funder dominates the agenda of the science festival. The funding mix mirrors that of many

other cultural festivals – and science festivals can provide an opportunity for a range of organisations with an interest in public engagement with science to collaborate on events and marketing to achieve
a shared goal.

Table 21.1 shows that the UK science festivals have a variety of
organisational structures, which influence their particular characteristics. The British Science Festival, as a long-standing festival which
includes scientists from across the UK, has a good track record in
achieving media coverage. The Manchester Science Festival benefits
from its hosting by the Museum of Science and Industry. Science festivals based at universities, as in Cambridge and Glasgow, benefit from
close access to and knowledge of scientific staff and students at those
universities, who can be encouraged to take part in the festivals. The
Cambridge Science Festival has a particularly high level of participation
by scientific students demonstrating science and arranging experiments which attendees can do. There are several student-run groups
organising events in the festival, including Cambridge Hands-on Science
(CHaOS), Time Truck (Earth scientists) and The Triple Helix, a society that
organises public and schools' debates on scientific, social and ethical
issues (Cambridge Science Festival, 2010).

Table 21.1. *Some UK science festivals and their organisational structure*

Examples of science festivals	Lead organisation for festival	Characteristics deriving from organisational structure
British Science Festival	National membership association/Government-funded	• Takes event submissions from its membership groups • Takes event submissions from scientists across UK • Tends to change location annually • Good media coverage
Edinburgh International Science Festival; Brighton Science Festival	Independent charity	• Numerous partner organisations • Benefits and challenges due to reputation of its host city for festivals

Table 21.1. (*cont.*)

Examples of science festivals	Lead organisation for festival	Characteristics deriving from organisational structure
Cheltenham Science Festival	Independent charity/city-based Festivals Trust	• Shares some programming and marketing possibilities with other festivals in Cheltenham, e.g. Literary • Several authors of scientific books and media personalities take part alongside scientists and science communicators
Cambridge Science Festival; Glasgow University Science Festival; Wrexham Science Festival	University	• High level of participation by university and partner institute scientists and students • Many events take place in university facilities • Collaboration with university widening participation activities
Oxfordshire Science Festival; Bristol Festival of Nature	Independent consortium organisation	• Events delivered by numerous participating organisations • These include universities, voluntary organisations, etc.
Newcastle Science Festival; Manchester Science Festival	Science museum or centre	• Access to high-quality exhibition and education spaces
TechFest (Aberdeen and north-east Scotland)	Setpoint/STEM Team: local agency brokering	• Good links with schools • Good contacts among

Table 21.1. (*cont.*)

Examples of science festivals	Lead organisation for festival	Characteristics deriving from organisational structure
York Science Festival	schools' science enrichment initiatives Science city: organisation which helps bring businesses and researchers based at universities etc. together	local providers of science enrichment • Access to promotional opportunities • Business partners

OTHER TYPES OF FESTIVALS THAT FEATURE SCIENCE

As well as those festivals that cover a broad range of scientific topics, there are also those that focus on specific areas of science such as Bristol's Festival of Nature, or Birmingham Science City's Climate Change Festival or Norwich and Norfolk's Sustainable Living Festival in June 2009, instigated by the Beacon for Public Engagement based at the University of East Anglia. Some science fairs and festivals target schools primarily: for example the Big Bang (the UK Young Scientists' and Engineers' Fair) in the UK, which includes the culmination of many science and engineering competitions for schools under the banner of the National Science and Engineering Competition. Some festivals have a link with special exhibitions: the Royal Society organises a Summer Science Exhibition each year, which is open to scientific research groups across the country, with stands staffed by researchers set up within the Society's central London premises for a week. In 2010 this exhibition moved to the South Bank cultural quarter in London to form a large part of a Festival of Arts and Science (Royal Society, 2010). There is also more and more science-based activity taking place at other types of festivals. For Einstein Year in 2005, members of the Science Communication Unit at the University of the West of England delivered 'Einstein at Glastonbury' which involved a team of young science communicators performing a huge variety of physics-based tricks, many music-related, at the annual Glastonbury Festival of Contemporary Performing Arts (Peters *et al.*, 2006). Guerilla Science is a group of musicians and science communicators who describe themselves as being dedicated to 'science by stealth'. Their website describes their remit as follows '*to combine "science" with "music festival" (which) may seem counterintuitive. Which is exactly why we do it.*' (Guerilla Science, 2010). Through their work at music festivals such as Latitude, Lovebox and Secret Garden, they aim to challenge negative misconceptions about science. Several festivals with a focus on literature or politics also include scientific content. The 'Battle of Ideas' is a weekend of debate on some of the most provocative questions facing society which takes place annually in November in London. Due to the nature of this festival it invariably features a healthy amount of science-based discussion and involves some of the country's leading scientific minds (Institute of Ideas, 2009).

SCIENTIST MOTIVATIONS AND BENEFITS

The turn to dialogue in the public engagement with science field has led many scientists to see the importance of engagement opportunities such as those offered by science festivals. Science festivals offer the potential for more or less formal types of interaction with non-specialists. They can be a chance to try out two-way dialogue with members of the public in a way that concentrating efforts on speaking to the media is less likely to provide, for example. A recent survey of factors affecting science communication by scientists and engineers asked whether respondents would be happy to take part in a science engagement activity that was organised by someone else, and 69% agreed or strongly agreed (Royal Society, 2006). This points to the importance of the infrastructure for science engagement: science centres, cafés scientifiques and science festivals all help to provide the places and occasions for public/scientist dialogue. The staff and volunteers who organise and market such events are performing a useful role in bringing together scientists and the public. They invite scientists to take part in events, provide or promote training opportunities in public communication and market events to the public. The existence of this support among science festival staff makes it attractive for a considerable number of scientists and students to take part in science festivals. In particular, if a scientist has an idea for a public engagement initiative, it is advantageous to collaborate with an event such as a science festival to benefit from the overall publicity plans which the festival will put into action.

It is increasingly common for science funding bodies such as the Research Councils and the Wellcome Trust to include a public engagement requirement into their funding proposal criteria. Science festivals provide an excellent platform for researchers to fulfil these public engagement requirements coupled with a motivation to engage others in discussion of their work. As disability ethicist Dr Tom Shakespeare says:

> There are so many reasons for scientists to engage with the public. They often receive public funds, and therefore have a duty to disseminate and share their results.

But also it is in their interests, because an ignorant public or a suspicious public can end up frightened or hostile to research. When scientists take the trouble to explain and to enter into dialogue, then many fears can be dispelled and the value of science is more widely appreciated. Hearing lay views also can suggest different ways of thinking about science, maybe even identify new research questions. Finally, young people often find science difficult and are put off studying it in school. Through meeting a working scientist, there is a chance that they will be inspired and see the utility of their learning. Some of them will later become the scientists of tomorrow. (Policy Ethics and Life Sciences, 2010).

It is possible that changes to the UK's system for assessing and rewarding researchers may recognise public engagement activity to a greater extent than before. The proposed new Research Excellence Framework includes 'public engagement with science' among the indicators of 'impact' for which research groups will be asked to provide evidence (HEFCE, 2009, p. 41). There has been some ambivalence among scientists about institutionalising public engagement. Some scientists feel that activities such as participating in science festivals are most successful when they are characterised by the 'goodwill' due to the current status of science communication as a 'voluntary, vocational, and somewhat exceptional activity' (Burchell *et al.*, 2009, p. 8). Others see the potential for participating in science festivals and related activity to become recognised as a more mainstream activity for scientists. But it will surely remain important for the scientists who take part in activities like festivals to be those who have enthusiasm for such events. Science festival organisers do not want scientists to take part who are merely doing it to 'tick a box'.

Case study

At the 2005 British Science Festival in Dublin, marine biologist Dr Jason Hall-Spencer showcased new video captured off the south-west of Ireland. The video not only revealed spectacular new species of corals but also showed that deep-sea trawling was inadvertently damaging coral reefs that were thousands of years old. This footage generated enormous media interest, and on the back of this publicity Jason was granted access to Government satellite tracking data showing where the international fleets of fishing boats were trawling. From these data Jason was able to show where deep-water fishing was having a catastrophic impact on coral habitats. Ultimately, the World Wide Fund for Nature joined Jason in lobbying the EU departments for the environment and fisheries to implement policy that was less detrimental to the marine environment. (British Science Association, 2007)

HOW TO GET INVOLVED

Science festivals offer researchers the golden opportunity to cut their public engagement teeth. Science festivals welcome participation by a wide range of scientists and scientific organisations, however also giving schools, businesses, voluntary/community groups and artists a chance to take part in addition to people from the large scientific institutions like universities, research institutes and companies, and science centres and museums. Science festivals provide contact details on their website, and may have festival event provider groups which interested parties can join. The process of event submission is more structured at larger festivals (e.g. British Science Festival) and some larger international festivals (e.g. US Science and Engineering Festival), with event submission forms on their website.

> **What you can do**
>
> As a scientific researcher or student, you may get an opportunity to become involved in communicating with the public at a science festival. This involvement may take numerous forms: from demonstrating hands-on activities for families, to taking part in a public panel discussion or giving a talk with a question-and-answer session. If a science festival regularly takes place near to where you work or study, then you can approach the festival organisers, with contacts usually found via their website. Many science festivals have limited budgets, so if you are keen to be involved, it will be worthwhile thinking about how much the activity you have in mind might cost and considering sources of funding that may be available to you.[2]
>
> It is important to remember that science festivals offer many more opportunities for communication than public lectures and presentations. The 'stands' at a science festival, staffed by scientists, students and other festival event contributors, can offer a good way for members of the public to engage with information and activities. These stands or display areas will often need to be staffed for a full day, perhaps over several days, so it can be an intensive way of engaging with the public. Science festivals also offer schools' programmes, either delivered to visiting school groups, or taken out to visit schools, and you may wish to propose an activity or talk to reach this target group. Most science festival

---

[2] Some sources of funding are listed here: http://www.britishscienceassociation.org/web/NSEW/GetInvolved/HowToGuides/NSEWFunding.htm

co-ordination teams are small, so if you wish to take part in a science festival, personal communication with the organisers will be crucial in establishing where you may fit best into the festival in terms of the spaces and time slots available, and the audience you are trying to reach.

Some festivals have competitive elements to them which researchers can get involved with. A great UK science festival success story is Famelab. Famelab began in 2005. It is a regional talent competition organised in the UK by the Cheltenham Science Festival. The competition takes place in a series of regional heats and is open to anyone over 18 working in or studying a science-related topic. Competitors have three minutes in which to impress a panel of judges with their communication skills on any science-related topic of their choice. Winners of the regional heats compete in the Famelab final at the Cheltenham Science Festival offering a five-minute talk on a different topic. With support from the British Council, Famelab has been rolled out into nine countries with the Famelab International Grand Final taking place at Cheltenham (Famelab, 2010).

Each year the British Science Association honours five outstanding young communicators with the opportunity to present an Award Lecture at the British Science Festival. The Award Lectures are aimed at professional scientists or engineers in the early stages of their career, who show outstanding skills in communication to a non-specialist audience. The Award Lectures aim to promote open and informed discussion on issues involving science and actively encourage young scientists to explore the societal aspects of their research, providing them with reward and recognition for doing so. The Lectures are a hugely popular component of the festival programme and have been awarded to scientists who went on to become some of the UK's best-known science communicators such as Professor Richard Wiseman, Professor Brian Cox and the co-director of the Cheltenham Science Festival, Dr Mark Lythgoe (British Science Association, 2010).

Preparing your activity

As with any piece of communication, in planning a science festival activity, as an event contributor, you will consider the messages you wish to communicate. You should take into account the potential level of knowledge among those with whom you will be communicating, as well as the likely range of attitudes and values you will encounter. Science festivals are not typically spaces for one-way communication solely from specialists to non-specialists, however, and those organising events should consider how you will build in the capacity for feedback from their audience. For example, Professor Roger Pedersen and Dr Kate Quinlan organised several public communication events around stem cell research. They found through participating in the Cambridge Science Festival that many attendees thought that a much higher number of human embryos were used in stem cell research than is actually the case. In fact, the vast majority of Professor Pedersen's group's research on human embryonic stem cells has been achieved using a line (the same one predominantly used by researchers across the world) that was derived in the late 1990s from a single fertilised egg. Through discussing the issues raised with attendees at talks and discussions, they and other stem cell researchers decided to provide more information to clarify this issue at future events (personal communication, 2010).

Event contributors will need to find out from the festival organisers the likely age range and numbers of visitors they can expect to attend their activity or talk. Speakers, demonstrators and workshop leaders may wish to practise their activity with friends or family who are not experts in their area of science or technology. The festival organisers should also offer the opportunity for event contributors and speakers to practise talks and activities with them. A range of methods may be used to interest and engage people in informal science learning: particularly popular methods include incorporating hands-on learning, games, arts/science activities, take-home information and activities, informal dialogue, question-and-answer opportunities and many more.

TRAINING

In its *Survey of Factors Affecting Science Communication by Scientists and Engineers*, the Royal Society found that the great majority (73% of those surveyed) had never undergone any training in communicating science to non-specialist publics (Royal Society, 2006). Before embarking upon taking part in a science festival activity, it is worthwhile to take advantage of training in communicating with the public. One-day courses are offered by various Research Councils, the Wellcome Trust and Royal Society among others in the UK and similar organisations in other countries. Some scientists choose to become STEM (Science, Technology, Engineering and Maths) Ambassadors, in a national scheme which arranges for working scientists to visit schools, and training is also available through that scheme. University outreach or staff development departments may also arrange training. For example, the Rising Stars course at the University of Cambridge provides 25 hours of training over a term in communicating about research with the public, and it requires participants to plan, deliver and evaluate an outreach activity over the course of the training period (University of Cambridge, 2010).

In 2009 Newcastle and Oxford Science Festivals started a poster competition modelled on one called 'perspectives', which took place at the British Science Festival between 2003 and 2009. 'perspectives' was a poster competition with a difference. It offered researchers at the beginning of their careers the training to develop their skills in discussing the ethical and social issues that arise from their research. Following this training competitors designed posters to convey the societal side of their research which they displayed in shopping centres as part of the British Science Festival, standing by their poster to discuss these aspects with passing members of the public. Festival events which can incorporate a training element like this are hugely valuable for those researchers interested in but lacking experience in public engagement.

Should participants in science festivals wish to take their development in public engagement and communication further, there are further training courses that go beyond one-day introductions. The University of the West of England runs a one-week masterclass in science communication, and there are short courses all the way up to Masters and PhDs in science communication and public engagement offered by Imperial College London, Birkbeck College London, the University of the West of England and the Open University among other providers in the UK.

EVALUATION

There are examples of evaluations from various festivals on their websites, or on those of their evaluators (Grant, 2004; British Science Association, 2009b; Jensen, 2009). Festival evaluations typically try to measure attitudinal changes to science and learning outcomes from festival activity. They also capture demographic data including ages, genders, ethnic backgrounds and so on of the visitors who came.

For a scientist planning a particular activity within a science festival, it will be worthwhile finding out whether there is a standard evaluation format which is to be used across various festival events: are there forms to give out, or evaluators on-site, or is an online survey being promoted? It is also important to check the reporting requirements of any funders of the activity. But the most important reason to evaluate an event is to ascertain whether it met its objectives, and to learn from the feedback in order to develop or change the activity in future.

A mix of quantitative and qualitative feedback data is often useful. Closed questions on surveys allow attendees to choose from a range of options to give their feedback, and these questions often allow for comparisons to be made between events. Open questions allow attendees to give written or verbal feedback freely, and these allow for a more personal and often deeper and more insightful glimpse into the impact of a particular event.

There is a wide range of evaluation methods that can be used. Sometimes more informal and creative forms of feedback are most useful: several science festivals have used hand-held voting technology, for example, which can measure changes in attitudes and knowledge over the course of an event. Or in art/science activity, it can be possible to ask participants to leave their comments on posters, notes or 'post-it' stickers. Observation of science festival events by experienced evaluators and science engagement specialists could be useful. Focus groups or interviews held after the festival offer the chance to probe further into the experience of a relatively small number of visitors (E. Jensen and N. Buckley, unpublished data).

One challenge in evaluating science festivals and other types of activity that tend to combine the twin aims of inspiring young people and engaging the public of all ages in science, is that there can be strong interest from Government and funders in whether this type of activity inspires young people to study science and technology further. If a particular science festival event is run solely or mainly for school pupils, then it will be important to find out whether it complemented school science provisions, and added anything to pupils' scientific understanding and interest. Both with events for young people, and for adults and all ages, it is worth thinking about scientific culture, and learning, in their widest senses. There are evaluation frameworks, and toolkits, that provide a guide towards setting your activity aims and objectives, and measuring these, and these guides can help event organisers to think through what they are trying to achieve and select mechanisms to assess whether the aims are being met (Research Councils UK, 2005; Cullen *et al.*, 2007; Museums, Libraries and Archives Council, 2009).

As the development of science festivals is largely a fairly recent phenomenon, the practice of science festival evaluation still has some way to go. Current challenges include how to measure the comparative quality of science festival events and to conduct more rigorous social scientific studies of science festivals. The vibrant mix of events, and the plethora of motivations and purposes for science festival activities, make it particularly interesting to assess what role science festivals play in attendees' understanding of science.

CONCLUSION

Science festivals comprise a diverse and growing area of activity. They offer a great opportunity for people working in science and technology together with community, schools, business and artistic representatives to come together to create special events which raise the profile of science, and raise questions and provoke debate.

As this book is intended for scientists, the focus of this chapter has been on illustrating how to get involved in science festivals, and some of the planning and evaluation considerations to take on board. There is comparatively little published information on the activities and impacts of science festivals, and there is considerable scope for further research into the effects that science festivals have on attendees and the organisations in their host towns and cities. The integration of science festivals in overall strategies for public engagement with science could also be more fully developed.

Anyone inspired to seek out a science festival to take part in is encouraged to pursue those plans. Sampling a science festival first as an attendee will be a good way to find out which events are most successful with their audiences. Thinking about training, funding, event design and key messages early on in the planning process for any activity will be helpful. You may then have a proposed event which will add an extra element to an exciting and diverse programme, to be marketed to a wide range of visitors of all ages. All science festivals rely on a high input of voluntary time from scientists and others, and a relatively small amount of co-ordinating staff time, so event contributors are asked to come to science festivals with that in mind, and collaborate on producing events which achieve high quality in creative forms of two-way communication.

Key resources

For more descriptive information on science festivals, see EUSCEA (2005). *White Book on Science Communication Events in Europe.* Vienna: European Science Events Association.

For training in public engagement prior to taking part in a science festival: Royal Society http://royalsociety.org/Communication-skills-training-course-programme/; and Wellcome Trust http://www.wellcome.ac.uk/Education-resources/Communicating-your-research/Training-and-support/index.htm

For evaluation of science festival activity, see British Science Festival and Cambridge Science Festival evaluations for examples, http://www.britishscienceassociation.org/NR/rdonlyres/4C205493-93D3-46DD-AC6C-CE9EDD8FA8B3/0/British ScienceFestivalevaluation2009.pdf and http://www.admin.cam.ac.uk/sciencefestival/reports.html

To fund science festival activity, see http://www.britishscienceassociation.org/web/NSEW/GetInvolved/HowToGuides/NSEWFunding.htm

References

BBC News (2008). Retrieved 12 May 2010, from http://news.bbc.co.uk/1/hi/uk/7603257.stm

British Science Association (2007). Retrieved 12 May 2010, from http://www.britishscienceassociation.org/web/AboutUs/AnnualReview/PastReviews.htm

British Science Association (2009a). *A History of the British Science Association.* Retrieved 28 June 2009, from http://www.britishscienceassociation.org/web/AboutUs/OurHistory/index.htm

British Science Association (2009b). *British Science Festival Evaluation 2009.* Retrieved 17 February 2010, from http://www.britishscienceassociation.org/NR/rdonlyres/4C205493-93D3-46DD-AC6C-CE9EDD8FA8B3/0/BritishScienceFestivalevaluation2009.pdf

British Science Association (2010). *Award Lectures.* Retrieved 12 May 2010, from http://www.britishscienceassociation.org/web/BritishScienceFestival/WhatsOn/The+Award+Lectures+2010.htm

Bultitude, K. (2009). *Global Science Events Survey 2008: Preliminary Findings.* Paper presented at the European Science Events Association Conference, 18 May.

Burchell, K., Franklin, S. and Holden, K. (2009). *Public Culture as Professional Science: Final Report of the ScoPE Project* (Scientists on public engagement: from communication to deliberation?) http://www.lse.ac.uk/collections/BIOS/scope/pdf/scope_final_report.pdf

Cambridge Science Festival (2010). Retrieved 12 May 2010, from http://www.cambridgescience.org

Comixed (2010). Retrieved 12 May 2010, from http://www.comixed.org.uk/

Cullen, J., Sullivan, F. and Junge, K. (2007). *Evaluating Science and Society Initiatives: A Framework for Evaluation.* London: Tavistock Institute.

Davies, S. (2009). Learning to engage; engaging to learn: the purposes of informal public-science dialogue. In R. Holliman, E. Whitelegg, E. Scanlon, S. Smidt and J. Thomas (eds.), *Investigating Science Communication in the Information Age,* pp. 72–85. Oxford: Oxford University Press.

Department of Innovation, Universities and Skills (2008). *Science and Society Consultation.* London: HMSO.

Eady, N., Singh, J., Taylor-Gee, A. and Wakeford, T. (2008). Community x-change: connecting citizens and scientists to policy makers. *Participatory Learning and Action*, **58**: 39–43.

Edinburgh International Science Festival (2010). Retrieved 12 May 2010, from http://www.sciencefestival.co.uk/

EUSCEA (2005). *White Book on Science Communication Events in Europe*. Vienna: European Science Events Association.

Famelab (2010). Retrieved 22 September 2010, from http://famelab.org/

Grant, L. (2004). *Evaluation of Cheltenham Festival of Science*. Liverpool: University of Liverpool.

Gribbin, J. and Gribbin, B. (1989). All the fun of the fair: the first Edinburgh Science Festival. *New Scientist*, 6 May.

Guerilla Science (2010). Retrieved 12 May 2010, from http://guerillascience.co.uk/

Higher Education Funding Council for England (2009). *Research Excellence Framework: Second Consultation on the Assessment and Funding of Research*. Retrieved 12 May 2010, from http://www.hefce.ac.uk/pubs/hefce/2009/09_38/09_38.pdf

Highfield, R. (2008). Embryo research: a source of hope or horror? *Daily Telegraph*, 6 May.

Holliman, R. and Jensen, E. (2009). (In)authentic science and (im)partial publics: (Re)constructing the science outreach and public engagement agenda. In R. Holliman, E. Whitelegg, E. Scanlon, S. Smidt and J. Thomas (eds.), *Investigating Science Communication in the Information Age: Implications for Public Engagement and Popular Media*, pp. 35–52. Oxford: Oxford University Press.

Institute of Ideas (2009). http://www.instituteofideas.com/events/battleofideas2009.html

Jensen, E. (2009). *Cambridge Science Festival 2009 External Evaluation Report*. Available from www.cambridgescience.org

Museums, Libraries and Archives Council (2009). *Measuring Outcomes*. Retrieved 28 June 2009, from http://www.inspiringlearningforall.gov.uk/toolstemplates/

Office of Science and Technology (2004). *UK Science Festivals: PEST or Not?* London: OST.

Peters, J., Stylianidou, F., Ingram, C., Malek, R., Reiss, M. and Chapman, S. (2006). *Evaluation of Einstein Year*. London: Institute of Education, University of London.

Policy Ethics and Life Sciences (2010). Retrieved 12 May 2010, from http://www.ncl.ac.uk/peals/people/profile/t.w.shakespeare

Research Councils UK (2005). *Evaluation: Practical Guidelines*. http://www.rcuk.ac.uk/aboutrcuk/publications/corporate/evaluationguide.htm

Royal Society (2006). *Survey of Factors Affecting Science Communication by Scientists and Engineers*. http://royalsociety.org/General_WF.aspx?pageid=7967

Royal Society (2010). Retrieved 12 May 2010, from http://royalsociety.org/Summer-Science/

Science for All Expert Group (2010). *Report and Action Plan from the Science for All Expert Group*. Retrieved 12 May 2010, from http://www.britishscienceassociation.org/NR/rdonlyres/D6B1ACFC-2F42–4F07-A5D1–938E1D83F3ED/0/ScienceforAllFinalReport.pdf

Sciencewise (2010). Retrieved 12 May 2010, from http://www.sciencewise-erc.org.uk/

TechFest (2010). Retrieved 12 May 2010, from http://www.techfestsetpoint.org.uk/

Technopolis Group (2008). *Evaluation of the ESRC Festival of Social Science 2008*. http://www.technopolis-group.com/

University of Cambridge (2010). *Rising Stars Scheme*. Retrieved 12 May 2010, from http://www.admin.cam.ac.uk/offices/communications/community/star/

Wellcome Trust (2010). *Communicating your Research: Festivals*. Retrieved 17 February 2010, from http://www.wellcome.ac.uk/Education-resources/Communicating-your-research/Public-engagement-opportunities/Festivals/index.htm

Wilsdon, J. and Willis, R. (2004). *See-Through Science*. London: Demos.

22

Things to see and do: how scientific images work

Clarity is not everything, but there is little without it.

Tufte (1990, p. 62)

INTRODUCTION

The first visions of a new world' is how the English scientist John Kendrew described the first crude three-dimensional representation of a protein in 1957 (Kendrew, 1961). The protein was myoglobin and the scientific group led by John Kendrew was from the Cavendish Laboratory in Cambridge, UK. The first study of the three-dimensional structural representation of myoglobin revealed a much more complicated and irregular structure than most of the earlier hypotheses of proteins had suggested (Kendrew *et al.*, 1958). Two years later Kendrew and colleagues produced an image with such a high resolution that it allowed them to deduce the actual arrangement in space of nearly all of myoglobin's 2600 atoms (Kendrew *et al.*, 1960).

Kendrew presented the results for *Scientific American*'s wide general audience in an article in 1961 (Kendrew, 1961). Visual representations were used throughout the article to clarify the process and to explain the scientific results and consequences of the discovery. Of the sixteen illustrations, a double-page watercolour of the entire structure by the renowned scientific illustrator Irving Geis stood out (Figure 22.1). The details and subtle colours contributing to the delicate three-dimensional illustration of the molecule were the result of the work of a dedicated scientist and a talented scientific illustrator working together, creating

Successful Science Communication, ed. D. J. Bennett and R. C. Jennings. Published by Cambridge University Press. © Cambridge University Press 2011.

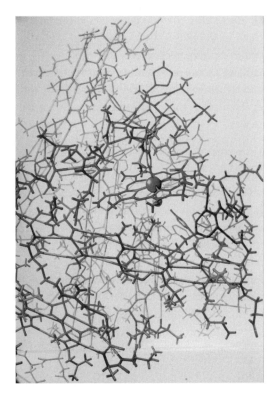

Figure 22.1 Detail of the watercolour of the sperm whale myoglobin, painted by Irving Geis for *Scientific American*. Illustration, Irving Geis. Image from the Irving Geis Collection/Howard Hughes Medical Institute. Rights owned by HHMI. Not to be reproduced without permission. See colour plate section.

a dazzling visual representation of the molecule. Other three-dimensional representations included an electron density map made of about fifty layers of transparent plastic Lucite sheets, a model of clips and rods, and a less detailed and rather rough sculpture. Throughout, Kendrew stressed the importance of producing three-dimensional representations of the molecule in search of explanations for chemical behaviours and physiological functions. This was how the work was done.

Visual representations are an important and integral part of understanding and developing new scientific concepts – both in the laboratory and when engaging a public audience. Images often serve as the primary evidence supporting the claims of the scientific publication (Goodsell & Johnson, 2007). Fifty years ago Kendrew and Geis aimed for the best possible visual representation of myoglobin. Geis later emphasised: *'We can only say "it's something like that" – and only create a visual metaphor*' (Paterlini, 2008). This chapter takes you through a series of visual representations made within a broad range of scientific areas, visual approaches and imaging technologies. It explores the way we look at scientific data, why some representations are better than others, and what you can do to achieve clarity, accuracy and aesthetic appearance in a visual representation that will represent your scientific data in the best possible way.

HOW DO WE VISUALISE SCIENTIFIC DATA?

One of the difficulties of visualising scientific information today is the scale of our data. One example is genetic sequence diagrams with billions of letters of genetic code made available through sequencing projects, another the expansion of phylogenetic trees trying to depict the characteristics of a vast and still growing number of different species. Simple design principles are valuable tools when we want to improve our visual communication of large data sets. When designing a phylogenetic tree a circular layout turns out to be most efficient but makes it more difficult to compare branch lengths, which, in phylograms, are used to establish similarity between species. The circular layout in Figure 22.2 can hold more information, whereas the rectangular layout makes it easier to communicate specific information. In the end it is not important how much information there is, but rather how effectively it is arranged (Tufte, 1990).

While data sets are growing, the sizes of the scientific objects we are able to measure are getting smaller. During recent decades we have developed new methods for visualising and manipulating things on the

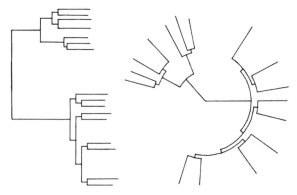

Figure 22.2 A rectangular and a circular layout of phylograms, redrawn from Procter *et al.* (2010, S22).

micro- and nanoscale. The desire to understand life's tiniest building blocks raises new questions of how to create visual representations. We use electrons and X-rays to create images through which we observe these objects, but these images may not be best for communicating science. To reach audiences outside the scientific community – or even across disciplines within the sciences – visual variety and simple designs are immensely important. Simple drawings or computer renderings can be fine complements to the more complex images produced in the laboratory. One such example is a nanoscale DNA box created by a group of scientists in 2009 (Andersen *et al.*, 2009). In addition to images produced by atomic force microscopy (AFM), cryo electron microscopy (cryo-EM) and small-angle X-ray scattering, the original paper used coloured drawings to show the principle in the controlled opening of the 'lid' of the DNA box (Figure 22.3). This example emphasises the importance of other visual representations beside the images produced by the advanced instruments in the laboratory. The drawing was taken as the single illustration when several popular media covered the story. In the scientific paper it was used to clarify the scientific message.

DYNAMIC DESIGN THROUGH INTERACTIVITY

More than 20 years ago Edward Tufte wrote about 'escaping flatland' (Tufte, 1990). His aim was to improve the endless two-dimensional flatland representations that we encounter every time we want to represent data. One way to escape flatland is to build models like the ones that Kendrew and colleagues created in the late 1950s. Another is to develop interactive software visualisation tools. Data designers, programmers and scientists are constantly developing new ways of representing scientific information through advanced computer software. Consequently, we have an enormous amount of computer software tools to choose from when we want to create three-dimensional representations of data.[1] The Protein Data Bank (PDB) is now an indispensable resource for researchers around the world. The database provides information about three-dimensional structures of biological molecules. It allows the users to visualise, rotate and analyse dynamic images of three-dimensional molecules and currently holds more than 65000 structures.[2]

---

[1] For an up-to-date collection of software tools for creating three-dimensional and interactive representations in the life sciences see *Nature Methods Supplement: Visualizing biological data*, **7**(3), 2010.

[2] For more information about the PDB resource see: www.pdb.org.

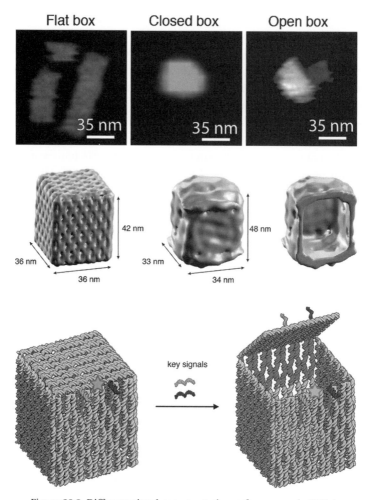

Figure 22.3 Different visual representations of a nanoscale DNA box with a controllable lid: pictures from atomic force microscopy (AFM) showing the flat box, the closed box and the open box (top), theoretical models and reconstructions based on cryo electron microscopy (middle), and finally a drawing showing the opening mechanism, where the blue and orange locking DNA strands recognise the complementary key DNA strands (bottom). (Courtesy of Ebbe Sloth Andersen.) See colour plate section.

An interactive software visualisation tool often combines several different ways of visualising the data into a single visual display. This interactive multiple view of data is a great advantage when dealing with large data sets. One example is a software tool developed by scientific data designer Ben Fry comparing the genetic profiles of different populations. There are many ways of looking at genetic variation data. The software provides a means of transition between these different views without loss of information. It shows that the many views are indeed related and highlights the diverse aspects in the data (Fry, 2004).[3]

Another good example is 'Walrus' – a software tool for interactively visualising large graphs (e.g. phylogenetic data) in three-dimensional space.[4] The software allows the viewer to simultaneously look at local details and the global context of the data. The user can browse through the data of, for example, a phylogenetic tree. Through the interactive module the viewer moves around inside the data set switching from one detailed view to another before yet again focusing on the global context (Figure 22.4) (Hughes et al., 2004).

The advantages of the interactivity, dynamics and large-scale data visualisation are obvious. We are able to convey information quickly through dynamic engagement and interactivity. However, since this chapter is written in 'flatland', actually visiting the relevant websites best demonstrates the advantages of the interactive software visualisation tools.

AESTHETIC AND FUNCTIONAL

Aesthetics is *not* the opposite of functionality in scientific imagery. It is a common misconception that aesthetic means 'not relevant' and function is something ugly. A better way of looking at this is trying to move back and forth between the two extreme views (Fry, 2004). Aesthetics not only makes the data look nice, it also makes it more understandable – it can help clarify the scientific message. Irving Geis's watercolour of myoglobin is a perfect example of combining aesthetics and function (Figure 22.1). Geis introduced visual elements that are now part of the standard conventions for representations of molecular structures used in, for example, contemporary modelling software.

---

[3] For more information on this interactive software visualisation tool see: http://benfry.com/isometricblocks. The project was originally part of the International HapMap Project (2002) aiming at the identification of genetic variations contributing to human disease through the development of a haplotype (haploid genotype) map of the human genome. For more information on the HapMap Project see: www.hapmap.org.

[4] For more information on Walrus see: www.caida.org/tools/visualization/walrus. From the website you can download examples, which give you a good idea of how the software works.

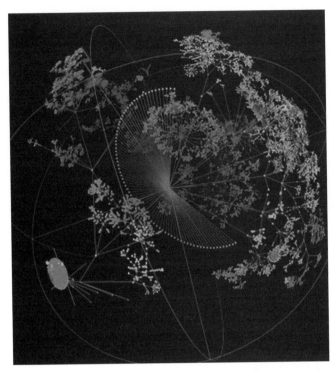

Figure 22.4 An example of phylogenetic data shown in three-dimensional space using the software tool 'Walrus'. (Copyright 2005 The Regents of the University of California. All Rights Reserved.) See colour plate section.

It is important to think about what to include in your represen-tation and what not to include. A well-prepared image, where unim-portant components are removed, will improve the visual expression of the work and result in an unambiguous representation of the data.

Photographs of data are frequently used as visual proof of the scientific process and outcome. The photograph of a floral structure made up of millions of yeast cells is a simple example of how minimal consideration can add aesthetic value to an image without losing any information or altering the data (Figure 22.5). The scientific message in the two images in Figure 22.5 is the same, but the photograph to the right is aesthetically better – the 'noise' has been removed. Science photographer Felice Frankel, who took the photograph of the yeast flower, emphasises through her work the visual strength of taking your visual representation just a bit further than the work required in the laboratory (Frankel, 2002; Frankel & Whitesides, 2009).

(a)   (b)

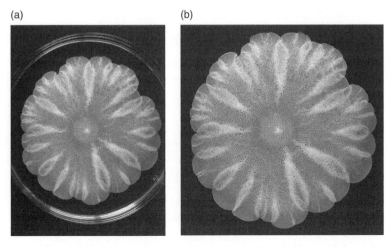

Figure 22.5 Photograph of a floral structure made of millions of yeast cells in a dish (left) and after digital alternation (right). (Courtesy of Felice Frankel.)

ARTISTIC SCIENCE OR SCIENTIFIC ART?

Thousands of artists and designers have looked for inspiration in the sciences. There is no reason why scientists should not seek inspiration in art and design. Visualising real data using simple design principles and artistic values is far more than just an interesting experiment across disciplines, it is a key step in exploring new ways of representing and communicating scientific information.

Visual representations of scientific information are first and foremost dependent on the type of data, the purpose of the particular communication, and the message we want to deliver. Kendrew's three-dimensional density map of the myoglobin crystal made up of layers of Lucite sheets was built to learn more about the configuration of the polypeptide chains (Kendrew, 1961). A related, but much more recent project is a glass representation of ATP synthase, the enzyme in all living organisms from bacteria to man that synthesises adenosine triphosphate (ATP) from adenosine diphosphate (ADP), by glass artist Colin Rennie.[5] Rennie used a powerful water-jet cutter to create the three-dimensional structure of the molecule in a 780-kilogram cube of 30 glass layers. Clear differences in why the models were built, who the audiences were and what

[5] The sculpture was originally made for the exhibition *Design4Science* (www.design4science.org). For a photograph of the sculpture see Paterlini (2008).

(a)

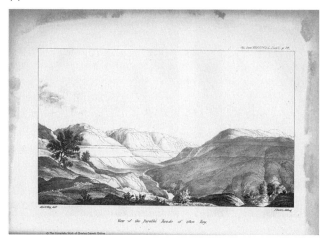

(b)

Figure 22.6 A drawing can provide greater clarity than for example a photograph of the same object as in this geological engraving of the 'Parallel Roads' on either side of Glen Roy. The engraving is from a paper Darwin read to the Royal Society in London in 1839 on the parallel roads. The drawing is reproduced with permission from John van Wyhe (ed.), *The Complete Work of Charles Darwin Online* (http://darwin-online.org.uk/). Photograph: courtesy of James Secord.

(scientific) message they each want to communicate defines them either as science or art. Where Irving Geis produced art in the service of science, Colin Rennie created art *inspired* by science.

A drawing can provide greater clarity than for example a photograph of the same object (Figure 22.6). Artistic representation can help the communication strategy by emphasising the traits you want your audience to focus on. Scientific or medical drawings used for scientific papers, textbooks, popular and children's publications, exhibit murals, advertising, education in general, newspapers and many other popular media outlets make a necessary step in the process of understanding scientific terms and processes. In such cases it is important to work with a professional science illustrator. The dialogue between artist and scientist can be time-consuming. However, many examples demonstrate that if the artist is good, it is worth your while. One early and well-known example of such a partnership is the Dutch painter Jan Steven van Calcar's impressive woodcut illustrations of anatomical studies for Andreas Vesalius's *De humani corporis fabrica libri septem* from the mid-sixteenth century. A mutual respect for each other's knowledge, work and field of expertise is crucial in order to arrive at a result that optimises the communication of the science. Irving Geis once pointed out to Richard Dickerson, a younger colleague and co-author of the articles uncovering the structure of myoglobin, that any artist working with scientific illustration had to be knowledgeable for the process and the collaboration to be successful: '*Most artists have no idea what they are drawing. [Geis] was once making an elaborate illustration of a folded protein, surrounded by space-filling H_2O molecules. A fellow artist watched him for a bit, and then remarked that Irv need to "put a few more lima beans over on the left"'* (Dickerson, 1997, p. 2484). If the artist does not respect or care for scientific detail there is little chance of success. On the other hand, if the scientist does not respect the illustrator's expertise, chances for success are equally minimal (Hodges, 2003).

USING COLOUR IN VISUAL REPRESENTATIONS

Molecular graphics is one of the most mature areas of visualisation in biology (O'Donoghue *et al.*, 2010). Twenty years ago only experts could create computer images of a protein structure. Today we are surrounded by images created by a large variety of software tools. We have familiarised ourselves with these more or less standard images of brightly coloured linked atoms, floating in space on the front covers of renowned scientific journals or in popular science magazines. Computer software lets us choose from a variety of colours for a visual representation of a molecule.

Colours relate to specific subjective associations, forms, perceptions and psychology. It is therefore likely that we will use the colours we prefer, for whatever reason, to visually represent our data. It is important though, to use colour appropriately. *'Colour is a language,'* Irving Geis said, *'and as with any other language, one mustn't babble!'* (Dickerson, 1997, p. 2484). When comparing structural representations of the sodium–potassium pump, a cell-membrane-bound ion pump belonging to the family of P-type ATPases, I found that there was very little consensus in choice of colour. The structure was first published and made the front cover of *Nature* in December 2007 (Morth *et al.*, 2007). Since then, more than a hundred articles have cited this original paper. In these articles, fifty images referred directly to the original visual representation of the structure. However, only one of the articles reproduced the colours of the original. Consequently, it is not easy to compare the structures, and chances for misinterpretation of important data increase. In any field of science, every time we make a visual representation, we have to consider existing colour conventions. It is also mandatory that we do our best to contribute to a possible extension of any colour conventions. Agreeing on colours will improve the communication process in any field of science.

Magnetic resonance imaging (MRI) is routinely used in medical investigations of a broad range of diseases. Figure 22.7 shows three visual representations used in a study comparing wild-type and so-called *peroneal muscle atrophy (pma)* mutant mice with clubfoot (Duce *et al.*, 2010). The images represent different considerations related to choice of colours. In the first two images the colours are chosen arbitrarily and colours are used for telling the different proximal bones from each other, which is a reasonable way of using colour. The image shows the leg of *pma* mice. Red, pink and purple shades are used for distinguishing different parts of muscles from each other. The gradations of red were chosen because of the high resemblance to real muscles and skin colour.

Colour can be a very powerful tool to highlight and clarify a scientific point as in the photograph of green and blue coloured squares of drops of water (Figure 22.8). The lines that separate the 4 × 4 millimetre squares provide new structures with which to manipulate the shapes of liquid drops (Abbott *et al.*, 1992). The surface underneath the water drops has been coated with a hydrophilic layer separated by hydrophobic bands 1 micron wide and 1/1000 of a micron high. This image was used on the front cover of *Science* in September 1992. Compared to a first attempt on a gold surface the redesign of both form and colour clearly improves the presentation of the data and makes it much

(a)

(b)

(c)

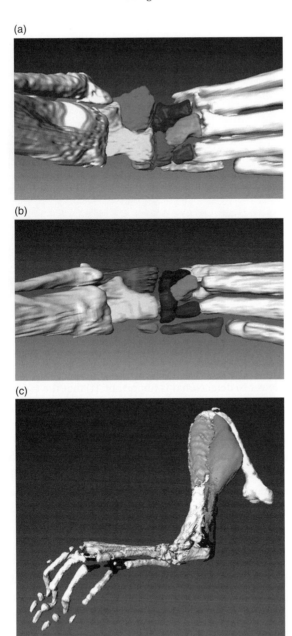

Figure 22.7 Three-dimensional reconstruction of wild-type and *pma* mice legs. The first two images compare the bones of wild-type mice and *pma* mice (top and middle). The third image shows the leg of *pma* mice (bottom). (Courtesy of Suzanne Duce, University of Dundee.) See colour plate section.

(a)   (b)

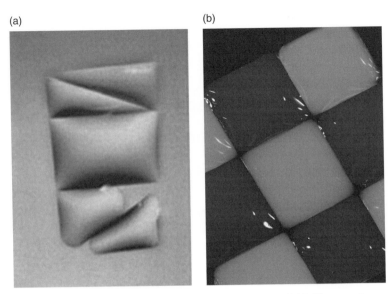

Figure 22.8 Drops of water on a hydrophilic surface divided by one micron wide hydrophobic strings on a gold surface (a) and coloured blue and green (b). (Courtesy of Felice Frankel.) See colour plate section.

easier for the viewer to detect what is important: (1) that the two shapes of liquid drops do not merge; and (2) that the shapes do not distract the observer from the actual scientific message (Frankel, 2002).

Colours are important to the way we interpret and understand visual representations, both when we work in the laboratory and when we communicate our results to a broader audience. Carefully chosen colours provide clarity. Lack of attention to colours leads to unnecessary confusion and increases the risk of misunderstandings.[6]

SCIENTIFIC IMAGES IN THE MEDIA

Images are crucial to the way we present, observe and interpret things – and audiences love them. New technologies have radically increased the number and types of visuals during the last decades and the media has become increasingly dependent upon great visual performance. This is equally important for Hollywood blockbusters, TV programmes, magazines, newspapers or professional scientific journals. People want visuals. When you read a newspaper, you look at the headlines and

[6] For a guide on choice of colours see Wong (2010).

the pictures before you start reading the text. The same is true when you browse a scientific journal. You first look at headlines and illustrations, and then, if you find it interesting, you start reading the text. Images lure in the audience, regardless of whether you are a layperson or a science professional.

Scientific images are rarely neutral when used in popular contexts. They often represent hyped promises or futuristic engineering of nature. Since the discovery by James D. Watson and Francis Crick in 1953 of the double helix structure of the DNA molecule, the simple visual representation of DNA has been widely used in almost every possible form and medium (Watson & Crick, 1953). The characteristic twisted structure has been reproduced in science and art, design and architecture, movies and advertisement, and generally in any media outlet (de Chadarevian & Kamminga, 2002). What has now turned into a cultural icon has multiple meanings ranging from great hopes for medical treatments to fear of genetic engineering. The point is that you don't have to be a specialist to recognise the icon. On the other hand, the simple double helix structure now carries so many connotations that it has become almost impossible to use in an unambiguous way.

A drawing of the structure by Odile Crick, Francis Crick's wife, was the sole image accompanying the original letter to *Nature* in 1953 (Figure 22.9). The simple drawing showed sugar chains as directional ribbons, while the bases were represented flat on. The plain spiral form resembling a twisted ladder makes any representation of DNA easy to depict and understand, by both layperson and specialist. The public success of the DNA design and idea was to a large extent due to the visually compelling and sculpturally ideal structure. The discovery was also a step towards the quest of unravelling 'the secret of life' (Watson, 2003). The structure is widely used in architectural elaborations and as sculptural inspiration (Figure 22.10).

Scientific images are reused, rearranged, manipulated and put into different contexts by different people all around the world, people who may know very little if anything about the science behind the visual representation. There is nothing you can do about this, and that is perhaps one of the best reasons for taking care in making good representations.

WHY ARE SOME REPRESENTATIONS BETTER THAN OTHERS?

When making a good visual representation you need to return to your data again and again. You will need to evaluate your choices and to redo your representation several times. In this process we move from our

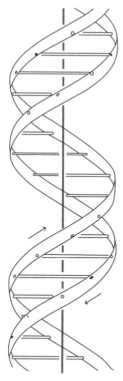

Figure 22.9 The schematic drawing accompanying the original article from 1953 by Francis Crick's wife, Odile Crick. (Reprinted by permission from Macmillan Publishers Ltd: *Nature* **171**(4356), 1953.)

sample to actually understanding the data. How you choose to design or arrange a visual representation is immensely important to how we understand and interpret the scientific message.

For example, consider '*small multiples*' introduced by Tufte (1990). Providing a continuous arrangement of images and a similarity in appearance helps the viewer focus on changes in information rather than changes in graphical composition (Figure 22.11). This simple design is used in thousands of scientific papers to show a connection, relation or flow in a series of images. The first example in Figure 22.11 was used as a front cover illustration for *Nature* in August 2009. The cover draws attention to the article on Platonic and Archimedean solids inside the journal and supplies an immediate overview of all the solids (Torquato & Jiao, 2009). The second example shows ten images structured as small multiples. These are MRI brain scans from native Colombians who learnt to read as adults (late-literates) compared with a

Figure 22.10 The DNA double helix sculpture at Clare College in Cambridge, UK (where James Watson was a graduate student and later an honorary fellow) by Charles Jencks, 2005. (Photograph: Rikke Schmidt Kjærgaard.)

carefully matched set of illiterates (Carreiras *et al.*, 2009). These two examples concentrate the viewer's attention on data rather than on data containers. Now contrast this with the third example, where the dark colours surrounding each image generate disruptive white stripes. The white stripes activate distracting negative spaces between the images, which should be avoided (Tufte, 1990).

Two different representations of so-called haplotype maps show how simple changes in design can improve visual representations of data and more clearly explain the scientific results (Figure 22.12). A software tool called 'HaploView', launched as one of the analytical tools for the so-called International HapMap Project, is used to analyse haplotype genetic variation data (Barrett *et al.*, 2005).[7] The triangular form shows the values when each so-called single-nucleotide polymorphism (SNP) is compared against the others. SNPs are defined as

[7] See note 2 above.

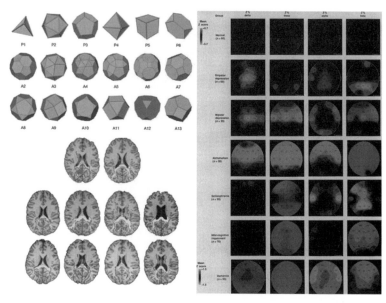

Figure 22.11 Examples of 'small multiples': an overview of the Platonic and Archimedean solids (top left); MRI brain scans from native Colombians who learnt to read as adults (late-literates) compared with a set of illiterates (bottom left); average topographic head maps related to a study about brain dysfunctions (right). (Sources: top left: Torquato & Jiao, 2009, image is on p. 877; bottom left: Carreiras *et al.*, 2009, image is on p. 984; and right: John *et al.*, 1988, image is on p. 163). See colour plate section.

variation in a genetic sequence that affects only one of the basic building blocks – adenine, guanine, thymine or cytosine – in a segment of a DNA molecule. The first image in Figure 22.12 shows the original design. In the new design by Ben Fry the values are multiplied with 100, which makes it easier to separate large numbers from small numbers. Values of 100 are not shown, reducing clutter in the image. These fields also have the strongest colouring and in that way stands out already. The diagram is tilted 45° in order for the associated sequence data to have a horizontal orientation. The most important feature in the new design is that it allows much larger data sets than the initial design. The diagram can be made much smaller and still be readable, which allows for data sets with several hundred markers (Fry, 2004).

The familiar beautiful images from the Hubble Space Telescope of the planets of our own solar system and stellar nebulae in deep space are representations of actual astronomical observations coloured by

(a)

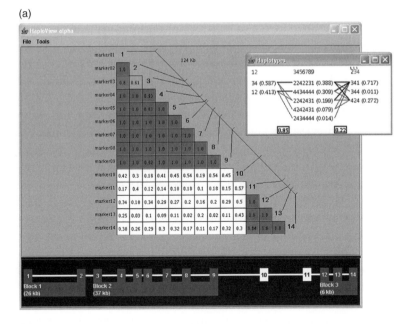

(b)

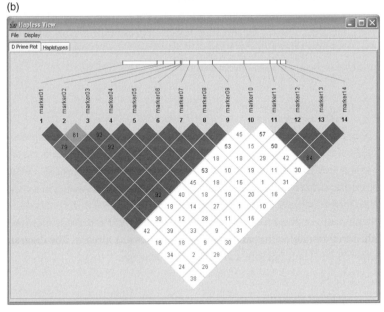

Figure 22.12 A screen shot from the initial release of the software tool called 'HaploView,' launched as one of the analysis tools for the HapMap project (a) and the redesigned diagram, which is now used in the HaploView programme (b). Courtesy of Ben Fry.

astronomers, imaging specialists and, in some cases, the media. All Hubble images are created from a combination of black-and-white images each representing different colours of light. The colours are often *not* what we would see in reality. If you bring a piece of lunar material to Earth it would look very dark. In many cases and for various reasons the human eye would not be able to see the colours in general, even if we were close to the object. Colours can be added because they might seem real, or to enhance an object's detail or simply to visualise what the human eye cannot normally see. When images are taken outside the visible light spectrum, e.g. in the infrared, the choice of colour is entirely up to the astronomers and photo processors. However, the process of colouring is never arbitrary. While coloured images of astronomical objects look far more appealing than black-and-white ones, the aim is to produce aesthetically beautiful images that represent information in the best possible way. The images must convey a maximum amount of information and a minimum amount of noise. The making of these images draws equally upon expertise from art and science.

Good representations are easier to understand, and they deliver the information the originators intend better than bad ones. Taking care in preparing your images greatly improves the success of getting your message across. Optimising visual representations of scientific data through simplicity of design provides greater clarity and gain in understanding without loss of information.

WHAT YOU CAN DO

There are many important questions you must ask before deciding on a particular visual layout. The first and most important is 'What is the key message that I want to communicate?' Next, you will need to consider what scientific data to include. The next and equally important question is 'Who is my target audience?' Different audiences and media need different images. Remember, in the process of making a good visual representation you need to evaluate your choices and to remake your representation several times. Some useful pointers are highlighted below.

Data

Make the right choice of data for your visual representations. Think about what to include in your image and what not to include. Decide on how much information is needed in one image. Prepare your data and remove 'noise'. A well-prepared image, where irrelevant components are removed, will improve the visual expression of the work and result in an unambiguous representation of the scientific results.

Context

Use different images for different purposes. Visual representations need to be adjusted accordingly to the context of the particular type of communication, for example a scientific paper, a poster, a scientific lecture or popular communication. Images work differently and should be used differently in different contexts. Even though scientific posters and popular magazines or newspapers serve different purposes it is equally important to get the attention of the intended audience, whether they are browsing through a poster session with two hundred posters, or skimming through a newspaper. The aim is the same: to attract attention to your work and results. But the means are different. In a scientific journal or in a scientific talk you will already have the audience's attention and can use your images differently.

Design

The design of your images should be motivated by the scientific questions first and the aesthetics next. However, aesthetics and simple design principles will always help clarify the scientific data. The choice of design will have a crucial influence on how audiences understand and interpret the intended scientific messages. Thus it has to be carefully planned. Add subtle colour coding when required, but do not exaggerate. Avoid surrounding words or images by boxes, which create distracting white spaces between object and box. That way you will concentrate the viewer's attention on the data rather on the data containers. Tables should not look like grids with every number enclosed generating a stripy texture fighting for space with important data information, nor should the grid of the graph drown out the data (Figure 22.13). Simple designs are valuable tools when we want to improve our visual communication.

Colour

Always consider your use and choice of colours carefully. Putting a good colour in the right place is a complex matter. However, to begin with, it is a good idea to use any existing colour conventions within your scientific field. Only change colours of original representations if you

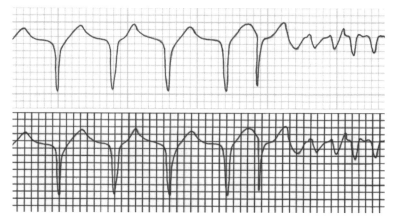

Figure 22.13 Different examples of graphs showing how the data can be caught up in a thick grid and how a subtle grid improves the visual appearance of the data. Redrawn from Tufte (1990).

have very good reasons for doing so. Colours can be used for labelling, for illustrating different quantities, as representation of something real, and to decorate and simply make the image more alive and nicer to look at. If you use colour for labelling, decorating or to illustrate quantities, do not use bright or very strong colours over large areas. It will leave a loud, disordered and unpleasant effect. Mixing bright colours with areas of white will also yield disagreeable results. Strong colours (red, blue, yellow and green) can be an advantage when you want to emphasise smaller areas. However, it is worth remembering that almost ten percent of the male population suffers from red–green colour blindness. In visuals representing real objects using subtle colours close to the real colours will most often offer the best result.

It makes a difference how you design and present your visuals. Creating first-class visual representations is about presenting data in an innovative, attractive and sometimes surprising way. You should always aim for an image that represents your data in the best possible way without loss of information. Optimising your visual communication skills is about discovering new ways of understanding and presenting your data and your scientific ideas.

Key resources

Frankel, F. (2002). *Envisioning Science: The Design and Craft of the Science Image.* Cambridge, MA: The MIT Press.
Tufte, E. R. (1990). *Envisioning Information.* Cheshire, CT Graphics Press.

O'Donoghue, S. I., et al. (2010) *Nature Methods Supplement: Visualizing biological data*, **7**(3): S42–S55.

VISBI, Visualizing biological data: http://vizbi.org/2010/

Wong, B. (2010–11). Monthly column in *Nature*. http://bang.clearscience.info/?p=S46

Data computer design: http://benfry.com/

Fry, B. J. (2004). Computational information design. PhD dissertation, Massachusetts Institute of Technology, Cambridge, MA. www.informationisbeautiful.net

References

Abbott, N. L., Folkers, J. P. & Whitesides, G. M. (1992). Manipulation of the wettability of surfaces on the 0.1- to 1-micrometer scale through micromachining and molecular self-assembly. *Science*, **257**: 1380–1382.

Andersen, E. S., Dong, M., Nielsen, M. M., et al. (2009). Self-assembly of a nanoscale DNA box with a controllable lid. *Nature*, **459**: 73–76.

Barrett, J. C., Fry, B., Maller, J. & Daly, M. J. (2005). Haploview: analysis and visualization of LD and haplotype maps. *Bioinformatics*, **21**: 263–265.

Carreiras, M., Seghier, M. L., Baquero, S., et al. (2009). An anatomical signature for literacy. *Nature*, **461**: 983–986.

de Chadarevian, S. & Kamminga, H. (2002). *Representations of the Double Helix*. Cambridge, UK: Whipple Museum of the History of Science.

Dickerson, R. E. (1997). Obituary: Irving Geis, molecular artist, 1908–1997. *Protein Science*, **6**: 2483–2484.

Duce, S., Madrigal, L., Schmidt, K., et al. (2010). Micro-magnetic resonance imaging and embryological analysis of wild-type and *pma* mutant mice with clubfoot. *Journal of Anatomy*, **216**: 108–120.

Frankel, F. (2002). *Envisioning Science: The Design and Craft of the Science Image*. Cambridge, MA: The MIT Press.

Frankel, F. & Whitesides, G. M. (2009). *No Small Matter*. Cambridge, MA: The MIT Press.

Fry, B. J. (2004). Computational information design. PhD dissertation, Massachusetts Institute of Technology, Cambridge, MA.

Goodsell, D. S. & Johnson, G. T. (2007). Filling in the gaps: artistic license in education and outreach. *PLoS Biology*, **5**: 2759–2762.

Hodges, E. R. S. (ed.) (2003). *The Guild Handbook of Scientific Illustration*. Hoboken, NJ: John Wiley & Sons.

Hughes, T., Hyun, Y. & Liberles, D. A. (2004). Visualising very large phylogenetic trees in three dimensional hyperbolic space. *BMC Bioinformatics*, **5**: 48.

John, E. R., Prichep, L. S., Fridman, J. & Easton, P. (1988). Neurometrics: computer-assisted differential diagnosis of brain dysfunctions. *Science*, **239**: 162–169.

Kendrew, J. C. (1961). The three-dimensional structure of a protein molecule. *Scientific American*, **205**: 96–110.

Kendrew, J. C., Bodo, G., Dintzis, H. M., Parrish, R. G., Wyckoff, H. & Phillips, D. C. (1958). A three-dimensional model of the myoglobin molecule obtained by X-ray analysis. *Nature*, **181**: 662–666.

Kendrew, J. C., Dickerson, R. E., Strandberg, B. E., et al. (1960). Structure of myoglobin: a three-dimensional Fourier synthesis at 2 Å resolution. *Nature*, **185**: 422–427.

Morth, J. P., Pedersen, B. P., Toustrup-Jensen, M. S., et al. (2007). Crystal structure of the sodium–potassium pump. *Nature*, **450**: 1043–1049.

O'Donoghue, S. I., Goodsell, D. S., Frangakis, A. S., et al. (2010). Visualization of macromolecular structures. *Nature Methods Supplement: Visualizing biological data*, **7**(3): S42–S55.

Paterlini, M. (2008). Exhibition: a protein ghost etched in glass. *Nature*, **452**: 155.

Procter, J. B., Thompson, J., Letunic, I., Creevey, C., Jossinet, F. & Barton, G. J. (2010). Visualization of multiple alignments, phylogenies and gene family evolution. *Nature Methods Supplement: Visualizing biological data*, **7**(3), S16–S25.

Torquato, S. & Jiao, Y. (2009). Dense packings of the Platonic and Archimedean solids. *Nature*, **460**: 876–879.

Tufte, E. R. (1990). *Envisioning Information*. Cheshire, CT: Graphics Press.

Watson, J. D. (2003). *DNA: The Secret of Life*. London: Arrow Books.

Watson, J. D. & Crick, F. H. C. (1953). Molecular structure of nucleic acids: a structure for deoxyribose nucleic acid. *Nature*, **171**: 737–738.

Figure 9.1 Global air volume at sea-level pressure. Conceptual computer artwork of the total volume of air within the Earth's atmosphere, seen as a sphere, centred over Europe. It dramatically shows how finite the available air supply actually is. The sphere measures 1999 kilometres across and weighs 5140 trillion tonnes. (© Adam Nieman/Science Photo Library.)

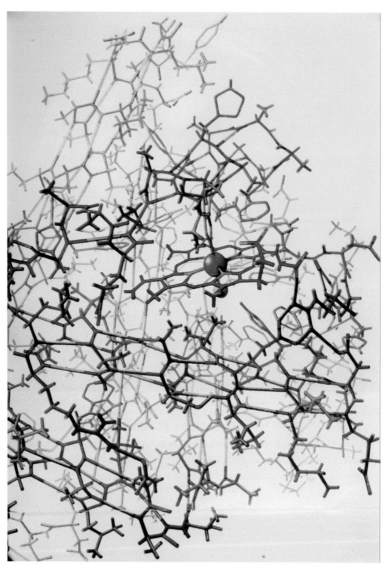

Figure 22.1 Detail of the watercolour of the sperm whale myoglobin, painted by Irving Geis for *Scientific American*. Illustration, Irving Geis. Image from the Irving Geis Collection/Howard Hughes Medical Institute. Rights owned by HHMI. Not to be reproduced without permission.

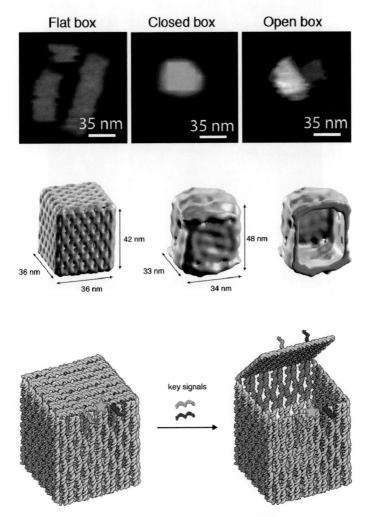

Figure 22.3 Different visual representations of a nanoscale DNA box with a controllable lid: pictures from atomic force microscopy (AFM) showing the flat box, the closed box and the open box (top), theoretical models and reconstructions based on cryo electron microscopy (middle), and finally a drawing showing the opening mechanism, where the blue and orange locking DNA strands recognise the complementary key DNA strands (bottom). (Courtesy of Ebbe Sloth Andersen.)

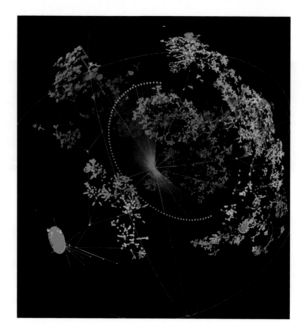

Figure 22.4 An example of phylogenetic data shown in three-dimensional space using the software tool 'Walrus'. (Copyright 2005 The Regents of the University of California. All Rights Reserved.)

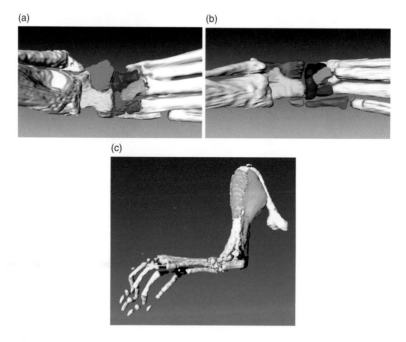

Figure 22.7 Three-dimensional reconstruction of wild-type and *pma* mice legs. The first two images compare the bones of wild-type mice and *pma* mice (left and right). The third image shows the leg of *pma* mice (bottom). (Courtesy of Suzanne Duce, University of Dundee.)

(a)   (b)

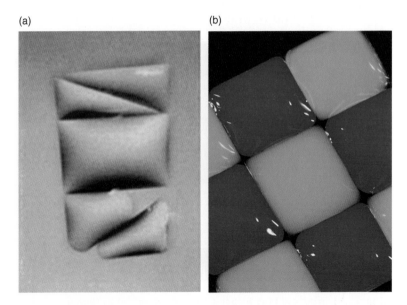

Figure 22.8 Drops of water on a hydrophilic surface divided by one micron wide hydrophobic strings on a gold surface (a) and coloured blue and green (b). (Courtesy of Felice Frankel.)

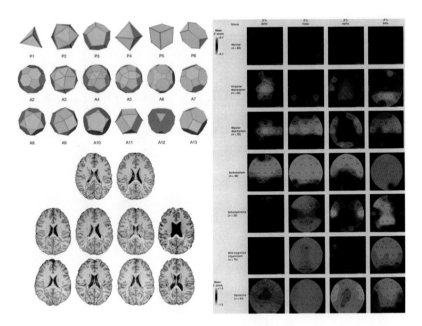

Figure 22.11 Examples of 'small multiples': an overview of the Platonic and Archimedean solids (top left); MRI brain scans from native Colombians who learnt to read as adults (late-literates) compared with a set of illiterates (bottom left); average topographic head maps related to a study about brain dysfunctions (right). (Sources: top left: Torquato & Jiao, 2009, image is on p. 877; bottom left: Carreiras *et al.*, 2009, image is on p. 984; and right: John *et al.*, 1988, image is on p. 163).

Figure 25.1 Winners of the 2010 *Imagine* competition: Julika Humme, Emily Allwood and Marleen Schuijer from the Christelijk Gymnasium Sorghvliet, The Hague, with the Biobag project by Jelmer Tamis, researcher at Delft University of Technology together with the Rector of the University, Professor Karel Luyben.

Figure 25.2 Contestants in the *Imagine* school competition using microscopes at Unesco IHE, Delft, the Netherlands preparing their project for the goldmines in Ghana, November 2009.

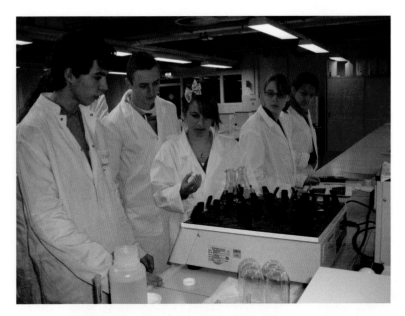

Figure 25.3 Contestants in the *Imagine* school competition in a laboratory experiment at Unesco IHE, Delft, the Netherlands, preparing their project for the goldmines in Ghana, November 2009.

Figure 25.5 Ghana, Enidado, with the *Imagine* Foundation sign at Oyster Mushroom Project in Aburi Ghana, with the winners of 2007, Marieke, Sandra and Nynke, August 2010.

Figure 25.6 The winners of *Imagine* 2007 in Ghana, Marieke and Nynke, singing and dancing with the children from Aburi Ghana at the Oyster Mushroom Project, August 2010.

23

The Triple Helix: the undergraduate student-run face of science communication

Undergraduates represent a huge and largely untapped resource for science communication. Recently, it has been found that a little under one-third of students become involved with voluntary work at some stage during their student career here at the University of Cambridge, and with 6000 students studying science or science-related subjects, this could be up to 2000 people at your disposal.[1] Who could pass up that kind of workforce?

The Triple Helix is a global undergraduate group for the communication of science and in particular how science interfaces with society. The organization achieves this through a mix of journalism through the production of literary material, engaging the public on topics of interest and explorations of science policy.

This vision is realized through the formation of a chapter or branch of The Triple Helix at a university and this is the story of the founding of one such branch at Cambridge. Along the way, there will be examples to illustrate how we have gone about organizing our activities, the ideas we've had and how well they worked, or, in some cases, how they didn't work.

Whilst written from an unashamedly personal perspective, it should be useful for:

---

[1] University of Cambridge: *Connecting with Communities Report 2007*, www.admin.cam.ac.uk/offices/communications/community/report/2007.pdf; University of Cambridge, *Facts and Figures: Key Data, 2007*, www.admin.cam.ac.uk/offices/planning/information/statistics/facts/2007_poster.pdf.

Successful Science Communication, ed. D. J. Bennett and R. C. Jennings. Published by Cambridge University Press. © Cambridge University Press 2011.

(1) People looking to start, or continue, an undergraduate society for science communication.[2]
(2) Students who are already involved in a science society, who want to diversify the activities that they're doing.
(3) Students who aren't already involved, and want a taste of (a) what science societies tend to do, (b) what these societies could do with your help.
(4) Non-students who want an example of what undergraduates can do for science communication.

WHAT WE'RE ABOUT

So what does The Triple Helix do at Cambridge? Perhaps surprisingly, the longer and more deeply you are involved with an organization, the harder it can be to explain it to other people. Especially when one of the biggest problems with communicating 'science in society' is that it's so very broad.

When we talk about 'science in society', we mean questions arising at the interface between the work of scientists and the broader community. These questions typically fall into one or more of several overarching categories:

• The application of scientific knowledge – what are the practicalities and implications of a resultant societal change?
• The acquisition of scientific knowledge – are there some things that shouldn't or can't be investigated?
• What happens when ongoing research hasn't reached a definite answer yet?
• The direction of future work in science – should greater priority be given to work in a certain area?
• Science education – can we do better in teaching the scientific and non-scientific communities of tomorrow?
• Interdisciplinary research – what can traditionally non-scientific institutions gain from science?

---

[2] If this inspires you to start a chapter of The Triple Helix, all the better. The application process for this starts by emailing our CEO at ceo@thetriplehelix.org.

On a practical level we:

- Produce a high-quality free termly journal, the *Science in Society Review*, written by undergraduates and distributed throughout the university. A strict editorial policy involving academic review ensures a mature and professional product.
- Run panel events, which are used to discuss wider topics with audience participation. (Think of these as journal articles where you're actually able to ask questions and give feedback in real time.)
- Hold outreach events that engage school students. The content and structure of these can vary wildly, from a one-hour workshop to a three-day competition held across months.
- Engage the public with *Café Scientifique* – informal science policy meetings aimed at the general public.
- Provide training for undergraduate students both through workshops where important skills are learnt (such as literary, interpersonal, management, leadership), and through practical application of these skills.

That said, from the point of view of someone who's involved, it's about something a bit more. This is a speech that I wrote for an audience who were previously unfamiliar with The Triple Helix:

> *The Triple Helix aims to raise awareness of the interdisciplinary aspects of science. Arguments that necessarily require voices from all sides.*
>
> *We think science in its correct context matters. When science is isolated outside the context of society it can't necessarily come to the right conclusions. This is true even of issues that are inherently scientific in nature (e.g. HIV/AIDS epidemic, man-made climate change). It is necessary to examine these from all the angles.*
>
> *We care when people are misled by bad science. We want to say something when people get it wrong. When politicians spin the science. We want scientists to listen a bit more to culture, e.g. when GM crops came to the UK, there was a misunderstanding of the public outrage at that scientific concept, and a mishandling of science in this cultural reaction. What will be our next example of this?*
>
> *We aim to provide a unique forum for this debate. We are interdisciplinary, but we are also an international network. Our aim is to get undergraduate voices heard across the globe.*
>
> *We back this up with a team here at Cambridge, a team that believes very much in what I've just said. And people who care about these issues are working together to raise awareness of them. We raise contentious issues because we're ambitious; we publish internationally; we put together dynamic and exciting events.*
>
> *We have a bright future, thriving on the talent of young scientists.*

So hopefully that gives you an idea of what we're trying to achieve on the local level.

THE BIGGER PICTURE

These activities don't just take place at Cambridge; they happen, in varying ways, across other chapters around the world. To give some feel for this I've included some numbers (see Box below). However, the important part of this is that the network created makes the whole much greater than the sum of its parts.

The Triple Helix in numbers

7 years since being founded

5000 undergraduates involved[3]

20 current universities

4 continents

500 articles written

60 journals produced

3 international conferences held

In particular, the international side of the organization provides a framework for management and leadership opportunities, whether it is regional or fully international. As a member of The Triple Helix it is possible to end up editing articles or managing editorial staff from across the globe. This network provides a unique opportunity to interact and exchange ideas with a diverse group of bright students at universities across the world.

Finally, this structure is also a source of support, inspiration and growth; founding new chapters in new places and developing new directions for us to pursue.

SOCIETIES

We will refer to The Triple Helix as a society. For those who either have not heard of these before, or alternatively know them by a different name, I will clarify. In the context of the University of Cambridge,[4] a society is a group of students who get together to do something. Good examples are the sports societies, drama clubs, or other well-defined special interests.

---

[3] Just an estimate, since we don't keep strict membership records.

[4] And probably other universities!

To set the scene, when I founded this chapter of The Triple Helix as a society at Cambridge in 2006, there were many societies that you could describe as 'communicating science', that ran one or two of the following list of activities:

(1) Evening lectures where invited speakers were asked to give a talk to an audience, usually undergraduates, on their own research.
(2) Social (networking) type events.
(3) Science experiments in schools, or bringing students to Cambridge to do 'sciency things'.
(4) Media-producing science communications – magazines, podcasts, videos.

There were also many organizations, external and internal to the university, that ran volunteering projects with undergraduates (far too many to list).

There were of course societies that also covered topics that could consider being bracketed as 'social', such as those founded for discussing international development.

It is worth pointing out that The Triple Helix was the first society I had seen that blended both science and social commentary explicitly, meaning that its work had broad appeal reaching out beyond those just interested in science. As a somewhat different form of communicating science, this demonstrates where science isn't just interesting, but is directly relevant and already affecting people's lives. Accordingly, our volunteers and contributors also came from a wide range of disciplines not usually represented in science societies.

HOW TO GET PEOPLE INVOLVED

It is very important to remember that university societies (and any other voluntary organizations) are always only as good as their volunteers. They live and die on the basis of whether you have enough dedicated, talented and keen people who want to do the same thing. This is even more important to university societies since even the most enthusiastic member is only around for three to four years before graduating and moving on.[5]

---

[5] It is arguably relatively easy to start up university societies, but difficult to keep them going.

Recruitment rapidly becomes the crux of your organization, and should be your primary concern. To recruit people, you want to talk to people. Endlessly. Tell them about your idea (in this case, a society) and tell them how wonderful you think it is. If they agree, chances are they won't mind helping out. Then it's just a case of engineering enough situations where you are doing this (for us, organizing our own events such as evening talks were pretty handy, since it's really rude to go to another society's event and chat about your own society!). This works best when it's *not* at a 'networking' event!

It's worth bearing in mind that few people have been involved with, or will have even heard of, science communication before coming to university. Although they may have unwittingly been the targets of science communication exercises, this is not something they will actively seek out, unlike say drama or sports, making recruitment more difficult.

Getting enough money to run activities through sponsorship is also vitally important, going hand-in-hand with recruitment. You don't want to end up with people who want to work for you, but have no budget to work with. There is quite a bit of funding out there if you look hard enough, for example from companies or charitable organizations.

HOW TO KEEP PEOPLE KEEN

Remember they are volunteers. And you've got some pretty hefty competition. If they're conscientious enough to be a good asset to your society they will have work in the forefront of their minds (with a few notable exceptions!), then they might have other societies, sports, friends and a social life.

So . . . hopefully you've got a team. When managing a team, what I've found handy to bear in mind is:

- Give people interesting things to do.
- Let them have input into the process.
- Design team structure carefully to allow for streamlined communication between staff, avoiding unnecessary hierarchies and bureaucracy.
- Make sure your team is going to get on with each other. There's nothing worse than in-fighting.
- Make sure you have enough people who care. It depends on what you want to do, but in publishing, where you have

a deadline it's very important that people are prepared to work very hard to get to the finished product on time. So if you have a problem at 2 a.m. because a writer has just phoned in and said they can't deliver, you want someone awake at 2.01 a.m. fixing this problem. You want people who are prepared to put in the effort tirelessly!

- Avoid taking on 'dead-weights', people who say they will do something but then will never deliver, especially if this is going to be infectious within the society.

- Be careful about recruiting your friends. This is just a caveat.

- Keep trying. I'm not convinced that management can be learnt, but even if it can there's probably no substitute for practice! Be part of teams, work out how you like to be treated, and then treat people like that. If they respond badly, try to find out why.

- See people regularly and don't forget to be friendly: since they're not contractually bound to work for you, a great deal rides on interpersonal interactions.

THE SCIENCE IN SOCIETY REVIEW

Every chapter of The Triple Helix aims to publish a journal, called the *Science in Society Review*, and to distribute this free as widely as possible to students, staff and members of public on their campus. A typical journal comprises ten articles that are all undergraduate-written – five of these are from international universities (they are very much supposed to represent the five best articles internationally!). The articles themselves are a review based around a 'science in society' theme (discussed previously). In the Cambridge edition, there are also editorial-style pieces where authors can express a viewpoint directly.[6]

Examples from Cambridge journals include:

Is Obesity Contagious? The Spread of Behaviour through Social Networks

Protecting the Terminally Ill: Is Present Medical Research Structure to Credit or to Blame?

Earthquake Deaths in the Third World: Preventable or Inevitable?

Choosing what articles to put into a journal is a key skill of a journal editor. Experience is important here, and this is why it is desirable to

---

[6] Traditionally these might be thought of as in line with a periodical's opinion, but for us these articles merely tend to express the opinions of the editorial team at the time.

choose experienced staff to lead the team of editors. But it's not just experience at editing and writing, it's also looking at how to form a coherent journal from a set of articles. What's required is a mixture of these two skill sets – and this is what we tend to look for at interview when recruiting for our editors.[7]

When choosing a topic, whether that's as an editor commissioning a piece, or as a writer finding something to write about, there is a vast array of things to bear in mind. But some of the most important are:

Is what I'm writing meaningful to a wider audience and does it make coherent sense?

Has someone else already said what I'm saying in a more convincing manner? Can I contribute to the debate by taking another angle?

Is the topic pertinent to the here and now? Have I artificially manufactured a problem that will never actually arise?

Have I talked to someone about this idea? Am I missing the obvious? Are there angles I haven't thought about? Am I being too narrow-minded (or even too broad-minded)?

All too often articles on the topic of science in society fail for one of these reasons.

A 'science in society' article differs from a 'straight' science article because the science itself is actually minimized, down to almost one paragraph if possible. The point of the article is to discuss the various offshoots, talking about society's reaction to the scientific discovery. This can make them a very different style.

The key difficulties of communicating science are:

- You have to deal with a lot of jargon
- You have to enthuse the reader
- You have to assume the reader knows nothing
- There is a 'right' answer – the correct science.

Since 'science in society' articles aim to discuss something different:

- The reader comes pre-enthused and can arrive at the article with preconceived notions about the way that this science is going to have its societal impact.

---

[7] It is worth bearing in mind that sometimes you won't find anyone who has previous experience, and in this case we simply muddle along. It's more important to find people who can learn quickly on the job, than to have someone who is trained at something that's not quite right, who can't change.

- There is a lot of misinformation (in common with science communication, but can be worse).
- Scientists can't be assumed to know and cover all the potential social, economic and cultural ramifications of the scientific subject.
- (Very broadly speaking) There is no 'right' answer. Even when there is scientific understanding, there is an imperfect way of applying it.

This tends to mean a long train of conditionals: supposing A, we can say B, ruling out C and solving our problem. If A isn't actually true, then we haven't solved our problem. The message can become much more like a day-to-day discussion.

One of the key aspects of the journal is actually the editorial process. In the best-case scenario the article will be read by the editor-in-chief, two student editors, a graduate editor and two academics. The most important part of this process is the academics who read our work as part of an 'academic review' process (a slightly toned-down version of peer review). We have found that academics can be invaluable editors. Even a cursory glance by someone who has been working with the subject matter, or in a nearby field, can help us make sure we are using the appropriate emphasis. We hope our articles, as a result of this thorough editing, become mature and professional products, not only good to read, but also well-argued and factually accurate.

PANEL EVENTS: A MEDIUM FOR PARTICIPATION

Sometimes there was only so much we could do with journalism. For some topics, it was far too difficult to distil the work of researchers at the 'front line' into print. Out of this inadequacy of print journalism, we decided we wanted to hear the science from the scientists, and to discuss the social aspects with people researching in those fields. We also felt that this would help bring the science to life.

What was our target audience going to be? First and foremost, people who would take part in a lively and engaging way. We've generally succeeded at this and at least in part this has been because of the breadth of attendees we have had: undergraduates, postgraduates, postdocs and members of the public. The range of backgrounds leads to a greater range of viewpoints.

So, assuming that we would get a lively audience, we secondly turned to recruiting this audience and brand awareness. Our primary target audience with this in mind was undergraduates – these were the people who we wanted to help us practically run the society, so they were good people to interest in coming along.

Next, we pondered the format our event was going to take. We wanted as much audience participation as possible so we chose the panel debate as the format of our events after dismissing other possibilities chosen by other student societies (keynote speeches at dinner or evening talk or lecture, to name two others). We ruled out the possibility of a day-long seminar or conference because we felt this was too inaccessible to our target audience.

After careful consideration, we decided to launch this venture with the highly controversial topic of why women appear to be underrepresented at the top of science. This seemed to be relevant to us as much as everyone else – since we hope to be the scientists of the future. We drew on a Public Library of Science (PLoS) article written Dr Peter Lawrence which briefly outlines the issues involved, as well as his own personal take on it, and invited him to be our key speaker. When running an event of this kind, we have found it very useful to have a source from the literature – it could be an article from *New Scientist*, the BBC, or similar – that acts as an inspiration. The reason for this is that it's hard to come up with an innovative topic on your own, find all the speakers, etc. without losing sight of the overall argument. A written source helps provide focus for an entire team as well.

Why women are no good at science (and how science stops them from being good)

Literature quote: 'Some have a dream that, one fine day, there will be equal numbers of men and women in all jobs, including those in scientific research. But I think this dream is Utopia.' Dr Peter Lawrence.[8]

Why we thought this would work: A combination of a controversial topic and controversial grammar was sure to bring a crowd in.

What we wanted to know: Is the under-representation of women at a high level in science due to discrimination of any form? What do social scientists say?

---

[8] Lawrence, P. A. (2006) Men, women and ghosts in science. *PLoS Biology* **4**, 13–15.

Target audience: Primarily, interesting people to debate the motion. Secondarily, undergraduates.

Speakers:

Dr Peter Lawrence

Professor Simon Baron-Cohen (author of *The Essential Difference*)

Professor Athene Donald (FRS and Director of University of Cambridge Women in Science, Engineering and Technology Initiative, WiSETI)

Dr Yulia Kovas (research into 'generalist genes' and mathematical ability in boys and girls)

Dr Helena Cronin (author of *The Ant and the Peacock: Altruism and Sexual Selection from Darwin to Today*)

Venue: Lecture theatre

Attendance: 180

Price: Free. (Very important)

What went best: The topic – we were the talk of campus for several days.

What went worst: The last-minute decision to change venue.

The podcast of this talk is available on our website.[9]

While aiming for a panel of speakers, there still needs to be a key speaker – someone who either has an interesting point of view, or is a good speaker (ideally both!). Think of this as someone who would carry the event all by him- or herself. The other panellists are then chosen as good additions to this central speaker; people who the key speaker recommends can make excellent co-panellists.

Once all the speakers had been prepared, we chose the final title, shortlisted potentials for the chair, chose the venue (a good compromise between a good location and a good cost) and prepared the poster and other publicity.[10]

We have since run many successful events and other examples of our topics include:

---

[9] http://www.camtriplehelix.com/

[10] It's worth bearing in mind that in hindsight, the title is one of the most important aspects of an event – needing to be both catchy and informative.

The World Under Assault: Can Science Beat Terrorism?
What Will It Take to Keep the Lights On?–Energy Security in Crisis
Science: Is It Really Ours? Public Ownership of Science.

SCHOOLS OUTREACH

In the meantime, once our first journal was printed, we began looking for things to do with it. We wanted to do something with the community, since we had volunteers who were keen to exploit our print product. So we thought about engaging with schools – something that we've termed 'schools outreach'.

So how old was our target audience going to be? Since we weren't just communicating science, but science, politics and current affairs, this immediately defined our age group as somewhat older than originally expected. Furthermore, we believed one of our key resources was the fact that we were undergraduates – we were uniquely able to be of a good age-match with participants who were doing GCSEs and A-levels so we could be 'on their wavelength'.

Something else to consider was the importance of establishing our message independently of the fact that we were Cambridge students interacting with potential applicants. Although we were always going to be fielding the question *'How do you get into Cambridge?'*, this was never our explicit aim. We therefore kept our agenda clear – we just wanted to communicate our message.

With one of the first groups of students, who were of GCSE age, we spoke to them on the subject of renewable energy and global warming. The session took the form of a group debate, where the students were given an article to read and analyse and they had to take a stand on it. They were then grilled on this view in an 'interview'-style setting almost as though they were the panellists at one of our events. This worked really well because it put them on the spot, giving them the opportunity to defend their views, and it allowed our sharp volunteers to dispel any myths and preconceptions they came up with. One of the most striking things we found was that some 90% of them had watched a then recent TV programme which was essentially a partisan view from climate-change denialists. Their recall of the 'soundbites' they had heard were astonishing. Moreover, there was already interest within the group to the topic – they were primed perfectly for the debate.

We had a second activity planned for the same group, one of a group debate led by facilitators. But it was far more challenging getting them to talk and discuss things without directly putting them on the spot. We found the same thing time and time again in our schools projects. When it came to getting responses and discussing material, small groups worked in a guaranteed way that didn't seem to be possible *en masse*. It also worked when we pitted two groups of students against one another – in debates.

At this point, we saw ourselves as somewhat offering a product: we have a journal, some interested volunteers, and if you contact us we can try to put on a show for some of your kids. We didn't actively seek out arrangements.

Another appealing aspect of this is that it can be run on a shoestring budget. Large costs are only involved if travelling is needed, and sometimes volunteers are prepared to shoulder the cost of taking a taxi if it's not too much each. But I wouldn't recommend running it on no budget!

Can you save our future: solutions to climate change

What: 30 year 11s, split into groups, given something to read (and told to discuss) then interviewed on the topic

Why we thought this would work: Age-match of participants was good. Putting people on the spot helps. Six-to-one tutoring is not accessible in many schools.

Price: Free.

What went best: The style – students really came to life in the six-to-one sessions.

What went worst: The topic was hard to engage with and the article was slightly too long (we have since lowered the length of articles for our normal readers too!)

This remains the way we do outreach to the present day. We have a portfolio of things that we can do and we go around doing them.

DEBATING COMPETITION

The layout of outreach changed a little when we wanted to hold a debating competition. This was very challenging, but we were helped by someone who had run an event like this before and used their guidelines as a model.

The format of this was to invite a group of say 50 students to a 'science in society day', which consisted of a variety of activities. One of the most successful activities we ran was a debating-style challenge. Once again we found that the ability to put people on the spot via the facilitators was very useful. But this was also beneficial because it allowed the students to argue from two different points of view.

Debating-style challenge

The students would read an article with four sides (it can be quite tricky to find so many good angles), and split up into groups. They would then be asked to argue the points of view they had been given. After a certain time had lapsed and debate had happened they were asked to vote on who had won, then they were allowed to swap sides to the point of view they wanted to represent. People who moved had to justify on the spot why they moved. Then the debate continued until the duration, when another vote was taken.

For example, the four sides for a debate about '*How to curb the obesity epidemic*':

(1) Ration-free healthcare

(2) Impose a 'Fat Tax'

(3) Encourage people through an optimal default, where for example exercise is necessary in everyday life

(4) Educate people to live a healthier lifestyle.

This was one of the hardest administration challenges we'd faced to date. We wrote to some 250 schools, got 50 students (from 30 different schools) but ultimately only had 30 or so attendees. This was an oversight: on thinking a bit more carefully we should have allowed many more than 50 to sign up since drop-outs for a one-day event were unavoidable. Surveying the people that came, our feeling was that allowing teachers to leave it up to the students to make contact on their own reduced the number of students who ultimately signed up, but making the students book the event themselves made them more likely to turn up. In spite of this setback it worked quite well.

We reran the same sort of competition the following year in association with the Darwin Festival, where we offered a prize in the competition of coming back to Cambridge again, to have mentoring and then finally to debate in front of an audience. This worked well again due to the small-groups mentoring, and also giving the opportunity for students to have conversations with academics.

CAFÉ SCIENTIFIQUE: PUBLIC ENGAGEMENT

At this stage we published a journal and ran events and outreach activities. Although we had reached out to schools, we still were not doing very much to engage the public. Whilst thinking of a way of doing this, an invitation came with an offer to set up a *Café Scientifique* in Cambridge. These are direct engagement events between what you might call 'practising scientists' and the public. A researcher is invited to sit in a bar, pub or café for an evening and briefly present their own work, or related themes, to a gathered crowd of the public. This is deliberately very informal, and people are invited to ask questions throughout.

For us this was a perfect opportunity to test out the skills we had learnt in our other projects. But this was also challenging – how do we engage public interest? We were fortunate in that up until now we hadn't done any 'real' science communication, in that we hadn't yet engaged the general public.

What we did bring to this was a wealth of academics (involved in the society through our academic review process) who were interested in what we were doing – so we knew plenty of people who we could ask to speak. In some sense, we hoped that we were able to act very well as an interface between lecturers and members of the public. Certainly one of the problems of *Cafés Scientifiques* nationally is that good speaker selection is tricky – one of the biggest challenges coming with science communication is when you're not doing the communicating!

Titles of these events have included:

> *Pandemic! Where do new infections come from?*
> *Shrinking down nutrition: nanofoods*
> *Jumping to delusions: how the brain takes dangerous shortcuts*
> *Are my genes to blame when my jeans don't fit?*

CONCLUDING REMARKS

There are a lot of activities that we do as one society. One of the best things about this is that you can work together as a large team with everyone supporting one another and complementing each other's skills.

It's just one more aspect of interdisciplinarity. Not only are we interdisciplinary in that we tackle science in society, but we are also interdisciplinary in the way we train people: all sorts of communicating skills, management skills and so on.

One of the best things about being an undergraduate is that you still haven't settled down to one discipline yet, and everyone you know is doing some very high-level stuff on one topic or another that probably isn't yours! So you should take advantage of that, and we do. And we learn from one another, not only on the perspectives we take on world issues (at least when it comes to science in society) but also from the skills we have. By accumulating the best writers, editors, organizers, planners, orators, teachers and putting them in the same place at the same time – knowledge and experiences are shared.

Hopefully you have a flavour of what's available to you as part of undergraduate science communications. If you want to get involved, then the next step is to look up what's going on at your university and above all work out whether there's a local branch of The Triple Helix! Though I haven't emphasized it enough perhaps, the Cambridge group is only one branch of an international organization. There will be a group far nearer to you (well, at least if you're in North America), called The Triple Helix, doing exactly the same thing.

And if there isn't and you think you have what it takes to start one, perhaps you should consider getting in touch.

WHY 'THE TRIPLE HELIX'?

One of the most common questions that we get asked is about our name: The Triple Helix. Ironically, some people think it's 'bad science', being a poor representation of the double helix of DNA. The three strands refer to Science, Society and Law, traditionally independent disciplines; the way in which they interweave is what we explore.

Acknowledgements

There are very many people who have helped me and The Triple Helix Cambridge to reach the stage that we're at now. They are too many and too numerous to mention individually; however, there are some individuals who have been exceptional.

Firstly, thanks to Hannah Price, whose hard work for two years (one year as President of the society) allowed us to go from just a journal to this diverse range of activities. Also, to Michaela de Clare, who was instrumental in our founding. Then to Jenny Molloy, who in her term as President launched *Café Scientifique* for us. Thanks also to Francesca Day, who currently runs the society, and Tanyella Allison who ran the society previously.

Thanks to our Academic Advisory Board for giving us their time in countless meetings; especially Dr David Summers, who was one of the first people I told about The Triple Helix – who has been enthusiastic ever since.

Thanks also to all of our generous sponsors. The whole operation needs a considerable amount of money to run, and since we provide services and products for free, none of our activities would be possible without them.

Thanks finally to the international team, a source of constant support and aid – one of the unique aspects of the society is our roots in North America. In particular, Kevin Hwang who founded The Triple Helix, and Manisha Bhattacharya, with whom we worked very closely when she ran the international management team for over a year.

Key resources

(1) I am more than happy to be contacted if you have any questions or want further information, at js615@cam.ac.uk or jamesjshepherd@googlemail.com.

(2) The Triple Helix Cambridge – www.camtriplehelix.com. For any further information about the activities at Cambridge, or to get involved or support the branch, please contact president@camtriplehelix.com.

(3) The Triple Helix International, www.thetriplehelix.org. The CEO can be contacted, for example if you wish to apply to start a chapter of The Triple Helix, at ceo@thetriplehelix.org.

(4) *Café Scientifique* are a UK-wide group who organize meetings where people from every walk of life meet to discuss science outside of the traditional academic environment. More information can be found at http://www.cafescientifique.org/.

24

Public understanding of research: the Open Research Laboratory at the Deutsches Museum

'Out of the ivory tower and into the public arena' – this could be the unofficial motto of the Open Research Laboratory, a fully equipped scanning probe microscopy laboratory for nano-scale research uniquely situated in the public area of the Deutsches Museum.[1] In this concept, young scientists are relocated from their dark, inaccessible basement laboratories and brought into the bright public space of the museum. They conduct their research work live in the midst of the exhibitions whilst answering questions and engaging the visitors in discussion, offering them insights into the processes and methods of a modern microscopic laboratory. Thus, the Open Research Laboratory creates a public space for dialogue and debate between scientists and lay persons in a neutral public setting, successfully tackling the problem posed by Field and Powell that *'few people [. . .] know what research is being conducted, much less understand why it is being done and what the potential implications may be'* (Field & Powell, 2001).

More than ever it is important for society to comprehend the processes of science as our communal future is being developed in research laboratories. Our ever-increasing dependency on technology, however, contrasts with a more and more sceptical, sometimes even critical, public view of modern research. Yet it is vital that lay people be given the opportunity to comprehend the aspects of science and

[1] Located in Munich, Germany, the Deutsches Museum is one of the largest museums for science and technology in the world. Founded in 1903, the main building features 50 exhibition areas covering some 47000 square metres.

Successful Science Communication, ed. D. J. Bennett and R. C. Jennings. Published by Cambridge University Press. © Cambridge University Press 2011.

technology that affect and even alter their daily lives. At the same time each individual researcher should strive to gain an understanding of the implications of their work, not only within their field as a whole, but also within society. As Bruno Latour says, *'Science and society cannot be separated, they depend on the same foundation. They are like two branches of power defined by the same constitution: If you alter the separation of powers, you immediately alter both the view of what science is and of what society can do'* (Latour, 1998). By giving young scientists an opportunity to conduct their work in public and challenging them to communicate it in a forum that encourages debate and discussion, the Open Research Laboratory responds to this need of reintegrating science into society.

Figure 24.1 The Open Research Laboratory at the Deutsches Museum.

But what exactly is the Open Research Laboratory? The whole concept is based on the public display of research and the corresponding interaction of the scientists with a broad public. In order to achieve this, a scanning probe microscopy laboratory was relocated from the Ludwig-Maximilians-University of Munich into the midst of the exhibits of the Deutsches Museum. Surrounded by a chest-high, glass-topped partition, young diploma and doctorate students conduct their measurements and the subsequent evaluation procedures in a public environment (see Figure 24.1). On outward-facing monitors which mirror those of the researchers' scanning probe microscope workstations, museum visitors can see the processes and results of this modern nano-scale research. From the acquisition of raw data through evaluation to the final publication, the Open Research Laboratory tries to present as many stages of the research process as possible. This transparent approach to science encourages discussion with the public. At all points the visitors are able to ask questions and inquire into the processes of the research and the underlying ideas and motivations of the individual scientists.

Despite the public environment and the resulting dialogue and engagement requirements, the scanning probe microscopy measurements in the Open Research Laboratory of the Deutsches Museum are conducted in a process identical to that of investigations in university laboratories, using duplicate preparation equipment and a standard microscope. This ensures that the research results gained in the Open Research Laboratory are identical in quality and relevance to those generated in a university environment. There are, however, a number of differences between the Open Research Laboratory and a standard university laboratory. These range from trivial factors such as general tidiness of the work surfaces in the museum over the obvious communication requirements to more substantial differences such as the necessity for different time management, for example. In the museum environment both research and communication have to be fitted into the limited time-frame dictated by the museum opening times (9 am to 5 pm), a restriction which does not exist in a university laboratory. Yet although these differences are significant enough to require researchers to adapt to them, they are not sufficient to seriously influence the quality of the scientific output of the laboratory.

Furthermore, there are additional benefits of the Open Research Laboratory. On the one hand researchers come to realise that communication of their work and dialogue with the public is an integral part of their professional identity, whilst on the other hand visiting young people who may be considering a career in a scientific or technological field will recognise the young researchers who are only a few years older than themselves as role models. This small age difference encourages both sides to identify with each other, enabling a peer-to-peer dialogue uncommon in typical science communication settings, especially within the 'deficit model' which adopts 'a one-way, top-down communication process' (Miller, 2001). Not only is it possible for the researchers of tomorrow to observe the daily routines that they will encounter and experience in a few years' time, but it is also possible to talk directly with people who are only a few steps ahead of them in their scientific careers. Hopes and fears, expectations and reality can thus be openly expressed and discussed. If there is immediate interest in experiencing research work directly, internships can be arranged. This has happened on numerous occasions at the Open Research Laboratory of the Deutsches Museum since it was established.

Secondary research also profits from the concept of relocating a laboratory into the public environment of a museum, as this approach offers great potential for investigations in the science and society field. Social scientists are, for example, able to analyse both the communication with the visitors as well as the everyday work processes in the laboratory. It is also conceivable that ethicists could investigate the topics being discussed or that behavioural scientists examine whether or how the behaviour and work processes of researchers change when working in public. A first study of the visitors' response to the Open Research Laboratory has already been concluded. Conducted over a period of three weeks by the research group of Professor Dr Doris Lewalter of the Technical University, the main result of the evaluation showed a high level of acceptance of the Open Research Laboratory in the Deutsches Museum amongst both public visitors and pupils, both stating that a visit to the laboratory is highly worthwhile (Pfuhl & Lewalter, 2008). A further in-depth evaluation of the concept is currently being conducted by the same group, with results expected in the latter half of 2011.

In order to further this novel approach to public engagement, one of the tasks in the immediate future is to identify other fields of current research where the Open Research Laboratory approach can be applied. We do not envisage this concept to be exclusive to nanotechnology, but hope to see it applied in many other scientific areas. First steps have already been taken in this direction with an Open Research Laboratory for conservation science investigations at the Berlin Old Museum. Operated by the Rathgen Research Laboratories, its success demonstrates that the concept is not restricted to nanotechnology, but can be utilised in a diversity of fields. Whether or not the approach sees widespread implementation, however, remains to be seen.

What were the reasons, however, for the Deutsches Museum to undertake the initial development and implementation of the Open Research Laboratory? Ultimately, this was a direct consequence of the fundamental approach of the Deutsches Museum to science communication and public engagement – the next logical step, as it were. Since its foundation the Museum has not only focused on presenting scientific results and technological developments in an understandable way, but has also tried to visualise the processes involved in the making of science. One of the most prominent examples of this is the masterpiece 'Otto Hahn Table', a collection of the original equipment used in the first-ever fission experiment conducted by Otto Hahn, Fritz Strassmann and Lise

Meitner presented on an old laboratory table. This has been described as an *'artefact which reminds some people of a child's experiment box'* which *'has in the meantime become something of a myth, a place where science history becomes manifest'* (Brandlmeier, 2004). Yet, despite both its authenticity and unquestionable scientific importance, it remains a collection of static objects in a display case which does not induce a public dialogue. On the contrary, without their attention being drawn to it by a museum employee, most visitors pass by and fail to recognise its significance.

As a second example, using a different approach, a publicly demonstrated scanning electron microscope in the Deutsches Museum allows visitors to interact personally with the operator of the microscope. The objects in the microscope are however almost all images for demonstration purposes, the focus being on visually attractive pictures and not on scientific evaluation. Only occasionally does a researcher from one of the local universities visit to use the microscope to investigate a current sample. The scanning electron microscope demonstration is thus a classical example of a public understanding of science approach, explaining and presenting a widely used instrument. Although clearly popular with museum visitors, this denies them both interesting insights into current research and also the possibility of dialogue and debate with the people directly involved in the making of science.

A third conventional approach applied in the Deutsches Museum is the DNA Visitors' Laboratory which, in comparison to the previous examples, encourages a hands-on approach to science. A researcher supervises and assists the visitors in the extraction and investigation of their own personal DNA, following methods used in contemporary genetics laboratories. This offers the participants a detailed insight into the processes and instruments of current research in this field and even enables a personal discussion with the scientist. However, as the focus of the laboratory is on the experimental procedures and not on the contents of current investigations or even on the background thoughts and ideas of the scientist, it is very difficult for the groups attending to even catch a glimpse of actual research going on. Also, as groups attending the DNA Visitors' Laboratory have to register in advance, this restricts accessibility and thus impact on the average museum visitor.

In comparison to these approaches, the Open Research Laboratory is exceptional as it focuses on depicting step-by-step the work procedures of the scientists involved in current research, offering both insights into the investigations as well as into the individual thought processes of the researchers. By integrating a laboratory environment complete with active scientists into the public area of the museum, the visitors are confronted live with the excitement and daily challenges of research, as well as with the multitude of tedious tasks and disappointments which are equally relevant to the work of a scientist. A comparison of the four approaches given above reflects the development of the Deutsches Museum from a place *'of "cold" science, where secure, closed and fixed knowledge is communicated, to [a place] that increasingly engages with "hot", controversial research and open debates'* (Meyer, 2009). According to Morgan Meyer, the static 'Otto Hahn Table' would be a prime example of 'cold' science, whilst the Open Research Laboratory would definitely represent 'hot', controversial research, with the other two somewhere in between, possibly being 'lukewarm'.

The Open Research Laboratory has thus taken the basic concept of public understanding of science and considerably transformed it by involving young researchers in a public arena, integrating dialogue, debate and reflection, and creating a relationship between scientists and public. It is safe to say that with this approach we have made the transition from the Public Understanding of Science to the Public Understanding of Research as defined by Field and Powell (Field & Powell, 2001). It is our belief that the public presentation of research by scientists on a day-to-day basis is the ideal way of engaging a wide public, and thus answering the needs of today's society concerning science and technology communication.

The need for such engagement by scientists is confirmed by a recent study of the public perception of nanotechnology in Germany. This showed that: *'many people see nanotechnology as a means to solving the urgent problems facing humanity, particularly in the context of medicine and the environment. This attitude is driven by hopes and expectations rather than knowledge'* (Simons et al., 2009). Hopes and expectations, however, will at some point be questioned and will then require a foundation based on knowledge. This process can be expected to be highly individualistic, requiring dialogue with a trusted source of information. At the same time this study showed that scientists enjoy a high level of confidence as sources of information about nanotechnology. On a scale from 1 (absolute confidence) to 4 (no confidence at all), scientists were rated a close second (at 1.6), just behind publicly funded consumer organisations (1.5), but well ahead of health and occupational safety authorities (1.9), NGOs (2.0) or government representatives (3.1). Thus, as scientists can be expected to have a deeper understanding of current scientific developments than consumer organisations, fundamentally they are ideally suited to the task of public dialogue.

Yet it cannot be expected that especially young researchers can accomplish this task without suitable preparation. In the Open

Figure 24.2 A scientist communicating his work to a public audience.
Note the younger researcher observing the engagement with the visitors.

Research Laboratory we carry out a systematic communication training programme. Ideally, the young scientists initially attend a one-day course outlining and rehearsing basic skills necessary for science communication. Once in the public laboratory area they can then spend some time simply observing the more experienced researchers engaging the visitors (see Figure 24.2). After a while they can then practise giving presentations and discussing their research with the public. This learning-by-doing approach on a day-to-day basis with individuals and groups of all ages and levels of knowledge enables the scientists to steadily improve their communication and dialogue skills to a high level in a short time. This is especially effective in the public venue of the museum as the social, ethical and educational background of interested visitors is almost never immediately apparent, challenging the scientists to continuously adapt and revise their approach to each encounter. It is completely possible that a young researcher will meet and talk to a group of high-school students, a university professor with her children, a retired engineer and a middle-aged couple visiting the museum on vacation all within the same day. Obviously, engaging people with such different backgrounds requires completely different methods. It can safely be said that learning to communicate and engage with the general public on an individual level is a continual learning process which is never fully completed. With up to ten scientists working concurrently in the laboratory, however, there are numerous opportunities to share experiences and give or receive advice, thus contributing to an ongoing improvement within this process.

Apart from the simple learning and practising of communication skills, the Open Research Laboratory concept has another important advantage for young scientists. The engagement with the wide variety of different museum visitors not only constantly challenges their communication skills but also their perceptions of their own field of work. This ranges from the smallest details to a general abstract view of science in society. In the former case it is obviously necessary to understand all processes and techniques of one's own work in order to explain these confidently on a level understandable to the various visitors. In the latter case the variety of questions ranging, for example, from motives for research, both individual and universal, over concerns about potential dangers of the work, to ethical and social aspects of the field prompt the scientists to see their work in its social context. This can be an eye-opening and sometimes unsettling experience for a young student in the initial stages of a career in science. We believe this to be an excellent learning process, however, shaping, preparing, equipping, and enabling the experienced researchers of tomorrow to redefine the position of science in society. Thus, in our opinion, the Open Research Laboratory concept not only fulfils, but exceeds, the recommendation of the House of Lords report that: *'communication training offered to research students should be broadened to include an awareness of the social context of their research and its applications'* (House of Lords, 2000).

In order to support the researchers in their engagement efforts, as well as to offer the visitors a comprehensive insight into nanoresearch and nanotechnology, the Open Research Laboratory encompasses various peripheral elements not present in a university setting. Information boards about the laboratory, its purpose and its research focus give an introduction into the work being done. These can either be read independently by the visitors, or can be utilised and integrated into the communication efforts of the scientist. A further element is a nanotechnology demonstration area, where the properties of a selection of nanotechnological innovations are shown. These enable the scientist to present some of the differences between the macroscopic and the nanoscopic worlds in a simple and easy-to-understand way, thus introducing visitors to the subject matter whilst at the same time generating interest. Such demonstrations can also be used to initiate a discussion, questioning, for example, the economic value of research by showing an effect for which an application is not immediately apparent, thus conveying the dilemma researchers sometimes encounter that it is often impossible to predict the potential economic value of scientific results and new inventions.

Yet there is an inherent risk in using these demonstrations of which the researchers working in the Open Research Laboratory have to be aware. Instead of acting as a supplement to explaining the research and thus leading to a scientific dialogue, it is possible that the visitor perceives these nano-effect presentations to be the central element of the Open Research Laboratory. On the one hand the researcher is often tempted to 'hide' behind such demonstrations, reducing interruptions and thus enabling more intense work. On the other hand it is also easy for the scientist to give a quick and fascinating explanation of the demonstrations, captivating the museum visitors with intriguing but scientifically trivial aspects of nanotechnology. Both these approaches, whether intentional or accidental, can hinder or even prevent discussion about current aspects of research and thus of its ethical and social implications. As this is contrary to the central goals of public understanding of research, the scientists have to be aware of this danger and take care to use the demonstrations accordingly.

A further useful supplement to the Open Research Laboratory is an exhibition of currently available products involving nanotechnology. This enables the visitor to realise the significance that nanotechnology has already attained in daily life. The range of products covers a variety of applications based on various nano-effects, including, for example, a selection of nanotechnology uses in medicine and sports. Although all these products are commercially available, some of them, such as a variety of nano-based car care products, openly advertise their nanotechnology content, whilst others omit mentioning this. This aspect of commercialisation reflects the attitudes of various consumer groups and presents an excellent opening for a dialogue on the ethical aspects of implementing nanotechnology. The products also represent the current state-of-the-art in nanotechnology which is backed up and explained by the demonstrations, whilst the research conducted in the Open Research Laboratory gives a view of the future of nanoscience and of its possible applications. Thus combined, the researchers in the laboratory are able to communicate a comprehensive overview of the nano-world to the visitor.

The communication aspects, however, are not the only challenge that young scientists face in the Open Research Laboratory. Conducting research in a public environment is, at first, an unusual and strange situation, especially to someone used to working in a university laboratory. Having every task and movement visible to the museum visitors can be unnerving at first and takes some time to get used to. Ranging from humorous moments *('He's alive!')* to trivialities *('Where can I get some coffee?')*, from general inquiries *('What are you doing?')* to specific questions *('How does the scanning movement of the tip affect the adsorbate molecules?')*, the scope of interaction with the general public requires patience and tenacity. It is necessary to learn to work effectively despite such interruptions and disturbances, focusing simultaneously on research and communication. Most of the time it is possible to find the correct balance between research and communication activities. During school holidays, especially at Christmas and Easter, however, the Deutsches Museum receives so many visitors that the possibilities for conducting effective research are often extremely limited. Although these periods are often great opportunities for engagement with the general public, it is vital for researchers in the Open Research Laboratory to realise that time and work schedules for important measurements or for paper deadlines have to be planned accordingly.

Apart from acquiring the skills necessary for working in public and adapting work processes accordingly, there are also deeper aspects to conducting open research which have to be addressed. Ramirez states: *'If researchers are willing to be vulnerable, we can use nanotechnology to demonstrate the business of science. More specifically, we could admit that sometimes we can build a tool but don't yet know its capabilities and applications, both positive and negative. [. . .] By letting our guard down and showing the unknowns and how we discover things, researchers may create a new science narrative, generate more public confidence and demystify science by adding a human element to it'* (Ramirez, 2008). Researchers working in an Open Research Laboratory need to be aware of such vulnerabilities. In dealing with the public you are exposed to criticism, ridicule and disbelief. There are doubts as to whether one's communication skills are sufficient for imparting essential insights and whether research in public will cause negative prejudices to surface which could be vented on the researchers. Additionally, the researcher also faces vulnerabilities within the scientific community. As working in public can be time-consuming, research output can be reduced in comparison with one's peers. The scientist is thus vulnerable to career setbacks due to a lower number of publications, often seen in the scientific community as the most important measure of success. Also, applying oneself to public communication and engagement is often not well regarded by colleagues, *'indeed, in many cases participation in events of this nature [is] considered to have negative repercussions on the participant's career'* (Martín-Sempere et al., 2008).

Thus, working in the Open Research Laboratory has an ambiguous aspect for a young scientist. On the one hand it is exciting and encouraging to acquire new skills whilst at the same time seeing visitors fascinated and captivated by one's work. Yet on the other hand both the public and the scientific community often do not appreciate the efforts of the individual researchers working in the laboratory and the disadvantages and vulnerabilities they have accepted in publicly conducting their work. This is a dilemma which is not likely to be solved in the near future as long as public communication and engagement still tends to be regarded by many within the scientific community as an idiosyncratic activity of minor importance. Obviously, we hope that our experience with the Open Research Laboratory concept will contribute to a change in this attitude, not only in the field of nanotechnology but in many other fields as this novel approach to science communication and public engagement spreads.

Key resources

Field, H., Powell, P. (2001). Public Understanding of Science vs. Public Understanding of Research. *Public Understanding of Science*, **10**, 421–426.
Meyer, M. (2009). *From 'Cold' Science to 'Hot' Research: The Texture of Controversy*, CSI Working Papers Series no. 016. Paris: Centre de Sociologie de l'Innovation.
Hix, P. (2009). *Professional Guidelines for Establishing an Open Nano Lab/A Nano Researcher Live Area*. München: Deutsches Museum.
Pfuhl, N., Lewalter, D. (2008). *Abschlussbericht: Studie zum Ausstellungsbereich Gläsernes Forscherlabor*. München: Technische Universität.

References

Brandlmeier, T. (2004). Ein Experiment, das die Welt erschütterte. *Meisterwerke aus dem Deutschen Museum*, vol. **1**, pp. 28–31. München: Deutsches Museum. [translation by Hix, P.]
Field, H., Powell, P. (2001). Public Understanding of Science vs. Public Understanding of Research. *Public Understanding of Science*, **10**, 421–426.
House of Lords (2000). *Science and Technology – Third Report*. London: HMSO.
Latour, B. (1998). From the world of science to the world of research? *Science* **280**, 208–209.
Martín-Sempere, M. J., Garzón-García, B., Rey-Rocha, J. (2008). Scientists' motivation to communicate science and technology to the public: surveying participants at the Madrid Science Fair. *Public Understanding of Science*, **17**, 349–367.
Meyer, M. (2009). *From 'Cold' Science to 'Hot' Research: The Texture of Controversy*, CSI Working Papers Series no. 016. Paris: Centre de Sociologie de l'Innovation.
Miller, S. (2001). Public understanding of science at the crossroads. *Public Understanding of Science*, **10**, 115–120.

Pfuhl, N., Lewalter, D. (2008). *Abschlussbericht: Studie zum Ausstellungsbereich Gläsernes Forscherlabor*. München: Technische Universität.

Ramirez, A. G. (2008). Nanotechnology as a catalyst for change. *ASTC Dimensions*, January/February 2008.

Simons, J., Zimmer, R., Vierboom, C., Härlen, I., Hertel, R., Böl, G.-F. (2009). The slings and arrows of communication on nanotechnology. *Journal of Nanoparticle Research*, **11**, 1555–1571.

25

Imagine: a communication project putting life sciences in the spotlight

INTRODUCTION

It was during a symposium about genomics in 2003, when we, myself (Patricia) and the communications advisor of our scientific centre, suddenly got the idea. One of those eureka moments when you know you are on to something special, it rings all the bells and the more you think about it, the more potential you see in the idea. We were working on a communication plan for a private–public partnership on industrial genomics and were wondering how we could engage people with genomics. We wanted to create a positive association in people's minds and avoid the rather negative connotations that 'biotechnology' had received. The idea for the project got us really enthusiastic. By involving scientists working with high-school students on investigations for application in developing countries, it would provide positive associations with the life sciences for a large public and the media, have the potential to interest school students in studies in the life sciences and, at the same time, be contributing to needy situations in developing countries. The idea was presented to the 300 scientists at the conference and it hit all the right buttons. The overall working concept finally grew into a full-blown annual competition and a legal foundation was established in 2005 to run it professionally.

I remember standing in a bus in Amsterdam thinking of a name for the competition. '*Imagine*' in recollection of John Lennon's verses came up and in our enthusiasm we tested it with some of the bus passengers. They liked it. So '*Imagine Life Sciences*' it became. The idea is simple. Scientists are asked to provide an idea for what one can do with

Successful Science Communication, ed. D. J. Bennett and R. C. Jennings. Published by Cambridge University Press. © Cambridge University Press 2011.

life sciences in a developing country. These ideas are collected and sent to secondary-school students who are asked to make a business plan of the original idea. In the Dutch secondary (pre-university level) school curriculum students are required to undertake an assignment of approximately 80 hours called the Profielwerkstuk (assignment related to the mainstream curriculum track). They need to work independently on a subject of their own choice and often they work in small groups of two to six students on the same subject, dividing the work. They have around four months to complete it during the final year of their high-school curriculum. The *Imagine* competition can therefore be easily incorporated into the standard curriculum.

In order to make the business plan, the school students need to do the experiments to test the science behind the proposal. They are invited to the university or company of the scientist who conceived the idea. They also need to become familiar with the social, economic and ethical issues in the developing country of their choice. The *Imagine* organisation provides contacts with development aid workers and organises a special 'development workers and experts meeting day' for the school students. After four months the business plans are submitted and assessed by a panel of experts consisting of scientists, development aid workers, teachers and key opinion leaders. The student groups providing the best plans have a special training day to prepare a presentation in English and a one-minute movie with the help of professionals. The final assessment takes place in a special session of an international scientific conference where the movies and presentations are presented led by a nationally well-known television personality. The group with the best presentation and business plan wins the competition (Figure 25.1) and their project is carried out in the chosen developing country. The winning school students receive funding to visit the project in the developing country (Schuurbiers *et al.*, 2006).

SOME FACTS ABOUT THE IMAGINE SCHOOL COMPETITION

The *Imagine* project was developed by the Delft University of Technology as an activity of the public–private partnership called the Kluyver Centre for Genomics of Industrial Fermentation[1] of which the Delft University is the coordinator. Genomics and its associated technologies in the life sciences have a major impact on society and their impact is growing. Because these developments affect everybody's lives it is

---

[1] See: www.kluyvercentre.nl

Figure 25.1 Winners of the 2010 *Imagine* competition: Julika Humme, Emily Allwood and Marleen Schuijer from the Christelijk Gymnasium Sorghvliet, The Hague, with the Biobag project by Jelmer Tamis, researcher at Delft University of Technology together with the Rector of the University, Professor Karel Luyben. See colour plate section.

important that people understand the main concepts behind these technologies and how they relate to society at large. Empowering people to make informed decisions about their future well-being, health-related or democratic and political, is a just aim of informing people about the possible social dimensions or influences of genomics (Waarlo *et al.*, 2002). However, effective science communication is not simple (Klop, 2008; Millar, 2006). Improvement of the communication between the scientific community and public remains an important subject for discussion and research and is a special objective of the Netherlands Centre for Society and Genomics with which the Kluyver Centre collaborates for the development of communication projects.

Imagine was conceived as an activity to improve education and communication for a broad public. It was first organised in 2004 and has since continued annually as an innovative science communication activity aiming to improve interaction between science and the wider world by presenting a constructive image of biotechnology and life sciences to the public. *Imagine* has been developed as a school competition involving scientists, school students and the media to achieve tangible results for developing countries. Set in an educational context, it aims to promote inspiring science education by encouraging communication between students and their teachers, and scientists in

Figure 25.2 Contestants in the *Imagine* school competition using microscopes at Unesco IHE, Delft, the Netherlands preparing their project for the goldmines in Ghana, November 2009. See colour plate section.

developed and developing countries. It involves school students in a self-motivating, open-learning and multidisciplinary approach address-ing the important social, ethical and economical issues in the applica-tions of biotechnology for developing countries (Figures 25.2 and 25.3). On the other hand, the project encourages scientists in being active in public communication and in considering the relevance of biotechnol-ogy for developing countries.

Since 2004, over 500 school students have been directly involved in making business plans for more than 50 selected scientific ideas for applying life sciences in developing countries (Table 25.1). More than 30 experts have been involved in the evaluation of business plans and presentations. *Imagine* has reached an extended public through over 175 media publications (newspapers, magazines, radio interviews) while a documentary was launched on the Dutch internet television channel *Goeddoel TV*, a channel presenting welfare projects, in 2009. *Imagine* has received very positive responses from school students, teachers, scientists, journalists and the wider public including from the Dutch Minister for Research and Education. In 2006 *Imagine* received the 'Silver Hourglass' award for best educational activity by the Nether-lands Biotechnology Society and was nominated for the European Com-mission's Descartes Prize for Science Communication in 2007.

Table 25.1. *Example of* Imagine *projects*

Underground water treatment (TUD)
Byxine in Surinam (TUD)
Composites from bamboo (TUD)
Soil improvement by microbial cement (TUD)
Biodegradable materials in the Philippines (TUD)
Artemisinine against malaria (Hanzeschool Groningen)
Fungi against malaria (WUR)
Food from waste (RUG)
Rice bran for added value (TUD + Oram, Quelimane)
The Star sun biogas reactor (WUR)
DNA Timber Check (personal initiative, supported by Forest Stewardship Council and WUR)

Notes: RUG, Rijksuniversiteit Groningen (University of Groningen); TUD, Technische Universiteit Delft (Delft University of Technology); WUR, Wageningen University and Research Centre.

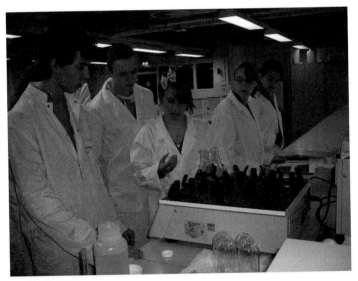

Figure 25.3 Contestants in the *Imagine* school competition in a laboratory experiment at Unesco IHE, Delft, the Netherlands, preparing their project for the goldmines in Ghana, November 2009. See colour plate section.

WHY DOES IT WORK?

The *Imagine* project is both an education and communication activity. It engages school students in life sciences including their ethical, social and legal issues. At the same time, the many media outlets of the activity also make *Imagine* a successful communication activity. In the field of education the project utilises several design principles such as hands-on learning, inquiry-based learning, etc. These principles can be found in the social constructivist perspective on learning. In this perspective the metaphor of 'participation' is often used to characterise this concept of 'learning' (Salomon & Perkins, 1998). In essence, social constructivist educational theories interpret learning as increasingly competent participation in the discourse, norms and practices associated with particular communities of practice (Lave & Wenger, 1991). Becoming a more central participant in society is not just a matter of acquiring knowledge and skills. It also implies becoming a member of a community of practice, in this case the life sciences. For this to happen, learning contexts must be chosen such that students can make sense of the subject matter and hence give them a feeling of responsibility to participate critically in the practice in question. Over the last decade, elements of social constructivist conceptions of learning have been used in science education (Frijters *et al.*, 2008; Ogborn, 1997). In particular, interest in how students learn to think critically about social issues is increasing (Driver *et al.*, 2000; Kolstø, 2001; Sadler & Zeidler, 2005). Improving science education is interpreted as helping young people to engage with the social practice of scientists. Against the background of this social constructivist perspective on learning, *Imagine* contains some key factors that establish this process.

When considering *Imagine* as a communication activity we can value it as an example of communicating sciences in the context of its impact. It also 'engages' the scientists and school students in the process. In the 1990s authors including Brian Wynne (1992) and John Durant (1993) discussed the idea of a paradigm shift in science communication. Several reasons were provided for the need of such a change, often based on the desirability of scientific progress and expressed as a need to increase acceptance or trust in science and technology (Gaskell *et al.*, 2006; Osseweijer, 2006a). It was suggested that science communication should be less limited to mass media and should make more use of interpersonal and other more interactive forms of communication. Over the years we have seen the development of the transition from public understanding of science (PUS) to public awareness of science (PAS) with a more active role given to the public in the communication process, to public engagement of science (PES) with a further increase in the role of the receiver responding to the (social) scientific debate on the notion of knowledge as a social construct (Latour, 1987; Nowotny *et al.*, 2001). The latter implies that scientific progress is the result of a continuous interaction process in which many stakeholders are involved. Accordingly, science communication should be seen as a means to optimise this mutual interaction or engagement in science. In this view, communication is a transaction process in which scientific as well as ethical and social considerations are taken into account. The role of the public however remains restricted to being consulted in the decision-making about the research agenda. The activities described for this (PES) process, such as surveys, citizen juries, consensus conferences, public consultations or referenda often reflect the limited influence on the decision-making process (e.g. Wynne, 2006).

So public participation in science (PPS) followed with the aim of improving the transparency and democratic quality of decision-making processes in the choice of scientific research that improves the quality of life in society. Public participation presupposes a certain level of public understanding and awareness, hence the experiences gained in activities focused on these aims are all relevant for the goals of PPS. However we urgently need to evaluate these types of projects. An important difficulty in this PPS approach is to actually get people involved. How can we interest people in 'engagement' with scientific subjects? As a possible answer the so-called Three-E model was suggested (Osseweijer, 2006b, c): *'Entertainment, Emotion and Education'* as a simple and universal approach applicable to all kinds of issues and not necessarily limited to the scientific domain. Entertainment triggers attention, emotion is found in identification with the subject, education is achieved by the raised curiosity. It provides an alternative to the long-existing AIDA (Attention, Interest, Desire and Action) model which is based on a simple hierarchy of effects and does not specifically involve an approach to include a reflexive element (Barry, 1987). It also differs essentially from the Entertainment–Education model used in health education for the same reason, because the emotions provoked through the Three-E model are intended to make the underlying values more explicit (Bouman, 2002). The Three-E approach will help in affecting a broader audience, involving a larger number of stakeholders and initiating more discussion on moral issues. As such it therefore also facilitates the easier recognition of possible societal issues and a smoother introduction of novel technologies. *Imagine* is based on this model, it entertains students and scientists, it touches the feelings of sharing benefit with people in less developed parts of the world and it educates all involved in the process.

Effective science education and communication is not simple. However, it seems that the *Imagine* project provides an example of an effective

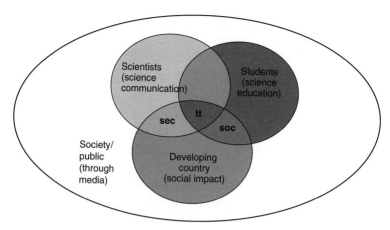

Figure 25.4 Four-circle model showing the different domains and interactions of the *Imagine* project, a science education and communication activity with a societal impact. (Sec, science education and communication; soc, societal impact; tt, technology transfer.)

and appreciated science education and communication activity with broad support from teachers, school students and politicians. The activity is placed in three domains: education, communication and societal valorisation with interaction between scientist and school student; scientists, school students and the public (through the media) and between scientists, school students and people in developing countries (Figure 25.4).

The overlapping interactions deal with:

science education and communication aspects
technology transfer aspects
ethical, legal and social aspects

As already indicated, *Imagine* can also be viewed in terms of its merit as a 'valorisation', value-creating activity. Technology developed in the Netherlands is transferred to a developing country. This part of the activity provides the greatest challenges, which we learned to tackle during the course of the years. Several authors describe the difficulties of introducing novel technologies in developing countries (e.g. Broerse & Bunders, 2000) and suggest using an iterative learning approach. Ownership of the activity is also an important issue as well as local knowledge, training and the availability of resources such as materials and repair skills. Problems encountered also include, for example, the local infrastructure of roads and ownership of land in which the project was located. Our original idea that we could easily find an ally to carry out the project was a little too naïve as it turned out.

Starting a school competition

When the idea was accepted and we decided to start *Imagine* we appointed a junior academic to develop and carry out the project. We assembled a team of four people to overlook the activity consisting of a Managing Director (the originator of the initiative), a financial manager, a communication advisor (all from the Kluyver Centre) and a person with a PhD in the social sciences. In order to limit any personal liability claims it was decided to set up a legal Foundation which was established in 2005 and associated with the Delft University of Technology. This group overlooking the project was established as the Foundation's first Board.

Funds were originally provided by the Kluyver Centre and raised from other similar centres in the Netherlands. The Netherlands Biotechnology Foundation also subsidised the activity and hosted the finals of the *Imagine* competition during their annual international symposia. A project was proposed to a government programme aimed at increasing the number of science students in Dutch universities (called WO Sprint) which provided additional income. Raising funds was carried out by the Board and took an enormous amount of time. We explored the possibility of raising funds from large charities such as the Dutch 'Postcode Loterij'. However it proved very difficult to obtain funds from these organisations and in general we can say that fund-raising is still an important issue of concern. In addition to fund-raising much time was spent initially in clarifying the rules of the competition and the drafting of clear guidelines both for the project ideas and the business plans.[2] Issues related to the execution of the project in the developing country were also anticipated – for example in relation to ownership and intellectual property rights which were handled with advice from the university's technology transfer officers. As we aimed to provide a competition that could withstand the criteria for responsible entrepreneurship, we also had our criteria checked by an expert in business ethics.

In order to increase support and solicit advice from experts we established a Board of Recommendation with renowned international people who could, when requested, open doors, put in a good word or cut a ribbon at a special ceremony. We also established

[2] See www.foundation-imagine.org

an Advisory Board with experts, chaired by the President of the Delft University of Technology. This Board provides the experts for jury tasks and is regularly asked for advice.

In 2009 we decided that the Foundation should be professionalised and a director and assistant were appointed. Fund-raising, links to industry and internationalisation are set as priorities for the further development of the Foundation.

Getting students involved

An advertising campaign was set up to attract school students, supported by a website to provide information. Biology and chemistry teachers were addressed by a general mailing with information on the *Imagine* competition, while the project was presented at teacher conferences and in articles published in teachers' magazines. In the first year 2004 a total of sixteen students (five groups) representing schools from throughout the Netherlands, subscribed to the competition. In the second year we received considerably more interest from students with 16 groups participating. Presently an average of 25 groups (about 100–120 students) take part in the competition each year. School students like the project, it appeals to their imagination and often they say they have put much more time into the project than expected from the school curriculum. It provides 'something worthwhile to do'.

Getting scientists involved

A request to scientists was circulated to suggest ideas for projects. Meetings were organised to inform scientists about the concept, the project was presented at national conferences in biotechnology and genomics, and articles were published in national science magazines. In addition the idea was communicated to key people in the field who also provided the experts we needed for the jury to judge the business plans. In the first year we received 25 ideas for projects in developing countries. We decided to appoint a jury to select five proposals that were consequently sent to schools. Also we realised that we needed to set some clear criteria including the feasibility of carrying out the plan in the period of one year; feasibility of carrying out the plan in the developing country; ethical soundness of the plan; a maximum for costs; etc.

In following years we were less lucky as on average we received five project ideas and it proved hard work to get them. While scientists often react enthusiastically to the project, many are quite reluctant to become involved with a scientific idea for proposals. This is seen as a major bottleneck within the *Imagine* project as it results in the organisers' struggling to collect enough high-quality project proposals on which secondary school students can base their business plans for the Profielwerkstuk. This potentially endangers the continuation of the *Imagine* project and affects the quality of the proposals. A Master's degree student research project (unpublished) revealed that clarity of information and support of superiors is crucial to maintaining the involvement of young scientists (which conforms with results from the Eurobarometer special study 'Citizens, science and technology', 2005 and the MORI–Wellcome Trust study (MORI, 2000)). In discussing this with the Director of the Kluyver Centre the suggestion was made to develop an advanced course for PhD students in genomics and the other life sciences linked to developing ideas for life science projects. In addition to increasing motivation and important skills (media training; dealing with ethical, legal and social issues in the context of global development), the course linked with a subsequent involvement in *Imagine* could count as training towards the PhD degree. Further ideas presently under consideration are the development of an university course for second-year undergraduate life science students on 'socially responsible design' with which it is hoped to increase the quality of ideas for *Imagine* business plans by validating the feasibility of projects for developing countries.

Carrying out the winning project in a developing country

The plan that won the first round of the competition was the production of biodiesel from algae in Mozambique. Although there were already-existing relationships between the scientist and an organisation in Mozambique, the *Imagine* organisation considered it preferable for the project to be adopted by a university. Contacts were therefore made with the University of Maputo. Implementing the plan was calculated to take at least €100 000, for which additional funding had to be found. A plan was written and submitted to the development aid programme, NCDO, in the Netherlands and approved. The scientist who originally put the idea forward decided to take time out from his job to carry out the project himself. This was of course an exceptional situation. However, it taught us that we should have limitations on the actual funds provided by *Imagine*, and that we should put a scheme in place determining how these winning projects should be embedded in developing countries. The students who won the competition went on a visit to Mozambique, which made us think hard about how to handle issues of liability. Declarations were drawn up as well as contracts with the university carrying out the project and specifying communication rights for *Imagine*. These experiences led to much clearer procedures on what we expect from the students, scientists and executors of the winning projects. It provided a learning trajectory which eventually led to the accommodation of three types of projects:

(a) projects that could be executed by the scientist who brought forward the original idea
(b) projects that could be executed by a named institution in the business plan
(c) projects that could be offered for carrying out by outsiders in a bid procedure.

The second winning project consisted of a plan to make avocado oil from overripe otherwise waste avocados in Kenya. As there were no already existing links with organisations in Kenya, a bid was circulated which led to a contract with a local farmer near the capital, Nairobi. Later projects used existing links with universities and research institutes. This part of the activity can still be improved in terms of technology transfer and development aid knowledge (Figures 25.5 and 25.6).

Media attention

The competition has several interesting opportunities for media coverage. The winning of the competition, the carrying out of the project itself, and the visit of the students to the developing country are all highly newsworthy activities. We circulate press briefings and actively maintain contacts with journalists to increase the chances that each of these is picked up. Recently the website has been improved to include special features and information for journalists. In addition to the media relations and activities by the organisers, the school students themselves also raise media coverage. They enthusiastically tell their stories to local newspapers, and national magazines have covered their activities. In addition to the website and media coverage we have the videos of the finalist school groups which make excellent entertaining material at conferences when talking about communication activities by scientists. We have also produced

Figure 25.5 Ghana, Enidado, with the *Imagine* Foundation sign at Oyster Mushroom Project in Aburi Ghana, with the winners of 2007, Marieke, Sandra and Nynke, August 2010. See colour plate section.

Figure 25.6 The winners of *Imagine* 2007 in Ghana, Marieke and Nynke, singing and dancing with the children from Aburi Ghana at the Oyster Mushroom Project, August 2010. See colour plate section.

a booklet telling the story of the implementation of the biodiesel plant in Mozambique and a documentary of the production of avocado oil in Kenya which is regularly posted at a Dutch internet TV channel.

THE FUTURE

Imagine has been established as a practical activity based on the long-term experience of the organisers with science communication activities but it has never been critically and methodologically examined as a case of good practice in science education and as a communication activity. Very little is known about what makes this activity so successful and appreciated. The *Imagine* project evokes important questions such as: *'What are the key factors that make this activity successful, and what impact do the interactions of the different components have on each other?'* (Figure 25.4). In other words, *'What can be learned from this specific case for other educational or communication activities?'* The project lends itself to studying several aspects which are related to either of two major questions: *'Are we doing the "right" things?'* and *'Are we doing things "right"?'* The first 'right' refers to a moral question, i.e. whether the goals of *Imagine* can be defined as 'good': are they appropriately chosen? The second question relates to the achievement of the defined goals of the activity, i.e. are the goals reached effectively and efficiently?

These are important questions and a research project has started to respond to these questions and learn from *Imagine*'s example. The project starts with the second question concerning achievement of the defined goals of the activity, as we wish to improve our understanding of how the activity reaches its goals and which factors are important for that success. However, in assessing the perceptions and opinions of the various groups involved in *Imagine* we will also collect data relating to the first question, 'Are the goals of *Imagine* supported?'

In summary, *Imagine* has a rich spectrum of different interactions and aspects for study. The research team has full access to all the data and has the opportunity to intervene in parts of the present interactions during the competition. Therefore, the *Imagine* project provides a perfect opportunity to evaluate qualitatively the fundamental theories and normative frameworks underlying the principles in this communication, education and societal valorisation activity in order to foster the broader use of the *Imagine* concept.

Acknowledgement

We would like to thank all those who have contributed to the *Imagine* project and concept over the years. This work is carried out within the research programmes of the Centre for Society and Genomics and the Kluyver Centre for Genomics of Industrial Fermentation which are part of the Netherlands Genomics Initiative/Netherlands Organisation for Scientific Research.

References

Barry, T. E. (1987) The development of the hierarchy of effects: an historical perspective. *Current Issues and Research in Advertising* **10**, 251–295.

Bouman, M. (2002) Turtles and peacocks: collaboration in Entertainment–Education television. *Communication Theory*, **30**, 331–346.

Broerse, J. E. W. & Bunders, J. F. G. (2000) Requirements for biotechnology development: the necessity for an interactive and participatory innovation process. *International Journal of Biotechnology*, **2**, 275–296.

Driver, R., Newton, P., & Osborne, J. (2000). Establishing the norms of argumentation in classrooms. *Science Education*, **84**, 287–312.

Durant, J. R. (1993) What is scientific literacy? In J. R. Durant & J. Gregory (eds.), *Science and Culture in Europe*, pp. 129–138. London: Science Museum.

Frijters, S., ten Dam, G., & Rijlaarsdam, G. (2008) Effects of dialogic learning on value-loaded critical thinking. *Learning and Instruction*, **1**, 66–82.

Gaskell, G., Stares, S., Allansdottir, A., Allum, N., Corchero, C., & Jackson, J. (2006) *Europeans and Biotechnology in 2005: Patterns and Trends*, Final Report of Eurobarometer 64.3. Luxembourg: Publications Office of the European Union.

Klop, T. (2008) Attitudes of secondary school students towards modern biotechnology. Thesis, Erasmus Universiteit Rotterdam, Rotterdam.

Kolstø, S. D. (2001) Scientific literacy for citizenship: tools for dealing with the science dimension of controversial socioscientific issues. *Science Education*, **85**, 291–310.

Latour, B. (1987) *Science in Action: How to Follow Scientists and Engineers through Society*. Cambridge, MA: Harward University Press.

Lave, J. & Wenger, E. (1991) *Situated Learning: Legitimate Peripheral Participation*. Cambridge, UK: Cambridge University Press.

Millar, R. (2006) Twenty-first century science: insights from the design and implementation of a scientific literacy approach in school science. *International Journal of Science Education*, **28**, 1499–1521.

MORI (2000) *The Role of Scientists in Public Debate, December 1999–March 2000*, Research Study conducted by MORI for the Wellcome Trust. London: Wellcome Trust.

Nowotny, H., Scott, P., & Gibbons, M. (2001) *Rethinking Science: Knowledge and the Public in an Age of Uncertainty*. Cambridge, UK: Polity Press.

Ogborn, J. (1997) Constructivist metaphors of learning science. *Science and Education*, **6**, 121–133.

Osseweijer, P. (2006a). A short history of talking biotech: fifteen years of iterative action research in institutionalising scientists'engagement in public communication. Thesis, Vrije Universiteit, Amsterdam.

Osseweijer, P. (2006b). A new model for science communication that takes ethical considerations into account: The Three-E model – Entertainment, Emotion and Education. *Science and Engineering Ethics*, **12**, 591–593.

Osseweijer, P. (2006c). *Imagine* projects with a strong emotional appeal. *Nature*, **444**, 422.

Sadler, T. D. & Zeidler, D. L. (2005) Patterns of informal reasoning in the context of socioscientific decision making. *Journal of Research in Science Teaching*, **42**, 112–138.

Salomon, G. & Perkins, D. N. (1998) Individual and social aspects of learning. In P. D. Pearson & A. Iran-Nejad (eds.), *Review of Research in Education*, pp. 1–24. Washington, DC: American Educational Research Association.

Schuurbiers, D., Blomjous, M., & Osseweijer, P. (2006) '*Imagine*': sharing ideas in the life sciences. In Cheng Donhong, J. Mecalfe, & B. Schiele (eds.), *At the Human Scale: International Practices in Science Communication*, pp. 107–122. Beijing: Science Press.

Waarlo, A. J., Brom, F. W. A., Nieuwendijk, G. M. T., Meijman, F. J., & Visak, T. (2002) Towards competence-oriented genomics education and communication. In *Societal Component of Genomics*. The Hague: NWO and The Netherlands Genomics Initiative.

Wynne, B. (1992) Public understanding of science research. *Public Understanding of Science*, **1**, 321–337.

Wynne, B. (2006) Public engagement as a means of restoring public trust in science: hitting the notes, but missing the music? *Community Genetics*, **9**, 211–220.

Part IV And finally, evaluating and
         embedding science
         communication

26

Evaluating success: how to find out
what worked (and what didn't)

1 WHY EVALUATE?

The question: '*So did it work?*' can be daunting for both new and experienced science communicators. The answer lies through effective evaluation, which can be one of the most interesting aspects of the engagement process. Kolb (1984) describes a cycle of conceptualisation, experiment, experience and reflection as crucial to the learning process, as recognised in Figure 26.1.

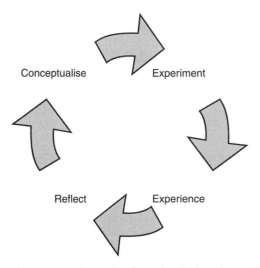

Figure 26.1 Kolb's cycle of experiential learning (Kolb, 1984).

Evaluators often talk about their work being used to 'prove' or 'improve' activities. Essentially evaluation can be used to improve an activity

Successful Science Communication, ed. D. J. Bennett and R. C. Jennings. Published by
Cambridge University Press. © Cambridge University Press 2011.

or programme by identifying and addressing limitations, or can look at an activity to arrive at a judgement of its success or worth. These findings are useful to check if your activity is achieving what it set out to, as well as in providing evidence for those interested in supporting your work such as funders.

This chapter will provide everything you need to get started in evaluation.

2 EVALUATION: DEFINITIONS AND TYPES

What is evaluation?

The UK Evaluation Society (2010) defines evaluation as:

> An in-depth study which takes place at a discrete point in time, and in which recognised research procedures are used in a systematic and analytically defensible fashion to form a judgement on the value of an intervention.

From this definition it is clear that evaluation is a form of social research. In fact approaching evaluation in a similar way to a scientific research study is often useful, although the methods are related to the social rather than natural sciences.

Evaluation is important in any area of activity where issues of effectiveness and impact are to be considered (Rossi and Freeman, 1989). This, of course, means that evaluations are conducted in a wide range of fields beyond science communication and there is much to learn from others' approaches.

Types of evaluation

In order to think about the different types of evaluation, it is first useful to model the system we wish to evaluate. Figure 26.2 provides a useful summary.

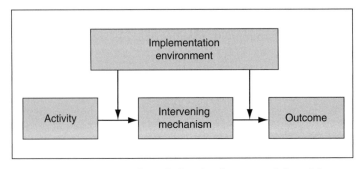

Figure 26.2 Summary of a typical evaluation system (adapted from Chen, 1990).

This evaluation system has the following elements:

- The **activity** (e.g. book, festival, website) that produces the change.
- An **intervening mechanism** that relates the activity to the outcome and can be explored in evaluations with a view to identifying causal factors. This can provide information on the reasons behind success or failure – far more valuable than simply reporting whether or not success was achieved.
- The intended and unintended **outcomes** of the activity.
- The **implementation environment** for the activity, which also affects the outcome. This could be something simple like a rainy day limiting festival attendance, or something much more complex like the cultural attitudes that participants bring to an activity and how they affect the outcomes.

Evaluations can focus on each of the individual elements above. In addition, **impact evaluations** aim to understand the impact of the activity on the outcome, and **generalising evaluations** provide information on how evaluation results for one activity or programme can be generalised to apply to future systems.

Despite the wide range of literature dealing with evaluation, science communication practitioners tend to use a much simpler way to distinguish evaluations: as either formative or summative. A single evaluation may contain both formative and summative elements.

Formative evaluation provides continuous feedback so that a project can be improved during the course of delivery. It's the best way to approach the evaluation of a new or innovative activity. It can also include some elements of **pre-research** with the target audience to identify needs or interests while the activity is in development.

Summative evaluation is usually conducted at the end of a project or activity, in order to 'sum up' its effectiveness. This type of evaluation usually focuses on impact, but information on delivery can also be collected. While summative evaluations are usually conducted too late to inform the project during its delivery, they provide useful lessons and good practice for future projects.

The best way to learn about evaluation is to apply it to a real activity or project. Evaluation is fairly straightforward and the remainder of this chapter will guide you through developing a meaningful approach to evaluating your science communication activities. Frequently, project managers find that thinking about how a project will be evaluated stimulates deeper reflection on the project goals and approach, so this is also a useful project management tool.

3 WHAT DOES SUCCESS LOOK LIKE?

Evaluation is about gauging success, so the first step is to decide what success looks like. Be as clear as you can about what you want to do, how you will go about it, who you want to involve and why. Even if your activity is something simple like a public talk, taking the time to write down a few objectives is invaluable.

Project managers talk about writing **SMART** objectives that are Specific, Measurable, Achievable, Relevant and Time-bound. With each objective ask yourself how easy it will be at the end of the activity to test whether it has been met. You may find that some are easier to test than others; it is acceptable to have a mix as long as they are not all impossible to test.

Outputs, outcomes and impacts for your audiences

Having decided what you intend to deliver, think about what your audience will get out of it. The terms outputs, outcomes and impacts are often interchanged, but to evaluators they have clear and differentiated meanings. The following definitions are adapted from Grant and Jenkins (2009).

Outputs are all the products and services that your activity or project will deliver. They are easy to count, but just measuring outputs tells you nothing about the value of a project. Examples of outputs include: numbers of visitors, web pages, events, resources, publications.

Outcomes are the changes or effects that occur *as a result of the outputs*. Outcomes can be short-term, e.g. visitors learn more about recycling; or longer-term, e.g. visitors change their behaviour to recycle more waste.

Impacts are lasting, long-term changes that the outcomes contribute to. However there are likely to be other factors that support or limit the extent to which these types of changes occur. Following the previous examples about recycling, an impact could be that the percentage of waste that is recycled in a particular city increases. Linking this impact to the project in question is problematic – evaluators call this challenge 'attribution' and it tends to become more difficult over time and as the number of possibly contributing factors increases.

It is important to be realistic about what we can evaluate. It is generally acceptable to focus on evaluating outputs and outcomes for science communication projects. Evaluation of impacts can be covered by longitudinal research over a period of time or broader social science research studies.

The Museums, Libraries and Archives Council (2008) has created a framework called *Inspiring Learning For All* that identifies sets of outcomes for museum projects. They are certainly not the only outcomes that may emerge from science communication activities, but they are a useful starting point. The Generic Learning Outcomes (GLOs) summarised in Figure 26.3 are especially helpful.

Figure 26.3 Summary of Generic Learning Outcomes (GLOs).

It can be useful to draw a table to help think about outcomes. Perhaps use the different audiences as column headings and have different GLOs in the rows, but remember not everyone will achieve all the outcomes (Table 26.1). During this exercise, ask yourself what you hope someone might tell a friend about the activity, or what they might be thinking as they leave.

Note that it is valuable to consider both internal and external audiences for your evaluation.

Mapping outcomes for your project

Some very valuable contributions to the field of evaluation have come from the international development sector. Here, programmes of work are directed towards creating social change in various communities and

Table 26.1. *The different Generic Learning Outcomes (GLOs) for different audiences*

Outcome – GLOs	School kids	Apprentices – explainers	Me – the activity leader
Experiences – enjoyment, creativity, inspiration	Fun Interesting	Fun Interesting Worthwhile	Fun Interesting Rewarding
Knowledge and understanding	About what a job in science is like		
Skills	Lab skills Teamwork Communication	Teamwork Communication Organisation	Teamwork Communication Organisation
Attitudes and values	Science is more interesting than I thought; science could be for me	More confident about public engagement	
Behaviour	More attentive in science lessons back at school?		
Anything else	A look inside the facility so it's not just 'that building on the hill'		Some links with local schools for other projects

it is not difficult to see how science communication activities also seek to create social change, albeit in a different way.

If your project is more complex than a one-off activity, or if you are looking to evaluate a series of activities (outreach activities across a university department for example) then some of these approaches may be valuable. They aim to draw maps of intended outcomes from activities and explore assumptions about how these outcomes might be affected by the implementation environment. Defining what successful outcomes are for a project is half the battle when it comes to measuring success.

Two approaches worth looking at here are **theory of change** and **outcome mapping**. They both use discussions, usually facilitated by an experienced moderator, to develop a rich understanding of the social changes that activities and projects aim to make. Interestingly, they take a more qualitative approach than many science communication evaluations, perhaps reflecting the backgrounds of practitioners working in this field. There is much material available online for both approaches; links are provided in the references.

Whatever approach is taken to identifying outcomes and defining success, once some intended outcomes have been identified it is time to think about how progress towards them will be measured.

4 EVALUATION QUESTIONS

Just as any scientific study has research questions it is useful to define evaluation questions based on your intended outcomes. Four or five evaluation questions are usually sufficient, as they should be relatively high level. Think of them as the questions you would ask someone else to answer if they were evaluating the project for you. Some examples from a hypothetical engineering project (developed by Grant and Paterson, 2009) are given in Table 26.2.

Table 26.2. Evaluation questions: *the questions you want your evaluation to address*

– What was the outcome of the project on engineers' knowledge of and attitudes towards public engagement?

– Did the impact differ for engineers at different stages of their careers, or for those with different levels of prior experience in public engagement? What other factors affected differences in impacts?

– What are the areas in which engineers needed the greatest amount of support to develop their activities?

– Did engaging in the activities change science festival visitors' perceptions of engineering? In what way?

– How useful was the DVD in sharing the learning from the project with others?

Next you will consider the research methods that can be used to evaluate the activity. The level of thinking that needs to happen before evaluation materials are designed is significant and this is crucial to ensuring that the evaluation is robust and its findings meaningful.

5 'MEASURING' SUCCESS

Quantitative and qualitative approaches

The two main approaches to answering evaluation questions are qualitative and quantitative.

Qualitative For evaluation questions that ask 'what', 'how' or 'why', qualitative methods provide a deep understanding of the ways in which your activity has had an impact on its participants. This approach is ideal if you are unsure of what outcome your activity will have, or if it aims to have a strong impact on a small number of participants. Often used in formative evaluations.

Quantitative For evaluation questions that ask 'how much' or 'how many', quantitative methods provide numbers and statistics to quantify participants' opinions. These methods work best if you have a good idea of the expected outcome or outcomes of your activity, if it or they can be easily counted or measured and if you are working with large numbers of participants. Often used in summative evaluations.

Many evaluation plans will contain both quantitative and qualitative elements (**mixed method**). For example, a new project may use qualitative methods at the start to find out what outcomes are emerging from activities. Later, quantitative methods may be used to measure the strength of the outcome, or what proportion of participants experience the different outcomes.

Figure 26.4 will help you think about which approach best suits your particular activity or project.

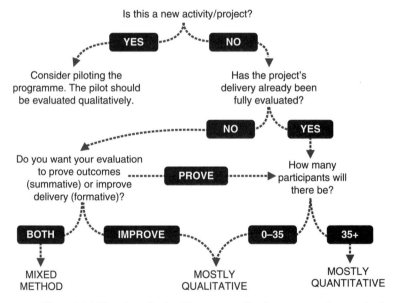

Figure 26.4 Flowchart for deciding on a qualitative, quantitative or mixed approach.

Which instrument?

There are many evaluation instruments to choose from, but the most popular are observations, questionnaires and individual or group interviews. Unfortunately no method is perfect, but an overview of the main methods including their strengths and weaknesses is provided in Table 26.3.

Table 26.3. *Overview of the main methods of evaluation*

Method	Advantages	Disadvantages
Observation	Suitable for collecting data related to behaviour	Subjects may change their behaviour if they are aware they are being observed
	Works well when subjects are involved in an interaction and unable to provide objective opinions	Potential for observer bias or difference in interpretation between observers
		Difficult to observe and record simultaneously
Questionnaire	Less expensive than interviewing Convenient Greater anonymity Can be distributed in a number of ways	Must be well designed Inappropriate for use with some groups, e.g. young children Self-selecting bias Not possible to clarify or explain questions Not enjoyable for participants
Interview	Appropriate for complex situations as collection of in-depth information is possible Responses can be probed further, questions can be explained	Potential for interviewer bias Requires skill on the part of the interviewer Time-consuming and expensive
Focus group	Very rich source of data Allows group interactions to be observed as well as opinions gathered	Requires skill on the part of the interviewer as group dynamic is crucial to collecting useful data

There are a large number of textbooks on the market that specialise in survey and interview design. Some are recommended in the **Key resources** at the end of this chapter. The next sections give a brief overview of questionnaire and interview design.

Questionnaire design

The key to effective questionnaire design is knowing exactly what you want to find out. Base your questionnaire on your evaluation questions and the outcomes you identified earlier. The **purpose** and **structure** of your questionnaire are important, as is the **wording** of the questions.

Purpose The questionnaire should always start with a brief sentence or two explaining the purpose of the questionnaire. A questionnaire is only as good as the questions it contains so ask yourself what you will do with the information each question yields. If you are unsure of the answer, consider removing the question. The aim is to end up with the smallest number of questions that can be answered quickly, but in a questionnaire that still provides the important information for your evaluation. Keeping it brief will encourage more people to answer your questionnaire and will encourage them to do so thoughtfully. The commonest 'mistake' is to keep on adding questions that it would be 'nice to know' without thinking whether they are really necessary.

Structure Your questionnaire should have a clear structure and questions dealing with similar aspects of the activity should be grouped together. Try and start with questions that participants will find easier to answer, such as why they came to the event or what their experience was like. This will ease your respondent into some potentially more probing questions about outcomes for them later.

It is often a good idea to ask personal information such as the respondent's age and ethnicity at the end of the questionnaire as these types of questions can put people off at the start. However, this information is important and if the questionnaire is too long respondents may not have the time to complete it.

Also, think about whether you will use closed form (multiple choice) or open form (where the respondent writes their response) items. Essentially, open-form items can tell you what the impacts of the programme are, while closed-form items will tell you how big each impact is, or how many people experienced it. If badly designed, closed-form items can skew data by not representing respondents' true range of opinions. This can also be frustrating for those completing the questionnaire, so closed-form items should only be used when you have a clear idea of what the potential responses will be. Open-form items, on the other hand, allow respondents complete freedom to report any opinions or impacts. However, using open form means that you have to develop a system for coding the responses and it will take much longer to enter the data into a spreadsheet and make sense of it in your report.

Wording Appropriate wording of questionnaire items is important in order to minimise bias in the questionnaire, i.e. leading people to answer one way or another. Here are a few points to guide you:

- Make sure materials are balanced, e.g. offer space for respondents to give both positive and negative feedback.
- Question wording should be non-leading, e.g. *'Please tell us whether or not the event was helpful and why'* is better than *'Do you agree that the event was helpful?'*
- A question should ask about a single issue and not be 'double' or 'multiply barrelled' by including more than one.
- If you can, make the questionnaires anonymous to elicit more honest feedback. Verbally pointing out that feedback is anonymous and you are interested in receiving balanced feedback can help reduce bias, as can ensuring forms are handed back to an evaluator who is not identifiable as a member of the core project team.
- Materials should be easy to complete, i.e. consider layout and instructions.
- All evaluation instruments should be piloted with a small group of people whenever possible before use to ensure that questions are easy to understand and that questionnaires and interviews are not too long or too short.

An example questionnaire is provided as an appendix to this chapter.

Interviews and focus groups

Interviews have been described by evaluators as conversations with a purpose. They are a very flexible and valuable evaluation technique.

Structured interviews collect data in an identical way for every interviewer, so the interview schedule (a guide that is used by the interviewer) can look very similar to a questionnaire. Structured interviews are a good way of collecting data when questionnaires are not appropriate, e.g. from those with poor written skills, or to achieve a random sample of participants.

Semi-structured interviews have a set of similar questions at the core of each interview, but the interviewer is free to move the questions around as he or she sees fit. The interviewer would also encourage respondents to expand on their answers and digress to include other relevant points. Semi-structured interviews are a useful way to collect quantitative and qualitative data at the same time.

Unstructured interviews are completely open-ended. The interviewer may note down a few topics of interest beforehand, but there is no formal interview schedule. The idea of the interview is to allow the respondent to define the situation and their opinions in their own words, so these types of interviews can be very useful at the start of an evaluation to help identify evaluation questions.

Group interviews (focus groups) typically bring together six to ten participants for a discussion around a particular topic, or set of topics. Respondents are encouraged to explain and qualify opinions, which can spark ideas from others in the group. For this reason, focus groups can provide a very rich source of information. It is important to select group members carefully: a diverse range of opinions is desirable, but some may feel intimidated and not speak up. Facilitators should ensure the discussion is not dominated by any individual, and should seek to bring out opinions from quieter group members. Flashcards and other exercises can be used to stimulate discussion.

Interview technique is a skill that can only really be developed through practice. A good interview should feel like an interesting chat between interviewer and interviewee. Try and encourage your interviewee to tell stories and give examples. Here are a few tips:

Do:

- Explain who you are and what the interview is for.
- Develop a rapport with the interviewee and show you're interested in their opinions.
- Ask questions clearly and clarify if necessary.
- Listen carefully so you can expand on relevant points. Make sure you know enough about the evaluation to ask good follow-up questions. It can be useful to prepare these in advance.
- Use non-leading probes like *'Could you tell me a bit more about that?'* or *'Why do you think you feel that way?'*

Don't:

- Feel you need to stick to the interview schedule: explore interesting issues as they arise.
- Ask leading questions or let your opinions come into the interview.
- Repeat exactly a question that you have already asked, rephrase it instead or drop it if you don't get a response.
- Do too much talking – you will know your interview is going well if your interviewee is doing most of the talking.

It is useful to record interviews (make sure you gain consent from your interviewee first) as you can then concentrate on interviewing rather than taking notes. There are many cheap, effective and unobtrusive small digital recorders now which can be put on the table during an interview or focus group discussion and played back through your computer. Take the opportunity to listen to the recording and reflect on your interviewing technique to help you improve.

Other data collection techniques

Questionnaires and interviews are not the only options when it comes to collecting data for your evaluation. You may like to think about incorporating some of the following more creative techniques:

- Electronic surveys or electronic voting to gather audience opinions.
- Using a graffiti wall, comment cards or 'post-it' notes during or at the end of an event as a lighter alternative to a questionnaire.
- Collecting 'vox pops' (short quotes) from audience members using a video camera or voice recorder, or giving audience members the camera and asking them to record their experiences.
- Having young children draw you a picture about their experience.
- Incorporating data collection into your activity, for example asking audience members to write down ideas about a topic near the start of a session and using these to stimulate discussion, then repeating as a reflection at the end to look at changes.
- Posing questions to an audience, who respond by lining up across the room on a scale of 'agree' to 'disagree'.
- Dropping pebbles in labelled boxes or using stickers and charts.

Mixing methods within the same evaluation can provide a range of perspectives on the success of your activity. This type of triangulation is useful to check whether the different sources of evidence are telling the same story about your project.

Sampling

The way you select your sample for the evaluation has a strong influence on the validity of your results. The sample will also determine, to some extent, the nature of your questions. For example, in an ideal research scenario participants would complete questionnaires both before and after an activity. In practice this is rarely feasible unless you have a generous amount of time to spend on evaluation. So you may wish to ask a question such as *'Before this activity, how would you rate your level of interest in. . .'*, or look at other ways of assessing baseline levels of interest (for example talking to the teacher of a school group or asking an event/venue organiser what they know about their regular audiences).

It is important that your sample is as unbiased as possible. A self-selected sample will usually include those with strongest opinions about the programme (either positive or negative) because those who were indifferent are not motivated enough to give feedback. Questionnaire evaluations are particularly susceptible to this, although it can be avoided. Instead of leaving questionnaires out to be completed by those who wish to do so, either ensure everyone completes a questionnaire or randomly select a sample of the audience to complete them, perhaps offering a small incentive or even just by asking nicely and explaining how important feedback is to you.

As a guideline, a quantitative evaluation will need a sample of 35 to 500. This figure could rise to 1000 if you are planning to use statistical analyses to explore relationships between subgroups in the sample, although this is well beyond the scope of most science communicators' own evaluations. It may however be possible (and is desirable) to involve someone with social science research methodology experience to help. If you are running an activity that involves a small number of participants, a full census sample (i.e. asking everyone) is a good way to avoid bias.

For qualitative work, much smaller samples are needed. Between 5 and 20 individuals or groups are usually sufficient. It is not possible to be representative in the same way as with quantitative work, so the individuals involved should be selected to include those with the widest-ranging experiences or opinions.

Ethics

Evaluators have a duty to conduct all research with an ethic of respect for the participants, and to ensure that findings are as robust and unbiased as possible. The British Educational Research Association's *Revised Ethical Guidelines for Educational Research* (2004) are a good guide in this area. They cover researchers' responsibilities to participants, sponsors and other researchers.

As well as taking an ethical approach to the evaluation overall, it is essential to comply with relevant legislation such as the Data Protection Act (1998) if in the UK or similar legislation elsewhere and legal requirements in relation to working with young people and vulnerable adults. If you are based at a university or research organisation you are likely to need approval from your ethics committee ahead of conducting evaluation fieldwork.

6   ENTERING, ANALYSING AND REPORTING ON YOUR DATA

Quantitative data

The easiest way to enter data is into a spreadsheet so that each row corresponds to one respondent. If you have used questionnaires or structured interviews, number each paper questionnaire or interview schedule. This will give you a unique code and will allow you to double-check responses later if necessary. If your questionnaire/interview included some open items, you can enter them into the spreadsheet in the relevant row. You can then compare responses to the closed and open items. Electronic survey software allows you to download your feedback in a spreadsheet format, removing the need to enter the data manually.

With the data entered, you can calculate frequencies and create charts to present the quantitative data. If you are using Excel, the PivotTable function is a useful way of cross-tabulating responses. More advanced analysis can be performed in statistical packages such as SPSS (Statistical Package for the Social Sciences, since 2009 called PASW (Predictive Analytics SoftWare) then changed again in 2010 to be called SPSS Statistics).

Qualitative data

Qualitative data is less straightforward. When analysing such data, look to identify common themes in the responses: a process known as 'coding' the responses. A simple way to do this is category analysis, which involves grouping similar responses into categories, then counting up the number of responses in each. Category analysis works well for open questionnaire items or open items in a semi-structured interview. If your responses are very brief (for example if respondents are asked to give their impressions of the activity in three words) you could present the findings visually in a 'word cloud' using free software such as www.wordle.net

If you have interview or focus group data, you may have hand-written notes or a typed transcript instead of columns in spreadsheets. If this is the case, take a photocopy of the originals to use while coding the responses. If possible, leave a wide margin on one side of the page to note down thoughts or ideas. You can write notes in the margins then organise these into codes, or use different-coloured highlighters to identify different themes, or cut up the (photocopied) document and organise the slips of paper into piles.

With qualitative analysis, you can code in as much or as little detail as you like (or have the time for). It works well to read through data briefly first, getting an idea of the big picture, then coming back to certain ideas again later if you get the chance.

Dealing with too much data

It is easy to get carried away with evaluation and collect large amounts of data that would take an unrealistically long time to analyse. The first thing to do in this situation is prioritise. Go back to your evaluation questions and identify a few key pieces of information from your feedback that will help answer them. You can then put the rest of the feedback to one side (and remember to use briefer instruments next time) or save it to come back to in future.

Reporting

Reporting is a crucial stage in your evaluation as you complete the 'reflection' part of Kolb's (1984) cycle and review what worked, what didn't and – most importantly – what you would do differently next time. It may not seem important to write up all the details of the evaluation if the project was a one-off, but it is essential to capture learning at this stage. If it is not reported it gets lost, meaning that you and other science communicators miss the opportunity to learn from your mistakes and build on your successes.

The easiest way to write a report is to work through the items in an interview schedule for example, reporting on findings in each. A better way is to theme the report sections according to your evaluation questions or intended outcomes, drawing on several sources of evidence for each. Report the findings as neutrally as possible in the main body of the report, then discuss them in a concluding section. Presenting quantitative data in graphs, bar or pie charts helps to make it easier for readers to see any trends you describe. Analysis of qualitative data should include plenty of quotes to help illustrate the themes you have identified. You may also wish to make recommendations for future projects based on the findings.

Increasingly, there are a number of arenas in which to share evaluations (by talking to colleagues, publishing through your own website, through the British Science Association's 'collective memory' database, or of course in academic journals).

By sharing evaluations across the science communication community we can develop more sophisticated answers to that tricky question: *'So did it work?'*

Key resources

Books

There are many books out there on research methods which can equally well be applied to evaluation. Have a look at the following:

- **Kumar R** (1996) *Research Methodology: A Step-by-Step Guide for Beginners.* London: Sage.
- **Weiss CH** (1972) *Evaluation Research.* Englewood Cliffs, NJ: Prentice Hall.
- **Chen HT** (1990) *Theory-Driven Evaluations.* Thousand Oaks, CA: Sage.
- Or have a browse through the journal *Evaluation* (Sage).

Guides

Alternatively, there are several guides that have been written specifically for those involved in public engagement:

- RCUK Evaluation: practical guidelines www.rcuk.ac.uk/ aboutrcuk/publications/corporate/evaluationguide.htm
- Ingenious evaluation toolkit (includes evaluation guide, FAQs and useful links) www.raeng.org.uk/societygov/ public_engagement/ingenious/evaluation.htm

Websites

- UK Evaluation Society www.evaluation.org.uk
- British Science Association collective memory www.collectivememory.britishscienceassociation.org
- Information Commissioner's Office (1998) *Data Protection Act* www.ico.gov.uk/what_we_cover/data_protection.aspx

- International Development Research Centre *Outcome Mapping* www.idrc.ca/en/ev-26586-201-1-DO_TOPIC.html
- Actknowledge www.theoryofchange.org

References

Actknowledge   www.theoryofchange.org   <http://www.theoryofchange.org/> (accessed 14 June 2010)

British Educational Research Association (2004) *Revised Ethical Guidelines for Educational Research.* www.bera.ac.uk/publications/guidelines/ (accessed 14 June 2010)

British Science Association evaluation database www.britishscienceassociation. org/forms/scicomm/evaluation/access (accessed 18 June 2010)

Chen HT (1990) *Theory-Driven Evaluations.* Thousand Oaks, CA: Sage.

Grant L and Jenkins S (2009) *Project Management Workbook.* London: Laura Grant Associates.

Grant L and Paterson L (2008) Ingenious evaluation planning template.

Information Commissioner's Office (1998) Data Protection Act http://www.ico.gov.uk/what_we_cover/data_protection.aspx <http://www.ico. gov.uk/what_we_cover/data_protection.aspx%20accessed%2014%20june% 202010> (accessed 14 June 2010)

International Development Research Centre Outcome Mapping http://www.idrc. ca/en/ev-26586-201-1-DO_TOPIC.html (accessed 14 June 2010)

Kolb DA (1984) *Experiential Learning: Experience as the Source of Learning and Development.* Englewood Cliffs, NJ: Prentice Hall.

Museums, Libraries and Archives Council (2008) *Inspiring Learning for All Framework.* www.mla.gov.uk (accessed 14 June 2010)

Rossi PH and Freeman HE (1989) *Evaluation: A Systematic Approach*, 4th edn. Thousand Oaks, CA: Sage.

UK Evaluation Society (2010) www.evaluation.org.uk (accessed 14 June 2010)

Wordle www.wordle.net (accessed 14 June 2010)

APPENDIX

What do you think about the science event?

Please take a few moments to tell us your thoughts on today's event. Your comments will help us improve future activities, so please be completely honest. Thanks!

1. Please write down **three words** that describe the event

2. Please circle the face that describes your opinion:

What did you think of the event overall?	Good	☺	☺	☹	Bad
Do you think you will **continue to discuss** science after the event?	Definitely will	☺	☺	☹	Definitely won't
Before the event, **how much did you know about science?**	I knew lots	☺	☺	☹	I knew nothing
How much do you think you have **learned about science** from the event?	I learned lots	☺	☺	☹	I learned nothing

3. Please tell us. . .

What you enjoyed **most** about the event:	What you enjoyed **least**, or what could be improved:

4. Did you **learn something new** at the event? If so, what?

5. Has the event changed how you **feel about science and engineering?**

More interested   ☺   ☺   ☹   Less interested

6. Please tell us why or why not:

```
┌─────────────────────────────────────────────────────┐
│                                                     │
│                                                     │
│                                                     │
└─────────────────────────────────────────────────────┘
```

7. Do you think any of this **relates to your own life**? Why or why not?

```
┌─────────────────────────────────────────────────────┐
│                                                     │
│                                                     │
│                                                     │
└─────────────────────────────────────────────────────┘
```

8. Do you have any other comments about the event?

```
┌─────────────────────────────────────────────────────┐
│                                                     │
│                                                     │
│                                                     │
└─────────────────────────────────────────────────────┘
```

9. What is **your age**?

    ☐ Under 16 (please tell us)   ☐ 16–25   ☐ 26–35   ☐ 36–45

    . . . .   ☐ 46–55   ☐ 56–65   ☐ 66+

10. What is **your gender**?

    ☐ Male   ☐ Female   **Thanks!**

27

Effectively embedding science communication in academia: a second paradigm shift?

INTRODUCTION

We know a great deal more now about the reasons for science communication and its effectiveness than when the Bodmer Report came out in 1985. Today scientists play an important role in all forms of public engagement, but have we internalised this effectively into our universities? And if not, how do we do so? This is the key question for this chapter. Universities recognise the ever-increasing need for showing and discussing the value of science and technology for society. So you would expect they are keen to support their scientists' efforts in science communication. And they certainly do, but demands are huge and competition for funding has made universities as research and teaching institutions into businesses in their own right. We still struggle with linking the scientists' praiseworthy but individual activities into our organisations' science communication efforts. We struggle to explain where we stand: are we a business institution, tainted by the industry money that is poured into research or can we maintain an 'objective' and critical point of view about science and its worth for society? Can we indeed build and maintain a trust relationship with the public? Are relations with the wider public shaped by collaboration with industry and others with financial and/or political interests? How *do* we maintain authenticity and trustworthiness?

A *second paradigm shift* for science communication is clearly needed – one in which scientists are encouraged by their professional academic institutions to strengthen and streamline their efforts in science communication and incorporate it into organisation policy – a

Successful Science Communication, ed. D. J. Bennett and R. C. Jennings. Published by Cambridge University Press. © Cambridge University Press 2011.

policy which provides a coherent approach to science communication throughout the university. Moreover, the science communication policy must manage the distinction between science communication for the *deliberative sharing* of scientific knowledge, and for the *instrumental promotion* of science – a distinction which is discussed by Alfred Nordmann in Chapter 7. Finally, the policy must be *communal* in the sense that not only are the scientists involved but so also are all the other staff of the organisation. The *communal science communication* policy must correspond to the mission of the university as an organisation and link individual science communication activities with the role of the university in society. Ideally such a policy will build trust and support the fruitful development of science and technology for society. However this *is* an ideal, and hopefully will be realised by policy, but it *cannot* simply be accomplished by making it 'a matter of policy' and will need communal commitment and effort to implement in practice.

During the last 25 years science communication has undergone its first paradigm shift – a shift in which scientists have searched for engagement with various audiences. Scientists can be seen again as 'normal people' busy with interesting things. But it has also made science vulnerable to outside eyes by revealing its fundamental uncertainty and economic dependency which often leads to polarisation of viewpoints, not infrequently based on non-scientific arguments. The second paradigm shift has to overcome this by embedding science communication in academic practice while paying attention to academic values such as scientific quality, integrity and transparency. This will require changes in our thinking about science communication, changes in the relations between scientists, institutional managers and professional communicators, and it will need a more critical focus on the goals of communication.

TIME FOR A SECOND PARADIGM SHIFT

The Bodmer Report clearly argued for a broader engagement of scientists in various ways but it did not pay a great deal of attention to embedding science communication in the organisation. We witnessed the increase in these activities in all fields of science by those who were willing to take on board Sir Walter and his committee's message. Funding for activities, often 'one-off', was often available and we learned a number of important things about what worked, and what didn't, and why. But the very purpose of these activities was often left implicit or was even neglected by organisers, or only vaguely referred to as 'explaining science and technology', or 'engaging people in science and technology to show how wonderfully amazing it all is'. What we lacked, at least until recently, was good, constructive discussion of the goals of science communication, but missing entirely was how we should effectively embed these new tasks for scientists in their organisations.

So where do we stand today? In the current academic enterprise we see large numbers of scientists who operate relatively autonomously in their daily endeavours. Although often more loyal to their (inter) national peers in their research community than to their university, they still depend on their university's fundamental reputation, a reputation that is built on the *combined* acquisition, production and reputation of its scientific staff. Influenced by the context in which it is operating, university management sets out the larger directions, the master plan for the institution. Periodically it decides on new fields to be developed and invested in, and those which need to be reorganised or even closed to maximise the institution's quality and standing in the longer term. Most universities maintain a marketing and communication department which is responsible for promoting the university to attract students, publicising its research and providing information for the media about its significant scientific discoveries and technological developments. This is the instrumental aspect of university science communication but it can be seen as consistent with the search for, and communication of, truth. Meanwhile the pressure to incorporate novel ways of science communication into its research programmes continues. This tendency continues to grow as large funding organisations, including the European Commission, require greater efforts to involve the wider public in research and development decisions. At the same time the changing relations between science and society as described by Gibbons (1999) in *Nature* and others require a more democratic process for defining research agendas. The university of today is depicted ideally as a trustworthy, transparent and integrated organisation. So the challenge is to:

(1) combine the autonomous scientist's communication with the agenda of the university *and* the scientific community;
(2) align the individual scientist's public interactive activities with the communications policy of the university;
(3) provide a transparent institution in which agenda setting of research is, in so far as is possible, a democratic process based on the values and norms described by Alfred Nordmann as 'communicative' (or 'deliberative') action.

And that, clearly, is not easy! It involves the integration of very different communication practices from the level of the individual scientist to that of the university as a whole, changing long-established customs and introducing novel forms of interaction. Plainly, a second paradigm shift towards *a communal science communication* for universities is necessary to fully integrate and align these objectives.

And while the heat is on, the demands on scientists to increase their efforts in these directions are also fully felt. But there is hope because, significantly, most of these constraints are actually related to the infrastructural arrangements of the university, providing not only a need for them to be addressed but also the hope that effective institutionalisation can and will indeed achieve results.

THE NEED FOR COMMUNAL SCIENCE COMMUNICATION

It is a truism that today's researchers are faced with ever-increasing acceleration and complexity of specialisation together with ever-continuing convergence of disciplines such as physics, biology and information technology into such as nano- and synthetic biology and the neurosciences. At the same time the global market in which science operates is characterised by the limitless stream of information and accompanying increasing complexity, and decrease in options for, its effective governance. The global challenges to which science is expected to contribute solutions are complex both in scientific terms as well as in social, economic and ethical demands. We need solutions for the effects of climate change that are more sustainable, we need more efficient food production for a growing world population and adequate measures to meet the challenges of poverty and disease in less-developed countries. The ageing populations of Western societies and the rapidly growing ones of less-developed economies require urgent responses to changing demographic demands.

Universities are seen as providers of the solutions. They need to report on the progress of their sciences and technologies and, more than ever before, orientate their research agendas to prioritise the most pressing questions. Science communication plays a crucial role in this relatively novel and recent relationship between science and society. To enable the provision of effective solutions, universities need to be trusted as institutions requiring the collaboration and coordination of individual scientists and their organisations. At the same time the same universities have become businesses in themselves. Competition for students and for research funds and deriving value from intellectual property has transformed universities into businesses. This is the challenge: producing 'glossies' to 'keep the business going' while encouraging open debate on the truth-seeking nature of the enterprise to maintain its status in society. And, above all, with as many publics as possible!

Individually scientists have responded to the challenge of creating novel ways of engaging with the general public – as is very well demonstrated by the many examples described in the earlier chapters of this book. But these activities need to be much more strongly embedded in the communication strategies and practices of their organisations in order, ultimately, to support the policy goals of individual scientists *and* their institutions. Scientists need the backing of their organisations and their organisations need to rely on the collaboration of their staffs. Differences and divergences all too easily lead to lack of trust and embarrassment with major international repercussions, as seen in cases such as Pusztai and the Roslin Institute over GM potatoes (Rampton and Stauber, 2001) and the more recent IPCC climate change debacle discussed by Andrew Revkin in his Chapter 9 on 'Tackling the climate communication challenge' and Tollefson in *Nature* (2010).

An integrated approach to science communication can reinforce the links between science, society, industry and academia. However, different organisations have different core values – universities value the pursuit of truth, industry the pursuit of profits. Hence, as we said at the outset, any such approach must involve managing the distinction between science communication for the deliberative sharing of scientific knowledge and for the instrumental promotion of science by industry and other sections of society. The overall university's science communication aim is to build trust by being open (transparent) and accountable, and by providing input to the process of research agenda setting. This requires close attention to the social, ethical and legal values and issues related to the research and development process. And, crucially, these objectives can only be realised by the genuine engagement of students, scientists, management and administrative staff in their social networks within the organisation and beyond. University strategy therefore requires a focus on identity, image and trustworthiness going far beyond individual activities by linking novel forms of public engagement rationally with traditional channels of mass communication. This strategic endeavour for the academic institution as a joined-up body or 'corpus' can be seen as *communal science communication*: an integrated and aligned communication approach based on shared values and aims while at the same time providing clarity on its desire to attract students and collaboration with industry.

WHAT CAN WE LEARN FROM GENERAL CORPORATE
COMMUNICATION PRACTICES?

Corporate communication is generally recognised to refer to *business* corporations, although other organisations such as the Red Cross have corporate communication policies and departments. So the term 'corporate communication', at least from the point of view of a practice, is used more widely than in solely the business context. However, to avoid any ambiguity in the discussion in this chapter the term *communal science communication* is used. And in contrast to corporate communication, communal science communication is certainly not a very well researched area. According to Van Riel and Fombrun (2007, p. 25), for example, corporate communication is:

> the set of activities involved in managing and orchestrating all internal and external communications aimed at creating favourable starting points with stakeholders on which the company depends. Corporate communication consists of the dissemination of information by a variety of specialists and generalists in an organisation, with the common goal of enhancing the organisation's ability to retain its licence to operate.

Corporate communication is an instrumental communication approach based on the idea that processes and messages at both the work floor and board levels are integrated. The processes and messages all contain the same core values and messages of the organisation. As Van Riel and Fombrun (2007, p. 9) also state:

> A strategic focus on what we call the total communication system [emphasis by original authors] is the only way to overcome the existing fragmentation of communications in most organisations. By developing an integrated communication system, an organisation can flesh out a structure for corporate communication that can assist in the implementation of strategic objectives, build brand and reputation, and thereby create economic value.

Communication therefore has to be embedded throughout the entire organisation. Even more so, it needs to be *owned* and *carried* by the whole organisation. Everyone needs to know and support the core mission and objectives so tasks can be divided to bring these objectives to the outside world. In this view communication is a condition for the organisational, i.e. the social and financial, well-being of the institution.

Communal science communication takes the same concepts of corporate communication into account but starts from the ethical values and principles discussed above which are attached to the university's deliberative sharing of information. This practically works out into various kinds of events, press relations, contacts with stake- and share-holders, and individual and institutional dealings that become part of the *organisation's* overall strategic communication plan. All need to be in tune and contribute to the communal standing and reputation. This makes the organisation and its members more effective in achieving their aims and enhancing their values on a personal, group and organisation level. The important questions now are *'How to support the scientist in his field to drive communication activities which are part of this communal perspective?'* and *'How to embed this undoubtedly complex process in the research organisation?'* And in short, the answers require both a bottom–up and a top–down approach.

CHALLENGES FOR COMMUNAL SCIENCE COMMUNICATION

As Simon Lock points out in his Chapter 1, advocacy, knowledge broker-ing and other novel (post-Bodmer) modes of science communication (such as dialogue) do indeed need different skills and competences. But is the development of these skills and competences provided and encouraged in the organisation? Michel Claessens (Chapter 8 and 2008) argues that the science–society dialogue is still insufficiently developed because a genuine communication culture is lacking in the science and technology sector. *'While communication of every kind is on everyone's lips, we are still far from the genuinely "intelligent" communication promised by the advent of the "knowledge society".'* (Claessens, 2008, p. 36).

Several problems immediately come to the fore. The first relates to the competences and skills of the individual scientist. Once scientists reach outside their laboratory they immediately enter a quite different realm in which their specific scientific knowledge has to be related to non-scientific policy or social issues. Public policy issues always have dimensions beyond science, and require more than technical responses as has been pointed out by Brian Wynne (2010): *'If the many factors that go into a policy commitment are recognized, science does not become the sole centre of authority and the sole target for opposition.'* This means for the scientists that they need to know and understand these issues, have formed opinions about them and have skills and competences to deal with this boundary process between science and society (Wynne, 1995; Osseweijer, 2006; Van der Sanden, 2008). Institutionalisation of science communication therefore also requires adequate reflection on, and training in, communi-cating about these issues by the university. In many universities scientists can obtain in-house training in writing and presentation skills, etc. But it is important that these skills and competences are meaningful in the complex context of ethical, social, economical and legal policy issues, and that the position of the scientist is linked to the overall strategic view of the university. But it is equally important that scientists are encouraged to take up these skills and are rewarded tangibly when they do so. The many tasks of the scientist in a university compete for time and attention. If training and communicating is not encouraged, it will not easily be taken on. Bottom–up activities by enthusiastic individual scientists need to be supported and also valued on their merits toward the communal communication plan before they are linked with top–down strategies.

The trustworthiness of the organisation and of the individual scientist, and the coordination of the two, is the second challenge to achieving communal science communication. The effects of climate change and vaccination programmes, for example, have become subjects for national and international debate. The putative failure of the IPCC and its email 'scandal' in November 2009 effectively became a discussion about the trustworthiness of science. Scientists need to be able to deliberate about uncertainty, as for example John Adams illustrates in his Chapter 6, 'Not 100% sure? The "public" understanding of risk'. In *Nature* Tollefson (2010) argued that public trust must be the scientific community's top priority. Borchelt (2008) called it the 'trust portfolio': the principal relationships that exist between the organisation and its many stakeholders. Within this portfolio important components include competence, integrity and dependability. According to Borchelt (2008, p. 156),

> Public relations is a strategic function of a successful organisation, as well as a tactical one. Too many scientific organisations see only the tactical value of PR, and are content to manage it through the human resources department, through laboratory administration, or through some other programme not at all connected functionally to PR.

So public relations is a function of entire organisations, not just of science communicators. We do not know of many studies about this function in the science communication field. What we do know is that it concerns more than just dialogue and engagement as it also relates to trust portfolios, positioning and branding. And that scientists' activities are influencing the public profiles of institutions, and this urgently needs to be evaluated and coordinated.

We have seen progressive increase in scientists' public presence in a variety of advisory, consultative, expert witness, debating, media and other roles in which they present opinions and views. Some claim that the opinions are often only loosely linked with proven findings (Peters, 2008; Trench, 2008) and that scientists are increasingly viewed as acting as advocates in their own political cause. In *Communicating Science in Social Contexts: New Models, New Practices,* Cascoigne (2008) refers to this new role of scientists as *'science advocacy'*. The primary motivation for the scientist's advocacy is seen as self-interested desire to maintain or increase funding. Cascoigne claims that despite a voiced reluctance to undertake lobbying activities, scientists have seen that they must engage with policy-makers, industry and other (even competing) scientists if they wish to maintain their influence on the research agenda and on funding. Increase in research funding from industry has also put strain on the perceived 'objectivity' of the individual scientist. According to Miedema (2009) the persona of a scientist as 'gentleman' is substituted by a much more business-like attitude. In such an attitude trust, accountability and reliability play an important role. So in addition to information about scientific development (the classical science communication), involvement and dialogue on the impact of science and technology on society is introduced. And this influences the trustworthiness and profile of the academic institution. The relative positioning of the scientist, science, society and the market is no longer taken for granted. It is changing constantly depending on the context. And this of course raises the question of whether the two forms of science communication – non-instrumental and instrumental – really can be kept separate, whether universities really can be credited with a pure interest in truth and companies solely motivated by profit. This is not new, as Gieryn already observed in 1983: *'Thus "science" is no single thing: its boundaries are drawn and redrawn in flexible, historically changing and sometimes ambiguous ways'* (Gieryn 1983, p. 781). But it is a key factor to be taken into account when linking individual scientists' communication into a communal science communication strategy.

Communal science communication of a university integrates issues in society, industry and science and aims to support the university as a coherent and consistent trustworthy partner. This also means, as Nordmann discusses in his Chapter 7, that well-designed experiments that fail to confirm hypotheses but give insight into the scientific process and its considerations are also part of the communication process. Its objective is to create and maintain a strong position (including being trustworthy, productive in research, good at teaching, socially sensitive, etc.) for the university and the individual researcher in the research and higher education market and to create and maintain a robust, integrated and credible position in society as a whole. To achieve this position *aims* (communal, departmental and individual), *functions* (deliberative communication and marketing) and the required *skills and competences* (scientist, communication professional) need to be embedded and coordinated in the organisation.

In summary, scientists and their organisations need to agree on the core goals of communal science communication, the development of communication competences and the integration of values (such as integrity and transparency) as an integral part of the organisation. Bottom–up initiatives need to be connected with top–down strategies and they need to be aligned to provide the unique profile of the academic institution. In this sense it is important to consider now the possible barriers for alignment and integration of the university's communal science communication.

BARRIERS TO COMMUNAL SCIENCE COMMUNICATION

We have already said that effective institutionalisation of science communication needs to be built with initiatives coming from both the bottom up and from the top down. Let us first focus on the bottom–up approach. In their analysis of the Wellcome Trust (2000) study on the involvement of scientists in communication Poliakoff and Webb (2007) point to the finding that 84% of scientists agreed that scientists have a duty to communicate their research findings to the public and that 56% want to spend more time on science communication activities. On the other hand, Bos (2010) found that despite the importance of science communication, scientists feel there is in fact a (perceived) lack of time and (expected) 'low profit on return' so it seems that practical barriers outweigh potential benefits. Moreover, Poliakoff and Webb (2007) conclude from their research on the intentions of scientists to participate in public engagement activities that scientists' decision not to participate is related to the following observations:

(1) they have not participated in the past;
(2) they have a negative attitude toward participation;
(3) they feel that they lack the skills to take part; and
(4) they do not believe that their colleagues participate in public engagement activities.

As the authors say, contrary to expected research outcomes, factors such as time constraints, money constraints, and (lack of) career recognition did not influence participation intentions very much. Similarly to Poliakoff and Webb, Van der Auweraert (2008) found that explanations for the science communication behaviour of researchers were first and foremost in 'willingness', 'permission' and 'ability'. She concluded the problem to be rather complex and that 'simply' focusing on external or internal barriers is clearly not enough. She advised paying closer attention to the personality of the researcher, and particularly to their perception of scientific research and their attitudes towards their profession and the tasks it entails. This could be achieved by adopting a much more bottom-up *coaching role* to support the scientist. Such a supportive role needs to be sustained by the institution's communal science communication policy and strategy.

A top–down approach establishing a profound communal science communication programme needs to relate science with society and with industry, and to combine integrity with social benefit and with commercial success, of the university, industry and society as a whole. Patricia Osseweijer (2006) has analysed a number of constraints on scientists in science communication processes from a more organisa-tional point of view. She suggested that the barriers to institutionali-sation of profound public science communication are:

(1) the lack of a strategy to determine and define which activities can be best organised and how;
(2) the financial allocation procedures of universities that focus mainly on scientific output rather than on output that is related to social impact.

Osseweijer also recognises that current changes in society affect interaction between science and society and therefore require change in scientists' roles. She wonders whether the researcher's capacity to reflect on their own work is perhaps the most crucial competence required to achieve this change. Reflection on their own research needs to relate to their own views about the potential applications of their science as a citizen, consumer or patient. She advises universities to:

(1) link science communication to university policies and strategies;
(2) include the task of science communication in the university (financial or goal-oriented) allocation system;
(3) implement appropriate training and reflection in curricula and departments; and
(4) select and reward personnel for public interaction skills.

The *Science for All* Expert Group (2010) published a report and action plan which is in line with the ideas raised by Osseweijer. This report on public engagement discusses the embedding of public engagement within institutions. The authors state, in line with what we have found, that public engagement is still not regarded strategically, or as of strategic importance, by many organisations. Their action plan provides similar and some additional points to those which Osseweijer advised, and include:

(1) embedding public engagement within institutional structures and processes;

(2) ensuring all researchers and practitioners have access to training for public engagement;

(3) including public engagement competencies within continuing professional development frameworks;

(4) improving understanding of mechanisms to recognise public engagement activities;

(5) ensuring that funders of the sciences have mechanisms in place to support and recognise public engagement;

(6) demonstrating public engagement on an institutional level;

(7) recognising by rewarding individuals who undertake public engagement;

(8) promoting successful knowledge exchange between the sciences, policy and business.

The picture for communal science communication is now emerging. It is no longer only about skills such as in media relations but also about genuine knowledge about communication, branding, positioning, identity, image and its overarching science communication management. It requires an awareness of communication goals and of the research and education market from a socially responsible perspective as well as from a commercial perspective. These are divergent aims and the challenge for communal science communication is to combine these perspectives in aligned communication processes in which the scientist, the group and the university as a whole participate. It engages in both deliberative and instrumental communication, and individual and communal communication. Both processes must be clearly distinguished by the communicator who must be clearly transparent in her or his aims to either engage and inform on the science or to promote it instrumentally. It must lead to a professional culture that values, recognises and supports public engagement as an essential component of its overall academic mission. Following the issues Osseweijer and the Expert Group raise at the institutional level and the insight into constraints at the individual level, we propose an outline for a communal science communication policy and strategy leading to embedded communal science communication consisting of three interrelated steps:

Step 1: Linking science communication with university policies and strategies;
Step 2: Aligning motivation with incentives;
Step 3: Providing a learning culture for coordinated communal science communication.

Step 1: Linking science communication with university policies and strategies

In most universities science communication staff are responsible for the development and implementation of a science communication policy and strategy while the board of the university identifies its priorities for positioning of scientific priorities, curriculum, acquisition of new students and branding. After agreement on the science communication strategy, professionals work together with scientists and the board of the university on the agreed plan. Unfortunately, and all too often, these plans are only designed and agreed upon at the top and lack meaningful input from individual scientists from the bottom up. The result is a continuing negotiation process between communication professionals and scientists about involvement in activities which is not always productive. Similarly, individual scientists often commit to activities organised by their disciplinary colleagues in their (inter) national community networks without in the process involving principles of communal communication such as we have discussed. In addition, other forms of collaboration, including in European Commission consortia and (inter)national public–private partnerships, develop their own communication and branding policies, further confusing communal communication strategy. Measures need to be taken to also coordinate these activities as much as possible by providing advice and support to the individual scientists participating in these consortia. Another important aspect of aligning and building communal science communication is the mutual learning process. Learning tends presently to be carried out individually and in different environments, and not fed back at the organisational level. The organisation's active approach to incorporating these lessons into its science communication training and practices may well help to overcome this problem.

Such *coaching* of scientists in their expert role can be carried out by communal science communication professionals and is already beginning to be taken on board by them as their function changes. Meyer (2010, p. 118) talks about 'knowledge brokers: people whose job it is to move knowledge around and create connections between researchers and their various audiences'. A professional communication and marketing department could achieve further alignment by supporting scientists directly from this coaching perspective as well as from that of the already-existing training of communication skills. This links with the earlier observations of Simon Lock in Chapter 1 that, after 25 years of Bodmer, we recognise the differing skills and competences required for science communication. This kind of approach will align professionals with scientists in a new relationship of bringing different knowledge to the societal interaction. It will bring knowledge about the science and about the impact of science on society together with knowledge on how to best communicate this with the broader community in line with the communal goals of the organisation.

Step 2: Aligning motivation with incentives

The majority of scientists feel restricted in their wish to increase their level of interaction with society. Internal factors such as 'willingness', and to a certain extent 'permission', need to be reconciled with incentives for motivation that need to be implemented at the laboratory level. The lack of 'ability', which refers to more external constraints, can be addressed by the top–down approach such as proposed and outlined before.

Motivation can best be tackled at the bottom. As pointed out previously, insecurity about abilities to deal with science in its broader social, ethical, economic and political contexts can be helped by training in skills on the relations with, and impact of, science and technology on society, and by reflecting on them. And other measures can also be introduced to increase these skills in individual scientists and to motivate them to become involved. One such method is the so-called *midstream modulation* developed by Erik Fisher and further described by Schuurbiers and Fisher (2009; Fisher *et al.*, 2010). Midstream modulation aims to bring about collaborative engagement between social and natural scientists in the laboratory in order to broaden research decisions incrementally (Schuurbiers and Fisher, 2009). Awareness of societal impacts is created by discussion about the possible adjustment of decisions about research in the light of societal factors. This process takes place actively in the laboratory and Fisher has shown that it does not interfere with the soundness or productivity of research (Schuurbiers and Fisher, 2009; Fisher *et al.*, 2010). This method may also motivate scientists to become more involved in science communication as it develops their ability to review their own position in relation to their 'own science'.

There are of course many other incentives to encourage scientists to become involved in communal science communication. The *Imagine* school competition described in Chapter 25 is just one of the many examples described in the previous chapters. Other incentives to increase reflection are the constructive embedding of soft law such as codes of conduct (Schuurbiers *et al.*, 2009a) or provision of courses on bioethics (Schuurbiers *et al.*, 2009b). Another approach is to incorporate a research group which studies the ethical, social and legal impact of a department's scientific research on society in the science department as is done in the Department of Biotechnology of the Delft University of Technology and elsewhere. Continuing interaction on a close personal, day-to-day basis is then secured providing a natural learning environment for both natural and social scientists mutually. Insights into possible new arrangements for public involvement in the decision-making processes and methods for interactive (risk) communication and constructive technology assessment such as those introduced by Arie Rip and colleagues (Rip *et al.*, 1995) provide other complementary approaches at the university and disciplinary level.

Incentives to accommodate these motivational efforts need to focus on embedding the task of science communication in the fabric of the university and linking it to communal planning. Financial and/or goal-oriented allocation systems need to recognise and reward integrated science communication efforts and, at the same time, evaluate them and provide feedback for their adjustment so they can be optimally coordinated in support of the communal strategy. This, in turn, needs to be supported by appropriate appointment, assessment, career progression and funding allocation, procedures for new and established personnel in which public interaction skills are valued as important together with research and teaching skills. Other incentives for scientists can be grant awards, sabbatical leaves, master classes, etc.

To align this policy with practice, scientific quality assessments need to recognise the importance of integrated science communication in the achievements of scientists. Quality assessments should not focus only on quality and quantity of scientific output and appropriateness of direction of research programmes, but also on the manner in which these are communicated with society. A new system is presently being explored in the Netherlands dubbed 'ERIC' (Evaluating Research in Context) with this objective. It includes the quantification of communication activities and an approach to validate these efforts in society by measuring the social impact of research. It would clearly be desirable to distinguish instrumental and deliberative communication activities in this evaluation.

In line with the observations of Poliakoff and Webb (2007) of the Royal Society Survey from 2006 which found that scientists who had received communication training were more likely to have participated in public engagement activities, efforts should be made to encourage and reward scientists to undergo this training. Scientists are presently often the managers of the communication and discussion of their projects' results. Such training, including how to evaluate their efforts as is illustrated by Laura Grant in her Chapter 26 'Evaluating success: how to find out what worked (and what didn't)', should help them in performing these tasks in a coordinated manner. This could well be embedded as a component of the tenure track planning of promising young staff members, and could include upstream engagement in which various external groups are engaged with a research project from its outset, reflecting on communal goals and on the impact of the science and technology involved on society and industry. Developing and carrying out this training as a collaboration between the science department and the university's communal science communication department builds the social networks needed for the continuity of the process. It will also be very worthwhile starting this training during the education of future scientists, embedding it as part of the undergraduate curriculum and of graduate training which has already begun from the grassroots in the Triple Helix network (James Shepherd, Chapter 23).

Finally it is of course important to keep in mind that not all scientists will want to be, or will need to be, good communicators. A first-class and effective organisation will recognise at the departmental level who is good at research, at teaching, at communication and at management, and share and distribute the tasks accordingly. It is possible at this level to ensure that the best talents are used to their best abilities, and that by sharing tasks according to talent, including communication, overall performance in all of these key areas is enhanced and certainly not detracted from by any of them.

Step 3: Providing a learning culture for coordinated communal science communication

It is great to see the enthusiastic scientist who is engaged in research that appeals to society, who feels comfortable with the social aspects of his research, who has communication skills and competences, and who is rewarded when a good job is done. But it is crucial that such efforts are coordinated so as to build and maintain a communal science communication culture. We need to connect the individual aims to the organisational aims, and to align the efforts and processes. We need to learn how to do this. So we need a mutual learning environment. Scientists, science communication professionals, university board members and administrators all need to be connected in this learning environment, to tackle this challenge of the second paradigm shift.

Decision support systems for communal science communication may help scientists and communication professionals in their efforts to link daily practice with their university's policies and strategies (Wehrmann and Van der Sanden, 2007; Van der Sanden, 2008; Van der Sanden and Dam, 2010). The *science communication spectrum* (Wehrmann and Van der Sanden, 2007) for example, interrelates organisation aims with communication aims and clarifies who is communicating what, and with what perspective, whether informing or instrumental. From this spectral viewpoint it becomes clear at what time, with whom and to what objective the scientist should communicate. Such novel approaches as these could ultimately support the effective implementation of communal science communication.

CONCLUSION

Most universities do not have a strategy for coordinating individual science communication with communal communication and for pursuing their role in deliberating about the relations of science and technology with society so as to provide the unified and integrated message that the university wants to convey. To institutionalise this new approach an interactive (learning) process needs to be implemented both from the bottom–up and the top–down. In order to achieve this a number of issues are involved – the manner and content of communal responsibility and governance (including financial allocation), assessment criteria for evaluation of scientific quality, and internalising the required competences among the scientific staff (such as selection criteria for staff and encouragement of competence building). As building trust and ability to reflect are important skills for interactive communication, it is also important to give attention to integrity, social responsibility and ethics at the institutional level while incentives to overcome lack of enthusiasm and ability need to be addressed at the lower level.

A VISION FOR 2035?

By 2035, a second paradigm shift will have completely changed science communication. It is now established as an integrated and valued part of the research organisation's overall strategy. Scientists negotiate on the content and context of their novel research ideas with particular groups of the wider public in order to relate to what is at stake from societal and industrial points of view. Universities have a clear and strong position in society, valued as trustworthy institutions in informing public discussion, reflecting on public policy and providing solutions for pressing challenges of society. In each research group some scientists really enjoy interacting with society, they are strongly supported by the communal science communication officers of the university, and engage in regular training and evaluation sessions. There is mutual agreement on the communal goals of the organisation, professional communicators are part of the social network of scientists, and management can rely on coordinated messages. Moreover, due to a smart allocation system, research groups have evolved into organisations with staff excelling in research, teaching, management and communication. Because communal science communication is integrated into the academic organisation, the organisation is flexible and responsive in its anticipation of social issues, it can easily react and steer processes and address issues in its context. Context and content, expert and scientist, board member and communication professional are all coordinated in support of the communal aims of the university.

This is the utopian outcome of the second paradigm shift in science communication described in this chapter. There is a long way to go, but 25 years after the Bodmer Report implementing the first paradigm shift, we can make the second paradigm shift happen within a similar period of time – one which will contribute to strong, high-class universities building bridges between science and society through profound and well-chosen research.

Key resources

Handbooks

Bucchi, M. and B. Trench (eds.) (2008) *Handbook of Public Communication of Science and Technology.* New York: Routledge.

Cheng, D. *et al.* (eds.) (2008) *Communicating Science in Social Contexts: New Models, New Practices.* New York: Springer.

Holliman, R. *et al.* (eds.) (2008) *Practising Science Communication in the Information Age: Theorising Professional Practices*. New York: Oxford University Press.
Riel, Van, C. B. M. and Fombrun, C. J. (2007) *Essentials of Corporate Communication: Implementing Practices for Effective Reputation Management*. New York: Routledge.

Websites

http://www.stempra.org.uk/

http://communicatingscience.aaas.org/

http://www.youtube.com/watch?v=gJpPEszAIAo (Science Communication, Science Literacy and Public Support)

References

Auweraert, A. van der (2008). De onderzoeker als communicator: een kwalitatief en verkennend onderzoek naar de determinanten van wetenschapscommunicatiegedrag (The researcher as a communicator: qualitative and exploratory research into the determinants of science communication behaviour). Thesis, Wageningen University and Research Centre.
Borchelt, R. E. (2008). Public relations in science: managing the trust portfolio. In *Handbook of Public Communication of Science and Technology*, pp. 147–158. M. Bucchi and B. Trench (eds.). New York: Routledge.
Bos, M. J. W. (2010). Making sense of ecogenomics: on information-seeking behaviors, attitude development and interactivity among adolescents. Thesis, Vrije Universiteit, Amsterdam.
Cascoigne, T. (2008). Science advocacy: challenging task, difficult pathways. In *Communicating Science in Social Contexts: New Models, New Practices*, pp. 227–242. D. Cheng, M. Claessens, T. Cascoigne, J. Metcalfe, B. Schiele and S. Shi (eds.) New York: Springer.
Claessens, M. (2008). European trends in science communication. In *Communicating Science in Social Contexts: New Models, New Practices*, pp. 27–38. D. Cheng, M. Claessens, T. Cascoigne, J. Metcalfe, B. Schiele and S. Shi (eds.). New York: Springer.
Fisher, E., Biggs, S., Lindsay, S. and Zhao, J. (2010). Research thrives on integration of natural and social sciences. *Nature*, **463**, 1018.
Gibbons, M. (1999). Science's new social contract with society. *Nature*, **402**, C81–C84.
Gieryn, T. F. (1983). Boundary-work and the demarcation of science from non-science: strains and interests in professional ideologies of scientists. *American Sociological Review*, **48**, 781–795.
Gregory, J. (2009). Scientists communicating. In *Practising Science Communication in the Information Age: Theorising Professional Practices*, pp. 3–18. R. Holliman, J. Thomas, S., Smidt, E. Scanlon and E. Whitelegg (eds.) New York: Oxford University Press.
Meyer, M. (2010). The rise of knowledge broker. *Science Communication*, **32**, 118–127.
Miedema, F. (2009). Het geïnspireerde genie als modelgeleerde: de geloofwaardigheid van de hedendaagse wetenschapper (The inspired genius as a model scholar: the credibility of the modern scientist). *Academische Boekengids*, **75**, 24–28.

Osseweijer, P. (2006). A short history of talking biotech: fifteen years of iterative action research in institutionalizing scientists' engagement in public communication. Thesis, Vrije Universiteit, Amsterdam.

Peters, H. P. (2008). Scientists as public experts. In *Handbook of Public Communication of Science and Technology*, pp. 131–146. M. Bucchi and B. Trench (eds.) New York: Routledge.

Poliakoff, E. and Webb, T. L. (2007). What factors predict scientists' intentions to participate in public engagement of science activities? *Science Communication*, **29**, 242–263.

Rampton, S. and Stauber, J. (2001). *Trust Us, We're Experts: How Industry Manipulates Science and Gambles with Our Future*. New York: Tarcher/Putnam.

Riel, Van, C. B. M. and Fombrun, C. J. (2007). *Essentials of Corporate Communication: Implementing Practices for Effective Reputation Management*. New York: Routledge.

Rip, A., Misa, T. J. and Schot, J. (eds.) (1995). *Managing Technology in Society: The Approach of Constructive Technology Assessment*. London: Pinter Publishers.

Schuurbiers, D. and Fisher, E. (2009). Lab-scale intervention. *EMBO Reports*, **10**, 424–427.

Schuurbiers, D., Osseweijer, P. and Kinderlerer, J. (2009a). Implementing the Netherlands Code of Conduct for Scientific Practice: a case study. *Science and Engineering Ethics*, **15**, 213–231.

Schuurbiers, D., Sleenhoff, S., Jacobs, J. F. and Osseweijer, P. (2009b). Multidisciplinary engagement with nanoethics through education: the Nanobio-RAISE Advanced Courses as a case study and model. *Nanoethics*, **3**, 197–211.

Science for All Expert Group (2010). *Science for All: Report and Action Plan from the Science for All Expert Group*. http://interactive.bis.gov.uk/scienceandsociety/site/all/files/2010/02/Science-for-All-Final-Report-WEB.pdf

Tollefson, J. (2010). An erosion of trust. *Nature*, **466**, 24–26.

Trench, B. (2008). Towards an analytical framework of science communication models. In *Communicating Science in Social Contexts: New Models, New Practices*, pp. 119–138. D. Cheng, M. Claessens, T. Cascoigne, J. Metcalfe, B. Schiele and S. Shi (eds.) New York: Springer.

Van der Sanden, M. C. A. (2008). Towards effective biomedical science communication: a composite theoretical framework making biomedical science communication on predictive DNA diagnostics understandable and manageable. Thesis, Vrije Universiteit, Amsterdam.

Van der Sanden, M. C. A. and Dam, K. H. van (2010). Towards an ontology of consumer acceptance in socio-technical energy systems. *Proceedings NGinfra 2010*, Shenzhen, China.

Wehrmann, C. and Van der Sanden, M. (2007). Communication spectrum: useful instrument in the science communication practice? The necessity of combining theory and practice. *Tijdschrift voor Communicatiewetenschap*, **35**, 79–98.

Wellcome Trust (2000). *The Role of Scientist in Public Debate*. London: Wellcome Trust.

Wynne, B. (1995). Public understanding of science. In *Handbook of Science and Technology Studies*, pp. 361–388. S. Jasanoff, G. E. Markle, J. C. Petersen, and T. Pinch (eds.) Thousand Oaks, CA: Sage.

Wynne, B. (2010). When doubt becomes a weapon. *Nature*, **466**, 441–442.

Index

443